Lecture Notes in Computer Science 13215

More information about this series at https://link.springer.com/bookseries/558

Michael Hanus · Atsushi Igarashi (Eds.)

Functional and Logic Programming

16th International Symposium, FLOPS 2022
Kyoto, Japan, May 10–12, 2022
Proceedings

 Springer

Editors
Michael Hanus ⓘ
Kiel University
Kiel, Germany

Atsushi Igarashi ⓘ
Kyoto University
Kyoto, Japan

ISSN 0302-9743   ISSN 1611-3349 (electronic)
Lecture Notes in Computer Science
ISBN 978-3-030-99460-0   ISBN 978-3-030-99461-7 (eBook)
https://doi.org/10.1007/978-3-030-99461-7

This Springer imprint is published by the registered company Springer Nature Switzerland AG
The registered company address is: Gewerbestrasse 11, 6330 Cham, Switzerland

Preface

This volume contains the papers presented at the 16th International Symposium on Functional and Logic Programming (FLOPS 2022) held during May 10–12, 2022, in Kyoto, Japan.

Writing down detailed computational steps is not the only way of programming. The alternative, being used increasingly in practice, is to start by writing down the desired properties of the result. The computational steps are then (semi-)automatically derived from these higher-level specifications. Examples of this declarative style include functional and logic programming, program transformation and rewriting, and extracting programs from proofs of their correctness.

FLOPS aims to bring together practitioners, researchers, and implementors of declarative programming, to discuss mutually interesting results and common problems: theoretical advances, their implementations in language systems and tools, and applications of these systems in practice. The scope includes all aspects of the design, semantics, theory, applications, implementations, and teaching of declarative programming. FLOPS specifically aims to promote cross-fertilization between theory and practice and among different styles of declarative programming.

FLOPS has a long tradition. Previous meetings were held at Fuji Susono (1995), Shonan Village (1996), Kyoto (1998), Tsukuba (1999), Tokyo (2001), Aizu (2002), Nara (2004), Fuji Susono (2006), Ise (2008), Sendai (2010), Kobe (2012), Kanazawa (2014), Kochi (2016), Nagoya (2018), and Akita (online, 2020).

The call for papers resulted in 32 abstract submissions from which 30 were finally submitted as full papers. The subsequent reviewing process was double-blind. Each submission was reviewed by at least three reviewers, either members of the Program Committee (PC) or external referees. After careful and thorough discussions, the PC accepted 12 regular research papers, two system descriptions, and a declarative pearl paper. The program also included three invited talks by Lindsey Kuper (University of California), Akimasa Morihata (University of Tokyo), and Peter J. Stuckey (Monash University).

We would like to thank all invited speakers and authors for their contributions. We are grateful to all PC members and external reviewers for their hard work, and to EasyChair for their conference management system that made our work of organizing FLOPS 2022 much easier. We thank the local co-organizers, Keigo Imai and Taro Sekiyama, who made an invaluable effort in setting up the conference and making sure everything ran smoothly.

Finally, we would like to thank our sponsor, the Japan Society for Software Science and Technology (JSSST) SIG-PPL, for their continued support. We acknowledge the cooperation of ACM SIGPLAN and the Asian Association for Foundation of Software (AAFS).

March 2022

Michael Hanus
Atsushi Igarashi

Organization

Program Chairs

Michael Hanus   Kiel University, Germany
Atsushi Igarashi   Kyoto University, Japan

Organizing Committee

Michael Hanus   Kiel University, Germany
Atsushi Igarashi   Kyoto University, Japan
Keigo Imai   Gifu University, Japan
Taro Sekiyama   National Institute of Informatics, Japan

Program Committee

Andreas Abel   Gothenburg University, Sweden
Elvira Albert   Universidad Complutense de Madrid, Spain
Nada Amin   Harvard University, USA
Davide Ancona   Università di Genova, Italy
William Byrd   University of Alabama, USA
Matteo Cimini   University of Massachusetts Lowell, USA
Youyou Cong   Tokyo Institute of Technology, Japan
Robert Glück   University of Copenhagen, Denmark
Makoto Hamana   Gunma University, Japan
Michael Hanus   Kiel University, Germany
Zhenjiang Hu   Peking University, China
Atsushi Igarashi   Kyoto University, Japan
Ekaterina Komendantskaya   Heriot-Watt University, UK
Shin-Cheng Mu   Academia Sinica, Taiwan
Koko Muroya   Kyoto University, Japan
Klaus Ostermann   University of Tübingen, Germany
Ricardo Rocha   University of Porto, Portugal
Tom Schrijvers   KU Leuven, Belgium
Harald Sondergaard   University of Melbourne, Australia
Hiroshi Unno   University of Tsukuba, Japan
Niki Vazou   IMDEA, Spain
Janis Voigtländer   University of Duisburg-Essen, Germany
Nicolas Wu   Imperial College London, UK

Ningning Xie	University of Cambridge, UK
Jeremy Yallop	University of Cambridge, UK
Neng-Fa Zhou	City University of New York, USA

Additional Reviewers

Aaron Bembenek	Anastasiya Kravchuk-Kirilyuk
Niels Bunkenburg	Leonid Libkin
Mário Florido	Enrique Martin-Martin
Samir Genaim	Marco Paviotti
Pablo Gordillo	Takehide Soh

Abstracts of Keynotes

There are No Integers in Discrete Optimisation Models!

Jip Dekker, Peter J. Stuckey, and Guido Tack

Department of Data Science and Artificial Intelligence, Monash University, Australia
{jip.dekker,peter.stuckey,guido.tack}@monash.edu

Abstract. Discrete optimisation problems make decisions from a finite set of choices. They encompass many important problem classes such as scheduling, rostering and resource allocation. MiniZinc is a leading modelling language for discrete optimisation. It allows the expression of discrete optimisation problems succinctly using high level global constraints, and automatically translates them to run on constraint programming (CP), mixed integer programming (MIP), Boolean satisfiability (SAT), SAT modulo theories (SMT), and local search solvers. Integers are a key type in MiniZinc since they are used represent all the finite decisions made during solving. Indeed, handling integer constraints efficiently is one of the key challenges in discrete optimisation solving. Each solving technology tackles this differently: CP by building specific integer propagation techniques for each different global constraint, MIP by relaxing integrality and using branching to enforce it, SAT by encoding integers using Boolean variables, SMT using a mix of all three methods above, and local search by converting constraints to penalty functions and using local moves. All the approaches require search, and for difficult problems this search can be enormous, requiring millions of decisions or moves to be explored. But in the latest development version of MiniZinc, we recommend **never** using integers in models. Why?

Finding errors in discrete optimisation models can be very challenging. In the worst case when a solver simply returns no answer, we don't know if this is because the problem we *want* to ask is too hard (for this solver) or the problem we *actually* asked (because of errors in the model) is too hard. Looking through solver traces of millions of events to find a problem is very hard work, and indeed there may be no error. Any errors we can detect *before* sending a model to the solver are invaluable. Hence, strong type systems are crucial for discrete optimisation models, since errors spotted by the type system may save us a huge amount of debugging work.

How can we model discrete optimisation problems without integers? Many discrete optimisation problems reason about sets of named objects. Since version 2.1 MiniZinc has supported (ordered) enumerated types (enums), which allow decisions over a such sets. This immediately improves type safety. But we also need to be able to reason about two or more sets of objects jointly. Enumerated type extension allows us to build a supertype that includes both types of objects. Unordered enumerated types allow us to further strengthen models, if it makes no sense to rank two different objects. With these tools we never confuse reasoning about different sets of objects.

But what about the many remaining integers in models, that don't represent objects? For these we rely on unit types to differentiate between different integers appearing in the model. All integer decisions in models are either about a set of objects or some measurable resource type. Using unit types we can add more type safety for our models by avoiding confusion of different types of decisions. Unit types in MiniZinc are somewhat unusual, since often models deal with multiple granularity of the same resource, e.g. scheduling to the minute, but doing resource allocation on the half day; or use an unspecified granularity, e.g. the same job-shop scheduling model could use task durations given in minutes or days. Unit types in MiniZinc also differentiate between absolute unit types, e.g. the time when an event occurred, and *delta* unit types, e.g. the time difference between two events. Errors arising from mixing absolute and delta can be very hard to debug, so we extend the type system to track this for us.

In a high-level modelling language like MiniZinc, the compiler ensures that models are type-safe. The underlying solvers can of course remain completely unaware of complex concepts like enums or unit types, since the MiniZinc compiler translates them into simple integers.

Overall, armed with a type system that supports enumerated types, type extension, unit types, and delta unit types, we find that no discrete optimisation model[1] needs to include raw, unsafe integer variables.

---

[1] With the possible exception of some combinatorics models which reason directly over the integers themselves.

Adventures in Building Reliable Distributed Systems with Liquid Haskell (Abstract)

Lindsey Kuper

University of California, Santa Cruz, USA
lkuper@ucsc.edu

Today's most important computer systems are distributed systems: those that consist of multiple components that communicate by sending messages over a network, and where individual components or network connections may fail independently. Programming such systems is hard due to messages being reordered or delayed and the ever-present possibility of failure. Many liveness guarantees are impossible in such a setting, and even safety properties (such as "received messages arrive in the order they were sent") can be challenging to prove. Protocols meant to ensure, say, a given message delivery order or a given data consistency policy are widely used in distributed systems, but verification of the correctness of those protocols is less common — much less machine-checked proofs about executable implementations.

Language-integrated verification techniques promise to bridge the gap between protocol specifications and executable implementations, letting programmers carry out verification directly in the same executable programming language used for implementation. One such language-level verification approach centers around refinement types: data types that let programmers specify logical predicates that restrict, or refine, the set of values that can inhabit the type, and that can be checked at compile time by an off-the-shelf SMT solver. Refinement types are beginning to make their way into general-purpose, industrial-strength programming languages through tools such as Liquid Haskell, which adds support for refinement types to the Haskell language. Liquid Haskell goes beyond last decade's refinement types: its powerful reflection capabilities let you prove theorems in an extrinsic style, by defining Haskell functions (with help from the underlying solver). Furthermore, its integration with an existing programming language lets programmers work with pre-existing code and add richer specifications as they go. But is it up to the task of verifying interesting correctness properties of practically deployable distributed systems?

In this talk, I'll report on my research group's recent and ongoing efforts to answer that question in the affirmative. For example, in a messaging system consisting of several peer nodes, we can use refinement types to express properties about the order in which broadcast messages are delivered at a node, and we can use Liquid Haskell to prove those properties extrinsically. Likewise, in a replicated storage system we can express and prove properties about the convergence of replicated data structures. I'll recount the pleasures and pitfalls of our journey so far, and discuss where we hope to go next.

From Program Synthesis to Program Transformation: Case Study in Reduction Parallelization

Akimasa Morihata [ID]

The University of Tokyo, 3-8-1, Komaba, Meguro-ku, Tokyo, Japan
morihata@graco.c.u-tokyo.ac.jp
https://www.graco.c.u-tokyo.ac.jp/labs/morihata/

Abstract. *Program synthesis* is the task of automatically constructing a program that implements the given specification. It is intensively studied in this decade, perhaps because of recent progress in constraint solvers and program verifiers. Unfortunately, even state-of-the-art methods tend to fail in generating large programs.

This talk discusses the effectiveness of combining program synthesis with *program transformations*. One may consider program transformations are merely a subcategory of program synthesis. In reality, they enable us to formally express the outline of the desired program and thereby lead to constructing complicated programs by filling the details by program synthesis. As case studies, we review two methods of automatically parallelizing programs for summarizing values in data structures. One is based on quantifier elimination (Morihata and Matsuzaki, FLOPS 2010 [1]), and the other is a recent proposal based on reverse engineering (Morihata and Sato, PLDI 2021 [2]).

Keywords: Program synthesis · Program transformation · Parallelization

References

1. Morihata, A., Matsuzaki, K.: Automatic parallelization of recursive functions using quantifier elimination. In: Blume, M., Kobayashi, N., Vidal, G. (eds.) Functional and Logic Programming. FLOPS 2010. LNCS, vol. 6009. Springer, Heidelberg (2010). https://doi.org/10.1007/978-3-642-12251-4_23
2. Morihata, A., Sato, S.: Reverse engineering for reduction parallelization via semiring polynomials. In Freund, S. N., Yahav, E. (eds.). In: 42nd ACM SIGPLAN International Conference on Programming Language Design and Implementation, Virtual Event PLDI '21, Canada, June 20–25, 2021, pp. 820–834. ACM (2021). https://doi.org/10.1145/3453483.3454079

Contents

Enhancing Expressivity of Checked Corecursive Streams

Davide Ancona[✉], Pietro Barbieri, and Elena Zucca

DIBRIS, University of Genova, Genoa, Italy
davide.ancona@unige.it

Abstract. We propose a novel approach to stream definition and manipulation. Our solution is based on two key ideas. Regular corecursion, which avoids non termination by detecting cyclic calls, is enhanced, by allowing in equations defining streams other operators besides the stream constructor. In this way, some non-regular streams are definable. Furthermore, execution includes a runtime check to ensure that the stream generated by a function call is well-defined, in the sense that access to an arbitrary index always succeeds. We extend the technique beyond the simple stream operators considered in previous work, notably by adding an *interleaving* combinator which has a non-trivial recursion scheme.

Keywords: Operational semantics · Stream programming · Runtime checking

1 Introduction

Applications often deal with data structures which are conceptually infinite; among those *data streams* (unbounded sequences of data) are a paradigmatic example, important in several application domains as the Internet of Things. Lazy evaluation is a well-established and widely-used solution to data stream generation and processing, supported, e.g., in Haskell, and in most stream libraries offered by mainstream languages, as `java.util.stream`. In this approach, data streams can be defined as the result of an arbitrary function. For instance, in Haskell we can write

```
one_two = 1:2:one_two    -- 1:2:1:2:1: ...
from n = n:from(n+1)     -- n:n+1:n+2: ...
```

Functions which only need to inspect a finite portion of the structure, e.g., getting the i-th element, can be correctly implemented, thanks to the lazy evaluation strategy as exemplified below.

```
get_elem 3 (one_two)   -- evaluates to 2
get_elem 3 (from 5)    -- evaluates to 7
```

More recently, another approach has been proposed [2,11,14,19], called *regular corecursion*, which exploits the fact that streams as `one_two` above are

© Springer Nature Switzerland AG 2022
M. Hanus and A. Igarashi (Eds.): FLOPS 2022, LNCS 13215, pp. 1–18, 2022.
https://doi.org/10.1007/978-3-030-99461-7_1

periodic, a.k.a. *regular* following the terminology in [8], meaning that the term
1:2:1:2:1: ... is infinite but has a finite number of subterms. Regular streams
can be actually represented at runtime by a finite set of equations involving only
the stream constructor, in the example $x = 1 : 2 : x$. Furthermore, function definitions are *corecursive*, meaning that they do not have the standard inductive
semantics; indeed, even though the evaluation strategy is call-by-value, thanks
to the fact that pending function calls are tracked, cyclic calls are detected,
avoiding in this case non-termination.

For instance, with regular corecursion[1] we have:

```
one_two() = 1:2:one_two()
from(n) = n:from(n+1)
get_elem(3,one_two())    -- evaluates to 2
get_elem (3,from(5))     -- leads to non-termination
```

Despite their differences, in both approaches programmers are allowed to
write intuitively ill-formed definitions such as bad_stream() = bad_stream(); any
access to indexes of the stream returned by this function leads to non-termination
both with lazy evaluation and regular corecursion. However, while in the regular
case it is simple to reject the result of calling bad_stream by checking a guard-
edness syntactic condition, the Haskell compiler does not complain if one calls
such a function. In this paper, we propose a novel approach to stream generation
and manipulation, providing, in a sense, a middle way between those described
above. Our solution is based on two key ideas:

- Corecursion is enhanced, by allowing in stream equations other typical operators besides the stream constructor; in this way, some non-regular streams
  are supported. For instance, we can define from(n)=n:(from(n)[+]repeat(1)),
  with [+] the pointwise addition and repeat defined by repeat(n)=n:repeat(n).
- Execution includes a runtime check which rejects the stream generated by
  a function call if it is ill-formed, in the sense that access to an index could
  possibly diverge. For instance, the call bad_stream() raises a runtime error.

In this way we achieve a convenient trade-off between expressive power and
reliability; indeed, we do not have the full expressive power of Haskell, where
we can manipulate streams generated as results of arbitrary functions, but,
clearly, the well-definedness check described above would be not decidable. On
the other hand, we significantly augment the expressive power of regular corecursion, allowing several significant non-regular streams, at the price of making
the well-definedness check non-trivial, but still decidable.

The main formal results are (1) Theorem 1 stating the soundness of the runtime check; (2) Theorem 2 stating that the optimized definition of the runtime
check in Sect. 5 is equivalent to the simpler one given in Sect. 4. In particular, for
contribution (1) the interleaving operator requires a more involved proof in comparison with [3] (see Sect. 6), while for (2) we show that the optimized definition
improves the time complexity from $O(N^2)$ to $O(N \log N)$.

---

[1] Here we use the syntax of our calculus, where, differently from Haskell, functions are
uncurried, that is, take as arguments possibly empty tuples delimited by parentheses.

In Sect. 2 we formally define the calculus, in Sect. 3 we show examples, in Sect. 4 we define the well-formedness check, and in Sect. 5 its optimized version. Finally, in Sect. 6 we discuss related and further work. More examples of derivations and omitted proofs can be found in the extended version [4].

2   Stream Calculus

Figure 1 shows the syntax of the calculus.

$$
\begin{array}{llll}
\overline{fd} & ::= fd_1 \dots fd_n & & \text{program} \\
fd & ::= f(\overline{x}) = se & & \text{function declaration} \\
e & ::= se \mid ne \mid be & & \text{expression} \\
se & ::= x \mid \textbf{if } be \textbf{ then } se_1 \textbf{ else } se_2 \mid ne : se \mid se\hat{\ } \mid se_1 \, op \, se_2 \mid f(\overline{e}) & & \text{stream expression} \\
ne & ::= x \mid se(ne) \mid ne_1 \, nop \, ne_2 \mid 0 \mid 1 \mid 2 \mid \dots & & \text{numeric expression} \\
be & ::= x \mid \textbf{true} \mid \textbf{false} \mid \dots & & \text{boolean expression} \\
op & ::= [nop] \mid \parallel & & \text{binary stream operator} \\
nop & ::= + \mid - \mid * \mid / & & \text{numeric operator}
\end{array}
$$

Fig. 1. Stream calculus: syntax

A program is a sequence of (mutually recursive) function declarations, for simplicity assumed to only return streams. Stream expressions are variables, conditionals, expressions built by stream operators, and function calls. We consider the following stream operators: constructor (prepending a numeric element), tail, pointwise arithmetic operators, and interleaving. Numeric expressions include the access to the i-th[2] element of a stream. We use $\overline{fd}$ to denote a sequence $fd_1, \dots, fd_n$ of function declarations, and analogously for other sequences.

The operational semantics, given in Fig. 2, is based on two key ideas:

1. some infinite streams can be represented in a finite way
2. evaluation keeps trace of already considered function calls

To obtain (1), our approach is inspired by *capsules* [13], which are expressions supporting cyclic references. That is, the *result* of a stream expression is a pair (s, ρ), where s is an *(open) stream value*, built on top of stream variables, numeric values, the stream constructor, the tail destructor, the pointwise arithmetic and the interleaving operators, and ρ is an *environment* mapping variables into stream values. In this way, cyclic streams can be obtained: for instance, $(x, x \mapsto n : x)$ denotes the stream constantly equal to n.

We denote by $dom(\rho)$ the domain of ρ, by $vars(\rho)$ the set of variables occurring in ρ, by $fv(\rho)$ the set of its free variables, that is, $vars(\rho) \setminus dom(\rho)$, and say that ρ is *closed* if $fv(\rho) = \emptyset$, *open* otherwise, and analogously for a result (v, ρ).

---

[2] For simplicity, here indexing and numeric expressions coincide.

$$
\begin{array}{ll}
c & ::= f(\overline{v}) & \text{(evaluated) call} \\
v & ::= s \mid n \mid b & \text{value} \\
s & ::= x \mid n : s \mid s\hat{} \mid s_1 \, op \, s_2 & \text{(open) stream value} \\
i, n & ::= 0 \mid 1 \mid 2 \mid \dots & \text{index, numeric value} \\
b & ::= \mathbf{true} \mid \mathbf{false} & \text{boolean value} \\
\tau & ::= c_1 \mapsto x_1 \, \dots \, c_n \mapsto x_n \quad (n \geq 0) & \text{call trace} \\
\rho & ::= x_1 \mapsto s_1 \dots x_n \mapsto s_n \quad (n \geq 0) & \text{environment}
\end{array}
$$

$$
\text{(VAL)}\frac{}{v, \rho, \tau \Downarrow (v, \rho)} \qquad
\text{(IF-T)}\frac{be, \rho, \tau \Downarrow (\mathbf{true}, \rho) \quad se_1, \rho, \tau \Downarrow (s, \rho')}{\mathbf{if} \ be \ \mathbf{then} \ se_1 \ \mathbf{else} \ se_2, \rho, \tau \Downarrow (s, \rho')} \qquad
\text{(IF-F)}\frac{be, \rho, \tau \Downarrow (\mathbf{false}, \rho) \quad se_2, \rho, \tau \Downarrow (s, \rho')}{\mathbf{if} \ be \ \mathbf{then} \ se_1 \ \mathbf{else} \ se_2, \rho, \tau \Downarrow (s, \rho')}
$$

$$
\text{(CONS)}\frac{ne, \rho, \tau \Downarrow (n, \rho) \quad se, \rho, \tau \Downarrow (s, \rho')}{ne : se, \rho, \tau \Downarrow (n : s, \rho')} \qquad
\text{(TAIL)}\frac{se, \rho, \tau \Downarrow (s, \rho')}{se\hat{}, \rho, \tau \Downarrow (s\hat{}, \rho')} \qquad
\text{(OP)}\frac{se_1, \rho, \tau \Downarrow (s_1, \rho_1) \quad se_2, \rho, \tau \Downarrow (s_2, \rho_2)}{se_1 \, op \, se_2, \rho, \tau \Downarrow (s_1 \, op \, s_2, \rho_1 \sqcup \rho_2)}
$$

$$
\text{(ARGS)}\frac{e_i, \rho, \tau \Downarrow (v_i, \rho_i) \quad \forall i \in 1..n \quad f(\overline{v}), \hat{\rho}, \tau \Downarrow (s, \rho')}{f(\overline{e}), \rho, \tau \Downarrow (s, \rho')} \qquad
\begin{array}{l}
\overline{e} = e_1, \dots, e_n \ \text{not of shape} \ \overline{v} \\
\overline{v} = v_1, \dots, v_n \\
\hat{\rho} = \bigsqcup_{i \in 1..n} \rho_i
\end{array}
$$

$$
\text{(INVK)}\frac{se[\overline{v}/\overline{x}], \rho, \tau\{f(\overline{v}) \mapsto x\} \Downarrow (s, \rho')}{f(\overline{v}), \rho, \tau \Downarrow (x, \rho'\{x \mapsto s\})} \quad
\begin{array}{l}
f(\overline{v}) \notin dom(\tau) \\
x \ \text{fresh} \\
fbody(f) = (\overline{x}, se) \\
wd(\rho', x, s)
\end{array} \qquad
\text{(COREC)}\frac{}{f(\overline{v}), \rho, \tau \Downarrow (x, \rho)} \quad \tau(f(\overline{v})) = x
$$

$$
\text{(AT)}\frac{se, \rho, \tau \Downarrow (s, \rho') \quad ne, \rho, \tau \Downarrow (i, \rho)}{se(ne), \rho, \tau \Downarrow (n, \rho)} \quad at_{\rho'}(s, i) = n
$$

$$
\text{(AT-VAR)}\frac{at_\rho(\rho(x), i) = n'}{at_\rho(x, i) = n'} \qquad
\text{(AT-CONS-0)}\frac{}{at_\rho(n : s, 0) = n} \qquad
\text{(AT-CONS-SUCC)}\frac{at_\rho(s, i) = n'}{at_\rho(n : s, i + 1) = n'}
$$

$$
\text{(AT-TAIL)}\frac{at_\rho(s, i + 1) = n}{at_\rho(s\hat{}, i) = n} \qquad
\text{(AT-NOP)}\frac{at_\rho(s_1, i) = n_1 \quad at_\rho(s_2, i) = n_2}{at_\rho(s_1[nop]s_2, i) = n_1 \ nop \ n_2}
$$

$$
\text{(AT-}\|\text{-EVEN)}\frac{at_\rho(s_1, i) = n}{at_\rho(s_1 \| s_2, 2i) = n} \qquad
\text{(AT-}\|\text{-ODD)}\frac{at_\rho(s_2, i) = n}{at_\rho(s_1 \| s_2, 2i + 1) = n}
$$

Fig. 2. Stream calculus: operational semantics

To obtain point (2) above, evaluation has an additional parameter which is a *call trace*, a map from function calls where arguments are values (dubbed *calls* for short in the following) into variables.

Altogether, the semantic judgment has shape $e, \rho, \tau \Downarrow (v, \rho')$, where e is the expression to be evaluated, ρ the current environment defining possibly cyclic stream values that can occur in e, τ the call trace, and (v, ρ') the result. The semantic judgments should be indexed by an underlying (fixed) program, omitted for sake of simplicity. Rules use the following auxiliary definitions:

- $\rho \sqcup \rho'$ is the union of two environments, which is well-defined if they have disjoint domains; $\rho\{x \mapsto s\}$ is the environment which gives s on x, coincides with ρ elsewhere; we use analogous notations for call traces.

- $se[\overline{v}/\overline{x}]$ is obtained by parallel substitution of variables $\overline{x}$ with values $\overline{v}$.
- $fbody(f)$ returns the pair of the parameters and the body of the declaration of f, if any, in the assumed program.

Intuitively, a closed result (s, ρ) is well-defined if it denotes a unique stream, and a closed environment ρ is well-defined if, for each $x \in dom(\rho)$, (x, ρ) is well-defined. In other words, the corresponding set of equations admits a unique solution. For instance, the environment $\{x \mapsto x\}$ is not well-defined, since it is undetermined (any stream satisfies the equation $x = x$); the environment $\{x \mapsto x[+]y, y \mapsto 1 : y\}$ is not well-defined as well, since it is undefined (the two equations $x = x \mapsto x[+]y, y = 1 : y$ admit no solutions for x). This notion can be generalized to open results and environments, assuming that free variables denote unique streams, as will be formalized in Sect. 4.

Rules for values and conditional are straightforward. In rules (CONS), (TAIL) and (OP), arguments are evaluated and the stream operator is applied without any further evaluation. That is, we treat all these operators as constructors.

The rules for function call are based on a mechanism of cycle detection [2]. Evaluation of arguments is handled by a separate rule (ARGS), whereas the following two rules handle (evaluated) calls.

Rule (INVK) is applied when a call is considered for the first time, as expressed by the first side condition. The body is retrieved by using the auxiliary function *fbody*, and evaluated in a call trace where the call has been mapped into a fresh variable. Then, it is checked that adding the association of such variable with the result of the evaluation of the body keeps the environment well-defined, as expressed by the judgment $wd(\rho, x, s)$, which will be defined in Sect. 4. If the check succeeds, then the final result consists of the variable associated with the call and the updated environment. For simplicity, here execution is stuck if the check fails; an implementation should raise a runtime error instead. An example of stuck derivation is shown in [4].

Rule (COREC) is applied when a call is considered for the second time, as expressed by the first side condition. The variable x is returned as result. However, there is no associated value in the environment yet; in other words, the result (x, ρ) is open at this point. This means that x is undefined until the environment is updated with the corresponding value in rule (INVK). However, x can be safely used as long as the evaluation does not require x to be inspected; for instance, x can be safely passed as an argument to a function call.

For instance, if we consider the program $\mathtt{f()=g()}$ $\mathtt{g()=1:f()}$, then the judgment $\mathtt{f()}, \emptyset, \emptyset \Downarrow (x, \rho)$, with $\rho = \{x \mapsto y, y \mapsto 1 : x\}$, is derivable; however, while the final result (x, ρ) is closed, the derivation contains also judgments with open results, as happens for $\mathtt{f()}, \emptyset, \{\mathtt{f()} \mapsto x, \mathtt{g()} \mapsto y\} \Downarrow (x, \emptyset)$ and $\mathtt{g()}, \emptyset, \{\mathtt{f()} \mapsto x\} \Downarrow (y, \{y \mapsto 1 : x\})$. The full derivation can be found in [4].

Finally, rule (AT) computes the i-th element of a stream expression. After evaluating the arguments, the result is obtained by the auxiliary judgment $at_\rho(s, i) = n$, whose straightforward definition is at the bottom of the figure.

Rules (AT-)∥(-EVEN) and (AT-)∥(-ODD) define the behaviour of the interleaving operator, which merges two streams together by alternating their elements.

When evaluating $at_\rho(s, i)$, if s is a variable free in the environment, then execution is stuck; again, an implementation should raise a runtime error instead.

3   Examples

First we show some simple examples, to explain how corecursive definitions work. Then we provide some more significant examples.

Consider the following function declarations:

```
repeat(n) = n:repeat(n)
one_two() = 1:two_one()
two_one() = 2:one_two()
```

With the standard semantics of recursion, the calls, e.g., `repeat(0)` and `one_two()` lead to non-termination. Thanks to corecursion, instead, these calls terminate, producing as result $(x, \{x \mapsto 0 : x\})$, and $(x, \{x \mapsto 1 : y, y \mapsto 2 : x\})$, respectively. Indeed, when initially invoked, the call `repeat(0)` is added in the call trace with an associated fresh variable, say x. In this way, when evaluating the body of the function, the recursive call is detected as cyclic, the variable x is returned as its result, and, finally, the stream value $0 : x$ is associated in the environment with the result x of the initial call. In the sequel, we will use `[k]` as a shorthand for `repeat(k)`. The evaluation of `one_two()` is analogous, except that another fresh variable y is generated for the intermediate call `two_one()`. The formal derivations are given below.

$$
\cfrac{\cfrac{\text{(VALUE)} \quad \mathbf{repeat}(0), \emptyset, \{\mathbf{repeat}(0) \mapsto x\} \Downarrow (x, \emptyset)}{0 : \mathbf{repeat}(0), \emptyset, \{\mathbf{repeat}(0) \mapsto x\} \Downarrow (0 : x, \emptyset)} \text{(CONS)}}{\mathbf{repeat}(0), \emptyset, \emptyset \Downarrow (x, \{x \mapsto 0 : x\})} \text{(INVK)} \;\; \text{(COREC)}
$$

$$
\cfrac{\text{(VALUE)} \quad \cfrac{\cfrac{\cfrac{\text{(VALUE)} \quad \mathbf{one\_two}(), \emptyset, \{\mathbf{one\_two}() \mapsto x, \ \mathbf{two\_one}() \mapsto y\} \Downarrow (x, \emptyset)}{2 : \mathbf{one\_two}(), \emptyset, \{\mathbf{one\_two}() \mapsto x, \ \mathbf{two\_one}() \mapsto y\} \Downarrow (2 : x, \emptyset)} \text{(CONS)}}{\mathbf{two\_one}(), \emptyset, \{\mathbf{one\_two}() \mapsto x\} \Downarrow (y, \{y \mapsto 2 : x\})} \text{(INVK)}}{1 : \mathbf{two\_one}(), \emptyset, \{\mathbf{one\_two}() \mapsto x\} \Downarrow (1 : y, \{y \mapsto 2 : x\})}}{\mathbf{one\_two}(), \emptyset, \emptyset \Downarrow (x, \{x \mapsto 1 : y, \ y \mapsto 2 : x\})} \text{(INVK)}
$$

For space reasons, we did not report the application of rule (VALUE). In both derivations, note that rule (COREC) is applied, without evaluating the body of `one_two` once more, when the cyclic call is detected.

The following examples show function definitions whose calls return non-regular streams, notably, the natural numbers, the natural numbers raised to the power of a number, the factorials, the powers of a number, the Fibonacci numbers, and the stream obtained by pointwise increment by one.

```
nat() = 0:(nat()[+][1])
nat_to_pow(n) =                 //nat_to_pow(n)(i)=i^n
  if n <= 0 then [1] else nat_to_pow(n-1)[*]nat()
fact() = 1:((nat()[+][1])[*]fact())
pow(n) = 1:([n][*]pow(n)) //pow(n)(i)=n^i
fib() = 0:1:(fib()[+]fib()^)
incr(s) = s[+][1]
```

The definition of `nat` uses corecursion, since the recursive call `nat()` is cyclic. Hence the call `nat()` returns $(x, \{x \mapsto 0 : (x[+]y), y \mapsto 1 : y\})$. The definition of `nat_to_pow` is a standard inductive one where the argument strictly decreases in the recursive call. Hence, the call, e.g., `nat_to_pow(2)`, returns

$$(x_2, \{x_2 \mapsto x_1[*]x, x_1 \mapsto x_0[*]x, x_0 \mapsto y, y \mapsto 1 : y, x \mapsto 0 : (x[+]y'), y' \mapsto 1 : y'\}).$$

The definitions of `fact`, `pow`, and `fib` are corecursive. For instance, the call `fact()` returns $(z, z \mapsto 1 : ((x[+]y)[*]z), x \mapsto 0 : (x[+]y'), y \mapsto 1 : y, y' \mapsto 1 : y')$. The definition of `incr` is non-recursive, hence always converges, and the call `incr(s)` returns $(x, \{x \mapsto s[+]y, y \mapsto 1 : y\})$.

The next few examples show applications of the interleaving operator.

```
dup_occ() = 0:1:(dup_occ() || dup_occ())
```

Function `dup_occ()` generates the stream which alternates sequences of occurrences of 0 and 1, with the number of repetitions of the same number duplicated at each step, that is, `(0:1:0:0:1:1:0:0:0:0...)`.

A more involved example shows a different way to generate the stream of all powers of 2 starting from 2^1:

```
pow_two=2:4:8:((pow_two^^[*]pow_two)||(pow_two^^[*]pow_two^))
```

The following definition is an instance of a schema generating the infinite sequence of labels obtained by a breadth-first visit of an infinite complete binary tree where the labels of children are defined in terms of that of their parent.

```
bfs_index() = 1:((bfs_index()[*][2])||(bfs_index()[*][2][+][1]))
```

In particular, the root is labelled by 1, and the left and right child of a node with label `i` are labelled by `2*i` and `2*i+1`, respectively. Hence, the generated stream is the sequence of natural numbers starting from 1, as it happens in the array implementation of a binary heap.

In the other instance below, the root is labelled by 0, and children are labelled with `i+1` if their parent has label `i`. That is, nodes are labelled by their level.

```
bfs_level() = 0:((bfs_level()[+][1])||(bfs_level()[+][1]))
```

In this case, the generated stream is more interesting; indeed, `bfs_level()(n)` = `floor(log_2(n+1))`.

The following function computes the stream of partial sums of the first $i+1$ elements of a stream s, that is, $\mathrm{sum}(s)(i) = \sum_{k=0}^{i} s(k)$:

```
sum(s) = s(0):(s^[+]sum(s))
```

Such a function is useful for computing streams whose elements approximate a series with increasing precision; for instance, the following function returns the stream of partial sums of the first $i+1$ elements of the Taylor series of the exponential function:

```
sum_expn(n) = sum(pow(n)[/]fact())
```

Function `sum_expn` calls `sum` with the argument `pow(n)[/]fact()` corresponding to the stream of terms of the Taylor series of the exponential; hence, by accessing the i-th element of the stream, we have the following approximation of the series:

$$\texttt{sum\_expn}(n)(i) = \sum_{k=0}^{i} \frac{n^k}{k!} = 1 + n + \frac{n^2}{2!} + \frac{n^3}{3!} + \frac{n^4}{4!} + \cdots + \frac{n^i}{i!}$$

Lastly, we present a couple of examples showing how it is possible to define primitive operations provided by IoT platforms for real time analysis of data streams; we start with `aggr(n,s)`, which allows aggregation by addition of data in windows of length `n`:

```
aggr(n,s) = if n<=0 then [0] else s[+]aggr(n-1,s^)
```

For instance, `aggr(3,s)` returns the stream s' s.t. $s'(i) = s(i) + s(i+1) + s(i+2)$. On top of `aggr`, we can easily define `avg(n,s)` to compute the stream of average values of `s` in windows of length `n`:

```
avg(n,s) = aggr(n,s)[/][n]
```

4   Well-Definedness Check

A key feature of our approach is the runtime check ensuring that the stream generated by a function call is well-defined, see the side condition $wd(\rho', x, s)$ in (INVK); in this section we formally define the corresponding judgment and prove its soundness. Before doing this, we provide, for reference, a formal abstract definition of well-definedness.

Intuitively, an environment is well-defined if each variable in its domain denotes a unique stream. Semantically, a stream σ is an infinite sequence of numeric values, that is, a function which returns, for each index $i \geq 0$, the i-th element $\sigma(i)$. Given a result (s, ρ), we get a stream by instantiating variables in s with streams, in a way consistent with ρ, and evaluating operators. To make this formal, we need some preliminary definitions.

A *substitution* θ is a function from a finite set of variables to streams. We denote by $[\![s]\!]\theta$ the stream obtained by applying θ to s, and evaluating operators, as formally defined below.

$$[\![x]\!]\theta = \theta(x)$$

$$([\![n : s]\!]\theta)(i) = \begin{cases} n & i = 0 \\ ([\![s]\!]\theta)(i-1) & i \geq 1 \end{cases}$$

$$([\![s\hat{\ }]\!]\theta)(i) = [\![s]\!]\theta(i+1) \quad i \geq 0$$

$$([\![s_1[nop]s_2]\!]\theta)(i) = [\![s_1]\!]\theta(i) \; nop \; [\![s_2]\!]\theta(i) \quad i \geq 0$$

$$([\![s_1\|s_2]\!]\theta)(2i) = [\![s_1]\!]\theta(i) \quad i \geq 0$$

$$([\![s_1\|s_2]\!]\theta)(2i+1) = [\![s_2]\!]\theta(i) \quad i \geq 0$$

Given an environment ρ and a substitution θ with domain $vars(\rho)$, the substitution $\rho[\theta]$ is defined by:

$$\rho[\theta](x) = \begin{cases} [\![\rho(x)]\!]\theta & x \in dom(\rho) \\ \theta(x) & x \in fv(\rho) \end{cases}$$

Then, a *solution* of ρ is a substitution θ such that $\rho[\theta] = \theta$.

A closed environment ρ is *well-defined* if it has exactly one solution. For instance, $\{x \mapsto 1 : x\}$ and $\{y \mapsto 0 : (y[+]x), \; x \mapsto 1 : x\}$ are well-defined, since their unique solutions map x to the infinite stream of ones, and y to the stream of natural numbers, respectively. Instead, for $\{x \mapsto 1[+]x\}$ there are no solutions. Lastly, an environment can be undetermined: for instance, a substitution mapping x into an arbitrary stream is a solution of $\{x \mapsto x\}$.

An open environment ρ is well-defined if, for each θ with domain $fv(\rho)$, it has exactly one solution θ' such that $\theta \subseteq \theta'$. For instance, the open environment $\{y \mapsto 0 : (y[+]x)\}$ is well-defined.

In Fig. 3 we provide the operational characterization of well-definedness. The judgment $wd(\rho, x, s)$ used in the side condition of rule (INVK) holds if $\mathsf{wd}_{\rho'}(x, \emptyset)$ holds, with $\rho' = \rho\{x \mapsto v\}$. The judgment $\mathsf{wd}_\rho(s, \emptyset)$ means well-definedness of a result. That is, restricting the domain of ρ to the variables reachable from s (that is, either occurring in s, or, transitively, in values associated with reachable variables) we get a well-defined environment; thus, $wd(\rho, x, s)$ holds if adding the association of s with x preserves well-definedness of ρ.

$$m ::= x_1 \mapsto n_1 \ldots x_n \mapsto n_k \quad (n \geq 0) \text{ map from variables to integer numbers}$$

$$(\text{MAIN})\frac{\mathsf{wd}_{\rho'}(x, \emptyset)}{wd(\rho, x, v)} \; \rho' = \rho\{x \mapsto v\} \qquad (\text{WD-VAR})\frac{\mathsf{wd}_\rho(\rho(x), m\{x \mapsto 0\})}{\mathsf{wd}_\rho(x, m)} \; x \notin dom(m)$$

$$(\text{WD-COREC})\frac{}{\mathsf{wd}_\rho(x, m)} \; \begin{array}{c} x \in dom(\rho) \\ m(x) > 0 \end{array} \qquad (\text{WD-DELAY})\frac{\mathsf{wd}_\rho(\rho(x), m\{x \mapsto 0\})}{\mathsf{wd}_\rho(x, m)} \; m(x) > 0$$

$$(\text{WD-FV})\frac{}{\mathsf{wd}_\rho(x, m)} \; x \notin dom(\rho) \qquad (\text{WD-CONS})\frac{\mathsf{wd}_\rho(s, m^{+1})}{\mathsf{wd}_\rho(n : s, m)} \qquad (\text{WD-TAIL})\frac{\mathsf{wd}_\rho(s, m^{-1})}{\mathsf{wd}_\rho(s\hat{\ }, m)}$$

$$(\text{WD-NOP})\frac{\mathsf{wd}_\rho(s_1, m) \quad \mathsf{wd}_\rho(s_2, m)}{\mathsf{wd}_\rho(s_1[nop]s_2, m)} \qquad (\text{WD-}\|)\frac{\mathsf{wd}_\rho(s_1, m) \quad \mathsf{wd}_\rho(s_2, m^{+1})}{\mathsf{wd}_\rho(s_1\|s_2, m)}$$

Fig. 3. Operational definition of well-definedness

The additional argument m in the judgment $\mathsf{wd}_\rho(s, m)$ is a map from variables to integer numbers. We write m^{+1} and m^{-1} for the maps $\{(x, m(x) + 1) \mid x \in dom(m)\}$, and $\{(x, m(x) - 1) \mid x \in dom(m)\}$, respectively.

In rule (MAIN), this map is initially empty. In rule (WD-VAR), when a variable x defined in the environment is found the first time, it is added in the map with initial value 0 before propagating the check to the associated value. In rule (WD-COREC), when it is found the second time, it is checked that constructors and right operands of interleave are traversed more times than tail operators, and if it is the case the variable is considered well-defined. Rule (WD-DELAY), which is only added for the purpose of the soundness proof and should be not part of an implementation[3], performs the same check but then considers the variable occurrence as it is was the first, so that success of well-definedness is delayed. Note that rules (WD-VAR), (WD-COREC), and (WD-DELAY) can only be applied if $x \in dom(\rho)$; in rule (WD-COREC), this explicit side condition could be omitted since satisfied by construction of the proof tree.

In rule (WD-FV), a free variable is considered well-defined.[4] In rules (WD-CONS) and (WD-TAIL) the value associated with a variable is incremented/decremented by one, respectively, before propagating the check to the subterm. In rule (WD-NOP) the check is simply propagated to the subterms. In rule (WD-)$\parallel$, the check is also propagated to the subterms, but on the right-hand side the value associated with a variable is incremented by one before propagation; this reflects the fact that, in the worst case, $at_\rho(s_1 \parallel s_2, i) = at_\rho(s_1, i)$, and this happens only for $i = 0$, while for odd indexes i we have that $at_\rho(s_1 \parallel s_2, i) = at_\rho(s_2, i - k)$, with $k \geq 1$; more precisely, $k = 1$ only when $i = 1$; for all indexes $i > 1$ (both even and odd), $k > 1$. For instance, the example $\mathsf{s()} = \mathsf{1:(s()\parallel s()\hat{\ })}$, which has the same semantics as $\mathsf{[1]}$, would be considered not well-defined if we treated the interleaving as the pointwise arithmetic operators.

Note that the rules in Fig. 3 can be immediately turned into an algorithm which, given a stream value s, always terminates either successfully (finite proof tree), or with failure (no proof tree can be constructed). On the other hand, the rules in Fig. 2 defining the $at_\rho(s, i) = n$ judgment can be turned into an algorithm which can possibly diverge (infinite proof tree).

Two examples of derivation of well-definedness and access to the i-th element can be found in [4] for the results obtained by evaluating the calls $\mathsf{nat()}$ and $\mathsf{bfs\_level()}$, respectively, with nat and $\mathsf{bfs\_level}$ defined as in Sect. 3. Below we show an example of failing derivation:

As depicted in Fig. 4, the check succeeds for the left-hand component of the interleaving operator, while the proof tree cannot be completed for the other side. Indeed, the double application of the tail operator makes undefined access to stream elements with index greater than 1, since the evaluation of $at_\rho(x, 2)$ infinitely triggers the evaluation of itself.

---

[3] Indeed, it does not affect derivability, see Lemma 4 in the following.
[4] Non-well-definedness can only be detected on closed results.

$$
\cfrac{
  \cfrac{
    \cfrac{
      \cfrac{\text{FAIL}}{\mathsf{wd}_\rho(x, \{x \mapsto 0\})}\ (\text{??})
    }{\mathsf{wd}_\rho(x^\wedge, \{x \mapsto 1\})}\ (\text{WD-TAIL})
  }{\mathsf{wd}_\rho(x^{\wedge\wedge}, \{x \mapsto 2\})}\ (\text{WD-TAIL})
  \qquad
  \cfrac{}{\mathsf{wd}_\rho(x, \{x \mapsto 1\})}\ (\text{WD-COREC})
}{
  \cfrac{
    \cfrac{\mathsf{wd}_\rho(x \,\|\, x^{\wedge\wedge}, \{x \mapsto 1\})}{\mathsf{wd}_\rho(0 : (x \,\|\, x^{\wedge\wedge}), \{x \mapsto 0\})}\ (\text{WD-CONS})
  }{\mathsf{wd}_\rho(x, \emptyset)}\ (\text{WD-VAR})
}\ (\text{WD-}\|)
$$

Fig. 4. Failing derivation for $\rho = \{x \mapsto 0 : (x \,\|\, x^{\wedge\wedge})\}$

To formally express and prove that well-definedness of a result implies termination of access to an arbitrary index, we introduce some definitions and notations. First of all, since the result is not relevant for the following technical treatment, for simplicity we will write $at_\rho(s, i)$ rather than $at_\rho(s, i) = n$. We call *derivation* an either finite or infinite proof tree. We write $\mathsf{wd}_\rho(s', m') \vdash \mathsf{wd}_\rho(s, m)$ to mean that $\mathsf{wd}_\rho(s', m')$ is a premise of a (meta-)rule where $\mathsf{wd}_\rho(s, m)$ is the conclusion, and $\vdash^\star$ for the reflexive and transitive closure of this relation.

Lemma 1.

1. *A judgment* $\mathsf{wd}_\rho(s, \emptyset)$ *has no derivation iff the following condition holds:*
   (WD-STUCK) $\mathsf{wd}_\rho(x, m') \vdash^\star \mathsf{wd}_\rho(\rho(x), m\{x \mapsto 0\}) \vdash \mathsf{wd}_\rho(x, m) \vdash^\star \mathsf{wd}_\rho(s, \emptyset)$
   for some $x \in dom(\rho)$*, and* m', m *s.t.* $x \notin dom(m)$*,* $m'(x) \leq 0$*.*
2. *If the derivation of* $at_\rho(s, j)$ *is infinite, then the following condition holds:*
   (AT-∞) $at_\rho(x, i + k) \vdash^\star at_\rho(\rho(x), i) \vdash at_\rho(x, i) \vdash^\star at_\rho(s, j)$
   for some $x \in dom(\rho)$*, and* $i, k \geq 0$*.*

Lemma 2. *If* $at_\rho(x, i') \vdash^\star at_\rho(s', i)$*, and* $\mathsf{wd}_\rho(s', m) \vdash^\star \mathsf{wd}_\rho(s, \emptyset)$ *with* $\mathsf{wd}_\rho(s, \emptyset)$ *derivable, and* $x \in dom(m)$*, then*

$$\mathsf{wd}_\rho(x, m') \vdash^\star \mathsf{wd}_\rho(s', m) \text{ for some } m' \text{ such that } m'(x) - m(x) \leq i - i'.$$

Proof. The proof is by induction on the length of the path in $at_\rho(x, i') \vdash^\star at_\rho(s', i)$.

Base. The length of the path is 0, hence we have $at_\rho(x, i) \vdash^\star at_\rho(x, i)$. We also have $\mathsf{wd}_\rho(x, m) \vdash^\star \mathsf{wd}_\rho(x, m)$, and we get the thesis since $m(x) = m(x) + i - i$.

Inductive step. By cases on the rule applied to derive $at_\rho(s', i)$.

(at-var) We have $at_\rho(x, i') \vdash^\star at_\rho(\rho(y), i) \vdash at_\rho(y, i)$. There are two cases:

- If $y \notin dom(m)$ (hence $y \neq x$), we have $\mathsf{wd}_\rho(\rho(y), m\{y \mapsto 0\}) \vdash \mathsf{wd}_\rho(y, m)$ by rule (WD-VAR), the premise is derivable, hence by inductive hypothesis we have $\mathsf{wd}_\rho(x, m') \vdash^\star \mathsf{wd}_\rho(\rho(y), m\{y \mapsto 0\})$, and $m'(x) \leq m\{y \mapsto 0\}(x) + i - i' = m(x) + i - i'$, hence we get the thesis.
- If $y \in dom(m)$, then it is necessarily $m(y) > 0$, otherwise, by Lemma 1-(1), $\mathsf{wd}_\rho(s, \emptyset)$ would not be derivable. Hence, we have $\mathsf{wd}_\rho(\rho(y), m\{y \mapsto 0\}) \vdash \mathsf{wd}_\rho(y, m)$ by rule (WD-DELAY), hence by

inductive hypothesis we have $\mathsf{wd}_\rho(x, m') \vdash^\star \mathsf{wd}_\rho(\rho(y), m\{y \mapsto 0\})$, and $m'(x) \leq m\{y \mapsto 0\}(x) + i - i'$. There are two subcases:

- If $y \neq x$, then $m\{y \mapsto 0\}(x) = m(x)$, and we get the thesis as in the previous case.
- If $y = x$, then $m\{x \mapsto 0\}(x) = 0$, hence $m'(x) \leq i - i' \leq m(x) + i - i'$, since $m(x) > 0$.

(at-cons-0) Empty case, since the derivation for $at_\rho(n : s, 0)$ does not contain a node $at_\rho(x, i')$.

(at-cons-succ) We have $at_\rho(n : s, i)$, and $at_\rho(x, i') \vdash^\star at_\rho(s, i - 1)$. Moreover, we can derive $\mathsf{wd}_\rho(n : s, m)$ by rule (WD-CONS), and by inductive hypothesis we also have $\mathsf{wd}_\rho(x, m') \vdash^\star \mathsf{wd}_\rho(s, m^{+1})$, with $m'(x) \leq m^{+1}(x) + (i - 1) - i'$, hence we get the thesis.

(at-tail) This case is symmetric to the previous one.

(at-nop) We have $at_\rho(s_1[op]s_2, i)$, and either $at_\rho(x, i') \vdash^\star at_\rho(s_1, i)$, or $at_\rho(x, i') \vdash^\star at_\rho(s_2, i)$. Assume the first case holds, the other is analogous. Moreover, we can derive $\mathsf{wd}_\rho(s_1[op]s_2, m)$ by rule (WD-NOP), and by inductive hypothesis we also have $\mathsf{wd}_\rho(x, m') \vdash^\star \mathsf{wd}_\rho(s_1, m)$, with $m'(x) \leq m(x) + i - i'$, hence we get the thesis.

(at-∥-even) We have $at_\rho(s_1 \| s_2, 2i)$ and $at_\rho(x, i') \vdash^\star at_\rho(s_1, i)$. By inductive hypothesis, we have $\mathsf{wd}_\rho(x, m') \vdash^\star \mathsf{wd}_\rho(s_1, m)$, with $m'(x) \leq m(x) + i - i'$. Moreover, $\mathsf{wd}_\rho(s_1, m) \vdash \mathsf{wd}_\rho(s_1 \| s_2, m)$ holds by rule (WD-)∥, hence we have $\mathsf{wd}_\rho(x, m') \vdash^\star \mathsf{wd}_\rho(s_1 \| s_2, m)$ with $m'(x) \leq m(x) + 2i - i'$ and, thus, the thesis.

(at-∥-odd) We have $at_\rho(s_1 \| s_2, 2i + 1)$ and $at_\rho(x, i') \vdash^\star at_\rho(s_2, i)$. By inductive hypothesis, we have $\mathsf{wd}_\rho(x, m') \vdash^\star \mathsf{wd}_\rho(s_2, m^{+1})$, with $m'(x) \leq m^{+1}(x) + i - i'$. Moreover, $\mathsf{wd}_\rho(s_2, m) \vdash \mathsf{wd}_\rho(s_1 \| s_2, m)$ holds by rule (WD-)∥, hence we have $\mathsf{wd}_\rho(x, m') \vdash^\star \mathsf{wd}_\rho(s_1 \| s_2, m)$ with $m'(x) \leq m(x) + 2i + 1 - i'$ and, thus, the thesis.

Lemma 3. *If $at_\rho(x, i') \vdash^\star at_\rho(s, i)$, and $\mathsf{wd}_\rho(s, \emptyset)$ derivable, then*

$$\mathsf{wd}_\rho(x, m) \vdash^\star \mathsf{wd}_\rho(s, \emptyset) \text{ for some } m \text{ such that } x \notin dom(m).$$

Proof. Easy variant of the proof of Lemma 2.

Theorem 1. *If $\mathsf{wd}_\rho(s, \emptyset)$ has a derivation then, for all j, $at_\rho(s, j)$ either has no derivation or a finite derivation.*

Proof. Assume by contradiction that $at_\rho(s, j)$ has an infinite derivation for some j, and $\mathsf{wd}_\rho(s, \emptyset)$ is derivable. By Lemma 1–(2), the following condition holds:

$$(\text{AT-}\infty) \quad at_\rho(x, i + k) \vdash^\star at_\rho(\rho(x), i) \vdash at_\rho(x, i) \vdash^\star at_\rho(s, j)$$
$$\text{for some } x \in dom(\rho), \text{ and } i, k \geq 0.$$

Then, starting from the right, by Lemma 3 we have $\mathsf{wd}_\rho(x, m) \vdash^\star \mathsf{wd}_\rho(s, \emptyset)$ for some m such that $x \notin dom(m)$; by rule (WD-VAR) $\mathsf{wd}_\rho(\rho(x), m\{x \mapsto 0\}) \vdash \mathsf{wd}_\rho(x, m)$, and finally by Lemma 2 we have:

$$(\text{WD-STUCK}) \quad \mathsf{wd}_\rho(x, m') \vdash^\star \mathsf{wd}_\rho(\rho(x), m\{x \mapsto 0\}) \vdash \mathsf{wd}_\rho(x, m) \vdash^\star \mathsf{wd}_\rho(s, \emptyset)$$
$$\text{for some } x \in dom(\rho), \text{ and } m', m \text{ s.t. } x \notin dom(m), m'(x) \leq -k \leq 0.$$

hence this is absurd by Lemma 1-(1).

5   An Optimized Algorithm for Well-Definedness

The definition of well-definedness in Fig. 3 can be easily turned into an algorithm, since, omitting rule (WD-DELAY), at each point in the derivation there is at most one applicable rule. Now we will discuss its time complexity, assuming that insertion, update and lookup are performed in constant time. It is easy to see that when we find a stream constructor we need to perform an update of the map ρ for every variable in its domain. If we consider the following environment:

$$\rho = (x_0, \{x_0 \mapsto 0 : x_1, x_1 \mapsto 0 : x_2, x_2 \mapsto 0 : x_3, x_3 \mapsto 0 : x_4, \ \dots \ , x_n \mapsto 0 : x_0\})$$

we get the derivation presented in Fig. 5. Here, the number of constructor occurrences for which we have to perform an update of all variables in the domain of the map is linearly proportional to the number N of nodes in the derivation tree; since the domain is increased by one for each new variable, and the total number of variables is again linearly proportional to N, it is easy to see that we have a time complexity quadratic in N.

$$\vdots$$

$$\cfrac{\cfrac{\cfrac{\cfrac{\cfrac{\cfrac{}{\mathsf{wd}_\rho(x_3, \{x_0 \mapsto 3, x_1 \mapsto 2, x_2 \mapsto 1\})} \text{ (WD-VAR)}}{\mathsf{wd}_\rho(0 : x_3, \{x_0 \mapsto 2, x_1 \mapsto 1, x_2 \mapsto 0\})} \text{ (WD-CONS)}}{\mathsf{wd}_\rho(x_2, \{x_0 \mapsto 2, x_1 \mapsto 1\})} \text{ (WD-VAR)}}{\mathsf{wd}_\rho(0 : x_2, \{x_0 \mapsto 1, x_1 \mapsto 0\})} \text{ (WD-CONS)}}{\mathsf{wd}_\rho(x_1, \{x_0 \mapsto 1\})} \text{ (WD-VAR)}}{\cfrac{\mathsf{wd}_\rho(0 : x_1, \{x_0 \mapsto 0\})}{\mathsf{wd}_\rho(x_0, \emptyset)} \text{ (WD-VAR)}} \text{ (WD-CONS)}$$

Fig. 5. wd worst case

We propose now an optimized version of the well-definedness check, having a time complexity of $O(N \log N)$. On the other hand, the version we provided in Fig. 3 is more abstract, hence more convenient for the proof of Theorem 1.

In the optimized version, given in Fig. 6, the judgment has shape $\mathsf{owd}_\rho(s, \mathsf{m}, \pi)$, where π represents a path in the proof tree where each element corresponds to a visit of either the constructor or the right operand of interleave (value 1 for both) or the tail operator (value -1), and m associates with each variable an index (starting from 0) corresponding to the point in the path π where the variable was found the first time. The only operation performed on a path π is the addition $\pi \cdot b$ of an element b at the end.

In rule (MAIN), both the map and the path are initially empty. In rule (OWD-VAR), a variable x defined in the environment, found for the first time, is added in the map with as index the length of the current path. In rule (OWD-COREC),

$m ::= x_1 \mapsto i_1 \ldots x_n \mapsto i_k \quad (i \geq 0)$ map from variables to indexes
$\pi ::= b_1 b_2 \ldots b_n$ sequence of either 1 or -1

$$(\text{MAIN}) \frac{\text{owd}_{\rho'}(x, \emptyset, \epsilon)}{wd(\rho, x, v)} \; \rho' = \rho\{x \mapsto v\} \qquad (\text{OWD-VAR}) \frac{\text{owd}_\rho(\rho(x), m\{x \mapsto i\}, \pi) \; x \notin dom(m)}{\text{owd}_\rho(x, m, \pi)} \; i = length(\pi)$$

$$(\text{OWD-COREC}) \frac{x \in dom(m)}{\text{owd}_\rho(x, m, \pi) \; sum(m(x), \pi) > 0} \qquad (\text{OWD-FV}) \frac{}{\text{owd}_\rho(x, m, \pi)} \; x \notin dom(\rho)$$

$$(\text{OWD-CONS}) \frac{\text{owd}_\rho(s, m, \pi \cdot 1)}{\text{owd}_\rho(n : s, m, \pi)} \qquad (\text{OWD-TAIL}) \frac{\text{owd}_\rho(s, m, \pi \cdot (-1))}{\text{owd}_\rho(s\hat{\ }, m, \pi)}$$

$$(\text{OWD-NOP}) \frac{\text{owd}_\rho(s_1, m, \pi) \quad \text{owd}_\rho(s_2, m, \pi)}{\text{owd}_\rho(s_1[nop]s_2, m, \pi)} \qquad (\text{OWD-}\|) \frac{\text{owd}_\rho(s_1, m, \pi) \quad \text{owd}_\rho(s_2, m, \pi \cdot 1)}{\text{owd}_\rho(s_1\|s_2, m, \pi)}$$

$$(\text{SUM-0}) \frac{sum(\pi) = n}{sum(0, \pi) = n} \qquad (\text{SUM-N}) \frac{sum(n - 1, b_2 \ldots b_n) = n'}{sum(n, b_1 b_2 \ldots b_n) = n'} \; n > 0$$

$$(\text{SUM-B}) \frac{}{sum(\epsilon) = 0} \qquad (\text{SUM-I}) \frac{sum(b_2 \ldots b_n) = n}{sum(b_1 b_2 \ldots b_n) = b_1 + n}$$

Fig. 6. Optimized operational definition of well-definedness

when the same variable is found the second time, the auxiliary function *sum* checks that more constructors and right operands of interleave have been traversed than tail operators (see below). In rule (OWD-FV), a free variable is considered well-defined as in the corresponding rule in Fig. 3. In rules (OWD-CONS), (OWD-TAIL) and (OP-WD), the value corresponding to the traversed operator is added at the end of the path (1 for the constructor and the right operand of interleave, -1 for the tail operator). Lastly, rules (OWD-NOP) behaves in a similar way as in Fig. 3. The semantics of the auxiliary function *sum* is straightforward: starting from the point in the path where the variable was found the first time, the sum of all the elements is returned.

Let us now consider again the example above:

$$\rho = (x_0, \{x_0 \mapsto 0 : x_1, x_1 \mapsto 0 : x_2, x_2 \mapsto 0 : x_3, x_3 \mapsto 0 : x_4, \; \ldots \; , x_n \mapsto 0 : x_0\})$$

By the new predicate owd, we get a derivation tree of the same shape as in Fig. 5. However, *sum* is applied to the path π only at the leaves, and the length of π is linearly proportional to the depth of the derivation tree, which coincides with the number N of nodes in this specific case; hence, the time complexity to compute $sum(0, \pi)$ (that is, $sum(m(x_0), \pi)$) is linear in N. Finally, since for inner nodes only constant time operations are performed[5] (addition at the end of the path, and map insertion and lookup), the overall time complexity is linear in N.

---

[5] This holds for any valid derivation tree and not for this specific case.

As worst case in terms of time complexity for the predicate owd, consider

$$\rho_i = (x_0, \{x_0 \mapsto 0 : x_1[+]x_1, x_1 \mapsto 0 : x_2[+]x_2, x_2 \mapsto 0 : x_3[+]x_3, \ldots, x_i \mapsto 0 : x_0\})$$

The derivation tree for this environment is shown in Fig. 7, where m_i abbreviates the map $\{x_0 \mapsto 0, x_1 \mapsto 1, \ldots, x_i \mapsto i\}$.

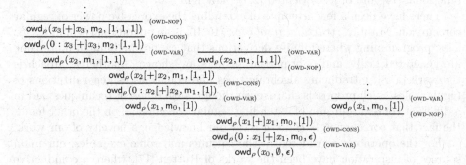

Fig. 7. owd worst case

As already noticed, for inner nodes only constant time operations are performed, and the length of the paths in the leaves is linearly proportional to the depth D of the derivation tree; however, in this worst case the number of leaves is not just one, but is linearly proportional to the total number N of nodes in the derivation tree, hence the depth D is linearly proportional to $\log N$. Therefore the overall time complexity is $O(N \cdot D)$, that is, $O(N \cdot \log N)$.

We now show that the optimized version of the judgment has the same semantics as its counterpart presented in Sect. 4. First of all we formally state that, in Fig. 3, rule (WD-DELAY) does not affect derivability.

Lemma 4. *A judgment* $\mathsf{wd}_\rho(s, \emptyset)$ *has a derivation iff it has a derivation which does not use rule* (WD-DELAY).

Proof. The right-to-left implication is obvious. If $\mathsf{wd}_\rho(s, \emptyset)$ uses rule (WD-DELAY), all the (first in their path) occurrences of the rule can be replaced by rule (WD-COREC), still getting a derivation.

Then, we define a relation between the auxiliary structures used in the two judgments:

For all m and (m, π), $m \bowtie (\mathsf{m}, \pi)$ holds iff
$dom(m) = dom(\mathsf{m})$ and, for all $x \in dom(m)$, $m(x) = sum(\mathsf{m}(x), \pi)$.

In this way, we have the following generalization, whose straightforward proof can be found in [4].

Theorem 2. *If* $m \bowtie (\mathsf{m}, \pi)$, *then, for all* s, $\mathsf{wd}_\rho(s, m)$ *is derivable iff* $\mathsf{owd}_\rho(s, \mathsf{m}, \pi)$ *is derivable.*

Corollary 1. $\mathsf{wd}_\rho(s, \emptyset)$ *is derivable iff* $\mathsf{owd}_\rho(s, \emptyset, \epsilon)$ *is derivable.*

6   Related and Future Work

As mentioned in Sect. 1, our approach extends regular corecursion, which originated from *co-SLD resolution* [1,6,18,19], where already considered goals (up to unification), called *coinductive hypotheses*, are successfully solved. Language constructs that support this programming style have also been proposed in the functional [14] and object-oriented [2,7] paradigm.

There have been a few attempts of extending the expressive power of regular corecursion. Notably, *structural resolution* [15,16] is an operational semantics for logic programming where infinite derivations that cannot be built in finite time are generated lazily, and only partial answers are shown. Another approach is the work in [8], introducing algebraic trees and equations as generalizations of regular ones. Such proposals share, even though with different techniques and in a different context, our aim of extending regular corecursion; on the other hand, the fact that corecursion is *checked* is, at our knowledge, a novelty of our work.

For the operators considered in the calculus and some examples, our main sources of inspiration have been the works of Rutten [17], where a coinductive calculus of streams of real numbers is defined, and Hinze [12], where a calculus of generic streams is defined in a constructive way and implemented in Haskell.

In this paper, as in all the above mentioned approaches derived from co-SLD resolution, the aim is to provide an *operational* semantics, designed to directly lead to an implementation. That is, even though streams are infinite objects (terms where the constructor is the only operator, defined coinductively), evaluation handles *finite* representations, and is defined by an *inductive* inference system. Coinductive approaches can be adopted to obtain more abstract semantics of calculi with infinite terms. For instance, [9] defines a coinductive semantics of the infinitary lambda-calculus where, roughly, the semantics of terms with an infinite reduction sequence is the infinite term obtained as limit. In coinductive logic programming, co-SLD resolution is the operational counterpart of a coinductive semantics where a program denotes a set of infinite terms. In [2], analogously, regular corecursion is shown to be sound with respect to an abstract coinductive semantics using *flexible coinduction* [5,10], see below.

Our calculus is an enhancement of that presented in [3], with two main significant contributions: (1) the interleaving operator, challenging since it is based on a non-trivial recursion schema; (2) an optimized definition of the runtime well-definedness check, as a useful basis for an implementation. Our main technical results are Theorem 1, stating that passing the runtime well-definedness check performed for a function call prevents non-termination in accessing elements in the resulting stream, and Theorem 2, stating that the optimized version is equivalent.

Whereas in [3] the well-definedness check was also a necessary condition to guarantee termination, this is not the case here, due to the interleaving operator. Consider, for instance, the following example: $\rho = \{s \mapsto (s\hat{}\,\|s)\|0{:}s\}$. The judgment $\mathsf{wd}_\rho(s, \emptyset)$ is not derivable, in particular because of $s\hat{}$, since $\mathsf{wd}_\rho(s, \{s \mapsto -1\})$ is not derivable and, hence, $\mathsf{wd}_\rho(s\hat{}, \{s \mapsto 0\})$, $\mathsf{wd}_\rho(s\hat{}\,\|s, \{s \mapsto 0\})$, and $\mathsf{wd}_\rho((s\hat{}\,\|s)\|0{:}s, \{s \mapsto 0\})$. However, $at_\rho(s, i)$ is well-defined for all indexes i; indeed, $at_\rho(s,1) = 0$ is derivable, $at_\rho(s,0) = k$ is derivable iff $at_\rho(s,1) = k$ is derivable, and, for all $i > 1$, $at_\rho(s,i) = k$ is derivable iff $at_\rho(s,j) = k$ is derivable for some $j < i$, hence $at_\rho(s,i) = 0$ is derivable for all i. We leave for future work the investigation of a complete check.

In future work, we plan to also prove soundness of the operational well-definedness with respect to its abstract definition. Completeness does not hold, as shown by the example `zeros() = [0] [*] zeros()` which is not well-formed operationally, but admits as unique solution the stream of all zeros.

Finally, in the presented calculus a cyclic call is detected by rule (COREC) if it is syntactically the same of some in the call trace. Although such a rule allows cycle detection for all the examples presented in this paper, it is not complete with respect to the abstract notion where expressions denoting the same stream are equivalent, as illustrated by the following alternative definition of function `incr` as presented in Sect. 3:

```
incr_reg(s) = (s(0)+1):incr_reg(s^)
```

If syntactic equivalence is used to detect cycles, then the call `incr_reg([0])` diverges, since the terms passed as argument to the recursive calls are all syntactically different; as an example, consider the arguments x and $x\hat{\ }$ passed to the initial call and to the first recursive call, respectively, in the environment $\rho = \{x \mapsto 0 : x\}$; they are syntactically different, but denote the same stream.

In future work we plan to investigate more expressive operational characterizations of equivalence.

Other interesting directions for future work are the following.

- Investigate additional operators and the expressive power of the calculus.
- Design a static type system to prevent runtime errors such as the non-well-definedness of a stream.
- Extend corecursive definition to *flexible* corecursive definitions [10,11] where programmers can define specific behaviour when a cycle is detected. In this way we could get termination in cases where lazy evaluation diverges. For instance, assuming to allow also booleans results for functions, we could define the predicate `allPos`, checking that all the elements of a stream are positive, specifying as result `true` when a cycle is detected; in this way, e.g., `allPos(one_two)` would return the correct result.

References

1. Ancona, D.: Regular corecursion in Prolog. Comput. Lang. Syst. Struct. **39**(4), 142–162 (2013)
2. Ancona, D., Barbieri, P., Dagnino, F., Zucca, E.: Sound regular corecursion in coFJ. In: Hirschfeld, R., Pape, T. (eds.) ECOOP'20 - Object-Oriented Programming. LIPIcs, vol. 166, pp. 1:1–1:28. Schloss Dagstuhl - Leibniz-Zentrum für Informatik (2020)
3. Ancona, D., Barbieri, P., Zucca, E.: Enhanced regular corecursion for data streams. In: ICTCS'21 - Italian Conference on Theoretical Computer Science (2021)

4. Ancona, D., Barbieri, P., Zucca, E.: Enhancing expressivity of checked corecursive streams (extended version) (2022). https://arxiv.org/abs/2202.06868
5. Ancona, D., Dagnino, F., Zucca, E.: Generalizing inference systems by coaxioms. In: Yang, H. (ed.) ESOP 2017. LNCS, vol. 10201, pp. 29–55. Springer, Heidelberg (2017). https://doi.org/10.1007/978-3-662-54434-1_2
6. Ancona, D., Dovier, A.: A theoretical perspective of coinductive logic programming. Fund. Inform. **140**(3–4), 221–246 (2015)
7. Ancona, D., Zucca, E.: Corecursive featherweight Java. In: FTfJP'12 - Formal Techniques for Java-like Programs, pp. 3–10. ACM Press (2012)
8. Courcelle, B.: Fundamental properties of infinite trees. Theoret. Comput. Sci. **25**, 95–169 (1983)
9. Czajka, L.: A new coinductive confluence proof for infinitary lambda calculus. Log. Methods Comput. Sci. **16**(1) (2020)
10. Dagnino, F.: Flexible coinduction. Ph.D. thesis, DIBRIS, University of Genova (2021)
11. Dagnino, F., Ancona, D., Zucca, E.: Flexible coinductive logic programming. Theory Pract. Logic Program. **20**(6), 818–833 (2020). Issue for ICLP 2020
12. Hinze, R.: Concrete stream calculus: an extended study. J. Funct. Program. **20**(5–6), 463–535 (2010)
13. Jeannin, J.-B., Kozen, D.: Computing with capsules. J. Autom. Lang. Comb. **17**(2–4), 185–204 (2012)
14. Jeannin, J.-B., Kozen, D., Silva, A.: CoCaml: functional programming with regular coinductive types. Fund. Inform. **150**, 347–377 (2017)
15. Komendantskaya, E., Johann, P., Schmidt, M.: A productivity checker for logic programming. In: Hermenegildo, M.V., Lopez-Garcia, P. (eds.) LOPSTR 2016. LNCS, vol. 10184, pp. 168–186. Springer, Cham (2017). https://doi.org/10.1007/978-3-319-63139-4_10
16. Komendantskaya, E., Power, J., Schmidt, M.: Coalgebraic logic programming: from semantics to implementation. J. Log. Comput. **26**(2), 745–783 (2016)
17. Rutten, J.J.M.M.: A coinductive calculus of streams. Math. Struct. Comput. Sci. **15**(1), 93–147 (2005)
18. Simon, L.: Extending logic programming with coinduction. Ph.D. thesis, University of Texas at Dallas (2006)
19. Simon, L., Bansal, A., Mallya, A., Gupta, G.: Co-logic programming: extending logic programming with coinduction. In: Arge, L., Cachin, C., Jurdziński, T., Tarlecki, A. (eds.) ICALP 2007. LNCS, vol. 4596, pp. 472–483. Springer, Heidelberg (2007). https://doi.org/10.1007/978-3-540-73420-8_42

Improving Type Error Reporting for Type Classes

Sheng Chen[✉] and Md Rabib Noor

UL Lafayette, Lafayette, LA 70503, USA
{chen,md-rabib.noor1}@louisiana.edu

Abstract. Debugging type errors when type inference fails is a challenging problem since there are many different ways to remove the type error, and it's unclear which way is intended. While numerous approaches have been proposed to more precisely locate the real error causes, most of them do not deal with popular type system extensions, such as type classes. A second problem is that most approaches do not provide enough information for removing the type error or do so for a few error causes only.

In this work, we develop an approach called TEC to address both problems. Given an ill-typed expression that may involve type classes, TEC finds comprehensive error causes and generates for each cause an error fix with detailed information for removing the type error. TEC computes all error fixes, ranks them, and iteratively presents the most likely error fix to the user until a fix is accepted. TEC reduces the problem of finding all error fixes to variational typing, which systematically reuses typing results. Our main technical innovation is a *variational context reduction* algorithm that simplifies type class constraints containing variations. We have evaluated the precision of TEC and found that it outperforms existing approaches in locating type errors arising from type class uses.

1 Introduction

Type inference allows programs to be statically typed, even without the presence of type annotations. However, it is particularly difficult to locate the real error causes and generate informative error messages when type inference fails. In the last thirty years, numerous approaches have been proposed to address this problem [4,5,10,13,17,18, 23–26,30,31,35,38,39,41–43].

However, while plentiful type system extensions have been proposed and integrated into languages like Haskell, most of the error debugging methods focused on the Hindley-Milner type system (HM) plus some basic extensions, such as algebraic data types. On one hand, as type classes in Haskell are so popular nowadays, it is hard to write a program without involving them, particularly as types for numbers (such as Int, Integer, and Double) are members of different classes (such as Num, Real, and Integral) and lists are a member of Traversable. On the other hand, type error debugging for type classes is rudimentary. All Haskell compilers and error debuggers SHErrLoc [43] and Chameleon [33,34] diagnose type errors only and do not provide change

---

This work is supported by the National Science Foundation under the grant CCF-1750886.

M. Hanus and A. Igarashi (Eds.): FLOPS 2022, LNCS 13215, pp. 19–38, 2022.
https://doi.org/10.1007/978-3-030-99461-7_2

suggestions. Moreover, they usually report only several likely error causes and in many cases miss the real cause.

Consider, for example, the erroneous expression `rank1 x = (x 1, x True)` adapted from [2]. This expression is ill-typed because it applies the argument to values of different types. For this expression the most widely used Haskell compiler GHC version 8.10.6 displays the following message.

```
* No instance for (Num Bool) arising from the literal '1'
* In the first argument of 'x', namely '1'
  In the expression: x 1
  In the expression: (x 1, x True)
```

This error message is not helpful for removing the type error for several reasons. First, the type information and the location information is inconsistent. The message seems to say that 1 requires the type system to prove `Bool` be an instance of the class `Num`. While 1 gives rise to the type class `Num`, it doesn't have anything to do with `Bool`. Second, it doesn't say how to remove the type error, for example, adding an instance definition `Num Bool`, changing 1 to something of `Bool`, and so on. In this small example, it is not hard to infer that `Num Bool` is caused by the conflict of 1 and `True`. However, when the program is large, the conflicting subexpressions may be far away, and figuring out the exact problem can be hard. Third, GHC only reports the problem at 1 while, in fact, changing any of `True` or either of x will make `rank1` well-typed. Moreover, there is no evidence that 1 is more likely to cause the type error than `True`. Thus, reporting the problem at 1 is biased for users. For this example, SHErrLoc produces a similar message, except that it mentions both 1 and `True`.

We will use the terms *error causes* and *error fixes* throughout the paper. Given an expression, an error cause is a set of subexpressions such that changing them appropriately can make the expression well-typed. We omit the set delimiters if the cardinality is 1. For example, all of x (either occurrence), 1, `True`, and $\{1, \text{True}\}$ are possible error causes for `rank1`. An error fix is an error cause plus change information, for each member of the error cause, to make the expression well-typed. For example, the error cause 1 plus the change of 1 to something of type `Bool` is an error fix for `rank1`. Given an oracle (for example, specified by the paper where the example was introduced), we say an error cause or error fix is correct if it is consistent with the oracle and incorrect otherwise. In these terms, both GHC and SHErrLoc only identify error causes and do not generate error fixes.

When multi-parameter classes and functional dependencies [22] are involved, the messages become worse. Consider, for example, the expression `insert2` adapted from [34]. The functional dependency `ce -> e` specifies that the container type `ce` uniquely determines the element type `e`. Many interesting `Collects` instances may be defined, such as lists, characteristic functions, bit sets for representing collections of characters, etc.

```
class Collects ce e | ce -> e where
    empty :: ce
    insert :: e -> ce -> ce

insert2 c = insert 1 (insert True c)
```

The expression `insert2` contains a type inconsistency between `1` and `True` because they violate the functional dependency [34]. For `insert2`, GHC generates a similar message as before while SHErrLoc generates the following message, where the text with a grey background is the error cause identified by SHErrLoc. The corresponding constraint for each error given by SHErrLoc is attached to the end of each message in italics. As a result, according to [34], these messages are incorrect.

```
2 errors found
A value with type cons_2 (ce_aL3) (e_aL4) is being used at type Collects
insert2 c = insert 1 (insert True c)   cons_2 (ce_aL3) (e_aL4) <= Collects

A value with type cons_2 (ce_aHQ) (e_aHR) is being used at type Collects
insert2 c = insert 1 (insert True c)   cons_2 (ce_aHQ) (e_aHR) <= Collects
```

Based on previous examples, we observe that the tool support for debugging type errors for type systems with type classes is inadequate. To address this problem, we develop TEC, which (1) finds comprehensive error causes, (2) generates an error fix for each cause, and (3) ranks all error fixes and presents them iteratively. For `insert2`, TEC generates the following error fix.

```
The expression contains type errors. Possible fix:
Change: "True", of type: "Bool", to something of type: "Num f => f"
the resulting type will be: (Collects c f, Num f) => c -> c

Show more one-change fixes? (y/n)
```

We can see that each fix includes the error cause (`True`), the type it has under normal type inference (`Bool`), the type it ought to have to remove the type error (`Num f => f`), and the type of the resulting expression after applying this fix. We will refer to these three type parts as *source type*, *target type*, and *consequent type*, respectively.

This message provides abundant information to remove the type error: the consequent type allows the user to quickly decide if this message is useful. For example, if the user's expected type of `insert2` is `Collects c Bool => c -> c`, then the user can simply skip this message and ask for the next one. Otherwise if the consequent type is intended, the user can turn to the target type to further decide how she can fix the type error. In this case, the user can figure out that she should change `True` to something that is an instance of the `Num` type class.

If this message is not useful, the user can hit the letter y to ask for the next message, which suggests to change `1`, with the source type `Num a => a`, the target type `Bool`, and the consequent type `Collects c Bool => c -> c`. This process continues until all error fixes are displayed. Later error fixes may involve multiple subexpressions. For example, after the first four fixes, TEC starts to generate fixes involving two subexpressions.

We have evaluated the precision of TEC in more depth for two benchmarks (Sect. 5) and the result shows that TEC is precise in locating type errors. Also, TEC is fast enough for practical use. For example, for programs of about 100 LOC and 300 LOC, TEC delivers the first error message within 1.6s and 5.7s, respectively. While the response time is still slower than compilers, this cost pays off as effective and informative error messages generated by TEC can save beginners dozens of minutes for fixing type errors, a view shared by [25].

Overall, our contributions in this paper is developing an error debugger, TEC, that considers type classes and functional dependencies, finds complete error fixes in leaves and their combinations under moderate conditions, and is fast enough for practical use. Each error fix provides abundant information to remove the type error. Along the way, we formally develop a type system for finding comprehensive error fixes and a variational context reduction for simplifying type class constraints.

We give an overview of TEC in Sect. 2, present a type system in Sect. 3, develop constraint generation and variational context reduction in Sect. 4, present evaluation in Sect. 5, discuss related work in Sect. 6, and conclude in Sect. 7.

2   TEC, Informally

TEC relies on the machineries developed in variational typing [6,7] to efficiently find comprehensive error fixes. In this section, we first present background on variational typing and then use an example to illustrate the idea of TEC.

Background. Variational typing introduces variations to the type syntax. For example, the type $A\langle \text{Int}, \text{Bool} \rangle$ contains a variation named A, which has two *alternatives*: Int and Bool. An expression having the type $A\langle \text{Int}, \text{Bool} \rangle$ means that the expression has either the type Int or Bool, depending on which alternative is taken. Variations can be considered as a binary type constructor, so $A\langle \text{Int}, B\langle \text{Bool}, \text{Int} \rangle \rangle$, $A\langle \text{Int}, \text{Bool} \rangle \rightarrow \text{Bool}$, and $A\langle \text{Int}, \text{Bool} \rangle \rightarrow B\langle \text{Bool}, \text{Int} \rangle$ are all valid types.

Variations can be eliminated through a process called *selection*, which takes a type ϕ and a selector s of the form $d.i$ and replaces all occurrences of variations named d with their ith alternatives in ϕ. We write $\lfloor \phi \rfloor_{d.i}$ for selecting ϕ with $d.i$. For instance, $\lfloor A\langle \text{Int}, \text{Bool} \rangle \rfloor_{A.2}$ yields Bool. A decision is a set of selectors. We use ω to range over decisions. Selection extends naturally to decisions as $\lfloor \phi \rfloor_{s\omega} = \lfloor \lfloor \phi \rfloor_s \rfloor_\omega$. Note that the ordering of selection doesn't matter. We say ω is complete with respect to ϕ if $\lfloor \phi \rfloor_\omega$ yields a *plain* type, which doesn't contain any choice. Selecting a plain type with any selector yields the type itself. For instance, $\lfloor \text{Int} \rfloor_{B.2} = \text{Int}$. Based on the definition of selection, choices with the same name are synchronized in the sense that we have to select the same alternatives from them and those with different names are independent. Thus, while $A\langle \text{Int}, \text{Bool} \rangle \rightarrow A\langle \text{Bool}, \text{Int} \rangle$ can generate two plain types, $A\langle \text{Int}, \text{Bool} \rangle \rightarrow B\langle \text{Bool}, \text{Int} \rangle$ can generate four with two different parameter types and two different return types.

An Example of Debugging with TEC. During type inference, compilers infer the most general types for all the subexpressions visited, which defers the detection of type errors. Thus, compiler error messages are often biased and incomplete. To find comprehensive error fixes, TEC systematically assume that each leaf may cause the type error and find the target type of each leaf to remove the type error in the expression. TEC also computes the source type and consequent type of changing each leaf (see Page 3 below our error message for the meanings of the terms source type and consequent type). In fact, TEC also finds error fixes in arbitrary combinations of leaves, and in this case computes related type information for each leaf in the error fix. After the computation is finished, TEC determines that a leaf indeed causes the type error if the source type differs from the target type for that leaf.

TEC reduces this computation process to variational typing by traversing the expression just once. For each leaf, TEC assigns a variational type whose left and right alternatives represent the source and target types, respectively. The source type is the type a leaf has under normal type inference and the target type is the type that makes the context well-typed. When a leaf is first visited, the target type is a fresh type variable, which will be refined to the correct type after the typing constraints are solved.

We illustrate this process with type error debugging for abs True, where abs has the type $\forall \alpha_1.\text{Num } \alpha_1 \Rightarrow \alpha_1 \to \alpha_1$. The following table lists types for subexpressions and the generated constraints, which are numbered. Each leaf receives a choice type that includes the source type and the target type for it. In the constraint (1), $\text{Num } \alpha_2$, the constraint in the left alternative, is come from the constraint of $\text{Num } \alpha_2 \Rightarrow \alpha_2 \to \alpha_2$, which is the type of abs. In that constraint, ε in the right alternative means that the type α_3 has no constraint. The constraint (2) expresses the equivalence constraint between two types, and we use $\equiv^?$ to denote such constraints.

Subexpr.	Types	Constraints	Idx
abs	$A\langle \alpha_2 \to \alpha_2, \alpha_3 \rangle$	$A\langle \text{Num } \alpha_2, \varepsilon \rangle$	(1)
True	$B\langle \text{Bool}, \alpha_4 \rangle$		
abs True	β_1	$A\langle \alpha_2 \to \alpha_2, \alpha_3 \rangle \equiv^? B\langle \text{Bool}, \alpha_4 \rangle \to \beta_1$ (2)	

In general, traversing an expression generates both type class constraints and type equivalence constraints. Type equivalence constraints are solved with the variational unification algorithm from [6]. In addition to a unifier, constraint solving also returns a *pattern* to indicate at which variants constraint solving is successful and at which it is not. Specifically, a pattern, written as π, can be $\top$ (denoting constraint solving success), $\bot$ (denoting solving failure), or a variation between two patterns (such patterns can be useful when constraint solving in one variant fails while in the other variant succeeds). For example, the pattern for solving the constraint $A\langle \text{Int}, \text{Bool} \rangle \equiv^? \text{Int}$ is $A\langle \top, \bot \rangle$ since the constraint solving in the second alternative fails. Type class constraints are solved using variational context reduction, to be developed in Sect. 4.1. Similarly, a pattern is returned to indicate where reduction is successful and where is not.

For the constraints (2) above, the solution is as follows. The returned pattern is $\top$, since constraint solving is successful for all variants. κs in the solution represent fresh type variables introduced during unification.

$$\theta = \{\alpha_2 \mapsto A\langle B\langle \text{Bool}, \alpha_4 \rangle, \kappa_1 \rangle, \alpha_3 \mapsto A\langle \kappa_3, B\langle \text{Bool}, \alpha_4 \rangle \to \kappa_2 \rangle, \beta_1 \mapsto A\langle B\langle \text{Bool}, \alpha_4 \rangle, \kappa_2 \rangle\}$$

After that, we apply θ to the constraint (1) and remove the dead alternative (κ_1), which yield the new constraint $C_1 = A\langle \text{Num } B\langle \text{Bool}, \alpha_4 \rangle, \varepsilon \rangle$. With variational context reduction, C_1 is reduced to (π, C) where $\pi = A\langle B\langle \bot, \top \rangle, \top \rangle$ and $C = A\langle B\langle \text{Num Bool}, \text{Num } \alpha_4 \rangle, \varepsilon \rangle$. The π indicates that C_1 can not be reduced to the normal form [21] in variant $\{A.1, B.1\}$. Overall, the result type is $\phi = C \Rightarrow \theta(\beta_1)$ with the pattern π.

With ϕ, θ, and π, we can generate error fixes by considering different decisions. For any ω, if $\lfloor \pi \rfloor_\omega$ is $\top$, then ω corresponds to an error fix that will remove the type error in the expression. The reason is that, as discussed earlier, only variants where both variational unification and context reduction are successful will receive $\top$. If either fails, then the variant contains a $\bot$. Given a ω, if $d.1 \in \omega$, it means that we do not change the subexpression where d is created. Otherwise, we change the corresponding subexpression to something of type $\lfloor \theta(\alpha) \rfloor_\omega$, where α is the target type for the subexpression. For example, let's consider generating the error fix for the decision $\omega = \{A.1, B.2\}$. Since $\lfloor \pi \rfloor_{\{A.1,B.2\}} = \top$, this fix will remove the type error. The decision ω corresponds to changing True only. The target type is α_4 and the constraint for the target type is $\lfloor C \rfloor_\omega$ = Num α_4, meaning that the overall target type for True is Num $\alpha_4 \Rightarrow \alpha_4$. The consequent type type is $\lfloor \phi \rfloor_\omega$, which is Num $\alpha_4 \Rightarrow \alpha_4$. This provides all the information needed for generating our error message in Sect. 1.

3   Type System

This section presents a type system for computing comprehensive error fixes and studies its properties. While supporting type class constraints, our formalization is made general so that it can be instantiated to support other type constraints.

3.1   Syntax

Figure 1 collects the syntax for types, expressions, and related environments. We consider a formalization for HM plus multiparameter type classes. We use c to range over constants. Our formalization omit functional dependencies for simplicity though our implementation supports them. Types are stratified into three layers. Monotypes include con-

Expressions	e, f	$::=$	$c \mid x \mid \lambda x.e \mid e\,e \mid \mathtt{let}\ x = e\ \mathtt{in}\ e$
Monotypes	τ	$::=$	$\gamma \mid \alpha \mid \tau \to \tau$
Variational types	ϕ	$::=$	$\tau \mid d\langle \phi, \phi \rangle \mid \phi \to \phi$
Type schemas	σ	$::=$	$\phi \mid \forall \overline{\alpha}.C \Rightarrow \phi$
Constraints	C	$::=$	$\varepsilon \mid \phi \equiv \phi \mid C \wedge C \mid \mathtt{G}\,\overline{\phi} \mid d\langle C, C \rangle$
Axiom schemes	Q	$::=$	$C \mid Q \wedge Q \mid \forall \overline{\alpha}.C \Rightarrow \mathtt{G}\,\overline{\tau}$
			$\mid \quad \forall \overline{\alpha}.C \Leftarrow \mathtt{G}\,\overline{\alpha}$
Typing patterns	π	$::=$	$\top \mid \bot \mid d\langle \pi, \pi \rangle$
Type environments	Γ	$::=$	$\varnothing \mid \Gamma, x \mapsto \sigma$
Substitutions	θ	$::=$	$\varnothing \mid \theta, \alpha \mapsto \phi$
Choice environments	Δ	$::=$	$\varnothing \mid \Delta, (l, d\langle \phi, \phi \rangle)$

Fig. 1. Syntax

stant types (γ), type variables (α), and function types. Variational types extend monotypes with choice types. We use τ and ϕ to range over monotypes and variational types, respectively. Type schemas, ranged over by σ, has the form $\forall \overline{\alpha}.C \Rightarrow \phi$, where C specifies the requirements of types substituting $\overline{\alpha}$ in ϕ. We use $FV(\sigma)$ to return the set of free type variables in σ.

There are two main forms of primitive constraints. The first form is the type equivalence requirement $\phi_1 \equiv \phi_2$, which specifies that ϕ_1 and ϕ_2 must be equivalent. Two types are equivalent if selecting them with the same decision always yields the same type. For example, $d\langle \mathtt{Int}, \mathtt{Int} \rangle \equiv \mathtt{Int}$. The second is the type class constraint $\mathtt{G}\,\overline{\tau}$. Compound constraints include $C_1 \wedge C_2$, where $\wedge$ is commutative, and $d\langle C_1, C_2 \rangle$, a variation between C_1 and C_2 under the name d.

E1 $\dfrac{}{Q \wedge C \Vdash C}$

E2 $\dfrac{Q \wedge C_1 \Vdash C_2 \quad Q \wedge C_2 \Vdash C_3}{Q \wedge C_1 \Vdash C_3}$

E3 $\dfrac{Q \Vdash C}{\theta(Q) \Vdash \theta(C)}$

E4 $\dfrac{Q \Vdash C_1 \quad Q \Vdash C_2}{Q \Vdash C_1 \wedge C_2}$

E5 $\dfrac{Q \wedge C_1 \Vdash C_2 \quad Q \wedge C_3 \Vdash C_4}{Q \wedge d\langle C_1, C_3\rangle \Vdash d\langle C_2, C_4\rangle}$

E6 $\dfrac{\forall \omega. \lfloor \pi \rfloor_\omega = \top \Rightarrow \lfloor Q \rfloor_\omega \Vdash \lfloor C \rfloor_\omega}{Q \Vdash_\pi C}$

T1 $\dfrac{Q \Vdash \phi_1 \equiv \phi_2}{Q \Vdash \phi_2 \equiv \phi_1}$

T2 $\dfrac{Q \Vdash \phi_1 \equiv \phi_2 \quad Q \Vdash \phi_2 \equiv \phi_3}{Q \Vdash \phi_1 \equiv \phi_3}$

T3 $Q \Vdash \phi \equiv \phi$

T4 $\dfrac{Q \Vdash \phi_1 \equiv \phi_2}{Q \Vdash C[\phi_1] \leftrightarrow C[\phi_2]}$

T5 $Q \Vdash d\langle \phi, \phi\rangle \equiv \phi$

T6 $Q \Vdash d\langle \phi_1, \phi_2\rangle \equiv d\langle \lfloor \phi_1 \rfloor_{d.1}, \lfloor \phi_2 \rfloor_{d.2}\rangle$

T7 $\dfrac{\forall \bar\alpha. C \Rightarrow G\,\bar\tau \in Q \quad Q \Vdash [\alpha \mapsto \phi](C)}{Q \Vdash [\alpha \mapsto \phi](G\,\bar\tau)}$

T8 $\dfrac{\forall \bar\alpha. C \Leftarrow G\,\bar\alpha \in Q \quad Q \Vdash [\alpha \mapsto \phi](G\,\bar\alpha) \quad C_G \in C}{Q \Vdash [\alpha \mapsto \phi](C_G)}$

Fig. 2. Entailment relation of constraints

Axiom schemes include constraints (C), abstractions of class declarations ($\forall \bar\alpha. C \Leftarrow$ G $\bar\alpha$), and those of instance declarations ($\forall \bar\alpha. C \Rightarrow$ G $\bar\tau$). For example, the declaration class Eq a => Ord a where... gives rise to $\forall \alpha.$Eq $\alpha \Leftarrow$ Ord α. We use a left arrow in the scheme to reflect that any type that is an instance of a subclass (Ord) is also an instance of the parent class (Eq). Similarly, the instance declaration instance Eq a => Eq [a] where... gives rise to $\forall \alpha.$Eq $\alpha \Rightarrow$ Eq $[\alpha]$.

We use l to range over program locations. Each program element has a unique location in the program. We use the function $\ell_e(f)$ to return the location of f in e. We may omit the subscript e when the context is clear. For simplicity, we assume that f uniquely determines the location. The exact definition of $\ell(\cdot)$ doesn't matter.

The definitions of the type environments Γ and the substitutions θ are conventional, mapping expression variables to type schemas and type variables to variational types, respectively. The choice environment Δ associates each program location l to a choice type $d\langle \phi_1, \phi_2\rangle$, where d, ϕ_1, and ϕ_2 are the choice, the source type, and the target type for the subexpression at l, respectively.

3.2 Type System

Constraint Entailment. Constraints are related together through the entailment relation defined in Fig. 2. The relation $Q \Vdash C$ specifies that under axiom Q, the constraint C is satisfied. The first three rules are standard in constrained type systems [19,28]. The rules E1 and E2 specify that the relation is reflexive and transitive. The rule E3 states

$$\boxed{C;\pi;\Gamma\vdash e:\phi|\Delta}$$

$$\text{CON}\ \frac{c\ \text{is of type}\ \gamma\qquad \exists d}{C;\pi;\Gamma\vdash c:d\langle\gamma,\phi\rangle|\{(\ell(c),d\langle\gamma,\phi\rangle)\}}$$

$$\text{VAR}\ \frac{\Gamma(x)=\forall\bar{\alpha}.C\Rightarrow\phi\qquad \exists d\qquad C_1\Vdash_{d\langle\lfloor\pi\rfloor_{d.1},\perp\rangle}[\alpha\mapsto\phi'](C)}{C_1;\pi;\Gamma\vdash x:d\langle[\alpha\mapsto\phi'](\phi),\phi_1\rangle|\{(\ell(x),d\langle[\alpha\mapsto\phi'](\phi),\phi_1\rangle)\}}$$

$$\text{UNBOUND}\ \frac{x\notin dom(\Gamma)\qquad \exists d\qquad \pi\leq d\langle\perp,\top\rangle}{C;\pi;\Gamma\vdash x:\phi|\{(\ell(x),\phi)\}}\qquad \text{ABS}\ \frac{C;\pi;\Gamma,x\mapsto\phi\vdash e:\phi'|\Delta}{C;\pi;\Gamma\vdash\lambda x.e:\phi\rightarrow\phi'|\Delta}$$

$$\text{LET}\ \frac{C;\pi;\Gamma,x\mapsto\phi\vdash e:\phi|\Delta\qquad \bar{\alpha}=FV(\phi)-FV(\Gamma)\qquad C_1;\pi;\Gamma,x\mapsto\forall\bar{\alpha}.C\Rightarrow\phi\vdash e_1:\phi_1|\Delta_1}{C\wedge C_1;\pi;\Gamma\vdash\textbf{let}\ x=e\ \textbf{in}\ e_1:\phi_1|\Delta\cup\Delta_1}$$

$$\text{APP}\ \frac{C;\pi;\Gamma\vdash e_1:\phi_1|\Delta_1\qquad C;\pi;\Gamma\vdash e_2:\phi_2|\Delta_2\qquad C\Vdash_\pi\phi_1\equiv\phi_2\rightarrow\phi}{C;\pi;\Gamma\vdash e_1\ e_2:\phi|\Delta_1\cup\Delta_2}$$

$$\boxed{Q;\pi;\Gamma\vdash_M e:\phi|\Delta}\qquad \text{MAIN}\ \frac{C;\pi;\Gamma\vdash e:\phi|\Delta\qquad \pi_1\leq\pi\qquad Q\Vdash_{\pi_1}C}{Q;\pi_1;\Gamma\vdash_M e:\phi|\Delta}$$

Fig. 3. Typing rules

that the entailment relation is stable under type substitution. Type substitution, written as $\theta(\sigma)$, substitutes free type variables in σ with their corresponding mappings in θ. For instance and class declaration constraints, substitution has no effect. For other constraints, substitution applies to their type components. The rules E4 and E5 show how to satisfy the compound constraints $C_1\wedge C_2$ and $d\langle C_3,C_4\rangle$. The rule E6 introduces the partial entailment relation $\Vdash_\pi$, which specifies that the validity of $\Vdash$ is only limited to the variants where π has $\top$s.

The rest of the rules in Fig. 2 specify the relations between type equivalence constraints. The rules T1 through T3 express that this relation is reflexive, symmetric, and transitive. In T4, we use $C[\ ]$ to denote a constraint context into which we can plug a type. The rule says that the satisfiability of a constraint is preserved if a type of it is replaced by an equivalent type. The notation $Q\Vdash C_1\leftrightarrow C_2$ is a shorthand for $Q\wedge C_1\Vdash C_2$ and $Q\wedge C_2\Vdash C_1$. The rule T5 states that a choice with same alternatives is equivalent to its alternatives. The rule T6 says that dead alternatives can always be removed without affecting type equivalence. Here $\lfloor\phi_1\rfloor_{d.1}$ removes all the second alternatives of d choices inside ϕ_1, which are unreachable because ϕ_1 is in the first alternative of d. For example, $Q\Vdash A\langle\text{Int},A\langle\text{Char},\text{Bool}\rangle\rangle\equiv A\langle\text{Int},\text{Bool}\rangle$. The rules T7 and T8 deal with entailments brought in by instance and class declarations, respectively. We use C_G to denote type class constraints having type variables as their arguments.

Typing Rules. Typing rules are presented in Fig. 3. Type judgment has the form $C;\pi;\Gamma\vdash e:\phi|\Delta$, which is read as: under the type environment Γ and constraint C the expression e has the type ϕ with the validity restriction π, with type change information collected in Δ. Here Γ, C, π, and e are inputs, and ϕ and Δ are outputs. The π indicates that the typing result is required to be correct only in the alternatives that π has $\top$s and is not required to be correct in alternatives that π has $\perp$s. For example, disregarding Δ, $\varepsilon; \top; \Gamma \vdash 1 : \mathtt{Int} | \Delta$ is valid. Interestingly, while 1 does not have the type $\mathtt{Bool}$, $\varepsilon; \bot; \Gamma \vdash 1 : \mathtt{Bool} | \Delta$ is also a valid type judgment since $\bot$ in the judgment says the result does not need to be correct. However, the judgment $\varepsilon; \top; \Gamma \vdash 1 : \mathtt{Bool} | \Delta$ is invalid because $\top$ requires the result to be correct but 1 does not have the type $\mathtt{Bool}$. Intuitively,

In many rules, we use the condition $\exists\, d$, where d can be a fresh or existing choice name. This condition allows us to maintain the flexibility of assigning variations to leaves. If we assign unique variations to leaves, we can change leaves independently. Otherwise, if some leaves receive the same variation, then either all or none of them will be changed. This condition is always satisfied.

The rule CON, dealing with unconstrained constants, says that for a constant c of the type γ, the source type is γ and the target type is ϕ, which is unconstrained, meaning that we can change c to anything to remove the type error. The π component can be any value since changing a constant will not introduce any error. Here Δ is assigned $\{(\ell(c), d\langle\gamma,\phi\rangle)\}$ to record the change information. The rule for constrained constants is very similar to VAR and we will not present it here. The rule VAR for variables has a similar pattern as CON has. The source type for a variable x is any valid instantiation of the polymorphic type $\Gamma(x)$ and the target type ϕ_1 is again unconstrained. Since typing a variable is always correct, π can be any value. The rule records a change for x in Δ.

We also need a rule for unbound variables since we do not want the typing process to be terminated. As always, the target type can be an unconstrained type. The question is, what should be the source type for the variable? Since the variable is unbound, we couldn't find out the correct source type. Fortunately, we can avoid this problem by choosing an appropriate π. Specifically, the first alternative of the typing pattern must be $\bot$, denoting that the typing result of the first alternative that accesses the unbound variable is invalid. As always, the second alternative can be any value.

To formally express this idea, we first define the *more-defined* relation between typing patterns as follows. We write $\pi_1 \leq \pi_2$ to express that π_2 is more-defined than π_1. Intuitively, $\pi_1 \leq \pi_2$ if for any alternative π_2 has an $\bot$ then so does π_1.

$$\pi \leq \top \qquad \bot \leq \pi \qquad \frac{\pi_1 \leq \pi_2 \qquad \pi_2 \leq \pi_3}{\pi_1 \leq \pi_3} \qquad \frac{\pi_1 \leq \pi_3 \qquad \pi_2 \leq \pi_4}{d\langle\pi_1,\pi_2\rangle \leq d\langle\pi_3,\pi_4\rangle} \qquad \frac{\Vdash \pi_1 \equiv \pi_2}{\pi_1 \leq \pi_2}$$

The first two rules indicate that all typing patterns are more-defined than $\bot$ and less-defined than $\top$. The third rule states that $\leq$ is transitive. The fourth rule says that two choice typing patterns satisfy $\leq$ if both corresponding alternatives satisfy this relation. Finally, the last rule reuses the entailment relation defined for variational types by interpreting $\top$ and $\bot$ as two distinct constant types. The rule says that two typing patterns that satisfy the equivalence relation also satisfy the $\leq$ relation. This allows us to derive $\top \leq d\langle\top,\top\rangle$ since the two sides are equivalent according to the rule T2 in Fig. 2.

We formalize the idea for typing unbound variables in the rule UNBOUND with the help of $\leq$. The rules ABS for abstractions and LET for **let** expressions are similar to those in the constraint-based formalization of HM, except for the threading information for π and Δ here. The rule APP deals with applications. The rules for deriving type equivalence ($\equiv$) are given in the upper part of Fig. 2.

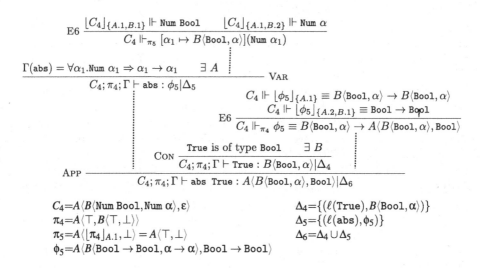

$C_4 = A\langle B\langle \text{Num Bool}, \text{Num } \alpha\rangle, \varepsilon\rangle$ $\Delta_4 = \{(\ell(\text{True}), B\langle \text{Bool}, \alpha\rangle)\}$

$\pi_4 = A\langle \top, B\langle \top, \bot\rangle\rangle$ $\Delta_5 = \{(\ell(\text{abs}), \phi_5)\}$

$\pi_5 = A\langle\lfloor \pi_4\rfloor_{A.1}, \bot\rangle = A\langle \top, \bot\rangle$ $\Delta_6 = \Delta_4 \cup \Delta_5$

$\phi_5 = A\langle B\langle \text{Bool} \to \text{Bool}, \alpha \to \alpha\rangle, \text{Bool} \to \text{Bool}\rangle$

Fig. 4. The derivation tree for the expression abs True.

In general, we are interested in generating error fixes for an expression given user defined axioms Q. We formalize this idea in the rule MAIN in Fig. 3. The type judgment for this rule is very similar to that for other rules and can be read similarly.

Example. Let's consider typing abs True under the constraint $C_4 = A\langle B\langle \text{Num Bool},$ Num $\alpha\rangle, \varepsilon\rangle$, where $\Gamma(\text{abs}) = \forall\alpha_1.\text{Num } \alpha_1 \Rightarrow \alpha_1 \to \alpha_1$ and True is of the type Bool. We present the derivation tree, together with values for symbols (such as C_4, π_4, etc.), for typing this expression in Fig. 4. Most of the derivations are simple instantiations of the typing rules in Fig. 3, except the two using E6. We defer the detailed explanation of deriving them to the long version of this paper [8]. Overall, we derive the typing result $C_4;\pi_4;\Gamma \vdash$ abs True : $A\langle B\langle \text{Bool}, \alpha\rangle, \text{Bool}\rangle|\Delta_6$ for the expression abs True.

We observe that C_4 includes the constraints Num Bool and Num α. What is the result of typing the expression under the axiom $Q_6 = $ Num α? Let $\pi_6 = A\langle B\langle \bot, \top\rangle, B\langle \top, \bot\rangle\rangle$, we have $\pi_6 \leq \pi_4$ and $Q_6 \Vdash_{\pi_6} C_4$. According to the rule MAIN, we have $Q_6;\pi_6;\Gamma \vdash_M$ abs True : $A\langle B\langle \text{Bool}, \alpha\rangle, \text{Bool}\rangle|\Delta_6$. From π_6, Δ_6, and the result type $A\langle B\langle \text{Bool}, \alpha\rangle, \text{Bool}\rangle$, we can extract error fixes as we did in Sect. 2. For example, changing abs to something of type Bool $\to$ Bool the resulting expression will have the type Bool.

Properties. We now investigate the properties of finding error fixes by our type system. We first present a few definitions. Given an ω and a Δ, we can generate an *alteration* for fix type errors as follows, where *locToChc(l)* returns the variation name generated at l during the typing process.

$$alt(\omega, \Delta) = \{(l, \lfloor\phi\rfloor_\omega)|(l, \phi) \in \Delta \wedge locToChc(l).2 \in \omega\}$$

An alteration specifies the target type of each location in it. We use δ to range over alterations. For example, $alt(\{A.2, B.1\}, \Delta_6)$ yields $\{(\ell(\text{abs}), \text{Bool} \to \text{Bool})\}$, where Δ_6 was introduced in Sect. 3.2 for typing abs True.

To reason about the correctness of our type system, we need a notion of applying alterations to the Hindley-Milner typing process extended with type classes for ill-typed expressions. For this purpose, we introduce the typing judgment $Q; \Gamma; \delta \vdash_{ALT} e : \tau$, which says that under Q, Γ, and the alteration δ, the expression e has the type τ. The type system is mostly standard but for each subexpression e' satisfying $\ell(e') \mapsto \tau' \in \delta$, e' has the type τ'. Since the specification of $\vdash_{ALT}$ is simple, we defer it to [8].

The correctness of our type system consists of the soundness and completeness of error fixes, shown in the following theorems. The proofs for both theorems are constructed through induction on the corresponding typing process.

Theorem 1 (Error fix soundness). *If* $Q; \pi; \Gamma \vdash_M e : \phi | \Delta$, *then for any* $\omega \lfloor \pi \rfloor_\omega = \top$ *implies* $Q; \Gamma; alt(\omega, \Delta) \vdash_{ALT} e : \lfloor \phi \rfloor_\omega$.

Theorem 2 (Error fix completeness). *Given* Q, e, *and* Γ, *if* $Q; \Gamma; \delta \vdash_{ALT} e : \tau$, *then there exists some* ϕ *and* Δ *such that* $Q; \pi; \Gamma \vdash_M e : \phi | \Delta$, $\lfloor \phi \rfloor_\omega = \tau$, *and* $alt(\omega, \Delta) = \delta$ *for some* ω.

4 Constraint Generation and Solving

When an expression is visited, both type constraints and class constraints are generated. Type constraints are solved using variational unification from [6], yielding substitutions, which will be applied to class constraints. After that, class constraints are simplified.

Constraint Generation. Since constraint generation rules can be systematically derived from the typing rules in Fig. 3, we present the rules only for variables and applications. Other constraint generation rules can be derived similarly.

$$\text{I-VAR} \frac{\Gamma(x) = \forall \overline{\alpha_1}.C \Rightarrow \phi \quad d, \overline{\alpha_2}, \alpha_3 \text{ fresh} \quad \phi_1 = [\overline{\alpha_1} \mapsto \overline{\alpha_2}](\phi)}{d \langle [\overline{\alpha_1} \mapsto \overline{\alpha_2}](C), \varepsilon \rangle; \Gamma \vdash_I x : d\langle \phi_1, \alpha_3 \rangle | \{(\ell(x), d\langle \phi_1, \alpha_3 \rangle)\}}$$

$$\text{I-APP} \frac{C_1; \Gamma \vdash_I e_1 : \phi_1 | \Delta_1 \quad C_2; \Gamma \vdash_I e_2 : \phi_2 | \Delta_2 \quad \beta \text{ fresh}}{C_1 \wedge C_2 \wedge \phi_1 \equiv^? \phi_2 \to \beta; \Gamma \vdash_I e_1 \, e_2 : \beta | \Delta_1 \cup \Delta_2}$$

The judgment for the inference rules has the form $C; \Gamma \vdash_I e : \phi | \Delta$, read as: given Γ, e has the type ϕ with the generated constraint C and the change information Δ. All components are output except e and Γ. The I-VAR rule is simple: the variable receives a choice type where the source type is an instantiation of the type schema and the target type is a fresh type variable. We use ε for the second alternative of the output constraint since that alternative is unconstrained. With these rules, we can generate the constraints shown in Sect. 2 for the example abs True.

4.1 Variational Context Reduction

Our algorithm in this subsection follows the idea of Jones [21] but has to deal with variations. Given a constraint, context reduction first transforms it into a head-normal form and then simplifies it with an entailment relation. We discuss them below in detail.

Constraint Transformation. We define the function $toHnf(C, Q)$ to transform C into the head-normal form with the given Q. A type class constraint is in head-normal form if at least one argument is a type variable. The result is (C_2, π), meaning that C_2 is the normal form for C but transformation was successful only in variants where π have $\top$s. When Q is ε, it means that no axiom is given. For example, $toHnf(A\langle \texttt{Num Bool}, \texttt{Num Int}\rangle, \varepsilon)$ yields $(\varepsilon, A\langle \bot, \top\rangle)$, meaning that the transformation is failed in $A.1$ but is successful in $A.2$. The operation $(C_1, \pi_1)\ (op_1, op_2)\ (C_2, \pi_2)$ below is defined as $(C_1\ op_1\ C_2, \pi_1\ op_2\ \pi_2)$ and $o_1\ d\langle, \rangle\ o_2$ yields $d\langle o_1, o_2\rangle$ where o denotes any object.

$$toHnf(C_1 \wedge C_2, Q) = toHnf(C_1, Q)\ (\wedge, \otimes)\ toHnf(C_2, Q)$$
$$toHnf(d\langle C_1, C_2\rangle, Q) = toHnf(C_1, Q)(d\langle, \rangle, d\langle, \rangle)toHnf(C_2, Q)$$
$$toHnf(C, Q) = toHnf'(inHnf(C), C, Q)$$

The operation $\otimes$ in the rule puts two patterns together. It is defined with three rules: (1) $\top \otimes \pi = \pi$, (2) $\bot \otimes \pi = \bot$, and (3) $d\langle \pi_1, \pi_2\rangle \otimes \pi = d\langle \pi_1 \otimes \pi, \pi_2 \otimes \pi\rangle$. $\otimes$ can be understood as logical **and** if we view $\top$ and $\bot$ as logical **true** and **false**, respectively.

When the constraint is a class constraint, $toHnf$ delegates the real task to $toHnf'$, which, in addition to C and Q, takes a ϖ, a *variational boolean value*, as its first argument. This argument indicates whether C is already normalized or not. It could be $\texttt{True}$, $\texttt{False}$, or a variation over ϖs.

$$toHnf'(\texttt{True}, C, Q) = (C, \top)$$
$$toHnf'(d\langle \varpi_1, \varpi_2\rangle, C, Q) = toHnf'(\varpi_1, \lfloor C \rfloor_{d.1}, Q)(d\langle, \rangle, d\langle, \rangle)\ toHnf'(\varpi_2, \lfloor C \rfloor_{d.2}, Q)$$

$$toHnf'(\texttt{False}, C, Q) = \begin{cases} (\varepsilon, \top) & byInst(C, Q) = (\varepsilon, \top) \\ toHnf(C_2, Q) & byInst(C, Q) = (C_2, \top) \\ (\varepsilon, \bot) & \text{otherwise} \end{cases}$$

$toHnf'$ pattern matches against ϖ. When ϖ is $\texttt{True}$, it means that C is already normalized and C itself, together with a $\top$, is returned. Note that ϖ equals $\texttt{True}$ doesn't mean that C is plain, but rather, all possible variants in C are normalized. When ϖ is a variational value, it means that at least some variant in C is not normalized. In this case, the constraint C is broken down into two constraints $\lfloor C \rfloor_{d.1}$ and $\lfloor C \rfloor_{d.2}$, which are normalized and the results are packed back using the choice d. When ϖ is $\texttt{False}$, then, due to how ϖ is computed, C must be plain. We call $byInst$ to possibly reduce C using instance declarations.

There are three possible outcomes of $byInst$. First, $byInst$ returns $(\varepsilon, \top)$, which means that C is successfully reduced with no new constraint generated. For example, $byInst(\texttt{Ord Bool}, Q)$ belongs to this case if Q includes the default instance declarations in Haskell. Second, $byInst$ returns $(C_2, \top)$, which means that C is successfully reduced to C_2, which is in turn normalized using *toHnf*. For example, *byInst*(Ord $[\alpha]$, Q) belongs to this case. Third, *byInst* returns $(\varepsilon, \bot)$, which means that no rule in Q can be used to reduce C and the reduction fails. For example, if Q includes Haskell default class instances, then *byInst*(Num Bool, Q) belongs to this case. For each case, *toHnf'* returns corresponding values. Since the argument C to *byInst* is always plain, the definition of *byInst* is very similar to that in [21]. We omit its definition here.

The value ϖ for C is computed with the function *inHnf*. Thus, the results from different arguments are combined together through the $\oplus$ operation, which is defined below. In this section, we use the notation $d\langle\overline{o}\rangle$ to denote $d\langle o_1, o_2 \rangle$ for any object o.

$$inHnf(\mathsf{G}\,\overline{\phi}) = \bigoplus \overline{hnf(\phi)}$$

$$\mathtt{True} \oplus \varpi = \mathtt{True} \quad \mathtt{False} \oplus \varpi = \varpi \quad d\langle\overline{\varpi}\rangle \oplus \varpi_3 = d\langle\overline{\varpi \oplus \varpi_3}\rangle$$

The following function $hnf(\phi)$ decides if ϕ is normalized. The notation $\mathtt{True} \,\|\, d\langle\overline{hnf(\phi)}\rangle$ means that $d\langle\overline{hnf(\phi)}\rangle$ is simplified to $\mathtt{True}$ if both alternatives of d are $\mathtt{True}$ and is unchanged otherwise.

$$hnf(\alpha) = \mathtt{True} \quad hnf(\gamma) = \mathtt{False} \quad hnf(\phi_1 \rightarrow \phi_2) = \mathtt{False} \quad hnf(d\langle\overline{\phi}\rangle) = \mathtt{True} \,\|\, d\langle\overline{hnf(\phi)}\rangle$$

Algorithmic Constraint Entailment. We define the function $entail(C_1, C_2, Q)$ to decide whether C_2 is entailed by C_1. In [21], *entail* returns a boolean value. However, here we need a variational boolean value, reflecting that entailment may only hold for certain variants. For example, $entail(A\langle\mathtt{Num}\,\alpha, \mathtt{Ord}\,\alpha\rangle, \mathtt{Ord}\,\alpha, Q)$ yields $A\langle\mathtt{False}, \mathtt{True}\rangle$, indicating that the entailment relation holds only in $A.2$.

Since a normalized constraint can not be simplified by instance declarations anymore, our definition of *entail* is quite simple: just checking if C_2 belongs to the super classes of C_1, as expressed below.

$$entail(C_1, C_2, Q) = belong(C_2; bySuper(C_1, Q))$$

$$bySuper(d\langle\overline{C}\rangle, Q) = d\langle\overline{bySuper(C, Q)}\rangle$$

$$bySuper(C_1 \wedge C_2, Q) = bySuper(C_1, Q) \wedge bySuper(C_2, Q)$$

$$bySuper(\mathsf{G}\,\overline{\phi}, Q) = \mathsf{G}\,\overline{\alpha} \wedge bySuper(C_G, Q) \quad \text{where } \forall\overline{\alpha}.C_G \Leftarrow \mathsf{G}\,\overline{\alpha} \in Q$$

The definition of *bySuper* is quite simple. In the third case we find super classes for constraints like $\mathsf{G}\,\overline{\phi}$, which can just be simplified to a sequence of type variables. Given C_1 and C_2, *belong* returns $\mathtt{True}$ if they are the same and $\mathtt{False}$ if they are primitive and have different class names. We omit the definition of *belong* here because it is quite simple. For plain class constraints, a simple equality testing is enough, and for variational class constraints, the definition recurse into their alternatives. When the second argument of *belong* is a $\wedge$ over two constraint operands, *belong* returns $\mathtt{True}$ if the first argument of *belong* belongs to any operand.

With *entail*, we can now define the simplification operation as follows. $simp(C_1, C_3, Q)$ simplifies the constraint C_1 with the already simplified constraint C_3

and the axiom Q.

$$simp(\varepsilon, C_3, Q) = C_3 \qquad simp(d\langle\overline{C}\rangle, C_3, Q) = d\overline{\langle simp(C, C_3, Q)\rangle}$$
$$simp(C_1 \wedge C_2, C_3, Q) = simp(C_2, entail(C_2 \wedge C_3, C_1, Q) \lhd C_1, Q)$$

When C_1 becomes ε, $simp$ terminates and returns C_3. For a variational constraint, $simp$ simplifies its individual alternatives. To simplify the compound constraint $C_1 \wedge C_2$, we check to see if we can simplify each of C_1 and C_2 by the other. Formally, we first decide the result of $\varpi = entail(C_2 \wedge C_3, C_1, Q)$. If the result is True, then C_1 can simply be dropped. However, the entailment may hold in certain variants only, and we can not drop the whole C_1 in this case. We handle this situation by replacing each variants in C_1 whose ϖ is True with a ε and leaving other variants unchanged. This process is defined through the operation $\varpi \lhd C_1$. Its definition is quite simple and is omitted here.

Overall, with *toHnf* and *simp*, context reduction for C under the axiom Q is defined as $(simp(C_1, \varepsilon, Q), \pi)$, where $(C_1, \pi) = toHnf(C, Q)$.

5   Evaluation

Following the ideas in this paper, we have implemented a prototype of TEC. The prototype supports functional dependencies using the idea from [20]. Our prototype is implemented into Helium [17] rather than GHC due to the overhead of implementing it into the latter. Our implementation generates constraints and solves them. During constraint generation, a Δ is generated to record location information and choices created. Constraint solving will update Δ with concrete type information. Type error messages are generated from Δ, the typing pattern from constraint solving, and the result type of the expression, following the method described in Sect. 2.

TEC reuses the heuristics in counter-factual typing [4] for ranking all the error fixes calculated and introduces two more heuristics. First, we favor fixes whose consequent types have lower ratios of unification variables. Given a type, the ratio is defined as the number of unification variables over the number of primitive types. The rationale of this rule is that less internal information should be leaked to the outside of the ill-typed expression. Second, we prefer fixes whose source type and target type have closer class constraints. Two class constraints are closer if they have a similar number of primitive constraints or share a class hierarchy. The rationale of this rule is to avoid exotic changes related to type classes.

Error Locating Precision. To evaluate the precision of TEC, we created two benchmarks. The first is created by taking all examples involving type classes from all the papers [33, 34, 39] in the literature (We do not include class directive examples from [17] since none of TEC, GHC, and SHErrLoc supports them). This benchmark contains 17 programs. The second benchmark is extracted from student programs [36], which were logged as undergraduate students in an introductory Haskell course were attempting their homework assignments. All intermediate program versions were logged. We obtained about 5000 programs in total, filtered out all programs that have type errors related to type classes, and then randomly chose 60 from them.

We next investigate how different tools perform in the presence of type classes. We consider TEC, GHC 8.10.6, and SHErrLoc. The precisions of these tools for Benchmarks 1 and 2 are shown in the following table. In both benchmarks, the first several messages are already correct and later messages (after 2 messages in Benchmark 1 and 3 in Benchmark 2) do not help.

Tool	Precision (%) after # of msgs (Bench. 1)			Precision (%) (Bench. 2)			
	1	2	> 2	1	2	3	> 3
TEC	65	88	88	55	72	78	78
SHErrLoc	47	59	59	42	58	63	63
GHC	41	53	53	33	40	40	40

Figure 5 presents the result for Benchmark 1 in more detail. A tool receives a filled circle if the first two messages from the tool help to locate the real error cause and an unfilled circle otherwise. Some examples from the paper contain an accompanying "oracle" stating how to remove the type error. For these examples, we compare reported error message against the oracles. For other messages, no oracles are given. Since there are usually many different causes for a type error, a message is regarded as correct if it points to at least one error cause. If the message is not helpful at all, then it is classified as incorrect. One such instance is that SHErrLoc says that Example 3 [34] is well-typed while in fact it is ill-typed, and the message of SHErrLoc is regarded as incorrect.

Both GHC and SHErrLoc are very good at locating type errors when the type annotations do not subsume the real inferred types. Both of them are successful for all the 6 examples of this kind. TEC also performs quite well for this kind. It can suggest a correct type annotation as well as find fixes in expressions so that the signature becomes valid. GHC also performs well in locating type errors violating functional dependencies when involved literals (for example '1' and True) have constant types (for example Char and Bool). However, when the involved literals have constrained types, the messages are always not helpful (for example the message for insert2). TEC always works well since it always finds an alternative type for the erroneous expression. SHErrLoc doesn't work well for functional dependencies. For other examples, TEC and SHErrLoc work better than GHC. The Example 6 [33] requires one to report that Integral and Fractional has no overlapping instances, and none of the evaluated tools are able to report this.

The following function demonstrates the shortcoming of TEC.

```
class Collects ce e where insert :: e -> ce -> ce

insert3 :: Collects ce Bool => ce -> ce
insert3 c = insert 1 (insert False c)
```

The type error is due to the mismatch between the type 1 and the Bool in the type signature. TEC doesn't work well because the target type α_4 of 1 gives rise to the wanted constraint Collects ce α_4, which can not be deduced from the given constraint Collects

Tool	Example # [33]		Example # [34]							Example # [39]					This paper		
	5	6	2	3	6	10	12	13	14	3	6	38	70	73	rank1	insert2	insert3
TEC	●	○	●	●	●	●	●	●	●	●	●	●	●	●	●	●	○
SHErrLoc	●	○	●	○	●	○	●	●	●	○	●	○	●	●	●	○	○
GHC	●	○	●	○	●	●	●	●	○	○	●	○	○	●	○	○	●

Fig. 5. A comparison of TEC, SHErrLoc and GHC for examples from the literature. Filled and unfilled circles denote that the first two messages from the corresponding tool are useful and not useful, respectively.

ce Bool. Moreover, suggesting (Collects ce Bool, Collects ce α_4) => ce -> ce as the type signature is incorrect since this type is ambiguous [39] as α_4 doesn't appear in ce -> ce. As a result, we can not identify 1 as an error cause. One way to fix this problem is to unify the wanted constraint with the given constraint if the deduction fails. However, it's unclear how to systematically apply this idea and we leave it for future work. SHErrLoc again reports that insert3 is well-typed. This example demonstrates that the folklore knowledge [3, 25] about the completeness of error debugging by searching does not hold when the type system extends to type classes. Note, this is not inconsistent with Theorem 2 because this happens when the condition $Q; \Gamma; \delta \vdash_{ALT} e : \tau$ of the Theorem does not hold.

Benchmark 2, among 60 programs, contains 13 programs where type errors are due to missing or extra parentheses. No existing tools are known to handle such errors well. The programs for which SHErrLoc doesn't perform well are those that are ill-typed but SHErrLoc reports that they are well-typed. GHC doesn't work well for programs where no type annotations are present: the reported locations are quite far away from the real error causes. TEC works well for both situations, and achieves a better precision. In this benchmark, we did not observe any program like insert3 that TEC could not find an error fix. In the future, we will investigate how often programs like insert3 happen in practice.

From the evaluation results of these benchmarks, we conclude that TEC is quite effective in locating the real error causes. We have also investigated the running time of TEC in detail. However, due to space limitation, we do not elaborate further. Briefly, the response time of TEC for programs around 100 LOC is about 1.6 s and that for about 300 LOC is 5.7 s. The reason that TEC has a long response time is that it first calculates all possible fixes (including changing 1 location, 2 locations, and up to all locations) at once before they are ranked. In the future, we will work on improving the response time by computing typing results in phases such that fixes that change only one or two locations will be returned and ranked before computing other fixes. This strategy works because in fixing type errors users prefer to change fewer locations.

6 Related Work

Approaches Supporting Type Classes. Besides GHC, SHErrLoc [42, 43], Chameleon [33, 34, 39], and the Top framework [17] also debug type errors involving type class constraints. SHErrLoc is a general method for locating static inconsistencies, including type errors. SHErrLoc treats many Haskell features, such as type classes, type families, and type signatures. Given a program, it works by calling GHC to generate typing constraints, builds a graph representation from the constraints, and then locates the most likely error cause using a Bayesian model. Chameleon is an extensible framework that supports HM and type classes. Given an ill-typed program, it first expresses typing constraints in constraint handling rules (CHRs) and then finds the minimal unsolvable constraints and reports the corresponding program source. Chameleon can also explain why a type error happens while our approach gives concrete messages for removing the type error. In this sense, they are complementary to each other. Another difference is that our approach finds all error causes while Chameleon doesn't.

Top aims to generate high quality error messages. It supports type classes through overloading of identifiers. A main feature of Top is that it uses type inference directives [16] and type class directives [15] to customize error messages. Directives allow certain type errors to be detected earlier. TEC doesn't support directives but focuses on how to change expressions to, for example, avoid class constraints, satisfy class constraints, and make context reduction successful. While TEC generates informative messages at all error causes, Top does so for several, usually one or two, locations only. Therefore, these two approaches are again complementary.

Other Approaches. Due to the large body of previous work in error debugging, we are able to only give a brief discussion. This work is similar to CFT [4] but we deal with type errors in type class uses while that does not. As type classes are prevalent in Haskell, we believe that this difference is significant. This work can be viewed as searching for type error fixes at the type level, and [37] searches error fixes at the expression level. Thus, while this work can reuse typing processes to scale to large programs, the scalability of that work is unclear. Also, the error messages from this work contains more information than that work. [4] discussed the relation between CFT and discriminative sum types for locating type errors [27]. As the difference between our work and [27] is similar, we will not discuss that work further in this paper.

It has been a long history of locating the most likely error cause in the research community. The first approach, developed by [18], is based on maximal flow of the graph representation of typing constraints. Essentially, it could be understood as majority voting. Numerous approaches based on reordering the unification process have been developed, including algorithms $\mathcal{M}$ [24], $\mathcal{G}$ [12], and the symmetrical versions of $\mathcal{W}$ and $\mathcal{M}$ [26]. Recent developments include dedicated heuristics [14] and a Bayesian model [42] for locating the most likely error cause.

Instead of just finding the mostly likely error causes, many error slicing approaches have been developed [13,31,35], which highlight all program text that contributes to the type error. The shortcoming of error slicing approaches, as noted in [17], is that they usually cover too many locations, and give no hint about which location more likely causes the type error. The approach by [29,30] takes the advantages of approaches locating most likely error causes and those slicing type errors in that it can find all error causes and iteratively presents the most likely one. TEC takes this approach one step further of providing an informative message for each error cause. A very different line of research explains type errors from various perspectives [1,9,11,32,38,40].

7 Conclusions

We have presented TEC, an efficient approach for debugging type errors in type systems with type classes and its extensions of multi-parameter classes and functional dependencies. For most expressions, TEC finds error causes in all possible combinations of leaves of the program AST and generates an informative error message for each error cause. We have evaluated TEC and the result shows that it can locate type errors quite precisely.

In some rare cases, TEC fails to find complete error fixes when the generalization of an error fix causes both context reduction failure and ambiguous types due to class usage. In the future, we will investigate how we can systematically fix this problem and integrate our solution into TEC. In the future, we also plan to perform a user study to find out how well TEC helps students in fixing type errors, such as how many type errors students investigate for fix type errors and whether TEC helps shorten students' type error debugging time. Finally, we plan to collect users' feedback for fine tuning our heuristics for ranking error fixes.

References

1. Beaven, M., Stansifer, R.: Explaining type errors in polymorphic languages. ACM Lett. Program. Lang. Syst. **2**, 17–30 (1994)
2. Bernstein, K.L., Stark, E.W.: Debugging Type Errors. State University of New York at Stony Brook, Technical report (1995)
3. Braßel, B.: Typehope: there is hope for your type errors. In: International Workshop on Implementation of Functional Languages (2004)
4. Chen, S., Erwig, M.: Counter-factual typing for debugging type errors. In: ACM SIGPLAN-SIGACT Symposium on Principles of Programming Languages, pp. 583–594 (2014)
5. Chen, S., Erwig, M.: Guided type debugging. In: Codish, M., Sumii, E. (eds.) FLOPS 2014. LNCS, vol. 8475, pp. 35–51. Springer, Cham (2014). https://doi.org/10.1007/978-3-319-07151-0_3
6. Chen, S., Erwig, M., Walkingshaw, E.: An error-tolerant type system for variational lambda calculus. In: ACM International Conference on Functional Programming, pp. 29–40 (2012)
7. Chen, S., Erwig, M., Walkingshaw, E.: Extending type inference to variational programs. ACM Trans. Program. Lang. Syst. **36**(1), 1:1–1:54 (2014)
8. Chen, S., Noor, R.: Improving Type Error Reporting for Type Classes. Technical report, UL Lafayette (2022). https://people.cmix.louisiana.edu/schen/ws/techreport/longtec.pdf
9. Chitil, O.: Compositional explanation of types and algorithmic debugging of type errors. In: ACM International Conference on Functional Programming, pp. 193–204, September 2001
10. Choppella, V.: Unification source-tracking with application to diagnosis of type inference. Ph.D. thesis, Indiana University (2002)
11. Duggan, D., Bent, F.: Explaining type inference. Sci. Comput. Program. **27**, 37–83 (1995)
12. Eo, H., Lee, O., Yi, K.: Proofs of a set of hybrid let-polymorphic type inference algorithms. New Gener. Comput. **22**(1), 1–36 (2004). https://doi.org/10.1007/BF03037279
13. Haack, C., Wells, J.B.: Type error slicing in implicitly typed higher-order languages. In: Degano, P. (ed.) ESOP 2003. LNCS, vol. 2618, pp. 284–301. Springer, Heidelberg (2003). https://doi.org/10.1007/3-540-36575-3_20
14. Hage, J., Heeren, B.: Heuristics for type error discovery and recovery. In: Horváth, Z., Zsók, V., Butterfield, A. (eds.) IFL 2006. LNCS, vol. 4449, pp. 199–216. Springer, Heidelberg (2007). https://doi.org/10.1007/978-3-540-74130-5_12

15. Heeren, B., Hage, J.: Type class directives. In: Hermenegildo, M.V., Cabeza, D. (eds.) PADL 2005. LNCS, vol. 3350, pp. 253–267. Springer, Heidelberg (2005). https://doi.org/10.1007/978-3-540-30557-6_19

16. Heeren, B., Hage, J., Swierstra, S.D.: Scripting the type inference process. In: Proceedings of the Eighth ACM SIGPLAN International Conference on Functional Programming, ICFP 2003, pp. 3–13. ACM, New York (2003). https://doi.org/10.1145/944705.944707

17. Heeren, B.J.: Top quality type error messages. Ph.D. thesis, Universiteit Utrecht, The Netherlands (2005)

18. Johnson, G.F., Walz, J.A.: A maximum-flow approach to anomaly isolation in unification-based incremental type inference. In: ACM Symposium on Principles of Programming Languages, pp. 44–57 (1986)

19. Jones, M.P.: A theory of qualified types. In: Krieg-Brückner, B. (ed.) ESOP 1992. LNCS, vol. 582, pp. 287–306. Springer, Heidelberg (1992). https://doi.org/10.1007/3-540-55253-7_17

20. Jones, M.P.: Simplifying and improving qualified types. In: Proceedings of the Seventh International Conference on Functional Programming Languages and Computer Architecture, FPCA 1995, pp. 160–169. ACM, New York (1995). https://doi.org/10.1145/224164.224198

21. Jones, M.P.: Typing Haskell in Haskell. In: Haskell Workshop (1999)

22. Jones, M.P.: Type classes with functional dependencies. In: Smolka, G. (ed.) ESOP 2000. LNCS, vol. 1782, pp. 230–244. Springer, Heidelberg (2000). https://doi.org/10.1007/3-540-46425-5_15

23. Lee, O., Yi, K.: Proofs about a folklore let-polymorphic type inference algorithm. ACM Trans. Program. Lang. Syst. **20**(4), 707–723 (1998)

24. Lee, O., Yi, K.: A generalized let-polymorphic type inference algorithm. Technical report, Technical Memorandum ROPAS-2000-5, Research on Program Analysis System, Korea Advanced Institute of Science and Technology (2000)

25. Lerner, B., Flower, M., Grossman, D., Chambers, C.: Searching for type-error messages. In: ACM International Conference on Programming Language Design and Implementation, pp. 425–434 (2007)

26. McAdam, B.J.: Repairing type errors in functional programs. Ph.D. thesis, University of Edinburgh. College of Science and Engineering. School of Informatics (2002)

27. Neubauer, M., Thiemann, P.: Discriminative sum types locate the source of type errors. In: ACM International Conference on Functional Programming, pp. 15–26 (2003)

28. Odersky, M., Sulzmann, M., Wehr, M.: Type inference with constrained types. Theor. Pract. Object Syst. **5**(1), 35–55 (1999)

29. Pavlinovic, Z., King, T., Wies, T.: Finding minimum type error sources. In: ACM International Conference on Object Oriented Programming Systems Languages and Applications, OOPSLA 2014, pp. 525–542. ACM, New York (2014). https://doi.org/10.1145/2660193.2660230

30. Pavlinovic, Z., King, T., Wies, T.: Practical SMT-based type error localization. In: ACM SIGPLAN International Conference on Functional Programming, pp. 412–423 (2015)

31. Schilling, Thomas: Constraint-free type error slicing. In: Peña, R., Page, R. (eds.) TFP 2011. LNCS, vol. 7193, pp. 1–16. Springer, Heidelberg (2012). https://doi.org/10.1007/978-3-642-32037-8_1

32. Seidel, E.L., Jhala, R., Weimer, W.: Dynamic witnesses for static type errors (or, ill-typed programs usually go wrong). In: Proceedings of the 21st ACM SIGPLAN International Conference on Functional Programming, ICFP 2016, pp. 228–242. ACM, New York (2016). https://doi.org/10.1145/2951913.2951915

33. Stuckey, P.J., Sulzmann, M., Wazny, J.: Interactive type debugging in Haskell. In: ACM SIGPLAN Workshop on Haskell, pp. 72–83 (2003)

34. Stuckey, P.J., Sulzmann, M., Wazny, J.: Improving type error diagnosis. In: ACM SIGPLAN Workshop on Haskell, pp. 80–91 (2004)
35. Tip, F., Dinesh, T.B.: A slicing-based approach for locating type errors. ACM Trans. Softw. Eng. Methodol. **10**(1), 5–55 (2001)
36. Tirronen, V., Uusi-Mäkelä, S., Isomöttönen, V.: Understanding beginners' mistakes with Haskell. J. Funct. Program. **25**, e11 (2015). https://doi.org/10.1017/S0956796815000179
37. Tsushima, K., Chitil, O., Sharrad, J.: Type debugging with counter-factual type error messages using an existing type checker. In: IFL 2019: Proceedings of the 31st Symposium on Implementation and Application of Functional Languages, ICPS. ACM, New York (2020). https://kar.kent.ac.uk/81976/
38. Wand, M.: Finding the source of type errors. In: ACM Symposium on Principles of Programming Languages, pp. 38–43 (1986)
39. Wazny, J.R.: Type inference and type error diagnosis for Hindley/Milner with extensions. Ph.D. thesis, The University of Melbourne (2006)
40. Yang, J.: Explaining type errors by finding the source of a type conflict. In: Trends in Functional Programming, pp. 58–66. Intellect Books (2000)
41. Yang, J.: Improving Polymorphic Type Explanations. Ph.D. thesis, Heriot-Watt University (2001)
42. Zhang, D., Myers, A.C.: Toward general diagnosis of static errors. In: ACM Symposium on Principles of Programming Languages, pp. 569–581 (2014)
43. Zhang, D., Myers, A.C., Vytiniotis, D., Peyton-Jones, S.: Diagnosing type errors with class. In: ACM SIGPLAN Conference on Programming Language Design and Implementation, pp. 12–21 (2015)

Asynchronous Unfold/Fold Transformation for Fixpoint Logic

Mahmudul Faisal Al Ameen$^{(\boxtimes)}$ [iD], Naoki Kobayashi [iD], and Ryosuke Sato [iD]

The University of Tokyo, Tokyo, Japan
`faisal@kb.is.s.u-tokyo.ac.jp`

Abstract. Various program verification problems for functional programs can be reduced to the validity checking problem for formulas of a fixpoint logic. Recently, Kobayashi et al. have shown that the unfold/fold transformation originally developed for logic programming can be extended and applied to prove the validity of fixpoint logic formulas. In the present paper, we refine their unfold/fold transformation, so that each predicate can be unfolded a different number of times in an asynchronous manner. Inspired by the work of Lee et al. on size change termination, we use a variant of size change graphs to find an appropriate number of unfoldings of each predicate. We have implemented an unfold/fold transformation tool based on the proposed method, and evaluated its effectiveness.

Keywords: Unfold/fold transformation · Fixed point logic · Size change graphs

1 Introduction

Unfold and fold transformation was originally proposed for logic programming [12], and recently generalized and applied for CHC solving [3] and fixpoint logics [5] in the context of program verification. To understand the idea, consider the following definitions of predicates Even and Odd:

$$\text{Even}(x) =_\mu x = 0 \vee \text{Odd}(x-1);$$
$$\text{Odd}(y) =_\mu \text{Even}(y-1).$$

Here, Even and Odd are defined as the least predicates that satisfy the equations (in other words, Even and Odd are inductively defined by the equations). Suppose we wish to prove $P(n) := \text{Even}(n) \vee \text{Odd}(n)$ holds for every $n \geq 0$. To this end, we transform $P(n)$ as follows.

$$
\begin{aligned}
P(n) &\equiv \text{Even}(n) \vee \text{Odd}(n) \\
&\equiv (n = 0 \vee \text{Odd}(n-1)) \vee \text{Even}(n-1) \quad \text{("unfold" Even and Odd)} \\
&\equiv n = 0 \vee (\text{Even}(n-1) \vee \text{Odd}(n-1)) \\
&\equiv n = 0 \vee P(n-1) \quad \text{("fold" } \text{Even}(n-1) \vee \text{Odd}(n-1))
\end{aligned}
$$

© Springer Nature Switzerland AG 2022
M. Hanus and A. Igarashi (Eds.): FLOPS 2022, LNCS 13215, pp. 39–56, 2022.
https://doi.org/10.1007/978-3-030-99461-7_3

Based on the transformation above, we obtain the following new definition of P:

$$P(n) =_\mu n = 0 \vee P(n-1).$$

We can then automatically prove that $P(n)$ holds for every $n \geq 0$, for example, by using the tool MU2CHC for fixpoint arithmetic [6].

The unfold/fold transformations like above require heuristics in general, to decide which predicate should be unfolded how many times, and how the resulting formulas should be folded. For example, suppose that we wish to prove the validity of $Q(n) := \mathrm{Div6}(n) \Rightarrow \mathrm{Even}(n)$, where Even, and Odd are as defined above, and Div6 is defined by:

$$\mathrm{Div6}(z) =_\mu z = 0 \vee \mathrm{Div6}(z-6).$$

Then, we need to transform $Q(n)$ in a specific manner, as follows.

$$
\begin{aligned}
Q(n) &\equiv \mathrm{Div6}(n) \Rightarrow \mathrm{Even}(n) \\
&\equiv (n = 0 \vee \mathrm{Div6}(n-6)) \Rightarrow (n = 0 \vee n = 2 \vee n = 4 \vee \mathrm{Even}(n-6)) \\
&\qquad\qquad \text{(unfold Div6 once and Even six times)} \\
&\equiv (n = 0 \Rightarrow (n = 0 \vee n = 2 \vee n = 4 \vee \mathrm{Even}(n-6))) \\
&\quad \wedge (\mathrm{Div6}(n-6) \Rightarrow (n = 0 \vee n = 2 \vee n = 4 \vee \mathrm{Even}(n-6))) \\
&\qquad\qquad \text{(by } A \vee B \Rightarrow C \equiv (A \Rightarrow C) \wedge (B \Rightarrow C)) \\
&\equiv \mathrm{Div6}(n-6) \Rightarrow (n = 0 \vee n = 2 \vee n = 4 \vee \mathrm{Even}(n-6)) \\
&\equiv n = 0 \vee n = 2 \vee n = 4 \vee (\mathrm{Div6}(n-6) \Rightarrow \mathrm{Even}(n-6)) \\
&\qquad\qquad \text{(by } A \Rightarrow (B \vee C) \equiv B \vee (A \Rightarrow C)) \\
&\equiv n = 0 \vee x = 2 \vee n = 4 \vee Q(n-6),
\end{aligned}
$$

and get the new definition:

$$Q(n) =_\nu n = 0 \vee n = 2 \vee n = 4 \vee Q(n-6),$$

where $=_\nu$ indicates that $Q(n)$ is the greatest predicate that satisfies the equation, which is **true**.[1] As shown above, in general, we need to unfold predicates in an asynchronous manner, by appropriately choosing the number of times each predicate is unfolded. Besides in the context of unfold/fold transformations, similar issues would also arise in tupling transformations (used for optimizations [4] and relational property verification of functional programs [1]), inductive methods for CHC solving [13], and cyclic proofs [2].

To address the issue above, this paper proposes a systematic method to determine how predicates should be unfolded. Inspired by size change termination graphs [8], from recursive definitions of predicates, we construct a graph

---

[1] Actually, because of the negative occurrences of Div6, we have to check some sanity conditions: see [5] for the sanity condition and the reason why $=_\mu$ can be replaced with $=_\nu$.

that represents how the arguments of predicates will change by unfoldings. For example, for the three predicates above, we prepare the following graphs:

The graphs represent that Div6 is unfolded to itself and Even and Odd are unfolded to each other. So we need two unfoldings (once from Even to Odd and, and once more from Odd to Even) to unfold Even to obtain Even again. The arguments of Div6 and Even will decrease by 6 and 2 respectively while they are unfolded to themselves. Based on this information, we can determine the numbers of unfoldings by solving the equation:

$$6i_1 = 2i_2,$$

where i_1 and i_2 are the numbers of times Div6 and combinedly Even and Odd should be unfolded. We formalize the idea above in a general setting, where predicates may have more than one argument and are defined in a mutually recursive manner.

The contributions of this paper are:

1. the formalization of the method sketched above for asynchronous unfold/fold transformations;
2. an implementation of the proposed method for improving the validity checker for a fixpoint logic [5,6]; and
3. evaluation of the proposed method through experiments.

The rest of this paper is structured as follows. Section 2 reviews MuArith [5,6], a first-order fixpoint logic with integer arithmetic, which is used as the target of our unfold/fold transformation. Section 3 describes our procedure for asynchronous unfold/fold transformation. Section 4 reports an implementation and experimental results. Section 5 discusses related work, and Sect. 6 concludes the paper.

2   Preliminaries: MuArith and Unfold/Fold Transformations

In this section, we review the first-order fixpoint logic with integer arithmetic MuArith [5,6], and set out the goal of unfold/fold transformation.

Definition 1 (MuArith formulas). *The set of* simple formulas, *ranged over by* φ, *is given by:*

$$t \ (\text{arithmetic terms}) ::= c \mid x \mid t_1 + t_2 \mid t_1 - t_2 \mid c \times t$$
$$\varphi \ (\text{simple formulas}) ::= t_1 \leq t_2 \mid X^{(k)}(t_1, \ldots, t_k) \mid \varphi_1 \vee \varphi_2 \mid \varphi_1 \wedge \varphi_2.$$

Here, c ranges over the set $\mathbf{Z}$ of integers, x represents an integer variable, and $X^{(k)}$ represents a predicate variable of arity k; we often omit the superscript k and just write X for a predicate variable. We write $\mathrm{FV}(\varphi)$ for the set of integer variables occurring in φ. A MuArith formula is a pair (D, φ), where φ is a simple formula, and D is a finite, possibly empty sequence of predicate definitions of the form $X_1^{(\ell_1)}(y_{1,1}, \ldots, y_{1,\ell_1}) =_{\sigma_1} \varphi_1; \cdots; X_m^{(\ell_m)}(y_{m,1}, \ldots, y_{m,\ell_m}) =_{\sigma_m} \varphi_m$, where $\sigma_i \in \{\mu, \nu\}$ and $\mathrm{FV}(\varphi_i) \subseteq \{y_{i,1}, \ldots, y_{i,\ell_i}\}$ for every $i \in \{1, \ldots, m\}$. We require that the predicate variables $X_1^{(\ell_1)}, \ldots, X_m^{(\ell_m)}$ are distinct from each other.

For the sake of simplicity, we have only $t_1 \leq t_2$ as primitive arithmetic constraints; other arithmetic constraints can be expressed as derived forms; for example, $t_1 = t_2$ can be expressed as $t_1 \leq t_2 \wedge t_2 \leq t_1$. We use them as if they were primitive constraints below. Intuitively, a predicate definition $X(x_1, \ldots, x_k) =_\mu \varphi$ ($X(x_1, \ldots, x_k) =_\nu \varphi$, resp.) defines X as the least (greatest, resp.) predicate such that $X(x_1, \ldots, x_k) \equiv \varphi$. For example, $X(y) =_\mu y = 0 \vee X(y - 1)$ defines X as the least predicate such that $X(y) \equiv y = 0 \vee X(y - 1) \equiv y = 0 \vee y - 1 = 0 \vee X(y - 2) \equiv y = 0 \vee y - 1 = 0 \vee y - 2 = 0 \vee \cdots$, i.e., the predicate $\lambda y.y \geq 0$. In contrast, $X(y) =_\nu y = 0 \vee X(y - 1)$ is equivalent to the predicate $\lambda y.\mathtt{true}$ (where $\mathtt{true}$ may be considered an abbreviation of $0 \leq 0$).

A universal quantifier $\forall x.\varphi$ can be represented as X where $(X(x) =_\nu \varphi \wedge X(x-1) \wedge X(x+1))\, 0$. Similarly, an existential quantifier $\exists x.\varphi$ can be represented as X where $(X(x) =_\mu \varphi \vee X(x - 1) \vee X(x + 1))\, 0$; below we also treat them as if they were primitives. As for the arguments of predicates, we sometimes consider terms representing recursive data structures such as lists, in addition to arithmetic terms.

Example 1. The formula $\mathrm{Div6}(x) \Rightarrow \mathrm{Even}(x)$ given in Sect. 1 can be represented as the MuArith formula $(D, \overline{\mathrm{Div6}}(x) \vee \mathrm{Even}(x))$, where D is:

$$\mathrm{Even}(x) =_\mu x = 0 \vee \mathrm{Odd}(x - 1);$$
$$\mathrm{Odd}(y) =_\mu \mathrm{Even}(y - 1);$$
$$\overline{\mathrm{Div6}}(z) =_\nu z \neq 0 \wedge \overline{\mathrm{Div6}}(z - 6).$$

Here, $\overline{\mathrm{Div6}}$ corresponds to the negation of Div6.   □

The order of the definitions of predicates does not matter in the example above, though it does matter in general [6]. We omit the (rather complex) formal semantics of MuArith formulas in the paper, as it is unnecessary for understanding the rest of this paper; interested readers are referred to [6].

We introduce some notations and terminologies to define the goal of unfold/fold transformation. A *(formula) context*, written C, is an expression obtained from a simple formula by replacing an atomic formula $X^{(k)}(t_1, \ldots, t_k)$ with a hole $[]$. We write $C[\varphi]$ for the simple formula obtained by replacing the hole in C with φ. For example, if $C = \overline{\mathrm{Div6}}(x) \vee []$, then $C[\mathrm{Even}(x)]$ is $\overline{\mathrm{Div6}}(x) \vee \mathrm{Even}(x)$. We write $[t_1/x_1, \ldots, t_k/x_k]\varphi$ for the simple formula obtained from φ by replacing each occurrence of x_i with t_i. If the predicate X is defined by $X(y_1, \ldots, y_k) =_\sigma \varphi$, then we write $C[X(t_1, \ldots, t_k)] \triangleleft_X C[[t_1/y_1, \ldots, t_k/y_k]\varphi]$, and say "$C[[t_1/y_1, \ldots, t_k/y_k]\varphi]$ is obtained from $C[X(t_1, \ldots, t_k)]$ by *unfolding* X" and also "$C[X(t_1, \ldots, t_k)]$ is obtained from $C[[t_1/y_1, \ldots, t_k/y_k]\varphi]$ by *folding* X". We write $\triangleleft^*_{X_1 \cdots X_\ell}$ for the composition of $\triangleleft_{X_1}, \ldots, \triangleleft_{X_\ell}$. We often omit the subscript and just write $\triangleleft$ and $\triangleleft^*$.

The goal of unfold/fold transformation considered in this paper is, given a MuArith formula (D, φ) with $\mathrm{FV}(\varphi) = \{x_1, \ldots, x_k\}$, to find an unfolding sequence $\varphi \triangleleft^* \varphi'$ such that φ' is logically equivalent to a formula of the form $C[[t_1/x_1, \ldots, t_k/x_k]\varphi]$ for some context C and terms $t_1, \ldots, t_k$. We can then replace the formula φ with $X(x_1, \ldots, x_k)$, where X is a new predicate variable defined by $X(x_1, \ldots, x_k) =_\sigma C[X(t_1, \ldots, t_k)]$. The replacement of φ with $X(x_1, \ldots, x_k)$ typically makes it easier to prove the validity of a formula containing φ. The soundness of such replacement depends on the shape of C and whether σ is μ or ν; see [5] for soundness criteria. In the present paper, we focus on the issue of how to find an appropriate unfolding sequence $\varphi \triangleleft^* \varphi' \equiv C[[t_1/x_1, \ldots, t_k/x_k]\varphi]$, ignoring the soundness criteria.

Example 2. Recall Example 1. The (simple) formula $\overline{\mathrm{Div6}}(x) \vee \mathrm{Even}(x)$ can be unfolded as follows.

$\overline{\mathrm{Div6}}(x) \vee \mathrm{Even}(x)$

$\triangleleft_{\overline{\mathrm{Div6}}} (x \neq 0 \wedge \overline{\mathrm{Div6}}(x - 6)) \vee \mathrm{Even}(x)$

$\triangleleft_{\mathrm{Even}} (x \neq 0 \wedge \overline{\mathrm{Div6}}(x - 6)) \vee x = 0 \vee \mathrm{Odd}(x - 1)$

$\triangleleft_{\mathrm{Odd}} (x \neq 0 \wedge \overline{\mathrm{Div6}}(x - 6)) \vee x = 0 \vee \mathrm{Even}(x - 2)$

$\triangleleft^*_{(\mathrm{EvenOdd})^2} (x \neq 0 \wedge \overline{\mathrm{Div6}}(x - 6)) \vee x = 0 \vee x - 2 = 0 \vee x - 4 = 0 \vee \mathrm{Even}(x - 6)$

$\equiv x = 0 \vee x - 2 = 0 \vee x - 4 = 0 \vee \overline{\mathrm{Div6}}(x - 6) \vee \mathrm{Even}(x - 6)$

Thus, we can replace $\overline{\mathrm{Div6}}(x) \vee \mathrm{Even}(x)$ with $X(x)$, where X is defined by: $X(x) =_\nu x = 0 \vee x = 2 \vee x = 4 \vee X(x - 6)$. The resulting formula $X(x)$ can be automatically proved to be valid by the existing tool Mu2CHC [6]. In contrast, Mu2CHC fails to prove the validity of the original formula $\overline{\mathrm{Div6}}(x) \vee \mathrm{Even}(x)$, although the original formula is equivalent to $X(x)$. □

3   Finding Unfolding Sequences via Size Change Abstraction

We now discuss our procedure for finding an appropriate unfolding sequence (like $\triangleleft_{\overline{\mathrm{Div6}}(\mathrm{EvenOdd})^3}$ in Example 2) to achieve the desired unfold/fold transformation. We make the following simplifying assumptions.

1. The target simple formula to be unfolded is either a conjunction $\bigwedge_i X_i(\tilde{t}_i)$ or a disjunction $\bigvee_i X_i(\tilde{t}_i)$ (where $\tilde{t}$ denotes a sequence of terms $t_1, \ldots, t_k$).
2. The righthand side of the definition of each predicate contains exactly one occurrence of a predicate variable. (Thus, $X(y) =_\mu y \leq 0 \vee X(y-1)$ is allowed but not $X(y) =_\mu y \leq 0 \vee X(y - 1) \vee X(y + 1)$.)

The first assumption is not a fundamental restriction: for nested formulas, we can apply unfold/fold transformation in a hierarchical manner as in [5]. For example, for $X(x) \wedge (Y(x) \vee Z(x))$, we can first apply the transformation to $Y(x) \vee Z(x)$ and replace it with $W(x)$, and then apply the transformation to $X(x) \wedge W(x)$. We discuss how to relax the second restriction later.

Our procedure for finding an appropriate unfolding sequence consists of the following steps.

Step 1: Abstract the recursive definitions of predicates to a size change graph, which represents how the arguments of each predicate are changed by unfolding the predicate.

Step 2: Compute finite summary information on possible unfolding sequences and their effects on the arguments of predicates.

Step 3: Compute candidates of appropriate unfolding sequences, based on the summary information and the target formula.

Step 4: Perform the actual unfolding transformations according to one of the candidate unfolding sequences; if it fails (i.e., if the formula obtained by the unfolding sequence cannot be matched with the original formula), try other candidate unfolding sequences.

To clarify the role of each step, let us explain how our procedure proceeds for the example of $\overline{\text{Div6}}(x) \vee \text{Even}(x)$ in Example 2.

Step 1: We prepare the graph in Sect. 1 (with Div6 replaced by $\overline{\text{Div6}}$).

Step 2: Based on the graph, we compute summary information like:

$$\{(\overline{\text{Div6}}^n, [z \overset{-6n}{\to} z]), ((\text{Even} \cdot \text{Odd})^n, [x \overset{-2n}{\to} x]), ((\text{Even} \cdot \text{Odd})^n \text{Even}, [x \overset{-2n-1}{\to} y]),$$

$$((\text{Odd} \cdot \text{Even})^n, [y \overset{-2n}{\to} y]), ((\text{Odd} \cdot \text{Even})^n \text{Odd}, [y \overset{-2n-1}{\to} x])\}.$$

(This notation of the summary information is informal; the actual formal notation will be introduced.) The first element $(\overline{\text{Div6}}^n, [z \overset{-6n}{\to} z])$ means that by unfolding $\overline{\text{Div6}}$ n times (where n is a parameter), the argument z of $\overline{\text{Div6}}$ will be decreased by $6n$. The second element $((\text{Even} \cdot \text{Odd})^n, [x \overset{-2n}{\to} x])$ means that by unfolding Even according to the sequence $(\text{Even} \cdot \text{Odd})^n$, the argument x of Even will be decreased by $2n$.

Step 3: Since the target formula $\overline{\text{Div6}}(x) \vee \text{Even}(x)$ consists of the predicates $\overline{\text{Div6}}$ and Even, we know that appropriate unfolding sequences should be the combination of $\overline{\text{Div6}}^m$ and $(\text{Even} \cdot \text{Odd})^n$ for some m, n (where $m + n > 0$). According to the summary information, the resulting formula is (equivalent to a formula) of the form $C[\overline{\text{Div6}}(x - 6m) \vee \text{Even}(x - 2n)]$. To match it with $C[[t/x](\overline{\text{Div6}}(x) \vee \text{Even}(x))]$ for some t, it must be the case that $3m = n$. By choosing the least such m, n, we obtain $m = 1$ and $n = 3$. Thus, we obtain $\overline{\text{Div6}} \cdot (\text{Even} \cdot \text{Odd})^3$ as a candidate unfolding sequence.

Step 4: We apply the unfold transformations according to the candidate sequence $\overline{\text{Div6}} \cdot (\text{Even} \cdot \text{Odd})^3$, and successfully obtain $X(x)$ where $X(x) =_\nu x = 0 \vee x = 2 \vee x = 4 \vee X(x - 6)$, as discussed in Example 2.

In the rest of this section, we discuss each step in more detail.

3.1   Step 1: Size Change Abstraction

Given a sequence D of predicate definitions, we construct a graph called a *size change graph* to represent information about how (the sizes of) arguments will change by unfolding of each predicate. For a predicate variable X, we write $\mathbf{Args}_D(X)$ for the set of formal parameters; we often omit D. For example, for Example 2, $\mathbf{Args}(\text{Even}) = \{x\}$, $\mathbf{Args}(\text{Odd}) = \{y\}$, and $\mathbf{Args}(\overline{\text{Div6}}) = \{z\}$.

Definition 2. *Let D be a (finite) sequence of predicate definitions, and $\mathbf{V}$ be the set of predicate variables defined in D. A size change graph for D is a labeled graph $(\mathbf{V}, E)$ where E is a set of labeled edges of the form (X_i, g, X_j) and $g \subseteq \mathbf{Args}(X_i) \times \mathbf{Z} \times \mathbf{Args}(X_j).$[2] We require that for each $y \in \mathbf{Args}(X_j)$, the label g contains at most one element of the form (x, n, y). A size change graph $G = (\mathbf{V}, E)$ is a sound abstraction of D, if whenever $(X_i, g, X_j) \in E$, (i) the definition of X_i is of the form $X_i(x_1, \ldots, x_k) = C[X_j(t_1, \ldots, t_\ell)]$, and (ii) for each $(x_i, n, y_j) \in g$ (where y_j is the j-th formal parameter of X_j), $t_j = x_i + n$.*

As indicated by the soundness criteria in the above definition, $(X_i, g, X_j) \in E$ means that $X_i(x_1, \ldots, x_k)$ can be unfolded to a formula of the form $X_j(t_1, \ldots, t_\ell)$, and g expresses information about how arguments flow from $x_1, \ldots, x_k$ to $t_1, \ldots, t_\ell$.

Example 3. Recall the definitions of Even, Odd, and $\overline{\text{Div6}}$ in Example 2. The (sound) size change graph for them consists of the following edges.

$$\{(\text{Even}, \{(x, -1, y)\}, \text{Odd}), (\text{Odd}, \{(y, -1, x)\}, \text{Even}), (\overline{\text{Div6}}, \{(z, -6, z)\}, \overline{\text{Div6}})\}.$$

□

Example 4. Let us consider the following definition.

$$\text{Mult}(x, y, z) =_\mu (x = 0 \wedge z = 0) \vee (x > 0 \wedge \text{Mult}(y, x - 1, z - y)).$$

The size change graph for it is $(\{\text{Mult}\}, \{(\text{Mult}, \{(x, -1, y), (y, 0, x)\}, \text{Mult})\})$. The edge $\{(x, -1, y), (y, 0, x)\}$ indicates that the first argument x is decremented by 1 and flows to the second argument, and the second argument y flows to the first argument. The label does not contain z, as the change of the third argument is not a constant; the size change graph expresses only information about arguments that change by a constant. □

The notion of size change graph is also applicable to predicates over data structures, by considering the change of the *size* of each argument. Thus, the method for calculating candidate unfolding sequences discussed in the next subsection can be applied also to predicates over data structures, although we focus on predicates over integers in the paper.

---

[2] In the original paper on size change termination [8], each label is called a size change graph; here we call the whole graph a size change graph.

Example 5. Consider the following definition of the predicate Shuffle on lists.

$$\text{Shuffle}(x, y, z) =_\mu (x = [] \wedge y = z) \vee (\text{hd}(x) = \text{hd}(z) \wedge \text{Shuffle}(y, \text{tl}(x), \text{tl}(z)))$$

By abstracting lists to their lengths, we obtain the following size change graph:
$(\{\text{Shuffle}\}, \{(\text{Shuffle}, \{(x, -1, y), (y, 0, x), (z, -1, z)\}, \text{Shuffle})\})$.   □

In the rest of this section, we impose a further restriction that each predicate variable X has exactly one outgoing edge (of the form (X, g, Y)); this restriction reflects the assumption that the righthand side of the definition of a predicate contains exactly one occurrence of a predicate variable.

3.2   Step 2: Computing Summary of Unfolding Sequences

The goal of this step is to construct summary information on all the possible unfolding sequences for each predicate variable.

For an edge $e = (X_i, g, X_j)$ of a size change graph, we write $\texttt{src}(e)$ and $\texttt{dst}(e)$ for X_i and X_j respectively. We call a sequence $e_1 \cdots e_m$ of edges of a size change graph a *path* from $\texttt{src}(e_1)$ to $\texttt{dst}(e_m)$ if $\texttt{dst}(e_i) = \texttt{src}(e_{i+1})$ for every $i \in \{1, \ldots, m-1\}$. Each path $e_1 \cdots e_m$ from X to Y expresses information about the effect of the unfolding sequence $\vartriangleleft^*_{\texttt{src}(e_1)\cdots\texttt{src}(e_m)}$ on the change of predicate arguments. By the assumption that each node of a size change graph has exactly one outgoing edge, the set of all the paths from X to Y can be expressed as $\pi_1 \pi_2^*$, where π_1 is a path from X to Y, and π_2 is a path from Y to Y. For instance, the set of all the paths from Even to Odd in the graph given in Example 3 is expressed as $(\text{Even}, \{(x, -1, y)\}, \text{Odd})((\text{Odd}, \{(y, -1, x)\}, \text{Even})(\text{Even}, \{(x, -1, y)\}, \text{Odd}))^*$.

To compress the information expressed by each path, we define the composition of edges as follows.

Definition 3. *Let $e_1 = (X, g_1, Y)$ and $e_2 = (Y, g_2, Z)$ be edges of a size change graph. The composition of e_1 and e_2, written $e_1 \circ e_2$, is (X, g, Z), where $g = \{(x, n_1 + n_2, z) \mid (x, n_1, y) \in g_1, (y, n_2, z) \in g_2\}$. Note that $e_1 \circ e_2$ is undefined if $\texttt{dst}(e_1) \neq \texttt{src}(e_2)$. We write id_X for $(X, \{(x, 0, x) \mid x \in \textbf{Args}(X)\}, X)$. For an edge $e = (X, g, X)$, we define $e^{\circ n}$ by $e^{\circ 0} = \text{id}_X$ and $e^{\circ n} = e^{\circ(n-1)} \circ e$.*

By this definition, $\circ$ is associative. The effect of each path $e_1 \cdots e_m$ can be computed by the composition $e_1 \circ \cdots \circ e_m$. For instance, the effect of the path:

$$(\text{Even}, \{(x, -1, y)\}, \text{Odd})((\text{Odd}, \{(y, -1, x)\}, \text{Even})(\text{Even}, \{(x, -1, y)\}, \text{Odd}))^3$$

is

$$(\text{Even},\{(x,-1,y)\},\text{Odd}) \circ ((\text{Odd},\{(y,-1,x)\},\text{Even}) \circ (\text{Even},\{(x,-1,y)\},\text{Odd}))^{\circ 3}$$
$$=(\text{Even},\{(x,-1,y)\},\text{Odd}) \circ (\text{Odd},\{(y,-2,y)\},\text{Odd})^{\circ 3}$$
$$=(\text{Even},\{(x,-7,y)\},\text{Odd}),$$

which implies that $\text{Even}(x)$ will be unfolded to a formula of the form $C[\text{Odd}(x - 7)]$. For a path $\pi = e_1 \cdots e_m$, we also write π° for $e_1 \circ \cdots \circ e_m$ ($\pi^\circ = \text{id}_X$ if $\pi = \epsilon$, where X depends on the context) and call it a *summary edge.*

The goal of the current step is to obtain a *finite* representation of information about the (infinite) set of paths $\pi_1\pi_2^*$. Since π_1 and π_2 are finite paths, they can be replaced by the summary edges π_1° and π_2°. Thus, the goal is reduced to the issue of how to represent the summary information for $(\pi_2^\circ)^*$. To that end, the lemma given below is a crucial lemma. We write $e_1 \approx e_2$ if they are identical except integer labels, i.e., if (i) $e_1 = (X, g_1, Y)$, (ii) $e_2 = (X, g_2, Y)$ and (iii) $(x, n, y) \in g_1$ if and only if $(x, m, y) \in g_2$ for some m. For example, $(X, \{(x_1, 1, y_2), (x_2, 2, y_1)\}, Y) \approx (X, \{(x_1, -1, y_2), (x_2, 3, y_1)\}, Y)$. When $e_1 \approx e_2$, we define $e_1 + e_2$, $e_1 - e_2$, and me as the pointwise extension of the operations on integer labels, i.e.,

$$(X, g_1, Y) + (X, g_2, Y) = (X, \{(x, n_1 + n_2, y) \mid (x, n_1, y) \in g_1, (x, n_2, y) \in g_2\}, Y)$$
$$(X, g_1, Y) - (X, g_2, Y) = (X, \{(x, n_1 - n_2, y) \mid (x, n_1, y) \in g_1, (x, n_2, y) \in g_2\}, Y)$$
$$m(X, g, Y) = (X, \{(x, mn, y) \mid (x, n, y) \in g\}, Y).$$

Lemma 1. *Let $e = (X, g, X)$ be an edge of a size change graph. Then, there exists k and ℓ (where $k \geq 0$ and $\ell > 0$) that satisfy the following conditions.*

1. $e^{\circ k} \approx e^{\circ(k+\ell)}$.
2. $e^{\circ(k+m\ell)} = e^{\circ k} + m(e^{\circ(k+\ell)} - e^{\circ k})$ *for every $m \geq 0$.*

Proof. Since $\mathbf{Args}(X)$ is finite, there are only finitely many (summary) edges of the form (X, g, X) up to $\approx$. Thus, by the pigeon hole principle, there exist $k \geq 0$ and $\ell > 0$ such that $e^{\circ k} \approx e^{\circ(k+\ell)}$. Since the relation $\approx$ is closed under the composition $\circ$, we have $e^{\circ m} \circ e^{\circ k} \approx e^{\circ m} \circ e^{\circ(k+\ell)}$ for every m, which implies $e^{\circ k} \approx e^{\circ(k+m\ell)}$ for any $m \geq 0$. Suppose $(x, n, y) \in g_{e^{\circ k}}$ and $(x, n', y) \in g_{e^{\circ(k+\ell)}}$. (Here, for an edge $e = (X, g, Y)$, we write g_e for g.) Since $e^{\circ(k+\ell)} = e^{\circ \ell} \circ e^{\circ k}$, it must be the case that $(x, n' - n, x) \in g_{e^{\circ \ell}}$ (recall that for each variable x, there exists at most one incoming edge of the form $(x', m, x) \in g$). Therefore, we have $(x, n + m(n' - n), y) \in g_{e^{\circ(k+m\ell)}}$ for every $m \geq 0$, which implies $e^{\circ(k+m\ell)} = e^{\circ k} + m(e^{\circ(k+\ell)} - e^{\circ k})$. $\quad\square$

Example 6. Let $e = (X, g, X)$ where $g = \{(x, 1, y), (y, 2, x), (y, -1, z)\}$. Then the lemma holds for $k = 1$ and $\ell = 2$. In fact,

$$e^{\circ 3} = (X, \{(x, 4, y), (y, 5, x), (y, 2, z)\}, X) \approx e,$$

and

$$e^{\circ(1+2m)} = (X, \{(x, 1 + 3m, y), (y, 2 + 3m, x), (y, -1 + 3m, z)\}) = e + m(e^{\circ 3} - e).$$

$\quad\square$

Based on the discussions above, we obtain the following procedure for computing a finite representation of the summary of unfolding sequences from X to Y.

1. Represent the set of paths from X to Y in the form $\pi_1\pi_2^*$.
2. For $e = \pi_2^\circ$, obtain the least k and ℓ that satisfy the conditions of Lemma 1.

3. Output the following set as the summary (where m is treated as a variable).

$$\{(\mathtt{src}(\pi_1), \pi_1^\circ), \ldots, (\mathtt{src}(\pi_1)\mathtt{src}(\pi_2)^{k-1}, \pi_1^\circ \circ e^{\circ(k-1)})\}$$
$$\cup\, \{(\mathtt{src}(\pi_1)\mathtt{src}(\pi_2)^{k+i+m\ell}, \pi_1^\circ \circ (e^{\circ(k+i)} + m(e^{\circ(k+\ell)} - e^{\circ k})))|0{\le}i{\le}\ell-1\}.$$

Here, for a path $\pi = e_1 \cdots e_n$, $\mathtt{src}(\pi)$ is defined as $\mathtt{src}(e_1) \cdots \mathtt{src}(e_n)$. The first component of each element of the summary represents an unfolding sequence, and the second component represents its effect.

Example 7. Recall Example 3. For the set of paths from Even to Even, $\pi_1 = \epsilon$, $\pi_2 = (\text{Even}, \{(x, -1, y)\}, \text{Odd})(\text{Odd}, \{(y, -1, x)\}, \text{Even})$, $k = 0$ and $\ell = 1$. Therefore, the summary information for all the possible unfolding sequences from Even to Even is: $\{((\text{Even} \cdot \text{Odd})^m, (\text{Even}, \{(x, -2m, x)\}, \text{Even}))\}$.   □

3.3   Step 3: Finding Candidate Unfolding Sequences

Now, we have the summary information of all pairs of predicates from the previous step. We denote summary information from X to Y by $s_{X,Y}$. We also have a target formula to unfold for folding. Our goal is to compute a set of candidate unfolding sequences in this step by (i) first enumerating the set of all unfolding sequences that unfold the target formula into a formula that contains the same set of predicate variables as the target, and (ii) then by filtering the sequences that gives a foldable formula w.r.t the size change graphs. We call the former sequences pre-candidate unfolding sequences and the later sequences candidate unfolding sequences.

Let $S = \langle(\pi_1, (X_1, w_1, Y_1)), \ldots, (\pi_n, (X_n, w_n, Y_n))\rangle$ be a tuple of summaries. We define $\text{Path}(S)$ to be $\langle\pi_1, \ldots, \pi_n\rangle$. For a path π_i without Kleene closure, we write $|\pi_i|$ for the length of π_i.

Definition 4. *Let $X_1, \ldots, X_n$ be the sequence of predicate variables occurring (in this order from left to right) in the target formula to be unfolded. A tuple $S = \langle(\pi_1, (X_1, w_1, Y_1)), \ldots, (\pi_n, (X_n, w_n, Y_n))\rangle$ of summaries is called a pre-candidate unfolding sequence if $\{X_1, \ldots, X_n\} = \{Y_1, \ldots, Y_n\}$ (as a multiset).*

A pre-candidate unfolding sequence gives a sequence of unfoldings by which the final unfolded formula contains enough predicate variables to match the target formula.

Example 8. Recall the target formula $\overline{\text{Div6}}(x) \vee \text{Even}(x)$ and definitions of the predicates in Example 2. Let

$$s_{\text{Even},\text{Even}} = \big((\text{Even} \cdot \text{Odd})^{m_1}, (\text{Even}, \{(x, -2m_1, x)\}, \text{Even})\big)$$
$$s_{\overline{\text{Div6}},\overline{\text{Div6}}} = \big((\overline{\text{Div6}})^{m_2}, (\overline{\text{Div6}}, \{(x, -6m_2, x)\}, \overline{\text{Div6}})\big).$$

Then, $\langle s_{\overline{\text{Div6}},\overline{\text{Div6}}}, s_{\text{Even},\text{Even}}\rangle$ is a pre-candidate unfolding sequence.   □

Example 9. Let the target formula be $\text{Odd}(x) \vee \text{Even}(x)$ for the definitions of the predicates in Example 2. Recall $s_{\text{Even},\text{Even}}$ in Example 8. Moreover, we have the following summaries:

$$s_{\text{Odd},\text{Odd}} = ((\text{Odd} \cdot \text{Even})^{m_3}, (\text{Odd}, \{(x, -2m_3, x)\}, \text{Odd}))$$
$$s_{\text{Even},\text{Odd}} = (\text{Even}(\text{Odd} \cdot \text{Even})^{m_4}, (\text{Even}, \{(x, -2m_4 - 1, x)\}, \text{Odd}))$$
$$s_{\text{Odd},\text{Even}} = (\text{Odd}(\text{Even} \cdot \text{Odd})^{m_5}, (\text{Odd}, \{(x, -2m_5 - 1, x)\}, \text{Even}))$$

Then, both $S_1 = \langle s_{\text{Even},\text{Even}}, s_{\text{Odd},\text{Odd}} \rangle$ and $S_2 = \langle s_{\text{Even},\text{Odd}}, s_{\text{Odd},\text{Even}} \rangle$ are pre-candidate unfolding sequences for the given target formula.   □

From a pre-candidate unfolding sequence, we construct constraints on parameters $m_1, m_2, \ldots$ for the formula obtained by the unfolding sequence to be folded. By solving the constraints, we obtain a *candidate unfolding sequence*.

Definition 5. *Let* $S = \langle (\pi_{1,1}\pi_{2,1}^{m_1}, (X_1, g_1, Y_1)), \ldots, (\pi_{1,n}\pi_{2,n}^{m_n}, (X_n, g_n, Y_n)) \rangle$ *be a pre-candidate unfolding sequence where*

$$g_i = \{(x_{i,1}, l_{i,1} + m_i w_{i,1}, y_{i,1}), \ldots, ((x_{i,k_i}, l_{i,k_i} + m_i w_{i,k_i}, y_{i,k_i}))\}$$

for $i = 1, \ldots, n$. *Let* $\varphi \equiv X_1(t_{1,1}, \ldots, t_{1,k_1}) \vee \cdots \vee X_n(t_{n,1}, \ldots, t_{n,k_n})$ *be the target formula* φ.[3] *Suppose* $\text{FV}(\varphi) = \{\tilde{y}\}$ *and* ρ *is a permutation over* $\{1, \ldots, n\}$ *such that* $Y_{\rho(i)} = X_i$ *for each* i. *We call* $[v_1/m_1,...,v_n/m_n]\text{Path}(S)$ *a candidate unfolding sequence if* $\{m_1 \mapsto v_1, \ldots, m_n \mapsto v_n\}$ *satisfies the constraint:*

$$\sum_{i=1}^{n} (|\pi_{1,i}| + |\pi_{2,i}| * m_i) > 0$$

$$\wedge \exists \tilde{f}(\forall \tilde{y}(\bigwedge_{i=1}^{n} \bigwedge_{j=1}^{k_i} \forall 1 \leq i \leq n([\tilde{f}(\tilde{y})/\tilde{y}]t_{i,j} = t_{\rho(i),j} + l_{\rho(i),j} + m_{\rho(i)}w_{\rho(i),j}))).$$

The first part of the constraint $\sum_{i=1}^{n}(|\pi_{1,i}| + |\pi_{2,i}| * m_i) > 0$ ensures that at least one unfolding must take place. The second part describes a necessary condition for the target formula $\varphi \equiv X_1(\tilde{t_1}) \vee \cdots \vee X_n(\tilde{t_n})$ to be unfolded to a formula of the form $C[[\tilde{f}(\tilde{y})/\tilde{y}]\varphi]$.

To solve the constraints above, we restrict $\tilde{f} = f_1, \ldots, f_k$ to be linear functions over $\tilde{y}$ in the form $c_{i,0} + c_{i,1}y_1 + \ldots$. Suppose $t_{i,j}$ is in the form $c'_{i,j,0} + c'_{i,j,1}y_1 + \ldots$. Then the part $\forall \tilde{y}([\tilde{f}(\tilde{y})/\tilde{y}]t_{i,j} = t_{\rho(i),j} + l_{\rho(i),j} + m_{\rho(i)}w_{\rho(i),j})$ can be rewritten to $\forall \tilde{y}(c'_{i,j,0} + c_{i,j,0}c'_{i,j,1} + c_{i,j,1}c'_{i,j,1}y_1 + \cdots = c_{\rho(i),j,0} + c_{\rho(i),j,1}y_1 + \cdots + l_{\rho(i),j} + m_{\rho(i)}w_{\rho(i),j})$, so that we can remove the universal quantifiers $\forall \tilde{y}$ by comparing the coefficients of $y_1, \ldots, y_k$ on both sides of the equation. Thus, the whole constraint becomes existentially quantified formulas on linear arithmetic, which can be solved by an SMT solver. By solving the resulting constraint, we get a candidate unfolding sequence.

---

[3] Similarly for the case $\varphi \equiv X_1(t_{1,1}, \ldots, t_{1,k_1}) \wedge \cdots \wedge X_n(t_{n,1}, \ldots, t_{n,k_n})$.

A candidate unfolding sequence $\langle \pi_1, \ldots, \pi_n \rangle$ of a target formula $\varphi = X_1(\tilde{t}_1) \vee \cdots \vee X_n(\tilde{t}_n)$ means that each X_i in φ should be unfolded along the path π_i. Below we often write $\langle \pi_1, \ldots, \pi_n \rangle$ as $\pi_1 \ldots \pi_n$ (hence the name "a candidate unfolding *sequence*") if the unfolding specified by $\pi_1 \ldots \pi_n$ is unambiguous (e.g., when the sets of predicate variables occurring in $\pi_1, \ldots, \pi_n$ are disjoint from each other).

Example 10. Recall the target formula and the pre-candidate unfolding sequence in Example 8. Then we have the following constraint.

$$\exists m_1 m_2 (2m_1 + 2m_2 > 0 \wedge \exists f(\forall x(f(x) = x - 2m_1 \wedge f(x) = x - 6m_2)))$$

Then it is reduced to the constraint $\exists m_1 m_2(m_1 + m_2 > 0 \wedge m_1 = 3m_2)$, and by solving the constraint, we get $m_1 = 3$ and $m_2 = 1$.

Therefore $\overline{\mathrm{Div6}}(\mathrm{Even} \cdot \mathrm{Odd})^3$ is a candidate unfolding sequence.   □

Example 11. Recall the target formula and the pre-candidate unfolding sequences in Example 9. Since $|\mathrm{Even}| = |\mathrm{Odd}| = 1$, we have the following constraints for the pre-candidate unfolding sequences S_1 and S_2 respectively.

$$\exists m_1 m_2 (2m_1 + 2m_2 > 0 \wedge \exists f_1(\forall x(f_1(x) = x - 2m_1 \wedge f_1(x) = x - 2m_2))), \text{ and}$$
$$\exists m_1 m_2 (1 + 1 + 2m_1 + 2m_2 > 0 \wedge \exists f_2(\forall x(f_2(x) = x - 1 - 2m_1 \wedge f_2(x) = x - 1 - 2m_2)))$$

Then it is reduced to the constraints $\exists m_1 m_2(m_1 + m_2 > 0 \wedge m_1 = m_2)$ and $\exists m_1 m_2(2 + m_1 + m_2 > 0 \wedge m_1 = m_2)$ respectively, and by solving the constraints, we get $m_1 = 1$ and $m_2 = 1$ for S_1 and $m_1 = 0$ and $m_2 = 0$ for S_1. Therefore, both $((\mathrm{Even} \cdot \mathrm{Odd}), (\mathrm{Odd} \cdot \mathrm{Even}))$ and $(\mathrm{Even}, \mathrm{Odd})$ are candidate unfolding sequences.

□

3.4   Step 4: Checking Candidate Unfolding Sequences

Once a candidate unfolding sequence is given, the actual unfold/fold transformation is essentially the same as the (synchronous) unfold/fold transformation given in [5]. Given a target formula φ, we just unfold it according to the unfolding sequence and obtain a formula φ'. When φ is a disjunctive (conjunctive, resp.) formula $\bigvee_i X_i(\tilde{t}_i)$, then convert φ' to a conjunctive (disjunctive, resp.) normal form. Then for each conjunct of the form $(\bigvee_i X_i(\tilde{s}_i)) \vee \varphi''$, check whether $\bigvee_i X_i(\tilde{s}_i)$ can be expressed in the form $[\tilde{u}/\tilde{x}](\bigvee_i X_i(\tilde{t}_i))$. If so, replace the target formula with $Z(\tilde{x})$, where Z is a fresh predicate variable defined by $Z(\tilde{x}) =_\sigma \cdots \wedge (Z(\tilde{u}) \vee \varphi'') \wedge \cdots$.

Here we give an example to demonstrate how CNF is used and folding is performed after the full unfolding for a candidate unfolding sequence.

Example 12. Recall the definition of Odd in Example 1. We also define the following predicates.

$$\overline{\mathrm{Even}}(x) =_\nu x \neq 0 \wedge \overline{\mathrm{Odd}}(x - 1);$$
$$\overline{\mathrm{Odd}}(y) =_\nu \overline{\mathrm{Even}}(y - 1);$$
$$\overline{\mathrm{S}}(x, y) =_\nu (x \neq 0 \vee y \neq 1) \wedge (x \leq 0 \vee \overline{\mathrm{S}}(x - 1, y - 1));$$

Here $\overline{S}$ is the dual of a successor predicate: $\overline{S}(x, y)$ means that y is not the successor of x. Suppose we wish to unfold and fold the formula $\varphi = \overline{S}(x, y) \vee \overline{\text{Even}}(y) \vee \text{Odd}(x)$. Using the candidate unfolding sequence $\langle \overline{S}^2, \overline{\text{Even}} \cdot \overline{\text{Odd}}, \text{Odd} \cdot \text{Even} \rangle$, we can unfold the target formula as follows.

$\overline{S}(x, y) \vee \overline{\text{Even}}(y) \vee \text{Odd}(x)$

$\lhd_{\overline{SS}} ((x{\neq}0 \vee y{\neq}1) \wedge (x{\leq}0 \vee ((x{\neq}1 \vee y{\neq}2) \wedge (x{\leq}1 \vee \overline{S}(x-2, y-2)))))$
$\qquad \vee \overline{\text{Even}}(y) \vee \text{Odd}(x)$

$\lhd_{\overline{\text{EvenOdd}}} ((x{\neq}0 \vee y{\neq}1) \wedge (x{\leq}0 \vee ((x{\neq}1 \vee y{\neq}2) \wedge (x{\leq}1 \vee \overline{S}(x-2, y-2)))))$
$\qquad \vee (y{\neq}0 \wedge \overline{\text{Even}}(y-2)) \vee \text{Odd}(x)$

$\lhd_{\text{OddEven}} ((x{\neq}0 \vee y{\neq}1) \wedge (x{\leq}0 \vee ((x{\neq}1 \vee y{\neq}2) \wedge (x{\leq}1 \vee \overline{S}(x-2, y-2)))))$
$\qquad \vee (y{\neq}0 \wedge \overline{\text{Even}}(y-2)) \vee (x{=}1 \vee \text{Odd}(x-2))$

Finally, we compute the CNF form of the unfolded formula as follows.

$(x \neq 0 \ \vee y \neq 1 \vee \overline{\text{Even}}(y-2) \vee \text{Odd}(x-2)) \wedge (x \leq 1 \vee y \neq 0 \vee \overline{S}(x-2, y-2) \vee$
$\text{Odd}(x-2)) \wedge (x \leq 1 \vee \overline{S}(x-2, y-2) \vee \overline{\text{Even}}(y-2) \vee \text{Odd}(x-2)).$

Finally we can fold it by defining a new predicate $F(x, y) =_\nu \ldots \wedge (x \leq 1 \vee F(x-2, y-2))$ and substituting φ by $F(x, y)$. $\qquad \square$

Example 13. Here we present another example to demonstrate the scenario where the predicate definitions have a non-constant change of an argument. Let $W(x, y, z) = \overline{\text{Mult}}(x, y, z) \vee \text{Mult}(y, x, z)$ be the target formula, where Mult was defined in Example 4. We also define the predicate $\overline{\text{Mult}}(x, y, z) =_\nu (x \neq 0 \vee z \neq 0) \wedge (x \leq 0 \vee \overline{\text{Mult}}(y, x-1, z-y))$. Similarly to Mult, the size change graph for $\overline{\text{Mult}}$ contains the edge $(\overline{\text{Mult}}, \{(x, -1, y), (y, 0, x)\}, \overline{\text{Mult}})$. The summary information for unfolding sequences on Mult and $\overline{\text{Mult}}$ contains:

$$s_{\text{Mult}, \text{Mult}} = \{((\text{Mult})^{2m_1}, (\text{Mult}, \{(x, -m_1, x)(y, -m_1, y)\}, \text{Mult}))\}$$
$$s_{\overline{\text{Mult}}, \overline{\text{Mult}}} = \{((\overline{\text{Mult}})^{2m_2}, (\overline{\text{Mult}}, \{(x, -m_1, x)(y, -m_1, y)\}, \overline{\text{Mult}}))\}$$

Therefore, $\langle s_{\text{Mult}, \text{Mult}}, s_{\overline{\text{Mult}}, \overline{\text{Mult}}} \rangle$ is a pre-candidate unfolding sequence or the given target formula. Then we have the following constraints for the precandidate unfolding sequence.

$$\exists m_1 m_2 (m_1 + m_2 > 0 \wedge \exists f_1 f_2 \ (\forall x, y, z(f_1(x, y, z) = x - m_1 \wedge f_1(x, y, z) = x - \dot{m}_2$$
$$\wedge f_2(x, y, z) = y - m_1 \wedge f_2(x, y, z) = y - m_2)))$$

Then it is reduced to the constraint $\exists m_1 m_2 (m_1 + m_2 > 0 \wedge m_1 = m_2)$, and by solving the constraint, we get $m_1 = 1$ and $m_2 = 1$. Therefore, $(\overline{\text{Mult}})^2 (\text{Mult})^2$ is a candidate unfolding sequence. By actually unfolding the target formula $W(x, y, z)$ according to the above candidate unfolding sequence, and then by computing CNF, we obtain a formula $C[\overline{\text{Mult}}(x-1, y-1, z-y-x+1) \vee \text{Mult}(y-1, x-1, z-x-y+1)]$ for some formula context C, which can be folded to $C[W(x-1, y-1, z-x-y+1)]$. $\qquad \square$

3.5   Extensions

We have so far imposed the restriction that the righthand side of each predicate definition contains exactly one occurrence of a predicate variable. This section briefly discusses how to remove the restriction.

To see what issues arise without the restriction, let us consider the following predicate definitions:

$$P(x) =_\mu x = 0 \vee P(x - 2) \vee P(x + 1)$$
$$Q(y) =_\mu y = 1 \vee Q(y - 2).$$

Here, the body of P contains two occurrences of P, combined with disjunction. The following two issues arise in unfolding a formula containing P and Q, depending on the logical connective that combines P and Q.

- If the target formula is $X(x) \equiv P(x) \vee Q(x)$, then the number of predicates increases each time P is unfolded. In fact, we obtain $x = 0 \vee P(x - 2) \vee P(x + 1) \vee x = 1 \vee Q(x - 2)$ by unfolding P and Q once. Thus, to fold the resulting formula, we have to choose between the two occurrences of P. (In this example, we should pick $P(x - 2)$, and fold the resulting formula to $x = 0 \vee x = 1 \vee P(x + 1) \vee X(x - 2)$.)
- If the target formula is $Y(x, y) \equiv P(x) \wedge Q(y)$, then by unfolding P, we obtain a formula of the form $(P(x - 2) \wedge Q(y)) \vee (P(x + 1) \wedge Q(y)) \vee (x = 0 \wedge Q(y))$. We should then fold each disjunct separately, possibly after further unfoldings of P and Q. For example, the formula above can be folded to $Y(x - 2, y) \vee Y(x + 1, y) \vee (x = 0 \wedge Q(y))$.

In general, the first case (where the number of predicate variables increases upon each unfolding) arises when the logical connectives of the target formula and the body of a predicate definition are the same, and the second case (where the unfolding process splits into multiple branches, although the number of predicates in each branch remains the same) arises when the logical connectives are dual. (We can also have a combination of the two cases, when predicates are combined with both conjunction and disjunction in the body of a predicate definition).

To deal with the first case, it suffices to allow multiple edges from each node. For example, the size change graph for P would consist of two edges $(P, \{(x, -2, x)\}, P)$ and $(P, \{(x, 1, x)\}, P)$, where the former (latter, resp.) edge corresponds to the case where we pick $P(x - 2)$ ($P(x + 1)$, resp.) as the target for further unfolding and folding. We can still compute the summary of all the possible unfolding sequences as in Sect. 3.2.

To deal with the second case, we need to generalize unfolding *sequences* to unfolding *trees*, and extend the representation of summary information accordingly. We leave it to future work to formalize the details and implement the extension.

Table 1. Experimental results for the first benchmark set [7].

#	Target formula φ	o/×?	MuHFL time $(T(\varphi))$ sec	MuHFL time (φ) sec
7	$\overline{\text{Plus}}(x,y,p) \vee \text{Neq}(p,z) \vee (\text{Plus}(y,x,q) \wedge \text{Eq}(q,z))$	×	N/A	Timeout
11	$\overline{\text{S}}(x,p) \vee \overline{\text{S}}(y,q) \vee \overline{\text{S}}(z,r) \vee \overline{\text{Plus}}(p,q,s) \vee \text{Neq}(s,r) \vee \exists m.\exists n.(\text{Plus}(x,y,m) \wedge S(m,n) \wedge \text{Eq}(n,z))$	o	0.656	14.343
13	$\overline{\text{S}}(x,z) \vee \overline{\text{S}}(y,w) \vee \overline{\text{Leq}}(z,w) \vee \text{Leq}(x,y)$	o	0.190	0.870
16	$\text{Leq}(x,y) \vee \text{Leq}(y,z) \vee \overline{\text{Leq}}(x,z)$	o	0.348	Timeout
17	$\overline{\text{Leq}}(y,x) \vee \exists z.(x+1 = z \wedge \text{Leq}(y,z))$	o	0.198	Timeout
20	$\overline{\text{Leq}}(z,x) \vee \exists w.(\text{Plus}(x,y,w) \wedge \text{Leq}(z,w))$	×	N/A	28.602
22	$\overline{\text{Plus}}(x,y,z) \vee \text{Leq}(y,z)$	o	0.328	Timeout
23	$\overline{\text{Even}}(x) \vee \overline{\text{Odd}}(x)$	o	0.180	Timeout
24	$\overline{\text{Even}}(x) \vee \text{Odd}(x+1)$	o	0.178	Timeout
25	$x < 0 \vee \overline{\text{Even}}(x+1) \vee Odd(x)$	o	0.179	Timeout

4   Experiments

We have implemented a transformation tool based on the discussions of this paper. It uses Z3 [9] in the backend for solving the constraints. Our tool currently supports only integers as basic data; an extension with data structures is left for future work.

We have conducted experiments to evaluate the effectiveness of our unfold and fold procedures and to know if it indeed transform formulas to aid to enhance their validity checking. To that end, we have first experimented our tool with the benchmark provided in the work of Kurita and Aoto [7] on automated theorem proving by rewriting induction. We have also evaluated the tool with our own benchmark set to further investigate its capabilities, limitations, and efficiency. The experiments were conducted on an Elementary OS 5.1.7 (on Ubuntu 18.04) system with 8 GB memory and 2.40 GHz Quad-Core Intel® Core™ i5-9300H CPU.

First we present a summary of the evaluation results for the first benchmark set. The original benchmark set [7] consists of 31 formula examples; we tested 28 instances and checked their validity by the automated theorem prover MuHFL (https://github.com/hopv/muhfl) for higher order mu-arithmetic formulas (which subsumes MuArith)) and the rest three examples are beyond the scope of the tool since they use 'List' data structure. Among 28 tested examples, there are 6 instances where validity checking of the original formula failed (due to timeout) but succeeded after transformation by our tool. For other 8 instances, our transformation clearly improved the time for validity checking and it failed to transform two other instances where a different transformation is needed. For the rest of the examples, the performance of validity checking was almost the

Table 2. Experimental results for our own benchmark.

Target formula	Transformed formula	Unfold T	Exec T (sec)
$\mathrm{Div6}(n) \Rightarrow \mathrm{Even}(n)$	$F(n-6)$	$(1,6)$	0.647
$\mathrm{Div2}(n) \wedge \mathrm{Div3}(n) \Rightarrow \mathrm{Div6}(n)$	$F(n-6)$	$(3,2,1)$	1.853
$\mathrm{Plus}(x,y,u) \wedge \mathrm{Plus}(u,z,v)$	$F(x-1,y,u-1,z,v-1)$	$(1,1)$	0.710
$\mathrm{Plus}(y,z,w) \wedge \mathrm{Plus}(x,w,v)$	$F(x-1,y,z,w,v-1)$	$(0,1)$	0.310
$\mathrm{Even}(x) \vee \mathrm{Odd}(x)$	$F(x-1)$	$(1,1)$	0.190
$\mathrm{Even}(x) \vee \overline{\mathrm{Odd}}(x-1)$	$F(x-2)$	$(2,2)$	0.370
$\overline{\mathrm{Even}}(x) \vee \mathrm{Odd}(x+1)$	$F(x-2)$	$(2,2)$	0.319
$\overline{\mathrm{Even}}(x) \vee \overline{\mathrm{Odd}}(x)$	$F(x-2)$	$(2,2)$	0.385
$\mathrm{Div1}(x) \vee \mathrm{Div2}(x) \vee \mathrm{Div3}(x)$	$F(x-6)$	$(6,3,2)$	0.436
$\mathrm{Div2}(x) \vee \mathrm{Div3}(x) \vee \mathrm{Div5}(x)$	$F(x-30)$	$(15,10,6)$	1.078
$\mathrm{Sum1}(x,y,z) \vee \mathrm{Sum2}(x,y,z)$	Not foldable	N/A	N/A
$\mathrm{Sum1}(x,y,2z) \vee \mathrm{Sum2}(x,y,2z)$	$F(x-1,y-1,z-1)$	$(4,4)$	0.162
$\mathrm{Sum1}(x,y,2z) \vee \mathrm{Sum2}(2x,2y,4z)$	$F(x-1,y-1,z-1)$	$(4,8)$	0.235
$\mathrm{Sum3}(x,y,2z) \vee \mathrm{Sum4}(2x,2y,4z)$	$F(x-1,y-1,z-1)$	$(4,8)$	110.121
$\mathrm{Sum1}(x,2y,2z) \vee \mathrm{Sum2}(2x,4y,4z)$	$F(x-2,y-1,z-2)$	$(8,16)$	0.182
$\mathrm{Sum3}(x,2y,2z) \vee \mathrm{Sum4}(2x,4y,4z)$	N/A	$(8,16)$	Timeout
$\mathrm{Sum1}(2x,3y,4z) \vee \mathrm{Sum2}(6x,9y,12z)$	$F(x-3,y-2,z-3)$	$(24,72)$	0.198
$\mathrm{Sum5}(2x,4y,5z) \vee$ $\mathrm{Sum6}(8x,16y,20z) \vee$ $\mathrm{Sum7}(4x,8y,10z)$	$F(x-10,y-5,z-8)$	$(120,480,240)$	0.347
$A(x) \vee A(2x-3) \vee C(3x-1) \vee$ $A(4x) \vee B(x) \vee D(x-2)$	$F(x-4)$	$(4,8,9,16,4,3)$	0.426
$\overline{\mathrm{Mult}}(x,y,z) \vee \mathrm{Mult}(y,x,z)$	$F(x-1,y-1,z-x-y+1)$	$(1,1)$	34.807

same for the original formula and the transformed formula. Table 1 summarizes interesting experimental results. In the table, the column 'o/×?' represents the transformation status of the target formula, where the successful transformations and the failures are indicated by ∘ and × respectively. The column 'MuHFL time $(T(f))$ sec' represents the time required for validity checking of the transformed formula by MuHFL. The next column 'MuHFL time (f) sec' does the same for the original formula (i.e. without transformation). The entry 'N/A' in the column 'MuHFL time $(T(f))$ sec' means that our unfold/fold transformation was inapplicable. The rows where 'MuHFL time (f) sec' is 'Timeout' (where the timeouts were set to 60 s). but 'MuHFL time $(T(f))$ sec' is not, indicate that validity checking by MuHFL was enabled by our transformation.

Table 2 summarizes the experimental results for our own benchmark set, which includes the examples presented in this paper. The column 'Unfold T' shows how many times the predicate variables in the target formula are unfolded to be transformed, and the column 'Exec T' shows the time our tool took to transform the given formula. For example, the first row presents that our tool took 0.647 s to transform $\mathrm{Div6}(n) \Rightarrow \mathrm{Even}(n)$ into $F(n-6)$ by first unfolding the predicate variables Div6 and Even respectively once and six times and then folding the resulting formula.

Among the predicates in the benchmarks presented in Table 2, the definitions of Even, Odd, Div6, Mult, and $\overline{\text{Mult}}$ are as given in examples given earlier in this paper. Among the rest of the predicates, here we provide definitions of some other predicates: $\text{Sum1}(p, q, r) =_\mu \text{Sum2}(q - 1, p, r - 1)$, $\text{Sum2}(s, t, u) =_\mu \text{Sum1}(s, t, u)$, $\text{Sum3}(p, q, r) =_\mu (q = 0 \wedge p = r) \vee (q > 0 \wedge \text{Sum4}(q - 1, p, r - 1))$, and $\text{Sum4}(s, t, u) =_\mu \text{Sum3}(s, t, u)$. Note that Sum3 and Sum4 are the same as Sum1 and Sum2 respectively, except that the definition of Sum3 contains an additional constraint. The timeout (at 60 s) for $\text{Sum3}(x, 2y, 2z) \vee \text{Sum4}(2x, 4y, 4z)$ is probably due to the bottleneck of the CNF and DNF computation, which is not currently optimized.

5   Related Work

As mentioned in Sect. 1, unfold/fold transformation was originally proposed by Tamaki and Sato [12] for logic programming, and various extensions have been studied [3,5,10,11]. In the present paper, we have addressed the issue of how to find an appropriate unfolding sequence efficiently, which has not been much studied, to our knowledge. The issue of how to unfold recursive definitions often arises also in other contexts, such as tupling transformations [1,4] and cyclic proofs [2]. We expect that our idea of using size change graphs would also be useful in those contexts.

The notion of size change graphs has been inspired by the work of Lee et al. [8] on size-change termination analysis, but the details are different (due to the difference of the applications). In their original work, the edges of a size change graph were either $(x, \downarrow, y)$ (which means $y < x$) or $(x, \overline{\mp}, y)$ (which means $y \leq x$). In contrast, the corresponding edges of our size change graph are of the form (x, c, y) (which means $y = x + c$), which represent information about a constant change. Consequently, (unlike in the original size change graphs) there can be infinitely many edges in the summary of unfolding sequences (because c can be an arbitrary integer), but since the set of possible c's is semi-linear, we can finitely represent the summary information, as discussed in Sect. 3.2.

6   Conclusion

We have proposed an unfold/fold transformation procedure for fixed-point logic formulas, which allows each predicate to be unfolded in an asynchronous manner. The key idea is the use of size change graphs to estimate an appropriate unfolding sequence. We have implemented the proposed method and confirmed its effectiveness through experiments.

Acknowledgments. We would like to thank anonymous referees for useful comments. This work was supported by JSPS KAKENHI Grant Numbers JP20H05703.

References

1. Asada, K., Sato, R., Kobayashi, N.: Verifying relational properties of functional programs by first-order refinement. Sci. Comput. Program. **137**, 2–62 (2017). https://doi.org/10.1016/j.scico.2016.02.007
2. Brotherston, J., Simpson, A.: Sequent calculi for induction and infinite descent. J. Log. Comput. **21**(6), 1177–1216 (2011)
3. De Angelis, E., Fioravanti, F., Pettorossi, A., Proietti, M.: Solving Horn clauses on inductive data types without induction. TPLP **18**(3–4), 452–469 (2018). https://doi.org/10.1017/S1471068418000157
4. Hu, Z., Iwasaki, H., Takeichi, M., Takano, A.: Tupling calculation eliminates multiple data traversals. In: Proceedings of the ICFP, pp. 164–175 (1997)
5. Kobayashi, N., Fedyukovich, G., Gupta, A.: Fold/unfold transformations for fixpoint logic. In: TACAS 2020. LNCS, vol. 12079, pp. 195–214. Springer, Cham (2020). https://doi.org/10.1007/978-3-030-45237-7_12
6. Kobayashi, N., Nishikawa, T., Igarashi, A., Unno, H.: Temporal verification of programs via first-order fixpoint logic. In: Chang, B.-Y.E. (ed.) SAS 2019. LNCS, vol. 11822, pp. 413–436. Springer, Cham (2019). https://doi.org/10.1007/978-3-030-32304-2_20
7. Kurita, T., Aoto, T.: Automated proofs of horn-clause inductive theorems for conditional term rewriting systems. Comput. Softw. **36**(2), 261–275 (2019). https://doi.org/10.11309/jssst.36.2_61. (in Japanese)
8. Lee, C.S., Jones, N.D., Ben-Amram, A.M.: The size-change principle for program termination. In: Hankin, C., Schmidt, D. (eds.) Conference Record of POPL 2001: The 28th ACM SIGPLAN-SIGACT Symposium on Principles of Programming Languages, London, UK, 17–19 January 2001, pp. 81–92. ACM (2001). https://doi.org/10.1145/360204.360210
9. de Moura, L., Bjørner, N.: Z3: an efficient SMT solver. In: Ramakrishnan, C.R., Rehof, J. (eds.) TACAS 2008. LNCS, vol. 4963, pp. 337–340. Springer, Heidelberg (2008). https://doi.org/10.1007/978-3-540-78800-3_24
10. Seki, H.: On inductive and coinductive proofs via unfold/fold transformations. In: De Schreye, D. (ed.) LOPSTR 2009. LNCS, vol. 6037, pp. 82–96. Springer, Heidelberg (2010). https://doi.org/10.1007/978-3-642-12592-8_7
11. Seki, H.: Proving properties of co-logic programs by unfold/fold transformations. In: Vidal, G. (ed.) LOPSTR 2011. LNCS, vol. 7225, pp. 205–220. Springer, Heidelberg (2012). https://doi.org/10.1007/978-3-642-32211-2_14
12. Tamaki, H., Sato, T.: Unfold/fold transformation of logic programs. In: Tärnlund, S. (ed.) Proceedings of the Second International Logic Programming Conference, Uppsala University, Uppsala, Sweden, 2–6 July 1984, pp. 127–138. Uppsala University (1984)
13. Unno, H., Torii, S., Sakamoto, H.: Automating induction for solving horn clauses. In: Majumdar, R., Kunčak, V. (eds.) CAV 2017. LNCS, vol. 10427, pp. 571–591. Springer, Cham (2017). https://doi.org/10.1007/978-3-319-63390-9_30

Program Logic for Higher-Order Probabilistic Programs in Isabelle/HOL

Michikazu Hirata[✉], Yasuhiko Minamide, and Tetsuya Sato

School of Computing, Tokyo Institute of Technology, Tokyo, Japan
hirata.m.ac@m.titech.ac.jp, minamide@is.titech.ac.jp, tsato@c.titech.ac.jp

Abstract. The verification framework PPV (Probabilistic Program Verification) verifies functional probabilistic programs supporting higher-order functions, continuous distributions, and conditional inference. PPV is based on the theory of quasi-Borel spaces which is introduced to give a semantics of higher-order probabilistic programming languages with continuous distributions. In this paper, we formalize a theory of quasi-Borel spaces and a core part of PPV in Isabelle/HOL. We first construct a probability monad on quasi-Borel spaces based on the Giry monad in the Isabelle/HOL library. Our formalization of PPV is extended so that integrability of functions can be discussed formally. Finally, we prove integrability and convergence of the Monte Carlo approximation in our mechanized PPV.

Keywords: Higher-order probabilistic programming language ·
Program logic · Formal verification · Isabelle/HOL

1 Introduction

Probabilistic programming languages provide a generic way to describe sophisticated probabilistic models. Programmers can directly write generative probabilistic models in the languages and work with the models without constructing the complicated inference algorithms by themselves.

Some languages, such as Anglican [32] and Church [12], support higher-order functions that make the languages more expressive. Unfortunately, its combination with continuous distributions causes difficulty in their semantics. Probabilistic programming languages without higher-order functions can be interpreted using the category of measurable spaces and a probability monad, called the Giry monad, on it [11]. However, Aumann's result [3] shows that we cannot interpret functions as first class objects using the category of measurable spaces. To overcome this difficulty, Heunen et al. introduced quasi-Borel spaces [15], which provide a suitable denotational model for higher-order probabilistic programs.

To verify the programs written in a higher-order probabilistic programs, Sato et al. introduced the verification framework PPV [28] (Probabilistic Program Verification framework). PPV consists of the language HPProg and three kind

© Springer Nature Switzerland AG 2022
M. Hanus and A. Igarashi (Eds.): FLOPS 2022, LNCS 13215, pp. 57–74, 2022.
https://doi.org/10.1007/978-3-030-99461-7_4

of logics PL, UPL, and RPL. The semantic foundation of the language is based on the theory of quasi-Borel spaces, and the language supports sampling, continuous distributions, conditional inference, and higher-order functions. With the framework PPV, we can verify properties of algorithms used in statistics and machine learning area.

Formal verification of probabilistic programs with proof assistants has been actively studied. Hurd et al. formalized an imperative probabilistic and nondeterministic language pGCL [20] in HOL4 [13], Cock also formalized pGCL [8] in Isabelle/HOL [27]. Audebaud and Paulin-Mohring shallowly embedded a functional probabilistic language [2] in Coq [6]. Eberl et al. constructed an executable first-order functional probabilistic programming language in Isabelle, and proved its correctness [10]. Lochbihler shallowly embedded a functional programming language, where the probabilities are restricted to only discrete spaces, in Isabelle/HOL, and verified cryptographic algorithms [22]. Bagnall and Stewart embedded MLCERT [5], a system for verified machine learning, in Coq. Tristan et al. partially automated probabilistic program verification [31] with Lean [26]. These previous works cannot support both higher-order functions and continuous distributions since they are based on the measure theory or restrict the probability spaces to discrete spaces.

Contributions of our work are the following.

- We formalize the theory of quasi-Borel spaces in Isabelle/HOL. Our formalization contains constructions of quasi-Borel spaces (product, coproduct, function space), the adjunction between the category of measurable spaces and the category of quasi-Borel spaces, and the probability monad on quasi-Borel spaces. Our formalization also contains the example of the Bayesian regression in the work of Heunen et al. [15], but we omit it in this paper due to space limitation.
- We construct the core part of the framework PPV in Isabelle/HOL which does not support the conditional inference. We formalize the programming language HPProg, the assertion logic PL and the program logic UPL. It should be noted that our system is extended so that we can formally reason about integrability.
- As an example of program verification, we prove the weak convergence (the weak law of large number) of the Monte Carlo approximation in our mechanized PPV. Our verification includes the integrability of the program, that is assumed implicitly in the previous work [28].

Our work enables verification of probabilistic programs with both higher-order functions and continuous distributions because we use the theory of quasi-Borel spaces. To the best of our knowledge, the theory of quasi-Borel spaces and verification based on the theory have not been implemented in any proof assistants.

There are two major differences between the original PPV and our formalized PPV. Firstly, the former supports the command `query` (`observe` in Anglican) for conditional inference, but the latter does not. Our formalization is based on the work of Heunen et al. [15], which introduces the monad P for probability measures on quasi-Borel spaces. However, the original PPV is based on the monad M for σ-finite measures introduced by Ścibior et al. [29], which supports denotational semantics for the command query. We choose the probability monad P because it is constructed from the Giry monad which has been already formalized in Isabelle/HOL. Secondly, we explicitly introduce the notion of integrability in the logics of PPV. There are informal discussions about expectations in the PPV of Sato et al. [28]. To mechanize the informal discussion, we need to introduce the notion of integrability in the logics. We explain the detail in Sect. 2.

Our source code is available online[1]. The formalization of quasi-Borel spaces is also available at [16].

2 Program Verification in PPV

We briefly review the verification framework PPV and show how a probabilistic program is verified with PPV.

2.1 A Verification Framework: PPV

PPV [28] is a verification framework for higher-order probabilistic programs. The basic structure comes from the program logic introduced by Aguirre et al. [1]. PPV consists of the probabilistic programming language HPProg and the logics PL and UPL[2]. The language HPProg supports sampling from distributions, conditional inference, higher-order functions, and terminating recursive functions. For a type T, $P[T]$ denotes the type of probability distribution on T.

The logic PL for assertions has the judgments $\Gamma \mid \Psi \vdash_{\mathrm{PL}} \phi$ where Γ is a typing context, Ψ is a set of assumptions, and ϕ is a conclusion. The judgment means that in the context Γ, if Ψ holds, then ϕ also holds.

The program logic UPL has the judgments $\Gamma \mid \Psi \vdash_{\mathrm{UPL}} e : T \mid \phi$ where e is an expression (program) and T is its type. In addition, the conclusion ϕ may contain the special variable $\mathbf{r}$ of type T that is used to refer to the value of e. The judgment means that in the context Γ, e has type T and if Ψ holds, then $\phi[e/\mathbf{r}]$ also holds. PL and UPL are equi-derivable in the sense Theorem 2.

The language HPProg has a denotational semantics based on quasi-Borel spaces. The notion of quasi-Borel spaces is introduced by Heunen et al. [15] in order to give denotational semantics to probabilistic programming languages with higher-order functions and continuous distributions. The assertions Ψ and ϕ in the logics PL and UPL are interpreted as predicates over quasi-Borel spaces.

2.2 Verification of Monte Carlo Approximation

We verify integrability and convergence of the Monte Carlo approximation in our mechanized PPV. For a given probability distribution d on X and $h : X \to \mathbb{R}$, it

---

[1] https://github.com/HirataMichi/PPV.
[2] The original PPV also includes the relational program logic RPL. Since we have not formalized RPL, we omit the explanation of RPL.

```
montecarlo : nat ⇒ P[real]
montecarlo n ≡ if (n = 0) then return 0
          else do {
              m ← montecarlo (n-1);
              x ← d;
              return ((1/n)*(h(x)+m*(n-1)))
          }
```

Fig. 1. Monte Carlo Approximation, written in pseudocode.

$\Gamma \equiv \varepsilon : \mathtt{real}, \mu : \mathtt{real}, \sigma : \mathtt{real}, \mathtt{d} : P[\mathtt{X}], \mathtt{h} : \mathtt{X} \Rightarrow \mathtt{real}$

$\Psi \equiv \{\sigma^2 = \mathbb{V}_{\mathtt{x} \sim \mathtt{d}}[\mathtt{h\ x}], \mu = \mathbb{E}_{\mathtt{x} \sim \mathtt{d}}[\mathtt{h\ x}], \varepsilon > 0, integrable\ \mathtt{d\ h}, integrable\ \mathtt{d\ h}^2\}$

$\Gamma \mid \Psi \vdash_{\mathrm{UPL}} montecarlo : \mathtt{nat} \Rightarrow P[\mathtt{real}] \mid \forall \mathtt{n} : \mathtt{nat}.\mathtt{n} > 0 \to \Pr_{\mathtt{y} \sim \mathtt{r\,n}}[|\mathtt{y} - \mu| \geq \varepsilon] \leq \sigma^2/\mathtt{n}\varepsilon^2$

$\Gamma \mid \Psi \vdash_{\mathrm{PL}} \forall \mathtt{n} : \mathtt{nat}.integrable\ (montecarlo\ \mathtt{n})(\lambda \mathtt{x}.\mathtt{x}) \wedge integrable\ (montecarlo\ \mathtt{n})(\lambda \mathtt{x}.\mathtt{x}^2)$

Fig. 2. Weak law of large numbers in PPV.

computes an approximation of the expectation $\mathbb{E}_{x \sim d}[h(x)]$. Let $x_1, \ldots, x_n$ be a sequence of samples generated from the distribution d, then the approximation value $\hat{\mu}_n$ is defined by

$$\hat{\mu}_n = \frac{h(x_1) + \cdots + h(x_n)}{n}.$$

The program in Fig. 1 is an implementation of this algorithm. It computes the mean value of $h(x_1), \ldots, h(x_n)$ recursively. In the program, $\mathtt{d} : \mathtt{P[X]}$ is a probability distribution on $\mathtt{X}$ and $\mathtt{h} : \mathtt{X} \Rightarrow \mathtt{real}$ is a function. Notice that the program is higher-order with respect to $\mathtt{h}$. The program *montecarlo* receives a natural number n, then returns the distribution of $\hat{\mu}_n$ on real numbers. The distribution of $\hat{\mu}_n$ has the following familiar property.

Proposition 1 (Weak law of large numbers). *Let $(X_i)_{i=1,2,\ldots}$ be a sequence of i.i.d. real-valued random variables with finite mean μ and variance σ^2. Then for any $\varepsilon > 0$, we have*

$$\lim_{n \to \infty} \Pr\left[\left|\frac{X_1 + \cdots + X_n}{n} - \mu\right| \geq \varepsilon\right] = 0. \tag{1}$$

This property is stated in UPL as in Fig. 2, where $\mathbb{V}_{\mathtt{x} \sim \mathtt{d}}[\mathtt{h\ x}]$ and $\mathbb{E}_{\mathtt{x} \sim \mathtt{d}}[\mathtt{h\ x}]$ are the variance and expectation of $\mathtt{h\ x}$ where $\mathtt{x}$ is sampled from $\mathtt{d}$, and $\Pr_{\mathtt{y} \sim \mathtt{r\,n}}[|\mathtt{y} - \mu| \geq \varepsilon]$ corresponds to the probability of the left hand side in the Eq. (1). The assertion Ψ provides the integrability assumptions on that ensures the existence of finite mean μ and variance σ^2. The UPL-judgment provides a concrete upper bound of the probability in the Eq. (1) for each n. To prove this UPL-judgment, we need to prove the PL-judgment of the integrability condition that ensures the existence of the expectation and the variance of $\hat{\mu}_n$ since we use the linearity of expectation, which requires the integrability assumptions, in the proof of the

UPL-judgment. The judgments in Fig. 2 are proved in our mechanized PPV. In Sect. 5, we will show how we mechanize them and their proofs.

The original PPV informally uses the linearity of expectation. The linearity of expectation $\mathbb{E}_{x \sim d}[f\ x + g\ x] = \mathbb{E}_{x \sim d}[f\ x] + \mathbb{E}_{x \sim d}[g\ x]$ holds if both f and g are non-negative. For general real-valued functions f and g, we additionally need to assume that f and g are integrable with respect to d. In the proof of the UPL-judgement, we use the following property.

$$\mathbb{V}_{(x,y) \sim d_1 \otimes d_2}[f\ x + g\ y] = \mathbb{V}_{x \sim d_1}[f\ x] + \mathbb{V}_{y \sim d_2}[g\ y]. \tag{2}$$

This equation is shown as follows.

$$
\begin{aligned}
&\mathbb{V}_{(x,y) \sim d_1 \otimes d_2}[f\ x + g\ y] \\
&= \mathbb{E}_{(x,y) \sim d_1 \otimes d_2}[(f\ x + g\ y - \mathbb{E}_{(x,y) \sim d_1 \otimes d_2}[f\ x + g\ y])^2] \\
&= \mathbb{E}_{(x,y) \sim d_1 \otimes d_2}[(f\ x - \mathbb{E}_{x \sim d_1}[f\ x])^2 + (g\ y - \mathbb{E}_{y \sim d_2}[g\ y])^2 \\
&\quad + 2(f\ x - \mathbb{E}_{x \sim d_1}[f\ x])(g\ y - \mathbb{E}_{y \sim d_2}[g\ y])] \\
&= \mathbb{E}_{x \sim d_1}[(f\ x - \mathbb{E}_{x \sim d_1}[f\ x])^2] + \mathbb{E}_{y \sim d_2}[(g\ y - \mathbb{E}_{y \sim d_2}[g\ y])^2] \\
&\quad + 2\mathbb{E}_{x \sim d_1}[f\ x - \mathbb{E}_{x \sim d_1}[f\ x]]\,\mathbb{E}_{y \sim d_2}[g\ y - \mathbb{E}_{y \sim d_2}[g\ y]] \\
&= \mathbb{V}_{x \sim d_1}[f\ x] + \mathbb{V}_{y \sim d_2}[g\ y].
\end{aligned}
\tag{3}
$$

Notice that the term $2(f\ x - \mathbb{E}_{x \sim d_1}[f\ x])(g\ y - \mathbb{E}_{y \sim d_2}[g\ y])$ in (3) may be negative, and hence we need the integrability assumptions to apply the linearity of expectation. In the original paper, they implicitly assume the integrability of functions and use the Eq. (2).

3   Quick Review: Measure Theory and the Giry Monad

The theory of quasi-Borel spaces is based on measure and probability theory. In this section, we recall some basic definitions and properties in those theories.

A measurable space is a pair (X, Σ_X) of a set X together with a σ-algebra Σ_X over X that is a nonempty family of subset of X closed under countable union and complement. Any topological space $(X, \mathcal{O}_X)$ is regarded as the measurable space $(X, \mathcal{B}[\mathcal{O}_X])$, called *Borel space*, whose σ-algebra $\mathcal{B}[\mathcal{O}_X]$ is the least one containing all its open sets. In this paper, we regard topological spaces, such as $\mathbb{R}$ and $\mathbb{N}$, as its Borel spaces. A measurable function from (X, Σ_X) to (Y, Σ_Y) is a function $f: X \to Y$ satisfying $f^{-1}(A) \in \Sigma_X$ for any $A \in \Sigma_Y$. Measurable spaces and measurable functions form the category **Meas**. It has small products and coproducts.

A measure μ on (X, Σ_X) is a σ-additive mapping $\mu: \Sigma_X \to [0, \infty]$ such that $\mu(\emptyset) = 0$. A measure space is a triple (X, Σ_X, μ) where (X, Σ_X) is a measurable space and μ is a measure on (X, Σ_X). If $\mu(X) = 1$, we call the measure space (X, Σ_X, μ) a *probability space*, and μ a *probability measure*. A measurable function $f: X \to \mathbb{R}$ is *integrable* with respect to a measure μ on X when $\int |f|\,d\mu < \infty$. Then the integral $\int f\,d\mu$ exists as a finite value.

The Giry Monad. Probabilistic computations with samplings from continuous distributions are captured by the *Giry monad* $(G, \eta^G, \ggg_G)$ on the category **Meas** [11]. For any measurable space X, $G(X)$ is the measurable space of all probability measures on X, and η_X^G assigns to each $x \in X$ the Dirac measure[3] δ_x centered at x. The bind assigns to all $f : X \to G(Y)$ and $\mu \in G(X)$ the probability measure $(\mu \ggg_G f) \in G(Y)$ defined by $(\mu \ggg_G f)(A) \overset{\text{def}}{=} \int_X f(x)(A) \, d\mu(x)$.

We can interpret first-order probabilistic programs with continuous random sampling using the Giry monad. A program of type $\Gamma \vdash e \colon P[T]$ can be interpreted as a measurable function $\llbracket e \rrbracket \colon \llbracket \Gamma \rrbracket \to G(\llbracket T \rrbracket)$ where $\llbracket \Gamma \rrbracket$ and $\llbracket T \rrbracket$ are measurable spaces. For example, the following program written in pseudocode

$$\mathtt{m} \colon \mathtt{real}, \mathtt{s} \colon \mathtt{real} \vdash \mathtt{x} \leftarrow \mathtt{Gauss(m, s)}; \mathtt{y} \leftarrow \mathtt{Gauss(m, s)}; \mathtt{return}(x + y) \colon P[\mathtt{real}]$$

is interpreted as the measurable function of type $\mathbb{R} \times \mathbb{R} \to G(\mathbb{R})$ given by

$$\lambda(m, \sigma). \, (\mathcal{N}(m, \sigma^2) \ggg_G (\lambda x. \, (\mathcal{N}(m, \sigma^2) \ggg_G (\lambda y. \, \eta_{\mathbb{R}}^G(x + y))))).$$

Here, $\mathcal{N}(m, \sigma^2)$ is the Gaussian distribution with mean m and standard deviation σ. The command $\mathtt{Gauss}$ is interpreted by $\llbracket \mathtt{Gauss} \rrbracket(m, \sigma) = \mathcal{N}(m, \sigma^2)$. This program computes the distribution of $x + y$ where both x and y are sampled independently from $\mathcal{N}(m, \sigma^2)$.

A Difficulty on Higher-Order Functions. However, the semantic model based on measurable functions does not support higher-order functions. Aumann [3] showed that the category **Meas** is *not* cartesian closed[4]: there is *no σ-algebra* over $\mathbb{R}^{\mathbb{R}} = \{f \colon \mathbb{R} \to \mathbb{R} \mid f \text{ is measurable}\}$ such that the evaluation mapping $(f, x) \mapsto f(x)$ is a measurable function of type $\mathbb{R}^{\mathbb{R}} \times \mathbb{R} \to \mathbb{R}$. Hence, a higher-order program

$$f \colon \mathtt{real} \Rightarrow \mathtt{real}, x \colon \mathtt{real} \vdash f(x) \colon \mathtt{real}$$

of function application *cannot* be interpreted as a measurable function. This means that there is no suitable interpretation of the function type $\mathtt{real} \Rightarrow \mathtt{real}$ as a measurable space.

4 Quasi-Borel Spaces

In this section, we review basic concepts on quasi-Borel spaces, and present our formalization of quasi-Borel spaces in Isabelle/HOL. We construct quasi-Borel spaces with the measure and probability theories in the standard Isabelle/HOL theory libraries: HOL-Analysis and HOL-Probability [4,10,17,18,22,27]. We expect that the theory of quasi-Borel spaces could be formalized in other proof assistants which have measure theory libraries [7,14,21,23,24,30].

---

[3] $\delta_x(U)$ is 1 if $x \in U$ and 0 otherwise.

[4] The standard Isabelle/HOL theory library includes a proof of this result:
   Isabelle2021-1.app/src/HOL/Probability/ex/Measure_Not_CCC.thy.

4.1   Standard Borel Spaces

Before formalizing quasi-Borel spaces, we first formalize *standard Borel spaces* which have not been formalized yet. Standard Borel spaces play an important role in the theory of quasi-Borel spaces. In general, a standard Borel space is the Borel space $(X, \mathcal{B}[\mathcal{O}_X])$ of a separable completely metrizable topological space $(X, \mathcal{O}_X)$. According to Kuratowski's theorem, a standard Borel spaces is either a countable discrete space or a space isomorphic to $\mathbb{R}$. In our work, we choose another, but equivalent, definition for standard Borel spaces.

Definition 1. *A measurable space X is called a standard Borel space if there exists a pair of measurable functions $X \xrightarrow{f} \mathbb{R} \xrightarrow{g} X$ such that $g \circ f = \mathrm{id}_X$.*

This form of definition is suitable for our purpose since we use these measurable functions in later proofs.

The following lemma is key to construct the probability monad on the category of quasi-Borel spaces.

Lemma 1. $\mathbb{N} \times \mathbb{R}$ *and* $\mathbb{R} \times \mathbb{R}$ *are standard Borel spaces.*

We have proved the second statement above according to the following proof sketch. Although it is not a main part of our formalization, it is one of the most cumbersome proofs in our formalization since we need to discuss about the limits. If we have two measurable functions $(0,1) \times (0,1) \xrightarrow{\alpha} (0,1) \xrightarrow{\beta} (0,1) \times (0,1)$ such that $\beta \circ \alpha = \mathrm{id}_{(0,1) \times (0,1)}$, we can construct two measurable functions $\mathbb{R} \times \mathbb{R} \xrightarrow{f} \mathbb{R} \xrightarrow{g} \mathbb{R} \times \mathbb{R}$ such that $g \circ f = \mathrm{id}_{\mathbb{R} \times \mathbb{R}}$ with isomorphisms between $\mathbb{R}$ and $(0,1)$. We construct α and β as follows: let us denote the binary fraction of $r \in (0,1)$ by $r = 0.r_1 r_2 \ldots$[5]. Let α be a function that maps $(r, r') \in (0,1) \times (0,1)$ to $0.r_1 r_1' r_2 r_2' \ldots$ and β be a function that maps $r \in (0,1)$ to $(0.r_1 r_3 \ldots, 0.r_2 r_4 \ldots)$.[6] These functions are limits of measurable functions. Hence they are measurable, and the composition $\beta \circ \alpha$ is equal to $\mathrm{id}_{(0,1) \times (0,1)}$ from the definitions.

4.2   Quasi-Borel Spaces

In the standard probability theory, we consider a measurable space (Ω, Σ_Ω), where Ω is called a sample space and Σ_Ω is a set of random events. We observe random events through a measurable function called a *random variable*. Thus we first axiomatize measurable spaces and then the notion of random variables comes later. In contrast, in the theory of quasi-Borel spaces, we first axiomatize random variables where the sample space is restricted to $\mathbb{R}$.

Definition 2 ([15, **Definition 7**]). *A quasi-Borel space is a pair of a set X and a set $M_X \subseteq \mathbb{R} \to X$ that satisfies*

---

[5] We choose the sequence that does not include infinite sequence of 1 at the tail. That is, we choose $0.100\ldots$ rather than $0.011\ldots$ for $1/2$.

[6] Actually, the domain of β is not $(0,1) \times (0,1)$ since β maps $0.1010\ldots$ to $(1,0)$. In the actual proof, some modification is needed when constructing f and g.

- If $\alpha \in M_X$ and $f : \mathbb{R} \to \mathbb{R}$ is measurable, then $\alpha \circ f \in M_X$.
- If α is a constant map, then $\alpha \in M_X$.
- If $\{\alpha_i\}_{i \in \mathbb{N}} \subseteq M_X$ and $P : \mathbb{R} \to \mathbb{N}$ is measurable, then $(\lambda r.\alpha_{P(r)}(r)) \in M_X$.

Intuitively, M_X is the set of random variables over the sample space $\mathbb{R}$. We sometimes write X for a quasi-Borel space (X, M_X) if the structure is obvious from the context. As an example, the standard Borel space $\mathbb{R}$ is the quasi-Borel space $(\mathbb{R}, M_\mathbb{R})$ where $M_\mathbb{R}$ is the set of measurable functions from $\mathbb{R}$ to $\mathbb{R}$.

We define the type of quasi-Borel spaces `'a quasi_borel` with the **typedef** command in Isabelle/HOL. The **typedef** command allows users to define a new type which denotes a non-empty subset of an existing type. For `X::'a quasi_borel`, we extract its components by the following projections.

$$\texttt{qbs\_space X::'a set} \qquad \texttt{qbs\_Mx X::(real} \Rightarrow \texttt{'a) set}$$

A function $f : X \to Y$ is called a *morphism* from (X, M_X) to (Y, M_Y) if $f \circ \alpha \in M_Y$ for all $\alpha \in M_X$. Quasi-Borel spaces and morphisms between them form the category **QBS**. It has products, countable coproducts and function spaces, where the function space Y^X is the set **QBS**(X, Y) of morphisms from X to Y (thus it is Cartesian closed). Our formalization includes binary products, binary coproducts, function spaces, products, and countable coproducts. In our formalization, for a product space $\prod_{i \in I} X_i$ and a coproduct space $\coprod_{i \in I} X_i$, every X_i has to be a quasi-Borel space over the same type due to Isabelle's type system.

4.3 Connection Between Measurable Spaces and Quasi-Borel Spaces

There are convenient conversions between measurable spaces and quasi-Borel spaces in both directions. Using the conversions, when we discuss about morphisms between quasi-Borel spaces, we can transform statements about morphisms to ones about measurable functions where we can use the Isabelle/HOL's automated measurability prover. Both directions of conversions are given by two functors $L\colon \mathbf{QBS} \to \mathbf{Meas}$ and $R\colon \mathbf{Meas} \to \mathbf{QBS}$ defined as follows:

$$L(X, M_X) \stackrel{\text{def}}{=} (X, \Sigma_{M_X}), \quad \Sigma_{M_X} \stackrel{\text{def}}{=} \{U \mid \forall \alpha \in M_X.\alpha^{-1}(U) \in \Sigma_\mathbb{R}\}, \quad L(f) \stackrel{\text{def}}{=} f,$$
$$R(X, \Sigma_X) \stackrel{\text{def}}{=} (X, M_{\Sigma_X}), \quad M_{\Sigma_X} \stackrel{\text{def}}{=} \{f\colon \mathbb{R} \to X \mid f\colon \text{measurable}\}, \quad R(f) \stackrel{\text{def}}{=} f.$$

These conversions do not change functions. Hence, we can regard a morphism $f\colon X \to Y$ of quasi-Borel spaces as a measurable function $f\colon (X, \Sigma_{M_X}) \to (Y, \Sigma_{M_Y})$, and conversely we can regard a measurable function $f\colon X \to Y$ as a morphism $f\colon (X, M_{\Sigma_X}) \to (Y, M_{\Sigma_Y})$. The conversions L and R have the following properties.

Lemma 2 ([15, **Propositions 15, 19**]).

- *For all quasi-Borel space X and measurable space Y, f is a measurable function from (X, Σ_{M_X}) to Y iff f is a morphism from X to (Y, M_{Σ_Y}).*
- *For any standard Borel space X, $L(R(X)) = X$ holds.*
- *R preserves products and countable coproducts of standard Borel spaces.*

4.4   The Probability Monad on QBS

We formalize probability measures on quasi-Borel spaces and the probability monad P on **QBS**. This monad inherits basic properties from the Giry monad.

First, we formalize probability measures on quasi-Borel spaces. In standard probability theory, a S-valued random variable Z is a measurable function from the probability space $(\Omega, \Sigma_\Omega, P)$ to S. The distribution of Z is the probability measure Z_*P on S where Z_*P is defined by $Z_*P(U) = P(Z^{-1}(U))$ for $U \in \Sigma_S$. Intuitively, a probability measure on a quasi-Borel space X is a distribution of a random variable $\alpha : (\mathbb{R}, \Sigma_\mathbb{R}, \mu) \to X$. Recall that $\alpha \in M_X$ is regarded as a random variable over the sample space $\mathbb{R}$.

Definition 3 (Probability measures, [15]). *A probability measure on a quasi-Borel space X is an equivalence class $[\alpha, \mu]_\sim$, where $\alpha \in M_X$ and $\mu \in G(\mathbb{R})$, and the equivalence relation $\sim$ is defined by $(\alpha, \mu) \sim (\alpha', \mu')$ iff $\alpha_*\mu = \alpha'_*\mu'$.*

We define the integral of a morphism $f : X \to \mathbb{R}$ with respect to a probability measure $[\alpha, \mu]_\sim$ on X by

$$\int f \, \mathrm{d}[\alpha, \mu]_\sim \overset{\text{def}}{=} \int f \, \mathrm{d}(\alpha_*\mu). \tag{4}$$

The notion of integrability is also defined similarly: a morphism $f : X \to \mathbb{R}$ is integrable with respect to $[\alpha, \mu]_\sim$ if f is integrable with respect to $\alpha_*\mu$.

We have defined the type of probability measure `'a qbs_prob_space` with the **quotient_type** command [19] in Isabelle/HOL. The **quotient_type** command enables users to define a quotient type when a equivalence relation over a raw type is given.

Next, we construct the probability monad $(P, \eta, \ggg\!=)$ on **QBS**.

Lemma 3 ([15]). *Let X be a quasi-Borel space and*

$$P(X) \overset{\text{def}}{=} \{\text{Probability measures on } X\}$$
$$M_{P(X)} \overset{\text{def}}{=} \{\beta \mid \exists \alpha \in M_X.\exists g \in \mathbf{Meas}(\mathbb{R}, G(\mathbb{R})).\forall r \in \mathbb{R}.\beta(r) = [\alpha, g(r)]_\sim\}.$$

Then $(P(X), M_{P(X)})$ is a quasi-Borel space.

We reconstruct the proof since the original paper have not suggested its hints. In the proof, we use Lemma 1 which says that $\mathbb{N} \times \mathbb{R}$ is a standard Borel space.

We define a function which converts a probability measure on a quasi-Borel space into the corresponding probability measure on a measurable space. Let l_X be a function that maps $[\alpha, \mu]_\sim \in P(X)$ to $\alpha_*\mu \in G(X)$. Then l_X is an injective measurable function from $L(P(X))$ to $G(L(X))$. Furthermore, l_X is bijective if X is a standard Borel space.

The monad operators η and $\ggg\!=$ are defined as follows. Let X be a quasi-Borel space and μ an arbitrary probability measure on $\mathbb{R}$. η_X is defined by $\eta_X(x) = [\lambda r.x, \mu]_\sim$. Let $[\alpha, \mu]_\sim \in P(X)$ and $f : X \to P(Y)$ be a morphism. Then we have $\beta \in M_Y$ and a measurable function $g : \mathbb{R} \to G(\mathbb{R})$, such that $f \circ \alpha = (\lambda r.[\beta, g(r)]_\sim)$. The bind operator is defined by $[\alpha, \mu]_\sim \ggg\!= f = [\beta, \mu \ggg\!=_G g]_\sim$.

Equations on η and $\ggg$ are inherited from ones of the Giry monad, because the injection $l_X : L(P(X)) \to G(L(X))$ satisfy the following equations:

$$l_X(\eta_X(x)) = \delta_x, \qquad l_X([\alpha, \mu]_\sim \ggg f) = l_X([\alpha, \mu]_\sim) \ggg_G l_Y \circ f.$$

Theorem 1 ([15, **Theorem 21**]). *The triple* $(P, \eta, \ggg)$ *is a commutative strong monad on* **QBS**.

For X::'a quasi_borel, we define the following functions in Isabelle/HOL.

    monadP_qbs X :: 'a qbs_prob_space quasi_borel

    qbs_return X :: 'a $\Rightarrow$ 'a qbs_prob_space

      qbs_bind :: 'a qbs_prob_space $\Rightarrow$ ('a $\Rightarrow$ 'b qbs_prob_space)

              $\Rightarrow$ 'b qbs_prob_space

In the proofs of the monad laws, strength and commutativity, we use the properties of the Giry monad and Lemma 1 indicating that $\mathbb{R} \times \mathbb{R}$ is a standard Borel space. We explicitly give the strength and reconstruct the proofs while the details are omitted in the original paper.

Translating Integrations to the Quasi-Borel Setting. As we mentioned, $l_X : L(P(X)) \to G(L(X))$ is bijective for a standard Borel space X. We can simulate integral on X with respect to a probability measure as follows. Let $f : X \to \mathbb{R}$ be a measurable function, equivalently $f : R(X) \to \mathbb{R}$ is a morphism (Lemma 2), and μ be a probability measure on X. Since X is standard Borel, we have some measurable function $\alpha : \mathbb{R} \to X$ and probability measure ν on $\mathbb{R}$ such that $\mu = \alpha_* \nu$. Then we have $\int f \, d\mu = \int f \, d(\alpha_* \nu) = \int f \, d[\alpha, \nu]_\sim$.

For instance, expectations for Gauss distribution and Bernoulli distribution is expressed as integrals on quasi-Borel spaces.

lemma qbs_normal_distribution_expectation:
  assumes "f $\in$ real_borel $\to_M$ real_borel" and "σ > 0"
  shows "($\int_Q$ x. f x ∂(qbs_normal_distribution μ σ))
        = ($\int$ x. normal_density μ σ x * f x ∂ lborel)"

The left hand side of the equation is the integral of the function f with respect to the probability measure on the quasi-Borel space $\mathbb{R}$ and the right hand side is the integral with respect to the probability measure on the measurable space $\mathbb{R}$. In the right hand side of the equation, respect to the probability measure normal_density μ σ x denotes the density function of Gauss distribution with mean μ and standard deviation σ, and lborel denotes the Lebesgue measure[7] on $\mathbb{R}$.

The expectation for Bernoulli distribution is described as integral on the quasi-Borel space of boolean in the similar way.

---

[7] Strictly speaking, completion lborel is the Lebesgue measure.

```
lemma qbs_bernoulli_expectation:
  assumes "0 ≤ p" "p ≤ 1"
  shows "(∫Q x. f x ∂qbs_bernoulli p) = f True * p + f False * (1 - p)"
```

5   Verification Framework PPV in Isabelle/HOL

PPV consists of the language HPProg, logic PL, and program logic UPL. In this section, we shallowly embed them on Isabelle/HOL.

5.1   Probabilistic Programming Language HPProg

HPProg is a functional probabilistic programming language used in PPV. The types and expressions of HPProg are defined as follows.

$$T ::= \text{unit} \mid \text{nat} \mid \text{bool} \mid \text{real} \mid \text{preal} \mid T \times T \mid T \Rightarrow T \mid P[T],$$
$$e ::= x \mid c \mid f \mid e\,e \mid \lambda x.e \mid \langle e, e \rangle \mid \pi_i(e) \mid \text{rec\_nat}\ e\ e$$
$$\mid \text{return}\ e \mid \text{bind}\ e\ e \mid \text{Bernoulli}(e) \mid \text{Gauss}(e, e).$$

The type preal denotes the type of non-negative extended real numbers $[0, \infty]$, and $P[T]$ is the type of probability measures on T.

The typing rules of expressions are standard. We show selected rules.

$$\frac{\Gamma \vdash e : T}{\Gamma \vdash \text{return}\ e : P[T]} \qquad \frac{\Gamma \vdash e : P[T] \qquad \Gamma \vdash f : T \Rightarrow P[T']}{\Gamma \vdash \text{bind}\ e\ f : P[T']}$$

$$\frac{\Gamma \vdash e : \text{real}}{\Gamma \vdash \text{Bernoulli}(e) : P[\text{bool}]} \qquad \frac{\Gamma \vdash e : \text{real} \qquad \Gamma \vdash e' : \text{real}}{\Gamma \vdash \text{Gauss}(e, e') : P[\text{real}]}$$

The semantics of HPProg is based on the Moggi's categorical denotational semantics [25]. In the semantics, a type T is interpreted as a quasi-Borel space $[\![T]\!]$ and a typed expression $\Gamma \vdash e : T$ is interpreted as a morphism $[\![\Gamma]\!] \to [\![T]\!]$ in **QBS**. In contrast to measurable spaces, we can interpret function types, lambda abstractions and function applications since **QBS** is Cartesian closed.

In Isabelle/HOL, the typing judgment is defined according to the semantics.

```
definition "hpprog_typing Γ e T ≡ e ∈ Γ →Q T"
```

Here, $\Gamma \to_Q$ T denotes the set of all morphisms from Γ to T. Each typing rule is obtained as a lemma. For instance, real constants and their typing rule are formulated as follows.

```
definition hp_const :: "'a ⇒ 'env ⇒ 'a" where
"hp_const k ≡ (λenv. k)"
lemma hpt_realc:"Γ ⊢t (hp_const (r :: real)) ;; ℝQ"
```

The programs are written with de Bruijn indices [9], thus the variables are distinguished by natural numbers. In the following examples, X,,Y denotes the binary product of quasi-Borel spaces X and Y.

```
definition var1 :: "'a × 'b ⇒ 'b" where "var1 ≡ snd"
lemma hpt_var1: "Γ,,Z ⊢ₜ var1 ;; Z"
definition var2 :: "('a × 'b) × 'c ⇒ 'b" where "var2 ≡ snd ∘ fst"
lemma hpt_var2: "Γ,,Z,,Y ⊢ₜ var2 ;; Z"
```

The lambda abstraction is currying according to the semantics.

```
definition "λₜ ≡ curry"
lemma hpt_abs:
  assumes "Γ,,X ⊢ₜ t ;; T"
  shows "Γ ⊢ₜ λₜ t ;; X ⇒_Q T"
```

For instance, the judgments $\Gamma, y \ : \ Y \vdash (\lambda x.x) \ y \ : \ Y$ and $\Gamma \vdash (\lambda\mu\sigma.\mathrm{Gauss}(\mu,\sigma)) : \mathrm{real} \Rightarrow \mathrm{real} \Rightarrow P[\mathrm{real}]$ are written in our formalization as follows.

```
lemma "Γ,, Y ⊢ₜ λₜ var1 $ₜ var1 ;; Y"
lemma "Γ ⊢ₜ λₜ (λₜ (hp_normal var2 var1)) ;; ℝ_Q ⇒_Q ℝ_Q ⇒_Q P_t ℝ_Q"
```

In the first lemma, the var1 in λ_t var1 is bound and the other var1 is free.

5.2   Assertion Logic PL

The logic PL is a higher-order logic for quasi-Borel spaces. The syntax of formulas in PL is defined by

$$\phi ::= (t = t) \mid (t < t) \mid \top \mid \bot \mid \phi \wedge \phi \mid \phi \rightarrow \phi \mid \forall x : T.\phi \mid integrable\ t\ t$$

where t is an expression of HPProg or an expectation $\mathbb{E}_{x\sim t}[t\ x]$. We abbreviate $\mathbb{E}_{x\sim t}[(t'\ x - \mathbb{E}_{x\sim t}[t'\ x])^2]$ to $\mathbb{V}_{x\sim t}[t'\ x]$ which denotes the variance. A PL judgment has the form $\Gamma \mid \Psi \vdash_{\mathrm{PL}} \phi$, where Γ is a context, Ψ is a set of assumptions, and ϕ is a conclusion. We show selected inference rules of PL.

$$\frac{\phi \in \Psi}{\Gamma \mid \Psi \vdash_{\mathrm{PL}} \phi}\ \mathrm{AX} \qquad \frac{\Gamma \mid \Psi \vdash_{\mathrm{PL}} \psi \rightarrow \phi \qquad \Gamma \mid \Psi \vdash_{\mathrm{PL}} \psi}{\Gamma \mid \Psi \vdash_{\mathrm{PL}} \phi}\ {\rightarrow}_E$$

$$\frac{\Gamma \mid \Psi \vdash_{\mathrm{PL}} \phi[t/x] \qquad \Gamma \mid \Psi \vdash_{\mathrm{PL}} t = u}{\Gamma \mid \Psi \vdash_{\mathrm{PL}} \phi[u/x]}\ \mathrm{SUBST}$$

We extend the logic with the integrability in our formalization. Another difference is the treatment of an expectation $\mathbb{E}_{x\sim t}[t\ x]$. In the original PL, it is defined through the σ-finite measure monad M on **QBS**. On the other hand, in our version of PL, it is formulated directly by the integral on a quasi-Borel space. The following are some of the inference rules related to integrability and expectations.

$$\frac{\Gamma \mid \Psi \vdash_{\mathrm{PL}} integrable\ \mu\ f \qquad \Gamma \mid \Psi \vdash_{\mathrm{PL}} integrable\ \mu\ g}{\Gamma \mid \Psi \vdash_{\mathrm{PL}} \mathbb{E}_{x\sim\mu}[f\ x] + \mathbb{E}_{x\sim\mu}[g\ x] = \mathbb{E}_{x\sim\mu}[f\ x + g\ x]}$$

$$\frac{\Gamma \vdash e : P[Y] \quad \Gamma, y : Y \vdash e' : Z \quad \Gamma \vdash e'' : Z \Rightarrow \mathbf{real}}{\Gamma \mid \varPsi \vdash_{\mathrm{PL}} \mathbb{E}_{x \sim \mathrm{bind}\ e\ (\lambda y.\mathrm{return}(e'))}[e''] = \mathbb{E}_{y \sim e}[e''[e'/x]]}$$

In the original PPV, PL/UPL judgments are interpreted with the category **Pred(QBS)** of predicates over quasi-Borel spaces. However, we interpret PL/UPL judgments as Isabelle/HOL's predicates, because it is easier to formalize and has the same mathematical meanings. The meaning of a PL judgment $\Gamma \mid \varPsi \vdash_{\mathrm{PL}} \phi$ is that for any $x \in [\![\Gamma]\!]$ if $\varPsi\ x$ holds then $\psi\ x$ holds. We formalize PL judgments according to its semantics.

definition "hp_conjall $\varPsi \equiv (\lambda \mathrm{env}.\ \forall \varphi \in \varPsi.\ \varphi\ \mathrm{env})$"
definition "pl_der $\Gamma\ \varPsi\ \varphi \equiv (\forall x \in$ qbs_space Γ. hp_conjall $\varPsi\ x \longrightarrow \varphi\ x)$"

Inference rules in PL are formalized as lemmas.

lemma pl_ax: **lemma** pl_impE:
  assumes "$\varphi \in \varPsi$"   **assumes** "$\Gamma \mid \varPsi \vdash_{PL} \psi \longrightarrow_{PL} \varphi$"
  shows "$\Gamma \mid \varPsi \vdash_{PL} \varphi$"   **and** "$\Gamma \mid \varPsi \vdash_{PL} \psi$"
                             shows "$\Gamma \mid \varPsi \vdash_{PL} \varphi$"

lemma pl_expect_add:
  assumes "$\Gamma \mid \varPsi \vdash_{PL}$ hp_integrable t e1"
    and "$\Gamma \mid \varPsi \vdash_{PL}$ hp_integrable t e2"
  shows "$\Gamma \mid \varPsi \vdash_{PL}$ hp_expect t (e1 $+_t$ e2) $=_{PL}$
                        hp_expect t e1 $+_t$ hp_expect t e2"

As other formalization of higher-order logics, the axiom SUBST is formalized by considering the predicate ϕ as a function.

lemma pl_subst:
  assumes "$\varphi = (\lambda t.\ \lambda k.\ \varphi'\ k\ (t\ k))$"
        "$\Gamma \mid \varPsi \vdash_{PL} t =_{PL} u$" **and** "$\Gamma \mid \varPsi \vdash_{PL} \varphi\ t$"
  shows "$\Gamma \mid \varPsi \vdash_{PL} \varphi\ u$"

We need to restrict the way the substitution applied with the first assumption.

5.3 Program Logic UPL

The PPV framework equips with the program logic UPL in the style of [1]. A UPL judgment has the form $\Gamma \mid \varPsi \vdash_{\mathrm{UPL}} e : T \mid \phi$, where e is an HPProg expression e and T is its type. The conclusion ϕ may refer to the special variable $\mathbf{r}$ of type T that is used to refer to the value of e. The following rules are some of the UPL inference rules.

$$\frac{\Gamma \mid \varPsi \vdash_{\mathrm{UPL}} e : T \mid \varphi_1 \quad \Gamma \mid \varPsi \vdash_{\mathrm{PL}} \varphi_1[e/\mathbf{r}] \to \varphi_2[e/\mathbf{r}]}{\Gamma \mid \varPsi \vdash_{\mathrm{UPL}} e : T \mid \varphi_2}$$

$$\frac{\Gamma \mid \varPsi \vdash_{\mathrm{UPL}} f : \tau \Rightarrow \sigma \mid \forall x.\phi'[x/\mathbf{r}] \to \phi[\mathbf{r}\ x/\mathbf{r}] \quad \Gamma \mid \varPsi \vdash_{\mathrm{UPL}} e : \tau \mid \phi'}{\Gamma \mid \varPsi \vdash_{\mathrm{UPL}} f\ e : \sigma \mid \phi[e/x]}$$

The meaning of a UPL judgment $\Gamma \mid \varPsi \vdash_{\mathrm{UPL}} e : T \mid \phi$ is that $\Gamma \vdash e : T$ and for any $x \in [\![\Gamma]\!]$ if $\varPsi\ x$ holds then $\psi[e/\mathbf{r}]\ x$ holds. UPL judgments are defined according to its semantics.

definition hp_montecarlo :: "('b × 'a qbs_prob_space) × ('a ⇒ real) ⇒
nat ⇒ real qbs_prob_space" **where** "hp_montecarlo ≡
hp_rec_nat (hp_return $\mathbb{R}_Q$ (hp_const 0))
　　　(λ_t (λ_t (var1 $\ggeq_t$
　　　　　　λ_t (var5 $\ggeq_t$
　　　　　　　　λ_t (hp_return $\mathbb{R}_Q$
　　　　　　　　　　(((var5 $\$_t$ var1) $+_t$ var2 $*_t$ hp_real var4) $/_t$
hp_real (hp_suc var4)))))))"

Fig. 3. Monte Carlo Approximation program, written in our formalization.

definition "$\varPhi$mon ≡
{hp_const 0 $<_{PL}$ var5, var4 $=_{PL}$ hp_expect var2 var1, var3^{-t}2 $=_{PL}$ hp_var
var2 var1, hp_integrable var2 var1, hp_integrable var2 (var1 $*_t$ var1)}"
lemma montecarlo_judgement:
"$,\mathbb{R}_Q,,\mathbb{R}_Q,,\mathbb{R}_Q,,P_t$ X,,(X $\Rightarrow_Q \mathbb{R}_Q$) | $\varPhi$mon
$\vdash_{UPL}$ hp_montecarlo ;; $\mathbb{N}_Q \Rightarrow_Q P_t \mathbb{R}_Q$
　| λr. $\forall_{PL}$ n $\in_{PL}\mathbb{N}_Q$. hp_const 0 $<_{PL}$ hp_const n
　　$\longrightarrow_{PL}$ hp_prob (r $\$_t$ hp_const n) {y. var5 $\leq_{PL}$ |hp_const y $-_t$ var4$|_t$}$_t$
　　　$\leq_{PL}$ (var3^{-t}2 $/_t$ hp_real (hp_const n)) $*_t$ (hp_const 1 $/_t$var5^{-t}2)"
lemma montecalro_integrable:
"$,\mathbb{R}_Q,,\mathbb{R}_Q,,\mathbb{R}_Q,,P_t$ X,,(X $\Rightarrow_Q \mathbb{R}_Q$) | $\varPhi$mon $\vdash_{PL} \forall_{PL}$ n $\in_{PL}\mathbb{N}_Q$.
　hp_integrable (hp_montecarlo $\$_t$ hp_const n) hp_id $\wedge_{PL}$
　hp_integrable (hp_montecarlo $\$_t$ hp_const n) (hp_id $*_t$ hp_id)"

Fig. 4. Weak law of large numbers and integrability, written in our formalization.

definition "upl_der Γ Ψ e T φ ≡
(($\Gamma \vdash_t$ e ;; T) $\wedge$ ($\exists\varphi$'. φ = (λt k. φ' k (t k)))
　$\wedge$ ($\forall$k∈qbs_space Γ. hp_conjall Ψ k $\longrightarrow \varphi$ e k))"

As the axiom SUBST, we need the formula $\exists\varphi$'. φ = (λt k. φ' k (t k)) to
restrict the way the substitution is applied. The special variable **r** in a conclusion
is represented as the bound variable of Isabelle/HOL's lambda expression. The
following is an example of UPL judgments, which is proved easily because $1 \leq$
$(\mathbf{r} + \mathbf{r})[1/\mathbf{r}]$.

lemma "Γ | $\Psi \vdash_{UPL}$ hp_const 1 ;; $\mathbb{N}_Q$ | λr. hp_const 1 $\leq_{PL}$ r $+_t$ r"

Each UPL rule is provided as lemma. The logic UPL is sound and complete with
respect to the logic PL.

Theorem 2 (Equi-derivability, [28, Theorem 6.1]). *A judgment* Γ | $\Psi \vdash_{\mathrm{PL}}$
$\phi[e/\mathbf{r}]$ *is derivable in PL iff* Γ | $\Psi \vdash_{\mathrm{UPL}}$ e : T | ϕ *is derivable in UPL.*

In Isabelle/HOL, the above completeness theorem is proved directly from the
definitions since we define the judgments semantically.

5.4   Verification of Monte Carlo Approximation

We have described the program of the Monte Carlo approximation in pseudocode and explained what we have proved in Sect. 2. In this section, we explain how we actually write the program and prove the PL and UPL judgments on it in our formalization.

The program of the Monte Carlo approximation is defined in our formalization as in Fig. 3. The program hp_montecarlo is a function from ('b × 'a qbs_prob_space) × ('a ⇒ real), where the second and third components correspond to the variables d and h in Fig. 1, respectively. Although they are obtained by var2 and var1 in the global context, both appear as var5 in the program because the indices are shifted by lambda abstractions. The extra context of type 'b is used to accommodate ε, μ, and σ in the PL and UPL judgments of Fig. 2. In those judgments, the program is a function from the following type:

((((unit × real) × real) × real) × 'a qbs_prob_space) × ('a ⇒ real)

where var3, var4, and var5 correspond to σ, μ, and ε, respectively.

We have first proved the PL judgment about integrability. This judgment is required for applying linearity of expectation used in the proof of the main UPL judgment. Then we have proved the main UPL judgment following the proof outline shown in [28]. Both of judgments in Fig. 4 require similar equational reasoning. There are no major difficulties in formalizing the proof. However, it requires a large number of steps of equational reasoning. For instance, let us consider the following equation appearing in the proof where $i > 1$.

$$\mathbb{V}_{y \sim montecarlo(i-1) \gg= (\lambda m.d \gg= (\lambda x.\text{return } (\frac{1}{i}(h(x)+m(i-1)))))}[y] = \sigma^2/i$$

Although the pen and paper proof spends only 7 lines[8], our formalization consists of more than 100 steps. A proper support of simplification may greatly reduces the number of steps which are manually conducted.

6   Conclusion

We have formalized quasi-Borel spaces and shallowly embedded a core part of the framework PPV. Fundamental properties of the Monte Carlo approximation are verified according to the proof outline shown in [28], although the proof in our formalization is rather lengthy and it is cumbersome to reason about programs written with de Bruijn indices. Our formalization contains around 13450 lines (9600 lines for quasi-Borel spaces and 3850 lines for PPV) including blank lines and comments.

There are two major future extensions of our formalized PPV. The first one is the query command for conditional inference. To support the query command, we need to implement the σ-finite measure M on **QBS**. We are planning

---

[8] It should be noted that the original proof does not include the discussion on integrability.

to formalize it. We expect more efforts to formalize the σ-finite measure monad M since there is no σ-finite measure monad on **Meas** while we have formalized the probability monad P on **QBS** using the Giry monad on **Meas** in the Isabelle/HOL library.

The second extension is the relational program logic. The original PPV contains a relational program logic RPL. It allows us to reason about relational properties of programs. For instance, we can prove a property of importance sampling algorithm and a property of Gaussian mean learning using RPL. We expect no essential difficulty to extend our formalization for RPL.

Acknowledgments. Minamide was supported by JSPS KAKENHI Grant Number 19K11899, and Sato was supported by JSPS KAKENHI Grant Number 20K19775.

References

1. Aguirre, A., Barthe, G., Gaboardi, M., Garg, D., Strub, P.Y.: A relational logic for higher-order programs. Proc. ACM Program. Lang. **1**(ICFP) (2017). https://doi.org/10.1145/3110265
2. Audebaud, P., Paulin-Mohring, C.: Proofs of randomized algorithms in CoQ. In: Uustalu, T. (ed.) MPC 2006. LNCS, vol. 4014, pp. 49–68. Springer, Heidelberg (2006). https://doi.org/10.1007/11783596_6
3. Aumann, R.J.: Borel structures for function spaces. Ill. J. Math. **5**(4), 614–630 (1961). https://doi.org/10.1215/ijm/1255631584
4. Avigad, J., Hölzl, J., Serafin, L.: A formally verified proof of the central limit theorem. J. Autom. Reason. **59**(4), 389–423 (2017). https://doi.org/10.1007/s10817-017-9404-x
5. Bagnall, A., Stewart, G.: Certifying the true error: machine learning in Coq with verified generalization guarantees. In: Proceedings of the AAAI Conference on Artificial Intelligence, vol. 33, pp. 2662–2669 (2019). https://doi.org/10.1609/aaai.v33i01.33012662
6. Bertot, Y., Castéran, P.: Interactive Theorem Proving and Program Development: Coq'Art: The Calculus of Inductive Constructions. Springer, Heidelberg (2013)
7. Boldo, S., Clément, F., Faissole, F., Martin, V., Mayero, M.: A Coq formalization of Lebesgue integration of nonnegative functions. Research Report RR-9401, Inria, France (2021). https://hal.inria.fr/hal-03194113
8. Cock, D.: Verifying probabilistic correctness in Isabelle with pGCL. Electron. Proc. Theor. Comput. Sci. **102**, 167–178 (2012). https://doi.org/10.4204/eptcs.102.15
9. de Bruijn, N.: Lambda calculus notation with nameless dummies, a tool for automatic formula manipulation, with application to the church-rosser theorem. Indagationes Mathematicae (Proceedings) **75**(5), 381–392 (1972). https://doi.org/10.1016/1385-7258(72)90034-0
10. Eberl, M., Hölzl, J., Nipkow, T.: A verified compiler for probability density functions. In: Vitek, J. (ed.) ESOP 2015. LNCS, vol. 9032, pp. 80–104. Springer, Heidelberg (2015). https://doi.org/10.1007/978-3-662-46669-8_4
11. Giry, M.: A categorical approach to probability theory. In: Banaschewski, B. (ed.) Categorical Aspects of Topology and Analysis. LNM, vol. 915, pp. 68–85. Springer, Heidelberg (1982). https://doi.org/10.1007/BFb0092872

12. Goodman, N.D., et al.: Church: a language for generative models. In: Proceedings of the 24th Conference in Uncertainty in Artificial Intelligence, UAI 2008, pp. 220–229. AUAI Press (2008)
13. Gordon, M.J.C., Melham, T.F.: Introduction to HOL (A Theorem Proving Environment for Higher Order Logic). Cambridge University Press (1993)
14. Harrison, J.: The HOL Light theory of Euclidean space. J. Autom. Reason. **50**, 173–190 (2013). https://doi.org/10.1007/s10817-012-9250-9
15. Heunen, C., Kammar, O., Staton, S., Yang, H.: A convenient category for higher-order probability theory. In: Proceedings of the 32nd Annual ACM/IEEE Symposium on Logic in Computer Science, LICS 2017. IEEE Press (2017). https://doi.org/10.1109/lics.2017.8005137
16. Hirata, M., Minamide, Y., Sato, T.: Quasi-Borel spaces. Archive of Formal Proofs (2022). https://isa-afp.org/entries/Quasi_Borel_Spaces.html. Formal proof development
17. Hölzl, J.: Markov processes in Isabelle/HOL. In: Proceedings of the 6th ACM SIGPLAN Conference on Certified Programs and Proofs, CPP 2017, pp. 100–111. Association for Computing Machinery (2017). https://doi.org/10.1145/3018610.3018628
18. Hölzl, J., Heller, A.: Three chapters of measure theory in Isabelle/HOL. In: van Eekelen, M., Geuvers, H., Schmaltz, J., Wiedijk, F. (eds.) ITP 2011. LNCS, vol. 6898, pp. 135–151. Springer, Heidelberg (2011). https://doi.org/10.1007/978-3-642-22863-6_12
19. Huffman, B., Kunčar, O.: Lifting and transfer: a modular design for quotients in Isabelle/HOL. In: Gonthier, G., Norrish, M. (eds.) CPP 2013. LNCS, vol. 8307, pp. 131–146. Springer, Cham (2013). https://doi.org/10.1007/978-3-319-03545-1_9
20. Hurd, J., McIver, A., Morgan, C.: Probabilistic guarded commands mechanized in HOL. Theor. Comput. Sci. **346**(1), 96–112 (2005). https://doi.org/10.1016/j.tcs.2005.08.005. Quantitative Aspects of Programming Languages (QAPL 2004)
21. Lester, D.R.: Topology in PVS: continuous mathematics with applications. In: Proceedings of the Second Workshop on Automated Formal Methods, pp. 11–20. AFM, Association for Computing Machinery (2007). https://doi.org/10.1145/1345169.1345171
22. Lochbihler, A.: Probabilistic functions and cryptographic oracles in higher order logic. In: Thiemann, P. (ed.) ESOP 2016. LNCS, vol. 9632, pp. 503–531. Springer, Heidelberg (2016). https://doi.org/10.1007/978-3-662-49498-1_20
23. Mathematical Components. https://math-comp.github.io. Accessed 12 Dec 2021
24. Mhamdi, T., Hasan, O., Tahar, S.: Formalization of measure theory and Lebesgue integration for probabilistic analysis in HOL. ACM Trans. Embed. Comput. Syst. **12**(1) (2013). https://doi.org/10.1145/2406336.2406349
25. Moggi, E.: Notions of computation and monads. Inf. Comput. **93**(1), 55–92 (1991). https://doi.org/10.1016/0890-5401(91)90052-4. Selections from 1989 IEEE Symposium on Logic in Computer Science
26. de Moura, L., Kong, S., Avigad, J., van Doorn, F., von Raumer, J.: The lean theorem prover (system description). In: Felty, A.P., Middeldorp, A. (eds.) CADE 2015. LNCS (LNAI), vol. 9195, pp. 378–388. Springer, Cham (2015). https://doi.org/10.1007/978-3-319-21401-6_26
27. Nipkow, T., Wenzel, M., Paulson, L.C.: Isabelle/HOL: A Proof Assistant for Higher-Order Logic. Springer, Heidelberg (2002)

28. Sato, T., Aguirre, A., Barthe, G., Gaboardi, M., Garg, D., Hsu, J.: Formal verification of higher-order probabilistic programs: reasoning about approximation, convergence, Bayesian inference, and optimization. Proc. ACM Program. Lang. **3**(POPL), 1–30 (2019). https://doi.org/10.1145/3290351

29. Ścibior, A., et al.: Denotational validation of higher-order Bayesian inference. Proc. ACM Program. Lang. **2**(POPL) (2017). https://doi.org/10.1145/3158148

30. The mathlib community: the lean mathematical library. In: Proceedings of the 9th ACM SIGPLAN International Conference on Certified Programs and Proofs, CPP 2020, pp. 367–381. Association for Computing Machinery (2020). https://doi.org/10.1145/3372885.3373824

31. Tristan, J.B., Tassarotti, J., Vajjha, K., Wick, M.L., Banerjee, A.: Verification of ML systems via reparameterization (2020). https://arxiv.org/abs/2007.06776

32. Wood, F., van de Meent, J.W., Mansinghka, V.: A new approach to probabilistic programming inference. In: Proceedings of the 17th International Conference on Artificial Intelligence and Statistics, pp. 1024–1032 (2014)

Generating C
System Description

Oleg Kiselyov[(✉)] [iD]

Tohoku University, Sendai, Japan
oleg@okmij.org

Abstract. Heterogeneous metaprogramming is using a generally higher-level host language to generate code in a lower-lever object language. Its appeal is taking advantage of the module system, higher-order functions, data types, type system and verification tools of the host language to quicker produce high-performant lower-level code with some correctness guarantees.

We present two heterogeneous metaprogramming systems whose host language is OCaml and object language is C. The first relies on *off-shoring*: treating a subset of (MetaOCaml-generated) OCaml as a different notation for (a subset of) C. The second embeds C in OCaml in tagless-final style. The systems have been used in several projects, including the generation of C supersets OpenCL and OpenMP.

Generating C with some correctness guarantees is far less trivial than it may appear, with pitfalls abound. Not coincidentally, the most subtle ones accompany the introduction of variables into the code. Maintaining the offshoring system has traps of its own. We expound the pitfalls we have came across in our experience, and describe counter-measures.

1 Introduction

Generating C is an odd problem: at first glance, it is trivial and nothing to write about. Beyond simple applications, however, complexity, traps, hazards snowball. One may as well write code directly in C to start with, or use a compiler.

Neither of these two choices may be palatable, especially in high-performance computing (HPC). For one, high-performant code is often voluminous and obscure – and hence hard to write directly by hand.[1] It also has to be re-adjusted for each new architecture and processor configuration. Hopes that an optimizing compiler save us such trouble were dashed two decades ago: see [3] for exposition and many references.[2] The alternative to writing performant low-level

---

[1] For an example, see the manually written high-performance BLAS code in https://www.openblas.net/, e.g., dot-product https://github.com/xianyi/OpenBLAS/blob/develop/kernel/x86_64/ddot.c and its kernel for a particular, already obsolete processor architecture https://github.com/xianyi/OpenBLAS/blob/develop/kernel/x86_64/ddot_microk_sandy-2.c.

[2] Furthermore, compiler-generated C code typically can only be executed within the specific run-time environment and cannot be freely linked with other C code.

© Springer Nature Switzerland AG 2022
M. Hanus and A. Igarashi (Eds.): FLOPS 2022, LNCS 13215, pp. 75–93, 2022.
https://doi.org/10.1007/978-3-030-99461-7_5

code by hand or to relying on a general-purpose compiler is code generation. Being domain-specific, a generator may employ very profitable but not widely-applicable expert knowledge and optimizations. Such code generation is being increasingly used in HPC, becoming dominant in some areas: ATLAS [23] for BLAS (Basic Linear Algebra Subroutines), FFTW [6] and SPIRAL [17] for FFT and related transforms, Halide [18] for image filtering, Firedrake [19] for partial differential equations using finite element method.

The present paper describes two orthogonal approaches for generating C using OCaml, with some guarantees and convenience. We take OCaml as a representative high-level language for writing generators, and C as a representative low-level language. The approaches extend to other languages (e.g., [21] for LLVM IR).

The first (also historically, [5]) approach is offshoring: It is based on the idea of generating simple OCaml code with certain correctness guarantees, and then translating this subset of OCaml to C, preserving the guarantees. The second approach is embedding C in OCaml as typed combinators, in tagless-final style [2,8]. Both ensure the generated C code compiles without errors or warnings. Both explore the metaphor of a subset of OCaml as a notation for C.

Offshoring is a particularly attractive idea – and has been implemented twice before, see Sect. 5. There are also pitfalls and challenges, which may explain why these implementations have become unmaintainable and are no longer available. The current implementation of offshoring in BER MetaOCaml is done from scratch, in complete re-design and re-thinking of the earlier implementations to clearly expose and address the challenges and ensure maintainability. It has been publicly available since 2018 (but privately, quite earlier) and used in several Master and Bachelor projects, among others, for generating performant OpenCL (GPGPU) [7] and OpenMP [1] code and for robot control code. Alas, there is no published description.

Our Contributions. (i) Explicate the challenges in generating low-level (C) code, many of which have only become clear from our experience; (ii) Present the implementations of the two approaches, which are freely available and have been used in practice, see Sect. 6; (iii) Describe how the two systems are designed to address or mitigate the challenges.

We concentrate on offshoring, with which we have more experience. The challenges and pitfalls are common to both approaches; the lessons learned with offshoring have directly carried towards the tagless-final embedding.

There are two sorts of challenges we have encountered in designing and using assured C code generation: technical and engineering.

Technically, the metaphor 'simple OCaml as a notation for C' does not actually hold: see, for example, control operators such as break, continue and goto, as well as the general for and do-while loops, which have no analogue in OCaml (Sect. 3.3). More subtly, and hence insidiously, is the difference between variables in C and variables of reference types in OCaml – which can easily lead to the generation of type-correct but ill-behaving code (Sect. 3.4). These problems make the embedding of C difficult, and all but doom offshoring.

The key idea reverberating throughout the paper is to keep the eyes on the goal: expressing an algorithm in an efficient-to-execute way – which can be done in a *subset* of C. For an example, see the manually written high-performance C code in OpenBLAS,[3] which is syntactically spartan. After all, C, as many languages, is redundant, with many ways of expressing the same algorithm. Some expressions may be more elegant or idiomatic – but we only care about efficiency. Covering all of C and generating every its construct is hence explicitly not the goal. A subset suffices, which is easier to put in correspondence with a subset of OCaml.

Among the engineering challenges is the unexpected need for type inference (Sect. 3.1), and, mainly, extensibility, Sect. 3.2. If a system is not easy to extend, it falls into disuse. We should be able to support architecture-specific types of C and its extensions (SIMD, CUDA, OpenMP, etc.) and generate code that interacts with external libraries.

The next section reminds the straightforward C generation, and the reasons one may quickly move beyond it. Section 3 describes the offshoring and its challenges, and Sect. 4 presents the tagless-final embedding of C. Section 6 briefly evaluates the usefulness and adequacy of the approaches and compares them.

MetaOCaml (which includes offshoring) is available from Opam,[4] among other sources (the current version is N111). The complete code for all examples and the tagless-final embedding are available at http://okmij.org/ftp/meta-programming/tutorial/0README.dr.

2   Prelude: Direct C Generation

What springs to mind when talking about code generation is directly emitting the code as strings. It also quickly becomes apparent why some abstractions and guarantees are desirable – as this section illustrates.

A notable example of directly emitting C code as strings is ATLAS [23]: a generator of automatically tuned linear algebra routines, which "is often the first or even only optimized BLAS implementation available on new systems and is a large improvement over the generic BLAS".[5] Figure 1 shows a typical snippet of ATLAS code, itself written in C and using fprintf to generate C code. The variable spc is whitespace for indentation, and the variables rC, i, and j are combined to name identifiers declared elsewhere. Nothing guarantees that these identifiers are indeed all declared and the declarations are in scope – nor that the result is syntactically well-formed. Even if a fprintf output is syntactically correct, the presence of loops and branching in the generator makes it hard to see that the overall generated code will be too. (It is also not at all obvious that the generated code performs matrix multiplication.)

Syntactically incorrect generated code (as well as code with unbound variables, etc.) will certainly be discovered when trying to compile it. However,

---

[3] https://www.openblas.net/.

[4] https://opam.ocaml.org/.

[5] https://en.wikipedia.org/wiki/Automatically_Tuned_Linear_Algebra_Software.

```
for (j=0; j < nu; j++) {
  for (i=0; i < mu; i++) {
    if (Asg1stC && !k)
      fprintf(fpout, "%s_%s%d_%d_=_%s%d_*_%s%d;\n", spc, rC, i, j, rA, i, rB, j);
    else fprintf(fpout, "%s_%s%d_%d_+=_%s%d_*_%s%d;\n", spc, rC, i, j, rA, i, rB, j);
    opfetch(fpout, spc, nfetch, rA, rB, pA, pB, mu, nu, offA, offB,
                   lda, ldb, mulA, mulB, rowA, rowB, &ia, &ib);
} }
```

Fig. 1. A snippet of ATLAS: generation of the inner loop body for matrix-matrix multiplication

figuring out which part of the generator to blame and to fix is non-trivial – as, e.g., [15] confirm from their experience of debugging unbound variables in the generated code. Incidentally, the implementor of ATLAS himself is quite frustrated:

> "As you have seen, this note and the protocols it describes have plenty of room for improvement. Now, as the end-user of this function, you may have a naturally strong and negative reaction to these crude mechanisms, tempting you to send messages decrying my lack of humanity, decency, and legal parentage to the atlas or developer mailing lists. ... So, the proper bitch format involves
> - *First,* thanking me for spending time in hell getting things to their present crude state
> - *Then,* supplying your constructive ideas"
>
> (R. Clint Whaley: User contribution to ATLAS. Conclusion. 2012-07-10. math-atlas.sourceforge.net/devel/atlas_contrib/)

That is why some correctness assurances are needed.

What comes to mind next is a sort of an abstract syntax tree for C (several of which are available just in OCaml, see Sect. 5 for details). The generator then produces the tree data structure, which is pretty-printed into C code at the end. The pretty-printing ensures the result syntactically well-formed – but makes no further guarantees. One would have liked, at the very least, that the generated code compiles without errors or warnings and contains no problematic expressions, like the ones involving several increment operators. Full correctness of the generated code is hard to assure; however, at least the above problems, which often arise by misediting or typos, should be preventable.

3   Offshoring

As we have seen, emitting C code is better done not directly but through a level of abstraction that provides some guarantees. Which guarantees is an engineering decision, balancing against the ease of use and the implementation and maintenance effort.

One particularly attractive balance is offshoring [5]: treating a *subset* of OCaml as if it were a (non-canonical) notation for C. For example, consider the following OCaml code for vector addition (a typical BLAS operation):

```
let addv = fun n vout v1 v2 → for i=0 to n−1 do vout.(i) ← v1.(i) + v2.(i) done
```

It is rather easy to imagine the C code it corresponds to:

```
void addv(int n, int* vout, int* v1, int* v2) {
  int i;
  for(i=0; i≤n−1; i++)
    vout[i] = v1[i] + v2[i];
}
```

One may even argue [5] that OCaml's addv is C's addv, written in a different but easily relatable way. Offshoring is the facility that realizes such correspondence between a subset of OCaml and C (or other low-level language). With offshoring, by generating OCaml we, in effect, generate C. Offshoring hence turns homogeneous metaprogramming into heterogeneous.

The first premise of offshoring is the ability to convert well-typed OCaml code into C code that surely compiles, without errors or warnings. Paper [5] formalized the OCaml subset-to-C translation and proved it type preserving. Bussone has formally (in Coq) shown the meaning preservation of the offshoring translation, in a yet unpublished work.[6]

The second premise is the ability to produce OCaml with some correctness guarantees. It is fulfilled by MetaOCaml [9,11], which generates OCaml code that surely compiles (meaning, i.a., it is well-typed and has no unbound variables). We now illustrate how it is all put together, continuing the vector addition example.[7]

Definition 1 (Generating C via offshoring).

1. *implement the algorithm in OCaml*
2. *stage it (add staging annotations) and generate possibly specialized code*
   (a) *test the generated OCaml code*
3. *convert the generated OCaml code to C, saving into a file*
4. (a) *compile and link the generated C code as ordinary C library code*
   (b) *compile the generated C code and (dynamically) link into an OCaml program, via an FFI such as [24].*

Definition 1 presents the overall flow of offshoring. In our example, the first step has already been accomplished, by addv above. The next step is to turn it into a generator of OCaml vector addition, with the help of MetaOCaml's *staging annotations* – specifically, so-called brackets .< and >., which enclose the code to generate, the code template:

---

[6] Grègoire Bussone, private communication.
[7] The complete code with tests and further examples is in **offshore_simple.ml** of the accompanying code.

```
let addv_staged =
  .<fun n vout v1 v2 → for i=0 to n−1 do vout.(i) ← v1.(i) + v2.(i) done>.
```

The result of evaluating addv_staged is

```
val addv_staged : (int → int array → int array → int array → unit) code =
  .<fun n_1 vout_2 v1_3 v2_4 →
    for i_5 = 0 to n_1 − 1 do
      Array.set vout_2 i_5 (Array.get v1_3 i_5 + Array.get v2_4 i_5)
    done>.
```

It is a so-called code value: a value of the type t code that represents the generated OCaml expression, where t is its type. Code values can be printed. In our case, the printout shows the original addv after desugaring and renaming of all identifiers. Such code value is the outcome of Step 2 of offshoring. Passing addv_staged to the function offshore_to_c, to be explained in detail later, accomplishes Step 3 and produces a .c file with exactly the addv C code shown earlier. It is an ordinary C code and can be linked with any C or other program that needs vector addition. It can also be called from OCaml, via an FFI such as [24].

Real-life use of offshoring is more interesting. For example, suppose that the size of vectors to add is known in advance, and is small enough to want to unroll the loop in addv. The generator of unrolled code cannot be obtained from addv merely by placing brackets; quite a few other modifications are required. It helps to generalize addv first:

```
let addvg n vout v1 v2 = iota n |> List.iter (fun i → vout.(i) ← v1.(i) + v2.(i))
```

where iota n generates a list of integers 0 through n−1 and List.iter performs a given action on each element of the list. We may stage it similarly to addv_staged, by enclosing everything in brackets:

```
let addvg_staged_full =
  .<fun n vout v1 v2 → iota n |> List.iter (fun i → vout.(i) ← v1.(i) + v2.(i))>.
```

Passing this code value to offshore_to_c, however, results in an exception: this code outside of domain of offshoring. It is not hard to see why: the argument of List.iter is a first-class function, which cannot be simply represented in C. If the array size n is known at the generation time, a different placement of brackets becomes possible:

```
let addvg_staged n =
  .<fun vout v1 v2 → .~(iota n |> iter_seq (fun i → .<vout.(i) ← v1.(i) + v2.(i)>.))>.
```

where

```
let iter_seq f = List.map f |> seq
let seq : unit code list → unit code = fun l → reduce (fun x y → .<.~x; .~y>.) l
```

Here, besides brackets we used the other staging annotation, .~ (pronounced 'escape') that denotes a hole in the code template (bracketed expression), to be filled by the code produced by the escaped expression. The function seq builds a sequence of code values. Evaluating addvg_staged 4 gives the fully unrolled code:

```
val addvg_staged4 : (int array → int array → int array → unit) code =
.<fun vout_16 v1_17 v2_18 →
    Array.set vout_16 0 ((Array.get v1_17 0) + (Array.get v2_18 0));
    Array.set vout_16 1 ((Array.get v1_17 1) + (Array.get v2_18 1));
    Array.set vout_16 2 ((Array.get v1_17 2) + (Array.get v2_18 2));
    Array.set vout_16 3 ((Array.get v1_17 3) + (Array.get v2_18 3))>.
```

MetaOCaml offers the facility to compile and run this code, so we can test it on sample 4-element arrays and compare the result with addv or addvg. It is easier to test OCaml code, if not for other reason that the out-of-bound indexing into an array results in an exception rather than undefined behavior.

Once we are satisfied that the generated OCaml code works, we pass it to offshore_to_c obtaining:

```
void addv4(int * vout_16,int * v1_17,int * v2_18)
{  (vout_16[0]) = (v1_17[0]) + (v2_18[0]);
   (vout_16[1]) = (v1_17[1]) + (v2_18[1]);
   (vout_16[2]) = (v1_17[2]) + (v2_18[2]);
   (vout_16[3]) = (v1_17[3]) + (v2_18[3]);}
```

It is unsettling that addv can be easily staged and offshored to produce a for loop but not an unrolled loop; addvg is the other way around. By generalizing addvg a bit more:[8]

```
let addv_abs vout v1 v2 = iter_assign vout (zip_with add v1 v2)
```

we not only express vector addition clearly but also, by appropriately instantiating iter_assign, zip_with and add combinators, may generate from the same expression a variety of programs (unrolled, not unrolled or partially unrolled for-loop) and apply strip mining and scalar promotion optimizations. App. A of the extended version of the paper, and addv.ml in the accompanying code show the details. We indeed produce the code with the look and feel of the HPC BLAS.[9]

As we have seen for addvg_staged_full, offshoring applies only to a small imperative subset of OCaml. Therefore, offshoring is much simpler than an OCaml-to-C compiler, which must deal with the full language and support closures, tail recursion, GC, etc. None of this matters in offshoring, which hence produces C code that does not need any special run-time. Albeit simple, the offshorable subset of OCaml is adequate for numeric and embedded programming.

Although the offshorable subset is easy to define in theory (see [5]) it is hard to express in types, especially in the extant OCaml type system. Therefore, nothing actually prevents offshore_to_c from being applied to the code outside

---

[8] see Sects. 4 and 5 of [10] for detailed explanation.

[9] https://raw.githubusercontent.com/xianyi/OpenBLAS/develop/kernel/x86_64/daxpy.c.

the supported subset – in which case it throws an exception. It is not a sound-ness problem: soundness is about C code, *if* successfully produced, being well-formed and well-typed. The problem is that this exception is raised late, after the code to offshore has all been generated. MetaOCaml (OCaml, actually) supports location information, which could be used to emit detailed error messages (not implemented in the current version however). The best mitigation is to generate OCaml code not via brackets and escapes but via further abstraction layers (combinators), with OCaml type system enforcing abstraction – as shown App. A.

As attractive the metaphor of OCaml as C is, upon close inspection it breaks down, as the rest of Sect. 3 describes. Fortunately, it can eventually be held together, by workarounds and the design of the library that implements, enforces and steers towards the workarounds, and away from the problematic cases. As our refrain goes, the goal is to express an algorithm in C efficiently, not to generate idiomatic code and every C construct.

3.1   Type Inference

Looking closer at the earlier addv OCaml and the corresponding C code one notices that the correspondence is not as straightforward as one may have initially thought: the OCaml code mentions no types, whereas in C any declaration, of arguments and local variables, must be accompanied by their type. The need for type inference is an unpleasant surprise.

Fortunately, a MetaOCaml compiler is an extension of an OCaml and hence may use the OCaml type checker to infer types in the code to offshore. The result is an OCaml compiler internal data structure typedtree: type-annotated abstract syntax tree. Unfortunately, this data structure, and especially the type representation, is rather difficult to deal with: for example, checking if a type is int is not a simple pattern-match but requires a sequence of obscure and undocumented internal compiler function calls.

For these reasons, the original implementation of offshoring [5] was tightly integrated with the OCaml type checker. Since the type checker (including the typedtree structure and often the type representation) notably change in every release of OCaml, the original offshoring almost immediately became unmaintainable and was removed when porting MetaOCaml to OCaml 3.12, which introduced especially many changes to the type checker.

The lesson was learned when resurrecting offshoring in BER MetaOCaml. The new offshoring is disentangled as much as possible from the OCaml type checker. The key idea is an intermediary language, Offshoring IR (Fig. 2), an abstraction barrier between typedtree and the rest of offshoring. In terms of Definition 1, Step 3 is hence split into two: converting the generated OCaml code to the Offshoring IR, and pretty-printing this IR as C code. The function offshore implements the first substep: takes the closed code value produced by MetaOCaml, invokes the OCaml type checker to infer types, and converts the resulting typedtree to the Offshoring IR. (The function's first argument, converters, is explained in Sect. 3.2). It raises an exception if the input is outside the supported subset of OCaml. The function encapsulates all peculiarities of the OCaml type checker. When OCaml internal data structures change, only that function needs to be adjusted. It is engineered to be an ordinary library function, outside the OCaml compiler and using only what is exposed in compiler-libs library. The offshoring function also enforces soundness side conditions, described in Sect. 3.4.

Offshoring IR, Fig. 2, is a simple, typed, imperative language, with expressions exp and statements cmd. The data structure proc_t represents the complete program, which is either a function returning a result or a procedure.

Continuing the example of vector addition from Sect. 3, the invocation offshore (**module** DefaultConv) addv_staged produces the following IR code:

```
Proc
  ([("n_1", TInt); ("vout_2", TArray1 TInt); ("v1_3", TArray1 TInt); ("v2_4", TArray1 TInt)],
  For {id = "i_5"; ty = TInt;
    lwb = Const (Const_int 0); upb = LocalVar ("n_1", TInt); step = Const (Const_int 1);
    body =
    FunCallC ("array1_set",
      [LocalVar ("vout_2", TArray1 TInt); LocalVar ("i_5", TInt);
      FunCall ("+",
        [FunCall ("array1_get",
          [LocalVar ("v1_3", TArray1 TInt); LocalVar ("i_5", TInt)]);
        FunCall ("array1_get",
          [LocalVar ("v2_4", TArray1 TInt); LocalVar ("i_5", TInt)])])])})
```

The translation from OCaml to OffshoringIR is really as straightforward as it looks from the example.[10] We see that in the IR, all identifier references and declarations are type-annotated, which makes it easy to produce C declarations later on. The local identifier names are all unique: courtesy of MetaOCaml. Therefore, no shadowing may occur – and identifier declarations may safely be lifted to a wider scope, which is sometimes necessary when emitting C, where all declarations must occur at the beginning of a block.

Pretty-printing this Offshoring IR expression to C gives the code we have seen in Sect. 3. The pretty-printing is straightforward, in this case (we describe the complications later on). One may just as easily pretty-print the IR to other low-level imperative language, such as Fortran or LLVM IR. Extensibility was another design decision behind the IR.

3.2 Extensibility

The original offshoring [5] was not extensible at all: any change required recompiling of the entire MetaOCaml system. Extensibility is the must however. We should be able to accommodate the ever increasing assortment of integer and floating-point types of C as well as the short-vector types of various SIMD extensions. The generated C code often needs to interact with external libraries:

---

[10] That said, offshore does need to do some work: e.g., function application is represented in typedtree in a rather complex way, due to OCaml's optional and named arguments. The type representation is far more involved than mere TInt.

```
type typ = ..                    (* Extensible type *)
type typ += | TUnit | TInt | TBool
   | TFloat                      (* 32—bit *)
   | TDouble                     (* 64—bit *)
   | TArray1 of typ              (* Usual array or Bigarray.Array1 *)
   | TArray2 of typ              (* Bigarray.Array2 *)
   | TRef of typ
   | TVariable        (* sometimes inevitably occurs. Transient *)

type varname = private string
type attribute = ..
type constant_t = | Const_unit | Const_int of int | Const_float of float
   | Const_bool of bool | Const_char of char | Const_string of string

type exp =
   | Const of constant_t         (* Constant/literal: int, bool,... *)
   | LocalVar of varname * typ   (* Locally—bound variable *)
   | KnownVar of varname         (* Global/library function,... *)
   | FunCall of varname * exp list (* Calls only to known identifiers *)
   | Let of {id: varname; ty: typ; bind: exp; body: exp; attrs: attribute list}
   | IfE  of exp * exp * exp
   | SeqE of cmd * exp
   | ArrayE of exp list          (* immediate array *)
 and cmd =
   | FunCallC of varname * exp list    (* Calls only to known identifiers *)
   | LetC of {id: varname; ty: typ; bind: exp; body: cmd; attrs: attribute list}
   | If of exp * cmd * cmd option
   | For of {id: varname; ty:typ; lwb: exp; upb: exp; step: exp; body: cmd}
   | While of exp * cmd
   | Seq of cmd * cmd
   | UnitC                       (* empty statement *)

type args_t = (varname * typ) list
type proc_t =
   | Fun  of args_t * typ * exp  (* Function with the result *)
   | Proc of args_t * cmd        (* Procedure, no result   *)

val offshore : (module converters) → α code → proc_t
```

Fig. 2. The intermediate language (IR) of offshoring (defined in offshoringIR.mli)

therefore, we have to generate calls to library functions and deal with their data types. OpenCL/CUDA and OpenMP bring further challenges: generating pragmas, local and global annotations, and their own vector and scalar data types. All these extensions in the target of offshoring have to be representatable in its source, i.e., OCaml.

The current implementation of offshoring is designed for extensibility. Not only it is an ordinary library, which can be changed and recompiled independently of the MetaOCaml compiler. It is designed so that no recompilation should be needed. We illustrate using the example of offshoring the code to print an array of 32-bit floating-point numbers into a file. The example shows off calls to external library functions (FILE i/o of C) with their own data types (the pointer to the FILE structure), as well as dealing with 32-bit floating-point numbers with no equivalent in OCaml (OCaml float corresponds to double in C). The example is designed to answer some of the most frequently asked questions about offshoring. The complete code accompanies the paper; Fig. 3 shows the salient parts.

The first puzzle is how to generate OCaml code that represents calls to external C functions and uses their data types – the functions that are not generally callable from OCaml as they are. The answer is to define a module to represent that external library: lines 1–11 of Fig. 3. For the purpose of offshoring, all the library data types can be abstract and all functions dummy: we only need their signatures.[11] The type float32 (line 7) is the type of short floats, introduced by the Offshoring IR interface as an alias to OCaml's float and translated to TFloat of OffshoringIR.[12]

With the module File_stub in scope we may generate code. Lines 13–19 show the result, the (well-typed) MetaOCaml code value. Passing it to offshore from Fig. 2 ends in an exception however: "unknown type: file". Indeed, the offshoring library knows nothing about this data type. We need to tell it. First, we add to the IR types the new base type TFile (meant to correspond to FILE of C). As OffshoringIR.typ is an extensible data type, its extension is as simple as line 21. Defining the correspondence between the OCaml type File_stub.file and the just introduced TFile is the job of the converters module, whose implementation DefaultConv is provided by default. Lines 23–32 extend this module: line 25 maps File_stub.file to TArray1 TFile (so that File_stub.fopen matches fopen in the C standard library). Lines 28–30 specify that the names in the File_stub module (namespace) are to be understood as OffshoringIR.KnownVar names: global identifiers. With thus set-up module Conv, offshoring succeeds and produces an IR program, which can then be straightforwardly pretty-printed to C (offshore_to_c combines the IR translation and pretty-printing). The result is shown at the end of Fig. 3.

The grouping of C library functions and types as an OCaml module, in the manner of File_stub, has an unexpected benefit: C gets a module system, which it never had.

---

[11] If one plans to run the generated code as OCaml as well, e.g., for testing, one needs the working implementation of File_stub. The complete code of the running example contains such an implementation, emulating C FILE i/o using OCaml i/o.

[12] The original OCaml float is translated to TDouble.

```
1   module File_stub : sig
2     type file                        (* abstract *)
3     val fnull : file                 (* null pointer FILE *)
4     val cassert : bool → unit        (* C assert *)
5     val fopen : string → string → file  (* standard C fopen, fclose *)
6     val fclose : file → unit
7     val write_f32 : file → float32 → unit  (* not in C standard library, but *)
8     val write_delim : file → unit         (* assume as also available, e.g. as a C macro *)
9   end = struct
10    type file = unit    let fnull = ()   let fopen = fun _ _ → assert false  ...
11  end
12
13  let write_arr =  .<fun arr n fname →
14    let fp = fopen fname "w" in cassert (fp ≠ fnull);
15    for i=0 to n−1 do
16      if i > 0 then begin write_delim fp end;
17      write_f32 fp arr.(i)
18    done;
19    fclose fp>.
20
21  type typ += TFile
22
23  module Conv = struct include DefaultConv
24    let type_conv : pathname → typ list → typ = fun pn args → match pn with
25      | "File_stub.file" → TArray1 TFile
26      | _               → DefaultConv.type_conv pn args
27    let id_conv : pathname → varname → string = fun pn v → match (pn,(v :> string)) with
28      | ("File_stub","cassert") → "assert"
29      | ("File_stub","fnull")   → "NULL"
30      | ("File_stub",v) → v
31      | _ → DefaultConv.id_conv pn v
32  end
33
34  let _ = Offshore_pp.offshore_to_c ~cnv:(module Conv) ~name:"writearr" write_arr
35
36  (* The code printed by offshore_to_c above: *)
37  void writearr(float * arr_1,int n_2,char * fname_3)
38  {
39    FILE * fp_4;
40    int i_5;
41    fp_4 = fopen(fname_3,"w");
42    assert(fp_4 != NULL);
43    for (i_5 = 0; i_5 < n_2; i_5 += 1)
44    {if (i_5 > 0)
45      write_delim(fp_4);
46      write_f32(fp_4,arr_1[i_5]);}
47    fclose(fp_4);}
```

Fig. 3. Extensibility example, slightly abbreviated

3.3   Control Structures: Loops and Exits

One place where C and OCaml differ significantly is control structures. Although while loop has the same syntax and meaning in both languages, do-while has no analogue in OCaml. The for loop is present in both, but rather restricted in OCaml: the loop variable must be an integer, stepping only by one, up or down. Since loops with an arbitrary stride are common in HPC, the offshoring library offers a workaround. It defines the function:

```
let forloop : int → int → int → (int → unit) → unit = fun lwb upb step body →
  let rec loop i = if i ≥ upb then () else (body i; loop (i+step))
  in loop lwb
```

It is an ordinary OCaml function and can be used as is, in OCaml and in the generated code, e.g.:

```
let sum_ar = .<fun arr n → let sum = ref 0 in
  forloop 0 n 4 (fun i → for j=i to min (i+3) (n−1) do sum := !sum + arr.(j) done);
  !sum>.
```

Its applications, however, are translated to OffshoringIR by a special rule, which is better understood by looking at the result of translating the two nested loops in sum_ar:

```
For {id = "i_4"; ty = TInt; lwb = Const (Const_int 0); upb = LocalVar ("n_2", TInt);
  step = Const (Const_int 4);
  body = For {id = "j_5"; ty = TInt; lwb = LocalVar ("i_4", TInt);
    upb = FunCall ("+", [Const (Const_int 1); FunCall ("min", [...])]);
    step = Const (Const_int 1); body = FunCallC (":=", [...])}}
```

Pretty-printing the result as C for-loops is straightforward (see App. A).

The do-while can be supported similarly; however, it rarely occurs in practice – and it can always be converted to the ordinary while.

C also has break, continue, return and goto. In principle, one may define dummy OCaml 'functions' like break : unit→unit, whose applications are pretty-printed as C in a special way. The code with those functions can only be offshored, not executed as OCaml. Mainly, nothing prevents using such 'functions' outside loop bodies, hence breaking the guarantee that the result of offshoring always compiles. A better idea is to introduce iteration combinators with an early exit, like forloop above (Example: cloop in Appendix).

3.4   Pointers and References

The metaphor of OCaml as C is strained the most when it comes to variables. In OCaml, names (variables) stand for values, which may be mutable-cell values. In C, ordinary variables always denote inherently mutable memory locations.

At first, the difference does not seem insurmountable. Compare

```
let exr1 = fun y → let x = ref 0 in x := 1; incr x; !x + y
```

```
int exr1(int y) {int x; x = 0; x = 1; x++; return (x+y);}
```

which suggests the correspondence in Table 1(a), to be used in offshoring. However, applying blindly this translation to

let exr2 = **fun** y → **let** x = **ref** 0 **in let** z = x **in** z := 42; !x + y

gives

int exr2(int y) {int x; int z; x = 0; z = x; z = 42; return (x+y);}

which has a very different meaning: in OCaml, exr2 0 returns 42, but in C, zero.

Table 1. Variables and pointers in OCaml vs. C (whereas in OCaml an introduced variable is immediately bound to a value, in C we split the declaration from initialization, because declarations have to be grouped at the beginning of a block.)

(a) with native C variables

OCaml	**let** (x:int **ref**) = **ref** e **in** ...		!x	x (in assignment)
C	int x; x = e; ...		x (as R-value)	x (as L-value)

(b) with C arrays

OCaml	**let** (x:int **ref**) = **ref** e **in** ...		!x	x (in assignment)
C	int x[1]; *x = e; ...		*x (as R-value)	*x (as L-value)

One modest proposal is to avoid ordinary mutable C variables completely – relying on array references instead. An array name in C refers to a mutable location, but itself is immutable – just like an OCaml variable of a reference type. The proposed translation is summarized in Table 1(b). With it, OCaml's exr1 and exr2 are translated into

int exr1_alt(int y) {int x[1]; *x = 0; *x = 1; (*x)++; return (*x+y);}
int exr2_alt(int y) {int x[1]; int * z[1]; *x = 0; *z = x; **z = 42; return (*x+y);}

The translation results in highly un-idiomatic C, but it compiles to the same machine code (gcc 8.2.2 -O2, x86_64): The efficiency does not suffer.

Although the proposal is attractive, BER MetaOCaml N111 implements a more conservative approach: using Table 1(a) but with side conditions that prohibit aliasing. (These side-conditions are used already in [5] but not described explicitly. They can be gleaned from typing rules in App. A2 of that paper.) That is, in the type t ref, t must be a base type, and the RHS of a let-expression must not be an expression of a ref-type, with an exception of **ref** e. In other words, when binding a reference-type OCaml variable, it should be clear, syntactically, that the mutable-cell value is fresh. The function offshore that translates OCaml to OffshoringIR checks these side conditions, raising an exception if they are violated. Although the side-conditions seem severe, (for example, preventing incr x, which has to be written as x:=!x+1; both result in the same machine code however), from our experience generating (mostly numeric) code, they do not seem overly restrictive.

4 Tagless-Final Embedding

A different way to generate C from OCaml is to embed it in OCaml, in tagless-final style [2,8]. This embedding is emphatically different from the mere representation of C AST in OCaml (Sects. 2, 5): the latter gives no assurances about well-typedness, absence of unbound variables or unexpected shadowing. Tagless-final embedding makes such assurances and hence guarantees that the generated C code compiles without errors or warnings.

In the tagless-final style, the embedded language is represented as a (multi-sorted) algebra whose operations are the syntactic forms of the language. The following collection of operations (an OCaml signature) represents a simple imperative language (not unlike the Offshoring IR, Fig. 2): a simple subset of C.

```
type α cde                    (* Abstract type of code *)

val int : int → int cde
val ( + ) : int cde → int cde → int cde
val ( = ) : int cde → int cde → bool cde
val if_ : bool cde → unit cde → unit cde → unit cde

val seq : unit cde → α cde → α cde
val for_ : int cde → int cde → (int cde → unit cde) → unit cde
val while_ : bool cde → unit cde → unit cde

val newref : α cde → (α ref cde → ω cde) → ω cde
val dref : α ref cde → α cde
val (:=) : α ref cde → α cde → unit cde
val array_get' : α array cde → int cde → α cde
val array_set : α array cde → int cde → α cde → unit cde
```

The body of the vector addition procedure (cf. addv_staged in Sect. 3 and especially its result) has then the form

```
for_ (int 0) (n − int 1) @@ fun i →
    array_set vout i ((array_get' v1 i) + (array_get' v2 i))
```

(given n, vout, v1, and v2 in scope). This OCaml expression, of the type unit cde, clearly describes the for-loop of the vector addition. Once again we use OCaml as a metaphor for C. The embedding is typed: t cde represents a C code expression (or statement, for unit cde) of C type t. The type of while_, for example, ensures that the loop condition is a comparison or dereference expression, and the loop body is a statement. A well-typed OCaml expression over the above signature thus represents well-typed C code.

An implementation of signature may realize α cde as string, of C code. Then while_ builds the code of while-loop from the code for loop condition and loop body. (The actual implementation uses the C AST, Sect. 5, pretty-printed at the end). Given an appropriate function header the above sample produces the code that looks quite like the addv C code in Sect. 3.

More extensive signature is in Appendix; it has been used in practice to generate stream-processing code. More operations can be added at any time: extensibility is the strongest point of the tagless-final style.

There are also complications, not unlike the ones described for offshoring. For example, newref can be used at several types, inferred by OCaml. Generating C variable declarations needs a run-time representation of that inferred type. Unlike offshoring, we implement our own inference (which is simple for a first-order language), relying on the OCaml type system to ensure OCaml's and our run-time types agree. The implementation also enforces side-conditions in Sect. 3.4. Another challenge is the handling of local variables, which in C have to be all declared at the beginning of a block. The salient points of the implementation are summarized in App. B.[13] The accompanying code also shows the advanced example in App. A implemented in the tagless-final style.

This approach can be traced back to C-code–generating combinators in [3]. Those combinators were monomorphic, and the explicit passing of the C variable environment made them ungainly: Compare [3, Fig. 18]

```
gen_inst (gen_assign y (gen_add (lvrv x) (gen_int_cst 3))) env
```

with y := x + int 3 in our approach. Ensuring well-scoping of the C code was also the responsibility of a programmer, to pass the environment env in the disciplined way.

5 Related Work

Offshoring was first proposed in [5], which we have discussed already. Its implementation is no longer available. Asuna [22] was an attempt to resurrect offshoring and extend to SIMD extensions, parallelism and LLVM. The paper presented a few applications of offshoring HPC kernels, with few details about the implementation. Curiously the paper does not mention any restrictions on let-bindings in the source language (raising doubts about correctness). The implementation has not been available.

KreMLin [16] introduces Low*, a subset of F* that is easily mapped to a small subset of C. Because F* is a dependently-typed language, one may state and verify sophisticated correctness properties (including functional correctness). The paper proves that the mapping preserves not just typing but also semantics and side-channel resistance. Like in offshoring, the translatable subset of F* is not easy to state in types; therefore, C code extraction ('offshoring') is best effort. Also related is C code extraction from constructive Coq proofs – although Coq is quite harder to program in; it is also harder to control the form of the produced C code and ensure high performance.

Among other heterogeneous metaprogramming system we should mention MetaHaskell [13], LMS [20] and Terra [4] (which offers weak guarantees: it does not assure the absence of unbound variables).

---

[13] Lack of space precludes the description of performing online partial evaluation and generating not only C but also OCaml (and flowcharts, WASM, etc.) from the same tagless-final expression.

FrontC by Hugues Cassé defines the abstract syntax for C, as an OCaml data structure, and includes the parser and the pretty-printer. It is used (with significant modifications) in CIL (C Intermediate Language)[14] [14] and Binary Analysis Platform.[15] Our abstract C syntax (produced by combinators in Sect. 4) is heavily influenced by Cassé's, but re-written from scratch. FrontC is developed to represent any existing C program (so to analyze it). We are interested only in C generation, and so chose a small but just as expressive and 'sane' subset of C – quite in the spirit of CIL but with different design choices: In our subset, a declaration introduces only one variable. Mainly, we distinguish statements and expressions, and regard assignment and increment as statements. Therefore, such C constructions as x=y=0 and --x * y++ are not representable in our abstract syntax and hence never produced.

6 Evaluation and Conclusions

We have presented two implemented approaches for generating high-performance C code that compiles without errors or warnings and can be freely linked with other C libraries. Offering correctness guarantees requires generator abstractions, which is a challenge to design and maintain. We have described the notable problems we experienced and the ways we mitigated them. One of the main problems turns out maintainability. The current systems are explicitly designed to be extensible and to last.

Offshoring was used in [1] to generate OpenMP matrix-matrix multiplication code that is faster, sometimes $2\times$, than the state of the art BLAS code generated by ATLAS; tuning was also faster. In [7] offshoring has generated GPGPU (OpenCL) matrix-matrix multiplication and k-means clustering code. The tagless-final approach is used in the new version of [12], e.g., to generate C code for the FM radio application ($\sim$3,000 lines of code). Both approaches thus proved adequate for their intended tasks.

The two approaches share the metaphor of OCaml as C: representing a small imperative language (a subset of C) in the form of OCaml expressions. One approach (offshoring) relies on MetaOCaml, thus offering a better syntax for loops and control structures, let-insertion and type inference. The other approach uses the bare OCaml and is more portable and extensible.

The future work involves proving the meaning preservation, designing let-insertion for tagless-final embedding, and emitting better error messages.

Acknowledgments. We thank anonymous reviewers for many, helpful comments and suggestions. This work was partially supported by JSPS KAKENHI Grants Number 18H03218, 17K12662 and 21K11821.

---

[14] http://cil-project.github.io/cil/doc/html/cil/cil001.html.
[15] https://githubhelp.com/BinaryAnalysisPlatform/bap.

References

1. Bussone, G.: Generating OpenMP code from high-level specifications, August 2020. Internship report to ENS
2. Carette, J., Kiselyov, O., Shan, C.: Finally tagless, partially evaluated: tagless staged interpreters for simpler typed languages. J. Funct. Program. **19**(5), 509–543 (2009)
3. Cohen, A., Donadio, S., Garzarán, M.J., Herrmann, C.A., Kiselyov, O., Padua, D.A.: In search of a program generator to implement generic transformations for high-performance computing. Sci. Comput. Program. **62**(1), 25–46 (2006)
4. DeVito, Z., Hegarty, J., Aiken, A., Hanrahan, P., Vitek, J.: Terra: a multi-stage language for high-performance computing. In: ACM SIGPLAN Conference on Programming Language Design and Implementation, PLDI 2013, Seattle, WA, USA, 16–19 June 2013, pp. 105–116. ACM (2013)
5. Eckhardt, J., Kaiabachev, R., Pasalic, E., Swadi, K.N., Taha, W.: Implicitly heterogeneous multi-stage programming. N. Gener. Comput. **25**(3), 305–336 (2007)
6. Frigo, M., Johnson, S.G.: The design and implementation of FFTW3. Proc. IEEE **93**(2), 216–231 (2005)
7. Hirohara, K.: Generating GPU kernels from high-level specifications using MetaOCaml, February 2019. Tohoku University, Master Thesis, in Japanese
8. Kiselyov, O.: Typed tagless final interpreters. In: Gibbons, J. (ed.) Generic and Indexed Programming. LNCS, vol. 7470, pp. 130–174. Springer, Heidelberg (2012). https://doi.org/10.1007/978-3-642-32202-0_3
9. Kiselyov, O.: The design and implementation of BER MetaOCaml. In: Codish, M., Sumii, E. (eds.) FLOPS 2014. LNCS, vol. 8475, pp. 86–102. Springer, Cham (2014). https://doi.org/10.1007/978-3-319-07151-0_6
10. Kiselyov, O.: Reconciling Abstraction with High Performance: A MetaOCaml Approach. Foundations and Trends in Programming Languages, Now Publishers (2018)
11. Kiselyov, O.: BER MetaOCaml N111, October 2020. http://okmij.org/ftp/ML/MetaOCaml.html
12. Kiselyov, O., Biboudis, A., Palladinos, N., Smaragdakis, Y.: Stream fusion, to completeness. In: Conference Record of the Annual ACM Symposium on Principles of Programming Languages, POPL 2017, pp. 285–299. ACM Press, New York, January 2017
13. Mainland, G.: Explicitly heterogeneous metaprogramming with MetaHaskell. In: ICFP, pp. 311–322. ACM Press, New York (2012)
14. Necula, G.C., McPeak, S., Rahul, S.P., Weimer, W.: CIL: intermediate language and tools for analysis and transformation of C programs. In: Horspool, R.N. (ed.) CC 2002. LNCS, vol. 2304, pp. 213–228. Springer, Heidelberg (2002). https://doi.org/10.1007/3-540-45937-5_16
15. Ofenbeck, G., Rompf, T., Püschel, M.: RandIR: differential testing for embedded compilers. In: Biboudis, A., Jonnalagedda, M., Stucki, S., Ureche, V. (eds.) Proceedings of the 7th ACM SIGPLAN Symposium on Scala, SCALA@SPLASH 2016, pp. 21–30. ACM, 30 October–4 November 2016
16. Protzenko, J., et al.: Verified low-level programming embedded in F*. Proc. ACM Program. Lang **1**(ICFP), 17:1–17:29 (2017)
17. Püschel, M., et al.: SPIRAL: code generation for DSP transforms. Proc. IEEE **93**(2), 232–275 (2005)

18. Ragan-Kelley, J., Barnes, C., Adams, A., Paris, S., Durand, F., Amarasinghe, S.P.: Halide: a language and compiler for optimizing parallelism, locality, and recomputation in image processing pipelines. In: Boehm, H.J., Flanagan, C. (eds.) ACM SIGPLAN Conference on Programming Language Design and Implementation, PLDI 2013, pp. 519–530. ACM, June 2013

19. Rathgeber, F., et al.: Firedrake: automating the finite element method by composing abstractions. ACM Trans. Math. Softw. **43**(3) (2016). https://www.firedrakeproject.org/

20. Rompf, T., Odersky, M.: Lightweight modular staging: a pragmatic approach to runtime code generation and compiled DSLs. Commun. ACM **55**(6), 121–130 (2012)

21. Takashima, N., Kiselyov, O., Kameyama, Y.: MetaOCaml as a high-level LLVM macro. In: Japan Society for Software Science and Technology (JSSST), 31st Annual Meeting, September 2014 (2014). (in Japanese)

22. Takashima, N., Sakamoto, H., Kameyama, Y.: Generate and offshore: type-safe and modular code generation for low-level optimization. In: Proceedings of the ACM SIGPLAN Workshop on Functional High-Performance Computing, FHPC@ICFP 2015, Vancouver, BC, Canada, 3 September 2015, pp. 45–53. ACM (2015)

23. Whaley, R.C., Petitet, A.: Minimizing development and maintenance costs in supporting persistently optimized BLAS. Softw.-Pract. Experience **35**(2), 101–121 (2005)

24. Yallop, J., Sheets, D., Madhavapeddy, A.: A modular foreign function interface. Sci. Comput. Program. **164**, 82–97 (2018)

Translation Certification for Smart Contracts

Jacco O.G. Krijnen[1]([✉]) [iD], Manuel M. T. Chakravarty[2], Gabriele Keller[1] [iD],
and Wouter Swierstra[1] [iD]

[1] Utrecht University, Utrecht, The Netherlands
{j.o.g.krijnen,g.k.keller,w.s.swierstra}@uu.nl
[2] IOHK, Singapore, Singapore
manuel.chakravarty@iohk.io

Abstract. Compiler correctness is an old problem, but with the emergence of *smart contracts* on blockchains that problem presents itself in a new light. Smart contracts are self-contained pieces of software that control (valuable) assets in an adversarial environment; once committed to the blockchain, these smart contracts cannot be modified. Smart contracts are typically developed in a high-level contract language and compiled to low-level virtual machine code before being committed to the blockchain. For a smart contract user to trust a given piece of low-level code on the blockchain, they must convince themselves that (a) they are in possession of the matching source code and (b) that the compiler has correctly translated the source code to the given low-level code.

Classic approaches to compiler correctness tackle the second point. We argue that *translation certification* also squarely addresses the first. We describe the proof architecture of a novel translation certification framework, implemented in Coq, for a functional smart contract language. We demonstrate that we can model the compilation pipeline as a sequence of translation relations that facilitate a modular verification methodology and are robust in the face of an evolving compiler implementation.

1 Introduction

Compiler correctness is an old problem that has received renewed interest in the context of *smart contracts*—that is, compiled code on public blockchains, such as Ethereum or Cardano. This code often controls a significant amount of financial assets, must operate under adversarial conditions, and can no longer be updated once it has been committed to the blockchain. Bugs in smart contracts are a significant problem in practice [5]. Recent work has also established that smart contract language compilers can exacerbate this problem [26, Section 3] (in this case, the Vyper compiler). More specifically, the authors report (a) that they did find bugs in the Vyper compiler that compromised smart contract security and (b) that they performed verification on generated low-level code, because they were wary of compiler bugs.

Hence, to support reasoning about smart contract source code, we need to get a handle on the correctness of smart contract compilers. On top of that, we

© Springer Nature Switzerland AG 2022
M. Hanus and A. Igarashi (Eds.): FLOPS 2022, LNCS 13215, pp. 94–111, 2022.
https://doi.org/10.1007/978-3-030-99461-7_6

do also need a *verifiable link* between the source code and its compiled code to prevent *code substitution attacks,* where an adversary presents the user with source code that doesn't match the low-level code committed on-chain.

In this paper, we are reporting on our ongoing effort to develop a certification engine for the open-source on-chain code compiler of the Plutus smart contract system[1] for the Cardano blockchain.[2] Specifically, we make the following contributions:

- We describe a novel architecture for a translation certifier based on *translation relations,* which enables us to generate *translation certificates*—proof objects that relate the source code to the resulting compiled code and establish the correctness of the translation (Sect. 2).
- We provide formal definitions for the transformation passes that step-by-step translate PIR (Plutus Intermediate Representation) to PLC (Plutus Core) and briefly discuss the challenges associated with the certification of each of these passes (Sect. 3).
- We present a summary of existing approaches to compiler correctness and discuss the importance of generating translation certificates in the domain of smart contracts (Sect. 4).

We also evaluate how our approach to gradual certification copes with changes to the compiler, which is being developed in an independent open source project. Finally, we discuss related work in Sect. 5 and future work in Sect. 6.

2   The Architecture of the Certifier

On-chain code in the Plutus smart contract system is written in a subset of Haskell called *Plutus Tx* [18]. The Plutus Tx compiler is implemented as a plugin for the widely-used, industrial-strength GHC Haskell compiler, combining large parts of the GHC's compilation pipeline with custom translation steps to generate Plutus Core. In this context, it seems infeasible to apply full-scale compiler verification à la CompCert [21]. We will therefore outline the design of a certification engine that, using the Coq proof assistant [6,9], generates a proof object, a *translation certificate*, asserting the validity of a Plutus Core program with respect to a given Plutus Tx source contract. In addition to asserting the correct translation *of this one program*, the translation certificate serves as a verifiable link between source and generated code.

We model the compiler as a composition of pure functions that transform one abstract syntax tree into another. Figure 1 illustrates the architecture for a single transformation, where the grey area marks the compiler implementation as a function $f_i : \mathrm{AST}_i \to \mathrm{AST}_{i+1}$. We use a family of types AST_i to illustrate that the representation of the abstract syntax might change after each transformation.

---

[1] https://developers.cardano.org/docs/smart-contracts/plutus/.
[2] http://cardano.org is, at the time of writing, the 5th largest public blockchain by market capitalisation.

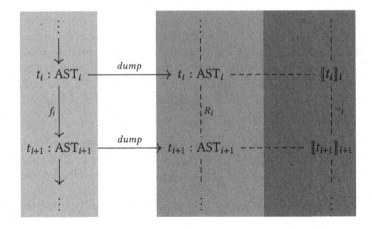

Fig. 1. Architecture for a single compiler pass. The grey area (left) represents the compiler, orange (center) and blue (right) represent the certification component in Coq. (Color figure online)

To support certification, the compiler outputs each intermediate tree t_i, so that we can parse these in our Coq implementation of the certifier. Within Coq, we define a high-level specification of each pass. We call this specification a *translation relation*: a binary relation on abstract syntax trees that specifies the intended behaviour of the compiler pass. The orange area in Fig. 1 displays the translation relation R_i of pass i, where the vertical dashed line indicates that $R_i(t_i, t_{i+1})$ holds. To establish this, we define a search procedure that, given two subsequent trees produced by the compiler, can construct a derivation relating the two.

The translation relation is purely syntactic—it does not assert anything about the correctness of the compiler—but rather *specifies* the behaviour of a particular compiler pass. To verify that the compilation preserves language semantics requires an additional proof, the blue area in Fig. 1, that establishes that any two terms related by R_i have the same semantics.

We have implemented this approach for a range of concrete passes of the Plutus Tx compiler. To illustrate our approach in this section, we will use an untyped lambda calculus, extended with non-recursive let-bindings.

$$t ::= x \mid \lambda x.\, t \mid t\, t \mid \texttt{let } x = t \texttt{ in } t$$

In the following section, we will extend this to a lambda calculus that is closer to the intermediate language used by the Plutus Tx compiler.

2.1   Characterising a Transformation

To assert the correctness of a single compiler stage f_i, we begin by defining a translation relation R_i on a pair of source and target terms t_i and t_{i+1},

$$\frac{\Gamma(x) = t' \qquad \Gamma \vdash t' \triangleright t}{\Gamma \vdash x \triangleright t} \text{ [Inline-Var}_1\text{]}$$

$$\frac{}{\Gamma \vdash x \triangleright x} \text{ [Inline-Var}_2\text{]}$$

$$\frac{\Gamma \vdash t_1 \triangleright t_1' \qquad (x, t_1), \Gamma \vdash t_2 \triangleright t_2'}{\Gamma \vdash \textbf{let } x = t_1 \textbf{ in } t_2 \triangleright \textbf{let } x = t_1' \textbf{ in } t_2'} \text{ [Inline-Let]}$$

$$\frac{\Gamma \vdash t_1 \triangleright t_1' \qquad \Gamma \vdash t_2 \triangleright t_2'}{\Gamma \vdash t_1 \ t_2 \triangleright t_1' \ t_2'} \text{ [Inline-App]}$$

$$\frac{\Gamma \vdash t_1 \triangleright t_1'}{\Gamma \vdash \lambda x.t_1 \triangleright \lambda x.t_1'} \text{ [Inline-Lam]}$$

Fig. 2. Characterisation of an inliner

respectively. This relation characterises the admissible translations of that compiler stage. That is, for all t_i, t_{i+1}, we have $f_i(t_i) = t_{i+1}$ implies $R_i(t_i, t_{i+1})$.

As a concrete example, consider an inlining pass. We have characterised this as an inductively defined relation in Fig. 2. Here, $\Gamma \vdash s \triangleright t$ asserts that program s can be translated into t given an environment Γ of let-bound variables, paired with their definition. According to Rule [Inline-Var$_1$] the variable x may be replaced by t when the pair (x, t') can be looked up in Γ and t' can be translated to t, accounting for repeated inlining. The remaining rules are congruence rules, where Rule [Inline-Let] also extends the environment Γ. We omitted details about handling variable capture to keep the presentation simple: hence, we assume that variable names are globally unique.

Crucially, these rules do *not* prescribe which variable occurrences should be inlined, since the [Inline-Var$_1$] and [Inline-Var$_2$] rules overlap. The choice in the implementation of the pass may rely on a complex set of heuristics internal to the compiler. Instead, we merely define a relation capturing the *possible* ways in which the compiler *may* behave. This allows for a certification engine that is robust with respect to changes in the compiler, such as the particular heuristics used to decide when to replace a variable with its definition or not.

We can then encode the relation $\cdot \vdash \cdot \triangleright \cdot$ in Coq as an inductive type `Inline`, which is indexed by an environment and two ASTs, as shown in Fig. 3. This type corresponds closely to the rules of Fig. 2: we define exactly one constructor per rule. However, there are some small differences. Since we cannot omit details about variable capture anymore, we choose a de Bruijn representation for variables and implement the environment Γ as a cons-list. In the `Inline_Let` constructor, we extend the list with the bound term and furthermore shift free variables in the other bound terms. For a let-bound variable n, its corresponding bound term can then be found at the n'th position in the list using Coq's `nth_error` list-indexing function. For this indexing to work properly, the

```
Inductive binding :=
  | LetBound    : term -> binding
  | LambdaBound : binding.

Inductive Inline : list binding -> term -> term -> Type :=
  | Inline_Var_1 : forall {env n t},
      nth_error env n = Some (LetBound t) ->
      Inline.env (Var n) t

  | Inline_Var_2 : forall {env n},
      Inline env (Var n) (Var n)

  | Inline_Let : forall {env s t s' t'},
      Inline env s s' ->
      Inline (LetBound s :: shiftEnv env) t t' ->
      Inline env (Let s t) (Let s' t')

  | Inline_Lam : forall {env s t},
      Inline (LambdaBound :: shiftEnv env) s t ->
      Inline env (Lam s) (Lam t)

  | Inline_App : forall {env s sx t tx},
      Inline env s t -> Inline env sx tx ->
      Inline env (App s sx) (App t tx)
```

Fig. 3. Characterisation of an inliner in Coq

environment also has to be extended at every lambda, as seen in `Inline_Lam`. We distinguish the two types of binding sites with the type `binding`.

These inductive types implement the translation relation: its inhabitants are proof derivations which will be a key ingredient of a compilation certificate.

2.2   Proof Search

After defining a translation relation R_i characterising one compiler stage, we now define a decision procedure to construct a proof that for two particular terms t_i and t_{i+1}, produced by a run of the compiler, the relation $R_i(t_i, t_{i+1})$ holds. To find and implement such a search procedure, we generally follow these steps:

1. We write proofs for specific compilations by hand using Coq's *tactics*, a form of metaprogamming. For simple relations, like the inline example sketched above, a proof can often be found with a handful of tactics such as `auto` or `constructor`. This is particularly useful for debugging the design of our relations describing compiler passes. The drawback of this approach is, however, that it is difficult to reason when such proof search may fail. Furthermore, proofs written using such tactics quickly become slow for large terms.

2. Once we are sufficiently confident that a relation accurately captures admissible compiler behaviour, we write a decision procedure of the form `forall (t1 t2 : term), option (R t1 t2)`. These procedures can still produce large proof terms and may not always successfully construct a proof, but they form a useful intermediate step towards full-on proof by reflection.

3. Finally, we write a boolean decision procedure in the style of ssreflect [17] of type `term -> term -> bool`, together with a soundness proof stating that it will only return `true` when two terms are related through R_i. Verifying such boolean functions for complex compilation passes is non-trivial; hence, we only invest the effort once we have a reasonable degree of confidence that the relation we have defined accurately describes a given compiler pass.

2.3 Semantics Preservation

Given the relational specification of each individual compiler pass, we can now establish the correctness properties for each pass. In the simplest case, this could be asserting the preservation of a program's static semantics, i.e., a proof of type preservation. On the other end of the spectrum, we can demonstrate that the translated term is semantically equivalent to the original program. Proving such properties for PIR and Plutus Core passes, however, requires advanced techniques such as step-indexed logical relations [2], which go beyond the scope of the current paper.

In Fig. 1, we denote R_i's correctness properties in the blue area by means of an abstract binary relation $\sim_i$ on the semantic objects $[\![t_i]\!]_i$ of ASTs t_i. In the case of static semantics, we can choose typing derivations as semantic objects, and (for most passes) relate these by simply comparing types syntactically.

We can construct these proofs independently and gradually for each step in the translation. In fact, even without any formal proof about the semantics, inspection of the (relatively concise) definition of a translation relation may already provide some degree of confidence that the translation step was performed correctly. After all, the translation relation asserts the specification of this compiler pass' admissible behaviour.

2.4 Certificate Generation

A complete translation certificate includes at least the entire set of ASTs $t_1, \ldots, t_n$ together with a proof term witnessing the translation relations of type $R_1(t_1, t_2) \wedge \ldots \wedge R_{n-1}(t_{n-1}, t_n)$. In addition, any semantic preservation results on translation relations can be instantiated and included as a proof of $[\![t_i]\!] \sim_i [\![t_{i+1}]\!]$.

Together with the source and compiled program, one can now independently check the certificate using a trusted proof checker, such as the Coq kernel [9]. The definitions of the abstract syntax, translation relations and semantic preservation can be inspected to confirm that the certificate proves the right theorem. One can then be confident that the compiled program is a faithful translation of the source code.

$$
\begin{aligned}
t ::=&\ x \mid \lambda(x:\tau).\,t \mid t\ t &&\text{variable, lambda, function application}\\
&\mid \Lambda(\alpha:\kappa).\,t \mid t\ \{\tau\} &&\text{type-abstraction, type application}\\
&\mid \mathtt{let}^s_r\ x = t\ \mathtt{in}\ t &&\text{term bindings}\\
&\mid \mathtt{data}\ T\ \overline{\alpha} = \overline{C_i\ \overline{\tau_i}}\ \mathtt{with}\ x\ \mathtt{in}\ t &&\text{datatype binding}\\
r ::=&\ \mathtt{rec} \mid \mathtt{nonrec} &&\text{recursion type of binding}\\
s ::=&\ \mathtt{strict} \mid \mathtt{nonstrict} &&\text{strictness of binding}\\
\tau ::=&\ \dots &&\text{types}
\end{aligned}
$$

Fig. 4. Simplified PIR

3 Translation Relations of the Plutus Tx Compiler

The Plutus Tx compiler translates Plutus Tx (a subset of Haskell) to Plutus Core, a variant of System F^μ_ω [13]. The Plutus Core code is committed to the Cardano blockchain, constituting the definitive reference to any deployed smart contract.

Plutus Core programs are pure, self-contained functions (i.e., they do not link to other code) and are passed a representation of the transaction whose validation they contribute to. The programs are run by an interpreter during the transaction validation phase of the blockchain.

The Plutus Tx compiler reuses parts of the GHC infrastructure and implements its custom passes by installing a core-to-core pass plugin [15] in the GHC compiler pipeline. On a high level, the compiler comprises three steps:

1. The parsing, type-checking and desugaring phases of GHC are reused to translate a surface-level Haskell program into a GHC Core program.
2. A large subset of GHC Core is directly translated into an intermediate language named Plutus Intermediate Representation (PIR). These languages are similar and both based on System F, with some extensions. Additionally, all referred definitions are included as local definitions so that the program is self-contained.
3. The PIR program is then transformed and compiled down into Plutus Core.

The certification effort reported here focuses on Step 3, which consists of several optimisation passes and translation steps. PIR is a superset of the Plutus Core language: it adds several conveniences, such as user-defined datatypes, strict and non-strict let-bindings that may be (mutually) recursive. The compilation steps translate these constructs into simpler language constructs.

In Fig. 4 we present a simplified version of the PIR syntax, where we omit some constructs for the sake of presentation. The full PIR language specification has been formalised elsewhere [13,19]. In particular, we ignore the fact that in PIR, let-bindings may contain a group of (mutually recursive) bindings. Similarly, we do not include mutually-recursive datatypes. Furthermore, we omit the syntax of types, and the term-level witnesses of iso-recursive types. We occasionally omit type annotations, when they are not relevant.

We introduce the individual compiler passes that the Plutus Tx compiler performs using the following Haskell program to illustrate their behaviour:

```
-- | Either a specific end date, or "never".
data EndDate = Fixed Integer | Never

pastEnd :: EndDate -> Integer -> Bool
pastEnd end current =
   let inlineMe = False
   in case end of
     Fixed n ->  (let floatMe = if current `greaterThanEqInteger` 0
       then n else 0 in floatMe) `lessThanEqInteger` current
     Never    -> inlineMe
```

This program is a basic implementation of a *timelock*, a contract that states that funds may be moved after a certain date, or not at all. It contains a few contrived bindings (`inlineMe` and `floatMe`) that will be useful to illustrate some transformations. After the program is desugared to GHC Core, it is converted to a term in PIR that corresponds to the following Simplified PIR term:

```
data Bool = True | False with Bool_match in
 data Unit = Unit with Unit_match in
  let nonrec strict lessThanEqInteger = ... in
    data EndDate = Fixed Integer | Never with EndDate_match in
     \(end : EndDate).
      \(current : Integer).
       let nonrec nonstrict inlineMe = False in
        EndDate_match end
          (\unit n -> lessThanEqInteger
            (let nonrect nonstrict floatMe =
               Bool_match (greaterThanEqInteger current 0)
                 (\unit -> n) (\unit -> 0)
                Unit
             in floatMe)
            current)
          (\unit -> inlineMe)
         Unit
```

Note that case distinction of a type `T` is encoded as the application of a pattern match function `T_match`, which is introduced as part of a data definition. Furthermore, branches of a case distinction are delayed by abstracting over a unit value, since PIR is a strict language.

Next we will discuss the compiler passes, we have included each intermediate form of the above program with some commentary in the appendix which can be found online[3].

---

[3] https://arxiv.org/abs/2201.04919.

3.1   Variable Renaming

In the renaming pass, the compiler transforms a program into an α-equivalent program, such that all variable names are globally unique, a property also known as the *Barendregt-convention*. The implementation of some subsequent compiler passes depend on it. We can express variable renaming as a translation relation $\Delta \vdash t \triangleright_\alpha t'$, stating that under the renaming environment Δ (consisting of pairs of variables), t is renamed to t'. The environment Δ records all variables that are free in t, paired with their corresponding name in t'.

The case for lambda abstractions is defined as follows:

$$\frac{(x,y), \Delta \vdash t \triangleright_\alpha t' \quad \{z \mid (z,y) \in \Delta\} \cap FV(t) = \emptyset}{\Delta \vdash \lambda x.t \triangleright_\alpha \lambda y.t'} \text{ [Rename-Abs]}$$

The [Rename-Abs] rule states that a lambda-bound variable x may be renamed at its binding-site to y, when t and t' are related under the extended environment. Of course, x may equal y, indicating that no renaming was performed. Additionally, the new binder y should not capture any other free variable z in t that was also renamed to y. Very similar rules can be stated for other binding constructs such as let.

Note that this relation does not establish global uniqueness of variables: we consider that an implementation detail internal to the compiler. If this property would be required or convenient in semantic preservation proofs, we will establish it separately, allowing this renaming relation to be as general as possible.

The variable case simply follows from the environment Δ:

$$\frac{(x,y) \in \Delta}{\Delta \vdash x \triangleright_\alpha y} \text{ [Rename-Var]}$$

3.2   Inlining

The rules of the translation relation for inlining in PIR are similar to those in Sect. 2.1. However, the Plutus Tx compiler does more than just inlining let-bound definitions. It also performs dead-code elimination (removing those let-bindings that have been inlined exhaustively) and it renames variables to ensure the global uniqueness of bound variables. This introduces a problem for our certification approach, as we cannot observe and dump the intermediate ASTs, since the transformations are fused into a single pass in the compiler.

We solve this by modeling the individual transformations, composing them using *relational composition*, $\exists t_2.R_1(t_1, t_2) \land R_2(t_2, t_3)$. To construct a proof relating two terms, then amounts to also finding the *intermediate term*, t_2 witnessing the composite transformation. To simplify the search of this intermediate AST, we adjust the compiler to emit supporting information about the performed pass; in this case, a list of the eliminated variables. If the compiler emits incorrect information, we may fail to construct a certificate, but we will never produce an incorrect certificate.

3.3   Let-Floating

During let-floating, let-bindings can be moved upwards in the program. This may save unnecessarily repeated computation and makes the generated code more readable. The Plutus Tx compiler constructs a dependency graph to maintain a correct ordering when multiple definitions are floated. For the translation relation, we first consider the interaction of a let expression with its parent node in the AST. For example, consider the case of a lambda with a non-strict let directly under it:

$$\frac{x \notin FV(t_1) \quad x \neq y \quad t_1 \ \triangleright_{let} \ t_1' \quad t_2 \ \triangleright_{let} \ t_2'}{\lambda x.\text{let}_r^{\text{nonstrict}} \ y = t_1 \ \text{in} \ t_2} \quad \text{[Float-Let-Lam]}$$
$$\triangleright_{let}$$
$$\text{let}_r^{\text{nonstrict}} \ y = t_1' \ \text{in} \ \lambda x.t_2'$$

This rule states that a non-strict let-binding may float up past a lambda, if the bound term does not reference the lambda-bound variable. Furthermore, we require $x \neq y$, to avoid variable capture in t_2. This rule does not apply to strict let-bindings, as floating them outside a lambda might change termination behaviour of the program. Similar rules express when a let may float upwards past the other language constructs. Most of these are much simpler, only binding constructs pose additional constraints on scoping and strictness. Since the compiler pass may float lets more than just one step up, we define the translation relation as the transitive closure of $\triangleright_{let}$. Note that we do not need to maintain a dependency graph in the certifier, but only need to assert that transformations do not break dependencies.

3.4   Dead-Code Elimination

By means of a live variable analysis, the compiler determines which let-bound definitions are unused. This is mainly useful for definitions that are introduced by other compiler passes. Since PIR is a strict language, however, the compiler can only eliminate those bindings for which it can determine they have no side-effects. For example, a let-bound expression that is unused but diverges cannot be removed, as that could change the termination behaviour of the program.

The analysis in the compiler is not as straightforward as counting occurences. Even a let-bound variable that does occur in the code, may be dead-code, if it is only used in other dead bindings. This is also known as strongly live variable analysis [16]. We define a translation relation $t \ \triangleright_{dce} \ t'$ that captures dead code elimination. The crucial rule is for let-bindings.

$$\frac{t_2 \ \triangleright_{dce} \ t_2' \quad x \notin FV(t_2')}{\text{let}_r^{\text{nonstrict}} \ x = t_1 \ \text{in} \ t_2 \ \triangleright_{dce} \ t_2'} \quad \text{[DCE-Let-nonstrict]}$$

Note that the condition $x \notin FV(t_2')$ mentions the *resulting* body of the let t_2'. This is justified since the rules of $\triangleright_{dce}$ can remove bindings only, but cannot change any other language constructs. This illustrates how succinct we can describe the specification of a complex compiler pass.

In practice, the Plutus Tx compiler also eliminates some strict bindings that obviously do not diverge, such as values.

3.5 Encoding of Non-strict Bindings

The PIR language allows both for strict and non-strict let-bindings, but Plutus Core does not. The *thunking transformation* is used to obtain semantic equivalent definitions which use a strict let-binding. We define the rules as a relation $\Gamma \vdash t \vartriangleright_{thunk} t'$, where Γ records for every bound variable whether it was bound strictly or non-strictly. The rule for a non-strict binding site is:

$$\frac{\Gamma \vdash t_1 \vartriangleright_{thunk} t_1' \qquad (x, \text{nonstrict}), \Gamma \vdash t_2 \vartriangleright_{thunk} t_2' \qquad y \notin FV(t_1)}{\begin{array}{c} \Gamma \vdash \\ \mathbf{let} \ ^{\text{nonstrict}}_{\text{nonrec}} \ x = t_1 \ \mathbf{in} \ t_2 \\ \vartriangleright_{thunk} \\ \mathbf{let} \ ^{\text{strict}}_{\text{nonrec}} \ x = \lambda y.\ t_1' \ \mathbf{in} \ t_2' \end{array}} \ [\text{Thunk-Let-nonstrict}]$$

This rule states that a right hand side is thunked by introducing a lambda abstraction that expects a trivial unit value y as its argument.

The rules for other variable binders extend Γ. The rule for a recursive let-binding also extends the environment under which t_1 is transformed. Finally, we also replace the occurrences of nonstrict variables, adding an application to the unit value, thereby forcing evaluation.

$$\frac{(x, \text{nonstrict}) \in \Gamma}{\Gamma \vdash x \vartriangleright_{thunk} x \ ()} \ [\text{Thunk-Var}]$$

3.6 Encoding of Recursive Bindings

The Plutus Tx compiler translates (mutually) recursive let-bindings in non-recursive ones using fixpoint combinators. Here we only consider the rule for individual recursive lets in simplified PIR:

$$\frac{t_1 \vartriangleright_\mu t_1' \qquad t_2 \vartriangleright_\mu t_2' \qquad y \notin FV(t_1)}{\begin{array}{c} \mathbf{let} \ ^s_{\text{rec}} \ x = t_1 \ \mathbf{in} \ t_2 \\ \vartriangleright_\mu \end{array}} \ [\text{EncRec-Let}]$$

$$\mathbf{let} \ ^{\text{strict}}_{\text{nonrec}} \ \mathit{fix} = \dots \ \mathbf{in} \ \mathbf{let} \ ^s_{\text{nonrec}} \ x = \mathit{fix} \ (\lambda x.\ t_1') \ \mathbf{in} \ t_2'$$

This rule relates recursive bindings to non-recursive ones, and expects an explicit definition of the fixpoint operator as well. Since PIR has no primitive construct for term-level fix-points, the compiler generates a definition fix. Note that fix is defined in a non-recursive let, its construction relies on recursive types [19].

The actual transformation for PIR is much more involved, since mutually recursive binding groups require a more involved fixpoint combinator of which the definition depends on the size of the group.

3.7 Encoding of Datatypes

Datatype definitions are encoded using lambda and type abstractions according to the Scott encoding [1]. To show the idea of the rather general $\triangleright_{data}$ translation relation, we show a rule specialised to the *Maybe* datatype.

$$\frac{t \;\triangleright_{data}\; t'}{\substack{\texttt{data } \textit{Maybe } \alpha = \textit{Just } \alpha \mid \textit{Nothing } \texttt{with } \textit{maybe } \texttt{in } t \\ \triangleright_{data} \\ (\Lambda \textit{Maybe}.\lambda \textit{Just}.\lambda \textit{Nothing}.\lambda \textit{maybe}.\ t')\ \tau_{Maybe}\ t_{Just}\ t_{Nothing}.t_{maybe}}} \text{[Scott-Maybe]}$$

The [Scott-Maybe] rule relates the datatype definition to a term that abstracts over the type *Maybe*, its constructors *Just* and *Nothing* and the matching function *maybe*, which are each lambda encoded. For the exact definitions of τ_{Maybe}, t_{Just}, $t_{Nothing}$ and t_{maybe} we refer to the general formalisation of PIR [19].

3.8 Encoding of Non-recursive Bindings

A non-recursive let-binding is simply compiled into a β redex:

$$\frac{t_1 \;\triangleright_\beta\; t_1' \qquad t_2 \;\triangleright_\beta\; t_2'}{\texttt{let }^{\texttt{strict}}_{\texttt{nonrec}}\ x = t_1 \texttt{ in } t_2 \;\triangleright_\beta\; (\lambda x.\ t_2')\ t_1'} \text{[Redex-Let]}$$

Note that at this point in the compiler pipeline, $\texttt{let}^{\texttt{strict}}_{\texttt{nonrec}}$ is the only type of let-binding that can still occur.

4 Evaluation

In this section, we evaluate our approach to proof engineering for an independently developed, constantly evolving compiler under the application constraints imposed by smart contracts.

4.1 Compilers and Correctness

The standard approach to compiler correctness is *full compiler verification*: a proof that asserts that the compiler is correct as it demonstrates that, for any valid source program, the translation produces a semantically equivalent target program. Examples of this approach include the CompCert [21] and CakeML [20] projects, showing that (with significant effort) it is possible to verify a compiler end-to-end. To do so, the compiler is typically implemented in a language suitable for verification, such as the Coq proof assistant or the HOL theorem prover.

In contrast, the technique that we propose for the Plutus Tx compiler is based on *translation validation* [27]. Instead of asserting an entire compiler correct, translation validation establishes the correctness of individual compiler runs.

A statement of full compiler correctness is, of course, the stronger of the two statements. Translation validation may fail to assert the correctness of some compiler runs; either because the compiler did not produce correct code or because the translation certifier is incomplete. In exchange for being the weaker property, translation validation is potentially (1) less costly to realise, (2) easier to retrofit to an existing compiler, and (3) more robust in the face of changes to the compiler.

The idea of *proof-carrying code* [23] is closely related to translation validation, shifting the focus to compiled programs, rather than the compiler itself. A program is distributed together with a proof of a property such as memory or type safety. Such a proof excludes certain classes of bugs and gives direct evidence to the users of such a program, who may independently check the proof before running it. Our certification effort, while related, differs in that we keep proof and program separate and in that we are interested in full semantic correctness and not just certain properties like memory and type safety.

4.2   Certificates and Smart Contracts

Smart contracts often manage significant amounts of financial and other assets. Before a user engages with such a contract, which has been committed to the blockchain as compiled code, they may want to inspect the source code to assert that it behaves as they expect. In order to be able to rely on that inspection, they need to know without doubt that (1) they are looking at the correct source code and (2) that the source code has been compiled correctly.

While a verified smart contract compiler addresses the second point, it doesn't help with the first. An infrastructure of *reproducible builds*, on the other hand, solves only the first point. The latter is the approach taken by Etherscan[4]: to verify that a deployed Ethereum smart contract was the result of a compiler run, one provides the source code and build information such as the compiler version and optimisation settings.

In contrast, a *certifying compiler* [24] that generates an independently verifiable certificate of correct translation, squarely addresses both points. By verifying a smart contract's translation certificate, a smart contract user can convince themselves that they are in possession of the matching source code and that this was correctly compiled to the code committed to the blockchain.

4.3   Engineering Considerations

Gradual Verification. The certifier architecture outlined in this paper allows for a gradual approach to verification: during the development of the certification engine, each individual step in the process increases our overall confidence in the compiler's correctness, even if we have not yet completed the end-to-end semantic verification of the compiler pipeline.

---

[4] https://etherscan.io/verifyContract.

By defining only the translation relations, we have an independent formal specification of the compiler's behaviour. This makes it easier to reason informally and to spot potential mistakes or problems with the implementation.

Implementing the decision procedures for translation relations ties the implementation to the specification: we can show on a per-compilation basis that a pass is sound with respect to its specification as a translation relation. Furthermore, we can test and debug translation relations by automatically constructing evidence for various input programs.

Finally, by proving semantics preservation of a translation relation, we gain full confidence in the corresponding pass for compiler runs that abide by that translation relation.

Agility. The Plutus Tx compiler is developed independently of our certification effort. Moreover, it depends on large parts of a large code base—namely, that of the Glasgow Haskell Compiler (GHC). In addition, both GHC and the Plutus Tx-specific parts evolve on a constant basis; for example, to improve code optimisation or to fix bugs.

In that context, full verification appears an insurmountable task and a proof on the basis of the compiler source code would constantly have to adapt to the evolving compiler source. Hence, the architecture of our certification engine is based on a *grey box approach*, where the certifier matches the general outline (such as the phases of the compiler pipeline), but not all of the implementation details of the compiler. For example, our translation relation for the inliner admits any valid inlining. Improvements of the compiler heuristics to produce more efficient programs by being selective about what precisely to inline don't affect the inliner's translation relation, and hence, don't affect the certifier.

Trusted Computing Base (TCB). The fact that the Plutus Tx compiler is not implemented in a proof assistant, but in Haskell complicates direct compiler verification. It might be possible to use a tool like hs-to-coq [29], which translates a subset of Haskell into Coq's Gallina and has been used for proving various properties about Haskell code [11]. However, given that those tools often only cover language subsets, it is not clear that they are applicable. More importantly, such an approach would increase the size of the trusted computing base (TCB), as the translation from Haskell into Coq's Gallina is not verified. Similarly, extraction-based approaches suffer from the same problem if the extraction itself is not verified, although there are projects like CertiCoq [3] that try to address that issue.

In any case, our architecture has a small TCB. We directly relate the source and target programs, taking the compiler implementation out of the equation. Trusting a translation certificate comes down to trusting the Coq kernel that checks the proof, the theorem with its supporting definitions and soundness of the Plutus Core interpreter with respect to the formalised semantics. Of course, these components are part of the TCB of a verified compiler too. This aspect also motivated our choice of Coq over other languages such as Agda, due to its relatively small and mature kernel.

5 Related Work

Ethereum was the first blockchain to popularise use of smart contracts, written in the Solidity programming language. Solidity is an imperative programming language that is compiled to EVM bytecode, which runs on a stack machine operating on persistent mutable state. The DAO vulnerability [12] has underlined the importance of formal verification of smart contracts. Notably, a verification framework has been presented [10] for reasoning about embedded Solidity programs in F*. The work includes a decompiler to convert EVM bytecode, generated by a compiler, into Solidity programs in F*. The authors propose that correctness of compilation can be shown by proving equivalence of the embedded source and (decompiled) target program using relational reasoning [7]. However, this would involve a manual proof effort on a per-program basis, and relies on the F* semantics since the embeddings are shallow. Furthermore, components such as the decompiler are not formally verified, adding to the size of the TCB.

The translation validation technique has been used for the verification of a particular critical Ethereum smart contract [26] using the K framework. The work demonstrates how translation validation can succesfully be applied to construct proofs about the low-level EVM bytecode by mostly reasoning on the (much more understandable) source code. The actual refinement proof is still constructed manually, however.

The Tezos blockchain also uses a stack-like language, called Michelson. The Mi-Cho-Coq framework [8] formalises the language and supports reasoning with a weakest precondition logic. There is ongoing work for developing a certified compiler in Coq for the Albert intermediate language, intended as a target language for certified compilers of higher-level languages. This differs from our approach as it requires the compiler to be implemented in the proof assistant.

ConCert is a smart contract verification framework in Coq [4]. It enables formal reasoning about the source code of a smart contracts, defined in a different (functional) language. The programs are translated and shallowly embedded in Coq's Gallina. Interestingly, the translation is proven sound, in contrast with approaches such as hs-to-coq [29], since it is implemented using Coq's metaprogramming and reasoning facility MetaCoq [28].

The Cogent certifying compiler [25] has shown that it is possible to use translation validation for lowering the cost of functional verification of low-level code: a program can be written and reasoned about in a high-level functional language, which is compiled down to C. The generated certificate then proves a refinement relation, capable of transporting the verification results to the corresponding C code. The situation is different from ours: the Cogent compiler goes through a range of languages with different semantic models and uses the forward-simulation technique as a consequence. In contrast, we are working with variations of lambda calculi that have similar semantics, allowing us to use logical relations and translation relations.

In their Coq framework [22], Li and Appel use a similar technique for specifying compiler passes as inductive relations in Coq. Their tool reduces the effort of implementing program transformations and corresponding correctness proofs. The tool is able to generate large parts of an implementation together with a partial soundess proof with respect to those relations. The approach is used to implement parts of the CertiCoq backend.

6   Conclusions and Further Work

The Plutus Tx compiler translates a Haskell subset into Plutus Core. The compiler consists of three main parts: the first one reuses various stages of GHC to compile the Haskell subset to GHC Core—GHC's principal intermediate language. The second part translates GHC Core to PIR and the final part compiles PIR to Plutus Core. As Plutus Core is strict and doesn't directly support datatypes, these parts are quite complex. Moreover, they consist of a significant number of successive transformation steps.

In this paper, we focused on the certification effort covering the third part of that pipeline; specifically, the translation steps from PIR to Plutus Core. We developed translation relations for all passes described in Sect. 3, such that we can, for example, produce a proof relating the previously described timelock example in PIR to its final form in Plutus Core. For some of these passes, such as inlining, we have implemented a verified decision procedure, but most of the evidence is generated semi-automatically by using Coq tactics. We have not yet covered all transformations in their full generality; for example, we do not cover (mutually) recursive datatypes yet. We have also started the semantic verification of key passes of the translation [14] and are investigating different ways to improve the efficiency of proof search for larger programs.

Our next steps comprise the following: (1) filling in the remaining gaps in translation relations (such as covering mutually recursive datatypes); (2) complete all decision procedures; (3) drive the semantic verification forward; and (4) develop techniques to further automate our approach and improve the efficiency of the certifier.

The first three steps pose a significant amount of work, but we do not expect major new conceptual questions or obstacles. This is different for Step (4), where we anticipate the need for further research work. This includes more compositional definitions of the translation relations, such that we can generate at least part of the decision procedures (semi-)automatically. Moreover, we already perceive efficiency to be a bottleneck and we plan to work on optimising the proof search. Finally, we plan to apply our approach to the first part of the Plutus Tx compiler (Haskell subset to GHC Core).

References

1. Abadi, M., Cardelli, L., Plotkin, G.: Types for the Scott numerals (1993)
2. Ahmed, A.: Step-indexed syntactic logical relations for recursive and quantified types. In: Sestoft, P. (ed.) ESOP 2006. LNCS, vol. 3924, pp. 69–83. Springer, Heidelberg (2006). https://doi.org/10.1007/11693024_6
3. Anand, A., et al.: CertiCoq: a verified compiler for Coq. In: The Third International Workshop on Coq for Programming Languages (CoqPL) (2017)
4. Annenkov, D., Nielsen, J.B., Spitters, B.: ConCert: a smart contract certification framework in Coq. In: Proceedings of the 9th ACM SIGPLAN International Conference on Certified Programs and Proofs, pp. 215–228 (2020)
5. Maffei, M., Ryan, M. (eds.): POST 2017. LNCS, vol. 10204. Springer, Heidelberg (2017). https://doi.org/10.1007/978-3-662-54455-6
6. Barras, B., et al.: The Coq proof assistant reference manual: Version 6.1. Ph.D. thesis, Inria (1997)
7. Barthe, G., Fournet, C., Grégoire, B., Strub, P.Y., Swamy, N., Zanella-Béguelin, S.: Probabilistic relational verification for cryptographic implementations. ACM SIGPLAN Not. **49**(1), 193–205 (2014)
8. Bernardo, B., Cauderlier, R., Hu, Z., Pesin, B., Tesson, J.: Mi-Cho-Coq, a framework for certifying tezos smart contracts. In: Sekerinski, E., et al. (eds.) FM 2019. LNCS, vol. 12232, pp. 368–379. Springer, Cham (2020). https://doi.org/10.1007/978-3-030-54994-7_28
9. Bertot, Y., Castéran, P.: Interactive Theorem Proving and Program Development: Coq'Art: The Calculus of Inductive Constructions. Springer, Heidelberg (2013). https://doi.org/10.1007/978-3-662-07964-5
10. Bhargavan, K., et al.: Formal verification of smart contracts: short paper. In: Proceedings of the 2016 ACM Workshop on Programming Languages and Analysis for Security, pp. 91–96 (2016)
11. Breitner, J., Spector-Zabusky, A., Li, Y., Rizkallah, C., Wiegley, J., Weirich, S.: Ready, set, verify! applying hs-to-coq to real-world Haskell code (experience report). In: Proceedings of the ACM on Programming Languages 2(ICFP), pp. 1–16 (2018)
12. Buterin, V.: CRITICAL UPDATE Re: DAO Vulnerability (2016). https://blog.ethereum.org/2016/06/17/critical-update-re-dao-vulnerability/, Accessed 10 Dec 2021
13. Hutton, G. (ed.): MPC 2019. LNCS, vol. 11825. Springer, Cham (2019). https://doi.org/10.1007/978-3-030-33636-3
14. Dral, J.: Verified Compiler Optimisations. Master's thesis, Utrecht University (2022)
15. GHC Team: GHC 9.0 User Manual. https://downloads.haskell.org/~ghc/9.0.1/docs/html/users_guide/extending_ghc.html
16. Giegerich, R., Möncke, U.: Invariance of approximative semantics with respect to program transformations. In: GI-11. Jahrestagung, pp. 1–10. Springer, Heidelberg (1981). https://doi.org/10.1007/978-3-662-01089-1_1
17. Gonthier, G., Le, R.S.: An Ssreflect Tutorial. Ph.D. thesis, INRIA (2009)
18. IOHK: The Plutus Platform and Marlowe 1.0.0 documentation. https://plutus.readthedocs.io/en/latest/plutus/tutorials/plutus-tx.html
19. Jones, M.P., Gkoumas, V., Kireev, R., MacKenzie, K., Nester, C., Wadler, P.: Unraveling recursion: compiling an IR with recursion to system F. In: Hutton, G. (ed.) MPC 2019. LNCS, vol. 11825, pp. 414–443. Springer, Cham (2019). https://doi.org/10.1007/978-3-030-33636-3_15

20. Kumar, R., Myreen, M.O., Norrish, M., Owens, S.: CakeML: a verified implementation of ML. ACM SIGPLAN Not. **49**(1), 179–191 (2014)
21. Leroy, X., Blazy, S., Kästner, D., Schommer, B., Pister, M., Ferdinand, C.: CompCert–a formally verified optimizing compiler. In: ERTS 2016: Embedded Real Time Software and Systems, 8th European Congress (2016)
22. Li, J.M., Appel, A.W.: Deriving efficient program transformations from rewrite rules. Proc. ACM Program. Lang. **5**(ICFP), 1–29 (2021)
23. Necula, G.C.: Proof-carrying code. In: Proceedings of the 24th ACM SIGPLAN-SIGACT Symposium on Principles of Programming Languages, pp. 106–119 (1997)
24. Necula, G.C., Lee, P.: The design and implementation of a certifying compiler. SIGPLAN Not. **39**(4), 612–625 (2004)
25. O'Connor, L., et al.: Cogent: uniqueness types and certifying compilation. J. Funct. Program. **31**, e25 (2021)
26. Lahiri, S.K., Wang, C. (eds.): CAV 2020. LNCS, vol. 12224. Springer, Cham (2020). https://doi.org/10.1007/978-3-030-53288-8
27. Pnueli, A., Siegel, M., Singerman, E.: Translation validation. In: Steffen, B. (ed.) TACAS 1998. LNCS, vol. 1384, pp. 151–166. Springer, Heidelberg (1998). https://doi.org/10.1007/BFb0054170
28. Sozeau, M., et al.: The MetaCoq project. J. Autom. Reas. **64**, 947–999 (2020)
29. Spector-Zabusky, A., Breitner, J., Rizkallah, C., Weirich, S.: Total Haskell is reasonable Coq. In: Proceedings of the 7th ACM SIGPLAN International Conference on Certified Programs and Proofs, pp. 14–27 (2018)

Zipping Strategies and Attribute Grammars

José Nuno Macedo[1(✉)], Marcos Viera[2], and João Saraiva[1]

[1] Department of Informatics and HASLab/INESC TEC, University of Minho,
Braga, Portugal
`jose.n.macedo@inesctec.pt`, `saraiva@di.uminho.pt`
[2] Universidad de la República, Montevideo, Uruguay
`mviera@fing.edu.uy`

Abstract. Strategic term rewriting and attribute grammars are two powerful programming techniques widely used in language engineering. The former relies on *strategies* (recursion schemes) to apply term rewrite rules in defining transformations, while the latter is suitable for expressing context-dependent language processing algorithms. Each of these techniques, however, is usually implemented by its own powerful and large processor system. As a result, it makes such systems harder to extend and to combine.

We present the embedding of both strategic tree rewriting and attribute grammars in a zipper-based, purely functional setting. The embedding of the two techniques in the same setting has several advantages: First, we easily combine/zip attribute grammars and strategies, thus providing language engineers the best of the two worlds. Second, the combined embedding is easier to maintain and extend since it is written in a concise and uniform setting. We show the expressive power of our library in optimizing Haskell let expressions, expressing several Haskell refactorings and solving several language processing tasks for an Oberon-0 compiler.

Keywords: Attribute grammars · Zippers · Strategic term rewriting

1 Introduction

Since Algol was designed in the 60's, as the first high-level programming language [38], languages have evolved dramatically. In fact, modern languages offer powerful syntactic and semantic mechanisms that improve programmers productivity. In response to such developments, the software language engineering community also developed advanced techniques to specify such new mechanisms.

Strategic term rewriting [19] and Attribute Grammars (AG) [14] have a long history in supporting the development of modern software language analysis, transformations and optimizations. The former relies on *strategies* (recursion schemes) to traverse a tree while applying a set of rewrite rules, while

M. Hanus and A. Igarashi (Eds.): FLOPS 2022, LNCS 13215, pp. 112–132, 2022.
https://doi.org/10.1007/978-3-030-99461-7_7

the latter is suitable to express context-dependent language processing algorithms. Many language engineering systems have been developed supporting both AGs [8,9,11,16,23,26,36] and rewriting strategies [4–6,17,30,37]. These powerful systems, however, are large systems supporting their own AG or strategic specification language, thus requiring a considerable development effort to extend and combine.

A more flexible approach is obtained when we consider the embedding of such techniques in a general purpose language. Language embeddings, however, usually rely on advanced mechanisms of the host language, which makes them difficult to combine. For example, Strafunski [17] offers a powerful embedding of strategic term rewriting in Haskell, but it can not be easily combined with the Haskell embedding of AGs as provided in [21,25]. The former works directly on the underlying tree, while the latter on a *zipper* representation of the tree.

In this paper, we present the embedding of both strategic tree rewriting and attribute grammars in a zipper-based, purely functional setting. Generic zippers [12] is a simple generic tree-walk mechanism to navigate on both homogeneous and heterogeneous data structures. Traversals on heterogeneous data structures (i.e. data structures composed of different data structures) is the main ingredient of both strategies and AGs. Thus, zippers provide the building block mechanism we will reuse for expressing the purely-functional embedding of both techniques. The embedding of the two techniques in the same setting has several advantages: First, we easily combine/zip attribute grammars and strategies, thus providing language engineers the best of the two worlds. Second, the combined embedding is easier to maintain and extend since it is written in a concise and uniform setting. This results in a very small library (200 lines of Haskell code) which is able to express advanced (static) analyses and transformation tasks. The purpose of this paper is three-fold:

- Firstly, we present a simple, yet powerful embedding of strategic term rewriting using generic zippers. This results in a concise library, named Ztrategic, that is easy to maintain and update. Moreover, our embedding has the expressiveness of the Strafunski library [17], as we showcase in Sect. 4.
- Secondly, this new strategic term rewriting embedding can easily be combined with an existing zipper-based embedding of attribute grammars [10,22]. By relying on the same generic tree-traversal mechanism, the zipper, (zipper-based) strategies can access (zipper-based) AG functional definitions, and vice versa. Such a joint embedding results in a multi-paradigm embedding of the two language engineering techniques. We show two examples of the expressive power of such embedding: First, we access attribute values in strategies to express non-trivial context-dependent tree rewriting. Second, strategies are used to define *attribute propagation patterns* [8,11], which are widely used to eliminate (polluting) copy rules from AGs.
- Thirdly, we apply Ztrategic in real language engineering problems, namely, in optimizing Haskell let expressions, expressing a set of refactorings that eliminate several Haskell smells, and solving the LDTA Tool Challenge [35] tasks for name binding, type checking and desugaring of Oberon-0 programs.

This paper is organized as follows: Sect. 2 presents generic zippers and describes Ztrategic, our zipper-based embedding of strategic term rewriting. In Sect. 3, we describe zipper-based embedding of attribute grammars and we show how the two techniques/embeddings can be easily combined. In Sect. 4 we use the library to define several usage examples, such as refactorings of Haskell source code and name binding, type checking and desugaring Oberon-0 source code. Section 5 discusses related work, and in Sect. 6 we present our conclusions.

2 Ztrategic: Zipper-Based Strategic Programming

Before we present our embedding in detail later in the section, let us consider a motivating example we will use throughout the paper. Consider the (sub)language of *Let* expressions as incorporated into most functional languages, including Haskell. Next, we show an example of a valid Haskell **let** expression and we define the heterogeneous data type *Let*, taken from [22], that models such expressions in Haskell itself.

$$
\begin{array}{ll}
p = \textbf{let}\ a = b + 0 & \textbf{data}\ Let\ = Let\ List\ Exp \\
\qquad c = 2 & \textbf{data}\ List = NestedLet\ String\ Let\ List \\
\qquad b = \textbf{let}\ c = 3\ \textbf{in}\ c + c & \quad\ |\ Assign\quad String\ Exp\ List \\
\textbf{in}\ \ a + 7 - c & \quad\ |\ EmptyList \\
& \textbf{data}\ Exp = Add\ Exp\ Exp\ |\ Sub\ Exp\ Exp \\
& \quad\ |\ Neg\ Exp\ |\ Const\ Int\ |\ Var\ String
\end{array}
$$

We can write p as a Haskell value with type *Let*:

$$
\begin{array}{l}
p = Let\ (Assign\quad \texttt{"a"}\ (Add\ (Var\ \texttt{"b"})\ (Const\ 0)) \\
\qquad\quad (Assign\quad \texttt{"c"}\ (Const\ 2) \\
\qquad\quad (NestedLet\ \texttt{"b"}\ (Let\ (Assign\ \texttt{"c"}\ (Const\ 3)\ EmptyList) \\
\qquad\qquad\qquad\qquad\qquad (Add\ (Var\ \texttt{"c"})\ (Var\ \texttt{"c"}))) \\
\qquad\quad EmptyList))) \\
\qquad\quad (Sub\ (Add\ (Var\ \texttt{"a"})\ (Const\ 7))\ (Var\ \texttt{"c"}))
\end{array}
$$

Consider now that we wish to implement a simple arithmetic optimizer for our language. Let us start with a trivial optimization: the elimination of additions with 0. In this context, strategic term rewriting is an extremely suitable formalism, since it provides a solution that just defines the work to be done in the constructors (tree nodes) of interest, and "ignores" all the others. In our example, the optimization is defined in *Add* nodes, and thus we express the worker function as follows:

$$
\begin{array}{ll}
expr :: Exp \rightarrow Maybe\ Exp \\
expr\ (Add\ e\ (Const\ 0)) = Just\ e \\
expr\ (Add\ (Const\ 0)\ e) = Just\ e \\
expr\ \_ \qquad\qquad\qquad = Nothing
\end{array}
$$

The first two alternatives define the optimization: when either of the sub-expressions of an *Add* expression is the constant 0, then it returns the other sub-expression. A type-specific transformation function returns a *Maybe* result, transformations that fail or do not change the input return *Nothing*. This is the case of the last alternative of *expr*, that defines the default behaviour.

This function applies to *Exp* nodes only. To express our *Let* optimization, however, we need a generic mechanism that traverses *Let* trees, applying this function when visiting *Add* expressions. This is where strategic term rewriting comes to the rescue: It provides recursion patterns (*i.e.*, strategies) to traverse the (generic) tree, like, for example, top-down or bottom-up traversals. It also includes functions to apply a node specific rewriting function (like *expr*) according to a given strategy. Next, we show the strategic solution of our optimization where *expr* is applied to the input tree in a full top-down strategy. This is a Type Preserving (*TP*) transformation since the input and result trees have the same type:

$$opt :: \textbf{Zipper } Let \rightarrow Maybe \ (\textbf{Zipper } Let)$$
$$opt \ t = applyTP \ (full\_tdTP \ step) \ t$$
$$\textbf{where } step = idTP \ `adhocTP` \ expr$$

We have just presented our first zipper-based strategic function. Here, *step* is a transformation to be applied by function *applyTP* to all nodes of the input tree *t* (of type **Zipper** *Let*) using a full top-down traversal scheme (function *full_tdTP*). The rewrite step behaves like the identity function (*idTP*) by default with our *expr* function to perform the type-specific transformation, and the *adhocTP* combinator joins them into a single function.

This strategic solution relies on our Ztrategic [20] library: a purely functional embedding of strategic term rewriting in Haskell. In this solution we clearly see that the traversal function *full_tdTP* needs to navigate heterogeneous trees, as it is the case of the *Let* expression *p*. In a functional programming setting, zippers [12] provide a simple, but generic tree-walk mechanism that we will use to embed strategic programming in Haskell. In fact, our strategic combinators work with zippers as in the definition of *opt*. In the remaining of this section, we start by briefly describing zippers, and, next, we present in detail the embedding of strategies using this powerful mechanism.

2.1   The Zipper Data Structure

Zippers were introduced by Huet [12] to represent a tree together with a subtree that is the *focus* of attention. During a computation the focus may move left, up, down or right within the tree. Generic manipulation of a zipper is provided through a set of predefined functions that allow access to all of the nodes of a tree for inspection or modification.

A generic implementation of this concept is available as the *generic zipper* Haskell library [1], which works for both homogeneous and heterogeneous data types. In order to illustrate the use of zippers, let us consider again the tree used as an example for our *Let* program. We build a zipper t_1 from the previous *Let* expression p through the use of the **toZipper** :: *Data* $a \Rightarrow a \to$ **Zipper** a function. This function produces a zipper out of any data type, requiring only that the data types have an instance of the *Data* and *Typeable* type classes[1].

$t_1 = $ **toZipper** p

We can navigate t_1 using pre-defined functions from the zipper library. The function **down'** moves the focus down to the leftmost child of a node, while **down** moves the focus to the rightmost child instead. Similarly, functions **right**, **left** and **up**, move towards the corresponding directions. They all have type **Zipper** $a \to Maybe$ (**Zipper** a), meaning that such functions take a zipper and return a new zipper in case the navigation does not fail.

Finally, the zipper function **getHole** :: *Typeable* $b \Rightarrow$ **Zipper** $a \to Maybe\ b$ extracts the actual node the zipper is focusing on. Notice that the type of the hole (b) can be different than the type of the root of the Zipper (a), since the tree can be heterogeneous. Using these functions, we can freely navigate through this newly created zipper. Consider our expression p, we can *unsafely*[2] move the focus of the zipper towards the $b+0$ subexpression and obtain its value as follows:

sumBZero :: *Maybe Exp*
sumBZero = (**getHole** . *fromJust* . **right** . *fromJust* . **down'** . *fromJust* . **down'**) t_1

The zipper library also contains functions for the transformation of the data structure being traversed. The function **trans** :: *GenericT* $\to$ **Zipper** $a \to$ **Zipper** a applies a generic transformation to the node the zipper is currently pointing to; while **transM** :: *GenericM* $m \to$ **Zipper** $a \to m$ (**Zipper** a) applies a generic monadic transformation.

2.2 Strategic Programming

In this section we introduce Ztrategic, our embedding of strategic programming using generic zippers. The embedding directly follows the work of Laemmel and Visser [17] on the Strafunski library [18].

We start by defining a function that elevates a transformation to the zipper level. In other words, we define how a function that is supposed to operate directly on one data type is converted into a zipper transformation.

zTryApplyM :: (*Typeable* a, *Typeable* b) $\Rightarrow$ ($a \to Maybe\ b$) $\to TP\ c$

The definition of *zTryApplyM*, which we omit for brevity, relies on transformations on zippers, thus reusing the generic zipper library **transM** function.

---

[1] These can be easily obtained via the Haskell data type **deriving** mechanism.

[2] By using the function *fromJust* :: *Maybe* $a \to a$ we assume a *Just* value is returned.

zTryApplyM returns a *TP c*, in which *TP* is a type for specifying Type-Preserving transformations on zippers, and *c* is the type of the zipper. For example, if we are applying transformations on a zipper built upon the *Let* data type, then those transformations are of type *TP Let*.

type *TP a* = **Zipper** *a* → *Maybe* (**Zipper** *a*)

Very much like Strafunski, we introduce the type *TU m d* for Type-Unifying operations, which aim to gather data of type *d* into the data structure *m*.

type *TU m d* = (*forall a* . **Zipper** *a* → *m d*)

For example, to collect in a list all the defined names in a *Let* expression, the corresponding type-unifying strategy would be of type *TU* [] *String*. We will present such a transformation and implement it later in this section.

Next, we define a combinator to compose two transformations, building a more complex zipper transformation that tries to apply each of the initial transformations in sequence, skipping transformations that fail.

adhocTP :: *Typeable a* ⇒ *TP e* → (*a* → *Maybe a*) → *TP e*
adhocTP f g z = *maybeKeep f* (*zTryApplyM g*) *z*

The *adhocTP* function receives transformations *f* and *g* as parameters, as well as zipper *z*. It converts *g*, which is a simple (*i.e.* non-zipper) Haskell function, into a zipper. Then, the zipper transformations *f* and *g* are passed as arguments to *maybeKeep*, which is an auxiliary function that applies the transformations in sequence, discarding either failing transformation (*i.e.* that produces *Nothing*). We omit the definition of *maybeKeep* for brevity.

Next, we use *adhocTP*, written as an infix operator, which combines the zipper function *failTP* with our basic transformation *expr* function:

step = *failTP* '*adhocTP*' *expr*

Thus, we do not need to express type-specific transformations as functions that work on zippers. It is the use of *zTryApplyM* in *adhocTP* that transforms a Haskell function (*expr* in this case) to a zipper one, hidden from these definitions.

The transformation *failTP* is a pre-defined transformation that always fails (returning *Nothing*) and *idTP* is the identity transformation that always succeeds (returning the input unchanged). They provide the basis for construction of complex transformations through composition. We omit here their simple definitions.

The functions we have presented already allow the definition of arbitrarily complex transformations for zippers. Such transformations, however, are always applied on the node the zipper is focusing on. Let us consider a combinator that navigates in the zipper.

$allTPright :: TP\ a \rightarrow TP\ a$
$allTPright\ f\ z = $ **case right** z **of**
$\qquad\qquad\quad Nothing \rightarrow return\ z$
$\qquad\qquad\quad Just\ r \quad \rightarrow fmap\ (fromJust\ .\ \textbf{left})\ (f\ r)$

This function is a combinator that, given a type-preserving transformation f for zipper z, will attempt to apply f to the node that is located to the right of the node the zipper is pointing to. To do this, the zipper function **right** is used to try to navigate to the right; if it fails, we return the original zipper. If it succeeds, we apply transformation f and then we navigate **left** again. There is a similar combinator $allTPdown$ that navigates downwards and then upwards.

With all these tools at our disposal, we can define generic traversal schemes by combining them. Next, we define the traversal scheme used in the function opt we defined at the start of the section. This traversal scheme navigates through the whole data structure, in a top-down approach.

$full\_tdTP :: TP\ a \rightarrow TP\ a$
$full\_tdTP\ f = allTPdown\ (full\_tdTP\ f)\ `seqTP`\ allTPright\ (full\_tdTP\ f)\ `seqTP`\ f$

We skip the explanation of the $seqTP$ operator as it is relatively similar to the $adhocTP$ operator we described before, albeit simpler; we interpret this as a sequence operator. This function receives as input a type-preserving transformation f, and (reading the code from right to left) it applies it to the focused node itself, then to the nodes below the currently focused node, then to the nodes to the right of the focused node. To apply this transformation to the nodes below the current node, for example, we use the $allTPdown$ combinator we mentioned above, and we recursively apply $full\_tdTP\ f$ to the node below. The same logic applies in regards to navigating to the right.

We can define several traversal schemes similar to this one by changing the combinators used, or their sequence. For example, by inverting the order in which the combinators are sequenced, we define a bottom-up traversal. By using different combinators, we can define choice, allowing for partial traversals in the data structure. We previously defined a rewrite strategy where we use $full\_tdTP$ to define a full, top-down traversal, which is not ideal. Because we intend to optimize Exp nodes, changing one node might make it possible to optimize the node above, which would have already been processed in a top-down traversal. Instead, we define a different traversal scheme, for repeated application of a transformation until a fixed point is reached:

$innermost :: TP\ a \rightarrow TP\ a$
$innermost\ s = repeatTP\ (once\_buTP\ s)$

We omit the definitions of $once\_buTP$ and $repeatTP$ as they are similar to the presented definitions. The combinator $repeatTP$ applies a given transformation repeatedly until a fixed point is reached, that is, until the data structure stops

$$expr :: Exp \rightarrow Maybe\ Exp$$
$$expr\ (Add\ e\ (Const\ 0)) \qquad\qquad = Just\ e$$
$$expr\ (Add\ (Const\ 0)\ t) \qquad\qquad = Just\ t$$
$$expr\ (Add\ (Const\ a)\ (Const\ b)) = Just\ (Const\ (a+b))$$
$$expr\ (Sub\ a\ b) \qquad\qquad\qquad = Just\ (Add\ a\ (Neg\ b))$$
$$expr\ (Neg\ (Neg\ f)) \qquad\qquad\ = Just\ f$$
$$expr\ (Neg\ (Const\ n)) \qquad\quad\ = Just\ (Const\ (-n))$$
$$expr\ \_ \qquad\qquad\qquad\qquad\quad = Nothing$$

$$add(e, const(0)) \rightarrow e \qquad\qquad (1)$$
$$add(const(0), e) \rightarrow e \qquad\qquad (2)$$
$$add(const(a), const(b)) \rightarrow const(a+b) \qquad (3)$$
$$sub(e1, e2) \rightarrow add(e1, neg(e2)) \qquad (4)$$
$$neg(neg(e)) \rightarrow e \qquad\qquad (5)$$
$$neg(const(a)) \rightarrow const(-a) \qquad (6)$$
$$var(id)\ |\ (id, just(e)) \in env \rightarrow e \qquad (7)$$

Fig. 1. Optimization rules

being changed by the transformation. The transformation being applied repeatedly is defined with the *once_buTP* combinator, which applies s once, anywhere on the data structure. When the application *once_buTP* fails, *repeatTP* understands a fixed point is reached. Because the *once_buTP* bottom-up combinator is used, the traversal scheme is *innermost*, since it prioritizes the innermost nodes. The pre-defined *outermost* strategy uses the *once_tdTP* combinator instead.

Let us return to our *Let* running example. Obviously there are more arithmetic rules that we may use to optimize let expressions. In Fig. 1 we present the rules given in [15].

In our definition of the function *expr*, we already defined rewriting rules for optimizations 1 and 2. Rules 3 through 6 can also be trivially defined in Haskell:

$$expr :: Exp \rightarrow Maybe\ Exp$$
$$expr\ (Add\ e\ (Const\ 0)) \qquad\qquad = Just\ e$$
$$expr\ (Add\ (Const\ 0)\ t) \qquad\qquad = Just\ t$$
$$expr\ (Add\ (Const\ a)\ (Const\ b)) = Just\ (Const\ (a+b))$$
$$expr\ (Sub\ a\ b) \qquad\qquad\qquad = Just\ (Add\ a\ (Neg\ b))$$
$$expr\ (Neg\ (Neg\ f)) \qquad\qquad\ = Just\ f$$
$$expr\ (Neg\ (Const\ n)) \qquad\quad\ = Just\ (Const\ (-n))$$
$$expr\ \_ \qquad\qquad\qquad\qquad\quad = Nothing$$

Rule 7, however, is context dependent and it is not easily expressed within strategic term rewriting. In fact, this rule requires to first compute the environment where a name is used (according to the scope rules of the *Let* language). We will return to this rule in Sect. 3.

Having expressed all rewriting rules from 1 to 6 in function *expr*, now we need to use our strategic combinators that navigate in the tree while applying the rules. To guarantee that all the possible optimizations are applied we use an *innermost* traversal scheme. Thus, our optimization is expressed as:

$$opt' :: \textbf{Zipper } Let \rightarrow Maybe \ (\textbf{Zipper } Let)$$
$$opt' \ t = applyTP \ (innermost \ step) \ t$$
$$\textbf{where } step = failTP \ `adhocTP` \ expr$$

Function *opt'* combines all the steps we have built until now. We define an auxiliary function *step*, which is the composition of the *failTP* default failing strategy with *expr*, the optimization function; we compose them with *adhocTP*. Our resulting Type-Preserving strategy will be *innermost step*, which applies *step* to the zipper repeatedly until a fixed-point is reached. The use of *failTP* as the default strategy is required, as *innermost* reaches the fixed-point when *step* fails. If we use *idTP* instead, *step* always succeeds, resulting in an infinite loop. We apply this strategy using the function *applyTP* :: *TP c* $\rightarrow$ **Zipper** *c* $\rightarrow$ *Maybe* (**Zipper** *c*), which effectively applies a strategy to a zipper. This function is defined in our library, but we omit the code as it is trivial.

Next, we show an example using a Type-Unifying strategy. We define a function *names* that collects all defined names in a *Let* expression. First, we define a function *select* that focuses on the *Let* tree nodes where names are defined, namely, *Assign* and *NestedLet*. This function returns a singleton list (with the defined name) when applied to these nodes, and an empty list in the other cases.

$$select :: List \rightarrow [String]$$
$$select \ (Assign \ s \ \_ \ \_) \quad = [s]$$
$$select \ (NestedLet \ s \ \_ \ \_) = [s]$$
$$select \ \_ \qquad\qquad = [\,]$$

Now, *names* is a Type-Unifying function that traverses a given *Let* tree (inside a zipper, in our case), and produces a list with the declared names.

$$names \ :: \textbf{Zipper } Let \rightarrow [String]$$
$$names \ r = applyTU \ (full\_tdTU \ step) \ r$$
$$\textbf{where } step = failTU \ `adhocTU` \ select$$

The traversal strategy influences the order of the names in the resulting list. We use a top-down traversal so that the list result follows the order of the input. This is to say that *names* $t_1 \equiv$ ["a", "c", "b", "c"] (a bottom-up strategy produces the reverse of this list).

As we have shown, our strategic term rewriting functions rely on zippers built upon the data (trees) to be traversed. This results in strategic functions that can easily be combined with a zipper-based embedding of attribute grammars [10,22], since both functions/embedding work on zippers. In the next section we present in detail the zipping of strategies and AGs.

3   Strategic Attribute Grammars

Zipper-based strategic term rewriting provides a powerful mechanism to express tree transformations. There are, however, transformations that rely on contextual information that needs to be collected so the transformation can be applied. Our optimization rule 7 of Fig. 1 is such an example. In this section we will briefly explain the Zipper-based embedding of attribute grammars, through the *Let* example. Then, we are going to explain how to combine strategies and AGs, ending with an implementation of rule 7.

3.1   Zipper-Based Attribute Grammars

The attribute grammar formalism is particularly suitable for specifying language-based algorithms, where contextual information needs to be collected before it can be used. Language-based algorithms such as name analysis [22], pretty printing [34], type inference [24], etc. are elegantly specified using AGs.

Our running example is no exception and the name analysis task of *Let* is a non-trivial one. Despite being a concise example, it has central characteristics of software languages, such as (nested) block-based structures and mandatory but unique declarations of names. In addition, the semantics of this implementation of *Let* does not force a declare-before-use discipline, meaning that a variable can be declared after its first use. Consequently, a conventional implementation of name analysis naturally leads to a processor that traverses each block twice: once for processing the declarations of names and constructing an environment and a second time to process the uses of names (using the computed environment) in order to check for the use of non-declared identifiers. The uniqueness of identifiers is efficiently checked in the first traversal: for each newly encountered name it is checked whether that it has already been declared at the same lexical level (block). As a consequence, semantic errors resulting from duplicate definitions are computed during the first traversal, and errors resulting from missing declarations in the second one. In fact, expressing this straightforward algorithm is a complex task in most programming paradigms, since it requires a complex scheduling of tree traversals[3], and intrusive code may be needed to pass information computed in one traversal to a specific node and used in a subsequent one[4].

In the attribute grammar paradigm, the programmer does not need to be concerned with scheduling of traversals, nor the use of intrusive code to glue traversals together. As a consequence, they do not need to adapt algorithms in order to avoid those issues. AGs associate *attributes* to grammar symbols (types in a functional setting), which are called *synthesized attributes* if they are computed bottom-up or *inherited attributes* if they are computed top-down.

---

[3] Note that only after building the environment of an outer block can nested ones be traversed: they inherited that environment. Thus, traversals are intermingled.

[4] This is the case when we wish to produce a list of errors that follows the sequential structure of the input program [27].

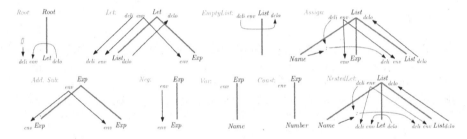

Fig. 2. Attribute grammar specifying the scope rules òf *Let*

$dclo :: \textbf{Zipper}\ Root \to Env$
$dclo\ t = \textbf{case}\ (constructor\ t)\ \textbf{of}$
  $Let_{Let}\qquad\quad \to dclo\ (t.\$1)$
  $NestedLet_{List} \to dclo\ (t.\$3)$
  $Assign_{List}\qquad \to dclo\ (t.\$3)$
  $EmptyList_{List} \to dcli\ t$

$lev :: \textbf{Zipper}\ Root \to Int$
$lev\ t = \textbf{case}\ (constructor\ t)\ \textbf{of}$
  $Let_{Let} \to \textbf{case}\ (constructor\ (parent\ t))\ \textbf{of}$
    $NestedLet_{List} \to (lev\ (parent\ t)) + 1$
    $Root_{Root} \to 0$
    $\_\qquad\quad \to lev\ (parent\ t)$

$dcli :: \textbf{Zipper}\ Root \to Env$
$dcli\ t = \textbf{case}\ (constructor\ t)\ \textbf{of}$
  $Let_{Let} \to \textbf{case}\ (constructor\ (parent\ t))\ \textbf{of}$
    $Root_{Root}\qquad\quad \to [\,]$
    $NestedLet_{List} \to env\ (parent\ t)$
  $\_\qquad \to \textbf{case}\ (constructor\ (parent\ t))\ \textbf{of}$
  $Let_{Let}\qquad\quad \to dcli\ (parent\ t)$

$env :: \textbf{Zipper}\ Root \to Env$
$env\ t = \textbf{case}\ (constructor\ t)\ \textbf{of}$
  $Let_{Let} \to dclo\ t$
  $\_\qquad \to env\ (parent\ t)$

  $NestedLet_{List} \to (lexeme_{Name}\ (\textbf{parent}\ t), lev\ (\textbf{parent}\ t), Nothing) : (dcli\ (\textbf{parent}\ t))$
  $Assign_{List}\qquad \to (lexeme_{Name}\ (\textbf{parent}\ t), lev\ (\textbf{parent}\ t), lexeme_{Exp}\ (\textbf{parent}\ t))$
    $: (dcli\ (\textbf{parent}\ t))$

Fig. 3. Definitions of *dclo*, *lev*, *dcli* and *env* attributes

Very much like strategic term rewriting, AGs also rely on a generic tree walk mechanism, usually called tree-walk evaluators [2], to walk up and down the tree to evaluate attributes. In fact, generic zippers also offer the necessary abstractions to express the embedding of AGs in a functional programming setting [10,22]. Next, we briefly describe this embedding, and after that we present the embedded AG that express the scope rules of *Let*. It also computes (attribute) *env*, that is needed by the optimization rule 7.

To allow programmers to write zipper-based functions as AG writers do, the generic zippers library [1] is extended with some combinators:

- The combinator "*child*", written as the infix function .$ to access the child of a tree node given its index (starting from 1).

  $(.\$) :: \textbf{Zipper}\ a \to Int \to \textbf{Zipper}\ a$

- The combinator parent to move the focus to the parent of a tree node.

  $parent :: \textbf{Zipper}\ a \to \textbf{Zipper}\ a$

Having presented these zipper-based AG combinators, we now show in Fig. 3 the scope rules specified in the *Let* AG directly as a Haskell-based AG. We also show a visual representation of the AG in Fig. 2. Productions are shown with the parent node above and children nodes below, inherited attributes are on their left and synthesized attributes on their right, and arrows show how information flows between productions and their children to compute attributes.

In this AG the inherited attribute *dcli* is used as an accumulator to collect all *Names* defined in a *Let*: it starts as an empty list in the *Root* production, and when a new *Name* is defined (productions *Assign* and *NestedLet*) it is added to the accumulator. The total list of defined *Name* is synthesized in attribute *dclo*, which at the *Root* node is passed down as the environment (inherited attribute *env*). The type of the three attributes is a list of triples, associating the *Name* to the level it is defined (used to distingish declarations with the same name) and its *Let* expression definition[5]. Thus, we define a type synonym

- **type** $Env = [(Name, Int, Maybe\ Exp)]$

We start by defining the equations of the synthesized attribute *dclo*. For each definition of an occurrence of *dclo* we define an equation in our zipper-based function. For example, in the diagrams of the *NestedLet* and *Assign* productions in Fig. 2 we see that *dclo* is defined as the *dclo* of the third child. Moreover, in production *EmptyList* attribute *dclo* is a copy of *dcli*. Let us consider the case of defining the inherited attribute *env*. In most diagrams an occurrence of attribute *env* is defined as a copy of the parent. There are two exceptions: in productions *Root* and *NestedLet* where *Let* subtrees occur. In both cases, *env* gets its value from the synthesized attribute *dclo* of the same non-terminal/type. We use the default rule of the case statement to express similar AG copy equations.

The inherited attribute *lev* is used to distinguish declarations with the same name in different scopes. We omitted this attribute in the visual AG of Fig. 2 since its equations are simple. This attribute is passed downwards as a copy of the parent node/symbol, with two exceptions: when visiting a *Let* subtree whose parent is a Root, and when visiting a *NestedLet*. In the former the (initial) level is 0, while in the latter since we are descending to a nested block, we increment the level of the outer one.

Finally, let us define now the accumulator attribute *dcli*. The zipper function, when visiting nodes of type *Let* (which have *dcli* attributes) has to consider two alternatives: the parent node can be a *Root* or a *NestedLet* (the two occurrences of *Let* as a child in the diagrams of Fig. 2). This happens because the rules to define its value differ: in the *Root* node it corresponds to an empty list (our outermost *Let* is context-free), while in a nested block, the accumulator *dcli* starts as the *env* of the outer block. When visiting all other subtrees (expressed by the default rule), we need to define the inherited attribute *dcli* of *List* subtrees. There are three different cases: when the parent is a *Let* node, *dcli* is a copy of the parent. When the parent is an *Assign* then the *Name*, *level* and the

---

[5] We will use this definition to expand the *Name* as required by optimization rule 7.

associated *Exp* are accumulated in the *dcli* of the parent. Finally, in the case of *NestedLet* the *Name*, *level* and a *Nothing* expression is accumulated in $dcli^6$.

In order to specify the complete name analysis task of *Let* expression we need to report which names violate the scope rules of the language. We can modular and incrementally extend our AG [28], and define a new attribute *errors* to report such violations. In the next section *errors* is expressed as a strategic function.

3.2   Strategic Attribute Grammars

By having embedding both strategic term rewriting and attribute grammars in the same zipper-based setting, and given that both are embedded as first-class citizens, we can easily combine these two powerful language engineering techniques. As a result, attribute computations that do useful work on few productions/nodes can be efficiently expressed via our Ztrategic library, while rewriting rules that rely on context information can access attribute values.

Accessing Attribute Values from Strategies: As we mentioned in Sect. 3, rule 7 of Fig. 1 cannot be implemented using a trivial strategy, since it depends on the context. The rule states that a variable occurrence can be changed by its definition. Thus, we need to compute an environment of definitions, which is what we have done with the attribute *env*, previously. If we had access to such attribute in the definition of a strategy, we would be able to implement this rule.

Given that both attribute grammars and strategies use the zipper to walk through the tree, such combinations can be easily performed if the strategy exposes the zipper, so it can be used to apply the given attribute. This is done in our library by the *adhocTPZ* combinator:

$$adhocTPZ :: Typeable\ a \Rightarrow TP\ e \rightarrow (a \rightarrow \textbf{Zipper}\ e \rightarrow Maybe\ a) \rightarrow TP\ e$$

Notice that instead of taking a function of type $(a \rightarrow Maybe\ a)$, as does the combinator *adhocTP* introduced in Sect. 2, it receives a function of type $(a \rightarrow \textbf{Zipper}\ e \rightarrow Maybe\ a)$, with the zipper as a parameter. Then, we can define a worker function with this type, that implements rule 7:

```
expC :: Exp → Zipper Root → Maybe Exp
expC (Var x) z = expand (i, lev z) (env z)
expC _        _ = Nothing
```

where *expand* is a simple lookup function that replaces a name *x* for its definition in the environment (given by attribute *env*). This strategic function also uses attribute *lev* to look for the current or closest scope where name *x* is defined.

---

[6] In this AG function we use boilerplate code $lexeme_{Name}$ and $lexeme_{Exp}$, which implement the so-called *syntactic references* in attribute equations [26]. They return the *Name* and *Exp* arguments of constructor *Assign*, respectively.

As a final step, we combine this rule with the previously defined *expr* (rules 1 to 6) and apply them to all nodes.

opt'' :: **Zipper** $Root \rightarrow Maybe$ (**Zipper** $Root$)
$opt''\ r = applyTP\ (innermost\ (failTP\ `adhocTPZ'\ expC\ `adhocTP'\ expr))\ r$

Synthesizing Attributes via Strategies: We showed how attributes and strategies are combined by using the former while defining the latter. Now we show how to combine them the other way around; i.e. to express attribute computations as strategies. As an example, let us define the *errors* attribute, that returns the list of names that violate the scope rules. Note that duplicated definitions are efficiently detected when a new *Name* (defined in nodes *Assign* and *NestedLet*) is accumulated in *dcli*. The newly defined *Name must not be in* the environment *dcli* accumulated prior to that definition. Invalid uses are detected when a *Name* is used in an arithmetic expression (*Exp*). In this case, the *Name must be in*[7] the accumulated environment *env*. This is expressed by the following zipper functions:

$decls$ :: $List \rightarrow$ **Zipper** $Root \rightarrow [Name]$
$decls\ (Assign\quad \_\,\_\,\_)\ z = mNBIn\ (lexeme_{Name}\ z, lev\ z)\ (dcli\ z)$
$decls\ (NestedLet\ \_\,\_\,\_)\ z = mNBIn\ (lexeme_{Name}\ z, lev\ z)\ (dcli\ z)$
$decls\ \_\,\_\qquad\qquad = []$

$uses$ :: $Exp \rightarrow$ **Zipper** $Root \rightarrow [Name]$
$uses\ (Var\ \_)\ z = mBIn\ (lexeme_{Name}\ z)\ (env\ z)$
$uses\ \_\ z\qquad = []$

Now, we define a type-unifying strategy that produces the list of errors.

$errors$ :: **Zipper** $Root \rightarrow [Name]$
$errors\ t = applyTU\ (full\_tdTU\ (failTU\ `adhocTUZ'\ uses\ `adhocTUZ'\ decls))\ t$

Although the applied function combines *decls* and *uses* in this order, the resulting list does not report duplicates first, and invalid uses after. The strategic function *adhocTUZ* combines the two functions and the default failing function into one, which is applied while traversing the tree in a top-down traversal, producing the errors in the order they occur. If we define *errors* as an attribute, most of the attribute equations are just propagating attribute values upwards without doing useful work! This is particularly relevant when we consider the *Let* sub-language as part of a real programming language (such as Haskell with its 116 constructors across 30 data types). Thus, combining attribute grammars with strategic term rewriting allows the leverage of the best of both worlds.

---

[7] Functions *mNBIn* and *mBIn* are trivial lookup functions. They are presented in [20].

4   Expressiveness and Performance

In order to evaluate our combined zipper-based embedding of attribute grammars and strategic term-rewriting we consider three language engineering problems: First, we define a refactoring that eliminates the monadic *do-notation* from Haskell programs. Second, we evaluate the performance of our library by comparing the runtimes of an implementation in Ztrategic of a Haskell smell eliminator with its Strafunski counterpart when processing a large set of smelly Haskell programs. Third, we express in Ztrategic the largest language specification developed in this setting: the Oberon-0 language. The construction of a processor for Oberon-0 was proposed in the LDTA Tool Challenge [35], and it was concisely and efficiently specified using AGs and strategies in Kiama [31].

Do-Notation Elimination: We start by defining a refactoring that eliminates the syntactic sugar introduced by the monadic *do-notation*. In order to automate this refactoring, a type-preserving strategy is used to perform a full traversal in the Haskell tree, since such expressions can be arbitrarily nested. The rewrite step behaves like the identity function by default with a type-specific case for pattern matching the *do-notation* in the Haskell tree (constructor *HsDo*).

The following type-specific transformation function *doElim* just matches *HsDo* nodes and returns the correct desugared node, expressed at abstract syntax tree level. We omit the details of its representation as Haskell data types.

```
refactor :: Zipper HsModule → Maybe (Zipper HsModule)
refactor h = applyTP (innermost step) h where step = failTP 'adhocTP' doElim

doElim   :: HsExp → Maybe HsExp
doElim (HsDo [HsQualifier e])              = Just e
doElim (HsDo (HsQualifier e : stmts))
    = Just ((HsInfixApp e (HsQVarOp (hsSymbol ">>")) (HsDo stmts)))
doElim (HsDo (HsGenerator _ p e : stmts)) = Just (letPattern p e stmts)
doElim (HsDo (HsLetStmt decls : stmts))   = Just (HsLet decls (HsDo stmts))
doElim _                                  = Nothing
```

We conclude that our library allows for the definition of powerful source code transformations in a concise manner. We also include a list desugaring implementation in our work's repository.

Smells Elimination: Source code smells make code harder to comprehend. A smell is not an error, but it indicates a bad programming practice. For example, inexperienced Haskell programmers often write $l \equiv [\,]$ to check whether a list is empty, instead of using the predefined *null* function. Next, we present a strategic function that eliminates several Haskell smells as reported in [7].

```
smellElim h = applyTP (innermost step) h
    where step = failTP 'adhocTP' joinList 'adhocTP' nullList
                 'adhocTP' redundantBoolean 'adhocTP' reduntantIf
```

where *joinList* detects patterns where list concatenations are inefficiently defined, *nullList* detects patterns where a list is checked for emptiness, *redundantBoolean* detects redundant boolean checks, and *reduntantIf* detects redundant **if** clauses.

In order to assess the runtime performance of our zipper-based strategic term rewriting implementation, we compare it with the state-of-the-art, fully optimized Strafunski system. A detailed analysis of runtime performance of the zipper-based embedding of AGs is presented in [10], in which *memoized* zipper-based attribute grammars with very large inputs are benchmarked, showing that this AG embedding is not only concise and elegant, but also efficient.

Let us consider the Haskell smell eliminator expressed in both Ztrategic and Strafunski. To run both tools with large *smelly* inputs, we consider 150 Haskell projects developed by first-year students as presented in [3]. In these projects there are 1139 Haskell files totaling 82124 lines of code, of which exactly 1000 files were syntactically correct[8]. Both Ztrategic and Strafunski smell eliminators detected and eliminated 850 code smells in those files. To compare the runtime performance of both implementations, we computed an average of 5 runs, on a Ubuntu 16.04 machine, i5-7200U Dual Core, with 8 GB RAM. In this case, the very first version of Ztrategic, while being more expressive, is only 60% slower than the Strafunski library (Table 1).

Table 1. Haskell smell eliminators in Ztrategic and Strafunski.

	Ztrategic	Strafunski
Lines of code	22	22
Runtime	16.2 s	10.2 s
Average memory	6607 Kb	6580 Kb

Oberon-0 in Ztrategic: The LDTA Tool Challenge [35] was a challenge focused on the construction of a compiler for the Oberon-0 language, with the goal of comparing the formalisms and toolsets used in it. The challenge was divided into 5 tasks: parsing and pretty-printing, name binding, type checking, desugaring and C code generation. These tasks were to be performed on the Oberon-0 language, which in itself was divided into 5 increasingly complex levels. We consider the level 2 (L2) of the Oberon-0 problem, and we specified the name binding, type checking and desugaring tasks in our Ztrategic AG approach. We use attributes for contextual information when needed, for example in name analysis to check whether a used name has been declared. This language level requires the desugaring of *For* and *Case* statements into semantically equivalent *While* and (nested) *If* statements. Such desugaring is implemented using Ztrategic type-preserving strategies, and the result is a new tree in which name analysis and type checking is performed through strategic traversals that use attributes. Because desugaring

Table 2. Numbers of lines of code for the Oberon-0 L2 tasks.

Task	Ztrategic	Kiama
Oberon-0 tree	57	99
Name analyzer	50	222
Type analyzer	34	117
Lifter	6	23
Desugarer	76	123
Total	223	584

---

[8] The student projects used in this benchmark are available at this work's repository.

a *For* statement induces a new assignment (before the new *WhileStmt* statement) whose variable needs to be added to the declarations part of the original AST, we use the attribute *numForDown* which is a synthesized attribute of the original tree. Having the desugared AST and the number of *For* statements refactored, then we return the final higher-order tree where the induced variables are properly declared.

$$
\begin{aligned}
desugar\ m = \textbf{let}\ &numberOfFors = numForsDown\ (\textbf{toZipper}\ m) \\
&step = failTP\ `adhocTP'\ desugarFor\ `adhocTPZ'\ desugarCase \\
&ata = fromJust\ (applyTP\ (innermost\ step)\ (\textbf{toZipper}\ m)) \\
\textbf{in}\ &injectForVars\ numberOfFors\ (fromZipper\ ata)
\end{aligned}
$$

We omit here the definition of the worker function *desugarFor*. Its definition is fully included in [20], and it is also similar to the Kiama definition presented in [31]. In Table 2, we compare our approach to the results presented in [31] for the L2 language level. Notably, we show that our approach, even in its earliest versions, is suited for large-scale and real world usage.

5   Related Work

The work we present in this paper is inspired by the pioneering work of Sloane who developed Kiama [13,30]: an embedding of strategic term rewriting and AGs in the Scala programming language. While our approach expresses both attribute computations and strategic term rewriting as pure functions, Kiama caches attribute values in a global cache, in order to reuse attribute values computed in the original tree that are not affected by the rewriting. Such global caching, however, induces an overhead in order to keep it updated, for example, attribute values associated to subtrees discarded by the rewriting process need to be purged from the cache [32]. In our purely functional setting, we only compute attributes in the desired re-written tree (as is the case of the let example shown in Sect. 3.1). Influenced by Kiama, Kramer and Van Wyk [15] present *strategy attributes*, which is an integration of strategic term rewriting into attribute grammars. Strategic rewriting rules can use the attributes of a tree to reference contextual information during rewriting, much like we present in our work. They present several practical application, namely the evaluation of λ-calculus, a regular expression matching via Brzozowski derivatives, and the normalization of for-loops. All these examples can be directly expressed in our setting. They also present an application to optimize translation of strategies. Because our techniques rely on shallow embeddings, we are unable to express strategy optimizations without relying on meta-programming techniques [29]. Nevertheless, our embeddings result in very simple libraries that are easier to extend and maintain, specially when compared to the complexity of extending a full language system such as Silver [36]. JastAdd is a reference attribute grammar based system [9]. It supports most of AG extensions, including reference and circular AGs [33]. It also supports tree rewriting, with rewrite rules that can reference attributes. JastAdd, however, provides no support for strategic programming, that is to say, there is no mechanism to control how the rewrite rules are applied. The zipper-based AG embedding we integrate in Ztrategic supports all modern AG extensions, including reference and circular AGs [10,22]. Because strategies and AGs are first-class citizens we can smoothly combine any such extensions with strategic term rewriting.

In the context of strategic term rewriting, our Ztrategic library is inspired by Strafunski [17]. In fact, Ztrategic already provides almost all Strafunski functionality. There is, however, a key difference between these libraries: while Strafunski accesses the data structure directly, Ztrategic operates on zippers. As a consequence, we can easily access attributes from strategic functions and strategic functions from attribute equations.

6 Conclusions

This paper presented a zipper-based embedding of strategic term rewriting. By relying on zippers, we combine it with a zipper-based embedding of attribute grammars so that (zipper-based) strategies can access (zipper-based) AG functional definitions, and vice versa. We developed Ztrategic, a small but powerful strategic programming library and we have used it to implement several language engineering tasks.

To evaluate the expressiveness of our approach we compared our Ztrategic solution to the largest strategic AG developed with the state-of-the-art Kiama system. In terms of runtime performance we compared our Ztrategic library to the well established and fully optimized Strafusnki solution. The preliminary results show that in fact zippers provided a uniform setting in which to express both strategic term rewriting and AGs that are on par with the state-of-the-art. Moreover, our approach can easily be implemented in any programming language in which a zipper abstraction can be defined. In order to improve performance, we are considering extending Ztrategic to work with a memoized version of the AG library.

Acknowledgements. This work is financed by National Funds through the Portuguese funding agency, FCT - Fundação para a Ciência e a Tecnologia, within project LA/P/0063/2020. The first author is also sponsored by FCT grant 2021.08184.BD.

References

1. Adams, M.D.: Scrap your zippers: a generic zipper for heterogeneous types. In: WGP 2010: Proceedings of the 2010 ACM SIGPLAN Workshop on Generic Programming, pp. 13–24. ACM, New York (2010). https://doi.org/10.1145/1863495. 1863499
2. Alblas, H.: Attribute evaluation methods. In: Alblas, H., Melichar, B. (eds.) SAGA School 1991. LNCS, vol. 545, pp. 48–113. Springer, Heidelberg (1991). https://doi. org/10.1007/3-540-54572-7_3

3. Almeida, J.B., Cunha, A., Macedo, N., Pacheco, H., Proença, J.: Teaching how to program using automated assessment and functional glossy games (experience report). Proc. ACM Program. Lang. **2**(ICFP) (2018). https://doi.org/10.1145/3236777

4. Balland, E., Brauner, P., Kopetz, R., Moreau, P.-E., Reilles, A.: Tom: piggybacking rewriting on Java. In: Baader, F. (ed.) RTA 2007. LNCS, vol. 4533, pp. 36–47. Springer, Heidelberg (2007). https://doi.org/10.1007/978-3-540-73449-9_5

5. van den Brand, M.G.J., et al.: The ASF+SDF meta-environment: a component-based language development environment. In: Wilhelm, R. (ed.) CC 2001. LNCS, vol. 2027, pp. 365–370. Springer, Heidelberg (2001). https://doi.org/10.1007/3-540-45306-7_26

6. Cordy, J.R.: TXL - a language for programming language tools and applications. Electron. Notes Theor. Comput. Sci. **110**, 3–31 (2004). https://doi.org/10.1016/j.entcs.2004.11.006

7. Cowie, J.: Detecting bad smells in haskell. Technical report, University of Kent, UK (2005)

8. Dijkstra, A., Swierstra, S.D.: Typing haskell with an attribute grammar. In: Vene, V., Uustalu, T. (eds.) AFP 2004. LNCS, vol. 3622, pp. 1–72. Springer, Heidelberg (2005). https://doi.org/10.1007/11546382_1

9. Ekman, T., Hedin, G.: The JastAdd extensible Java compiler. SIGPLAN Not. **42**(10), 1–18 (2007). http://doi.acm.org/10.1145/1297105.1297029

10. Fernandes, J.P., Martins, P., Pardo, A., Saraiva, J., Viera, M.: Memoized zipper-based attribute grammars and their higher order extension. Sci. Comput. Program. **173**, 71–94 (2019). https://doi.org/10.1016/j.scico.2018.10.006

11. Gray, R.W., Levi, S.P., Heuring, V.P., Sloane, A.M., Waite, W.M.: Eli: a complete, flexible compiler construction system. Commun. ACM **35**(2), 121–130 (1992). https://doi.org/10.1145/129630.129637

12. Huet, G.: The zipper. J. Funct. Program. **7**(5), 549–554 (1997)

13. Kats, L.C.L., Sloane, A.M., Visser, E.: Decorated attribute grammars: attribute evaluation meets strategic programming. In: de Moor, O., Schwartzbach, M.I. (eds.) CC 2009. LNCS, vol. 5501, pp. 142–157. Springer, Heidelberg (2009). https://doi.org/10.1007/978-3-642-00722-4_11

14. Knuth, D.E.: Semantics of context-free languages. Math. Syst. Theory **2**(2), 127–145 (1968)

15. Kramer, L., Van Wyk, E.: Strategic tree rewriting in attribute grammars. In: Proceedings of the 13th ACM SIGPLAN International Conference on Software Language Engineering, SLE 2020, pp. 210–229. Association for Computing Machinery, New York (2020). https://doi.org/10.1145/3426425.3426943

16. Kuiper, M., Saraiva, J.: Lrc - a generator for incremental language-oriented tools. In: Koskimies, K. (ed.) CC 1998. LNCS, vol. 1383, pp. 298–301. Springer, Heidelberg (1998). https://doi.org/10.1007/BFb0026440

17. Lämmel, R., Visser, J.: Typed combinators for generic traversal. In: Krishnamurthi, S., Ramakrishnan, C.R. (eds.) PADL 2002. LNCS, vol. 2257, pp. 137–154. Springer, Heidelberg (2002). https://doi.org/10.1007/3-540-45587-6_10

18. Lämmel, R., Visser, J.: A Strafunski application letter. In: Dahl, V., Wadler, P. (eds.) PADL 2003. LNCS, vol. 2562, pp. 357–375. Springer, Heidelberg (2003). https://doi.org/10.1007/3-540-36388-2_24

19. Luttik, S.P., Visser, E.: Specification of rewriting strategies. In: Proceedings of the 2nd International Conference on Theory and Practice of Algebraic Specifications, Algebraic 1997, p. 9. BCS Learning & Development Ltd., Swindon (1997)

20. Macedo, J.N., Viera, M., Saraiva, J.: The Ztrategic library (2022). https://bitbucket.org/zenunomacedo/ztrategic/

21. Martins, P., Fernandes, J.P., Saraiva, J.: Zipper-based attribute grammars and their extensions. In: Du Bois, A.R., Trinder, P. (eds.) SBLP 2013. LNCS, vol. 8129, pp. 135–149. Springer, Heidelberg (2013). https://doi.org/10.1007/978-3-642-40922-6_10

22. Martins, P., Fernandes, J.P., Saraiva, J., Van Wyk, E., Sloane, A.: Embedding attribute grammars and their extensions using functional zippers. Sci. Comput. Program. **132**(P1), 2–28 (2016). https://doi.org/10.1016/j.scico.2016.03.005

23. Mernik, M., Korbar, N., Žumer, V.: LISA: a tool for automatic language implementation. SIGPLAN Not. **30**(4), 71–79 (1995). https://doi.org/10.1145/202176.202185

24. Middelkoop, A., Dijkstra, A., Swierstra, S.D.: Iterative type inference with attribute grammars. In: Proceedings of the Ninth International Conference on Generative Programming and Component Engineering, GPCE 2010, pp. 43–52. Association for Computing Machinery, New York (2010). https://doi.org/10.1145/1868294.1868302

25. de Moor, O., Backhouse, K., Swierstra, D.: First-class attribute grammars. Informatica (Slovenia) **24**(3) (2000). citeseer.ist.psu.edu/demoor00firstclass.html

26. Reps, T., Teitelbaum, T.: The synthesizer generator. SIGPLAN Not. **19**(5), 42–48 (1984). https://doi.org/10.1145/390011.808247

27. Saraiva, J.: Purely functional implementation of attribute grammars. Ph.D. thesis, Utrecht University, The Netherlands, December 1999

28. Saraiva, J.: Component-based programming for higher-order attribute grammars. In: Batory, D., Consel, C., Taha, W. (eds.) GPCE 2002. LNCS, vol. 2487, pp. 268–282. Springer, Heidelberg (2002). https://doi.org/10.1007/3-540-45821-2_17

29. Sheard, T., Jones, S.P.: Template meta-programming for haskell. In: Proceedings of the 2002 ACM SIGPLAN Workshop on Haskell, Haskell 2002, pp. 1–16. Association for Computing Machinery, New York (2002). https://doi.org/10.1145/581690.581691

30. Sloane, A.M., Kats, L.C.L., Visser, E.: A pure object-oriented embedding of attribute grammars. Electron. Notes Theor. Comput. Sci. **253**(7), 205–219 (2010). https://doi.org/10.1016/j.entcs.2010.08.043

31. Sloane, A.M., Roberts, M.: Oberon-0 in kiama. Sci. Comput. Program. **114**, 20–32 (2015). https://doi.org/10.1016/j.scico.2015.10.010. lDTA (Language Descriptions, Tools, and Applications) Tool Challenge

32. Sloane, A.M., Roberts, M., Hamey, L.G.C.: Respect your parents: how attribution and rewriting can get along. In: Combemale, B., Pearce, D.J., Barais, O., Vinju, J.J. (eds.) SLE 2014. LNCS, vol. 8706, pp. 191–210. Springer, Cham (2014). https://doi.org/10.1007/978-3-319-11245-9_11

33. Söderberg, E., Hedin, G.: Circular higher-order reference attribute grammars. In: Erwig, M., Paige, R.F., Van Wyk, E. (eds.) SLE 2013. LNCS, vol. 8225, pp. 302–321. Springer, Cham (2013). https://doi.org/10.1007/978-3-319-02654-1_17

34. Swierstra, S.D., Azero Alcocer, P.R., Saraiva, J.: Designing and implementing combinator languages. In: Swierstra, S.D., Oliveira, J.N., Henriques, P.R. (eds.) AFP 1998. LNCS, vol. 1608, pp. 150–206. Springer, Heidelberg (1999). https://doi.org/10.1007/10704973_4

35. van den Brand, M.: Introduction - the LDTA tool challenge. Sci. Comput. Program. **114**, 1–6 (2015). https://doi.org/10.1016/j.scico.2015.10.015

36. Van Wyk, E., Bodin, D., Gao, J., Krishnan, L.: Silver: an extensible attribute grammar system. Electron. Notes Theor. Comput. Sci. **203**(2), 103–116 (2008). https://doi.org/10.1016/j.entcs.2008.03.047
37. Visser, E.: Stratego: a language for program transformation based on rewriting strategies system description of Stratego 0.5. In: Middeldorp, A. (ed.) RTA 2001. LNCS, vol. 2051, pp. 357–361. Springer, Heidelberg (2001). https://doi.org/10.1007/3-540-45127-7_27
38. van Wijngaarcien, A., et al.: Revised report on the algorithmic language Algol 68. SIGPLAN Not. **12**(5), 1–70 (1977). https://doi.org/10.1145/954652.1781176

Unified Program Generation and Verification: A Case Study on Number-Theoretic Transform

Masahiro Masuda[✉] and Yukiyoshi Kameyama

University of Tsukuba, Tsukuba, Japan
masa@logic.cs.tsukuba.ac.jp,kameyama@acm.org

Abstract. Giving correctness assurance to the generated code in the context of generative programming is a poorly explored problem. Such assurance is particularly desired for applications where correctness of the optimized code is far from obvious, such as cryptography.

This work presents a unified approach to program generation and verification, and applies it to an implementation of Number-Theoretic Transform, a key building block in lattice-based cryptography. Our strategy for verification is based on problem decomposition: While we found that an attempt to prove functional correctness of the whole program all at once is intractable, low-level components in the optimized program and its high-level algorithm structure can be separately verified using procedures of appropriate levels of abstraction.

We demonstrate that such a decomposition and subsequent verification of each component are naturally realized in a program-generation approach based on the tagless-final style, leading to an end-to-end functional correctness verification of a highly optimized program.

1 Introduction

State-of-the-art multi-stage programming languages and systems can generate highly performant code [14,15,24,25]. In terms of reliability, however, assuring correctness beyond type safety of generated code has been rarely provided and thus it remains a relatively unexplored problem. For applications where code correctness is as important as performance, this is an undesirable situation.

Cryptography is an example of such application domains. Expert cryptographers still write performance-critical code in assembly. Assembly code makes it hard to be confident in the correctness of its implementation, as well as complicates the development and maintenance process. Although there has been remarkable progress on verifying and generating code for low-level cryptographic primitives that are used today [11,26], doing full-scale verification of bleeding-edge primitives that are still being developed is costly and unrealistic. Number-Theoretic Transform (NTT) is one example of recent primitives that is of increasing interest in lattice-based cryptography. More specifically, NTT is a variant of Fast Fourier Transform specialized to a finite field; It is used to accelerate

© Springer Nature Switzerland AG 2022
M. Hanus and A. Igarashi (Eds.): FLOPS 2022, LNCS 13215, pp. 133–151, 2022.
https://doi.org/10.1007/978-3-030-99461-7_8

polynomial multiplication on prime-field coefficients, which is at the heart of cryptographic constructions based on the Ring learning with errors (RLWE) problem [18]. Since the RLWE problem is widely recognized as a promising hardness assumption for post-quantum cryptography, many cryptographic schemes based on the hardness of the RLWE problem have been developed, along with optimized assembly implementations of NTT [3,13,17,23]. We believe that the programming language community should be able to help implement correct and efficient code for such state-of-the-art primitives.

This work contributes a DSL-based approach to an NTT implementation, which uniformly represents code generation and verification in a single framework. Our approach is based on module-based abstraction techniques for embedded DSL implementations that are well-known in the functional programming community: Specifically, the tagless-final style [9] is used for code generation. Our framework extends our previous work on code generation [19] to accommodate program verification as an instance of interpretations of a DSL program. By exploiting the highly parameterized nature of the framework, we can realize interval analysis and symbolic computation at the level of an abstract DSL, while taking into account low-level details that are present in the generated code.

We have performed both safety property and functional correctness verification, which led us to several interesting findings. First, we found that a DSL framework based on the tagless-final style naturally enables a custom implementation of interval analysis, and that it can yield more precise bounds than those estimated by the state-of-the-art static analyzer for C programs, Frama-C value analysis tool [7], applied to the generated code. Moreover, the more precise bounds allowed us to discover a new optimization opportunity that was not known before. Second, we found that decoupling the low-level details of modular reductions from the high-level structure of the NTT algorithm is the key to carrying out the end-to-end equivalence checking against the DFT reference. We summarize our contributions as follows[1].

- A unified treatment of code generation and verification in a single framework
- Interval analysis for NTT that verifies the absence of integer overflow (Sects. 4.1 and 4.2)
- A verified derivation of a new code optimization based on interval analysis (Sect. 4.3)
- End-to-end verification of functional correctness of the highly optimized NTT code against a textbook DFT algorithm (Sect. 5)

The rest of the paper is organized as follows: Sect. 2 gives background to this work. We describe our verification tasks concretely in Sect. 3 before we go into our technical contributions in Sects. 4 and 5. We recap the pros and cons of our approach in Sect. 6. Section 7 discusses related work and we conclude in Sect. 8.

---

[1] Our code is available in https://github.com/masahi/nttverify.

2   Background

2.1   Number-Theoretic Transform

NTT is an $O(n \log n)$ time algorithm to compute Discrete Fourier Transform (DFT) on a finite field. DFT is defined as follows: Given an input $a = (a_0, a_1, ..., a_{n-1})$ such that $a_i \in \mathbb{Z}_q$, the finite field of integers modulo q, it computes $y = (y_0, y_1, ..., y_{n-1}), y_i \in \mathbb{Z}_q$ by the following formula [10]:

$$y_k = \sum_{j=0}^{n-1} a_j \omega_n^{kj} \tag{1}$$

Here, ω_n is the nth primitive root of unity modulo q, satisfying $\omega_n^n \equiv 1$ (mod q). All addition and multiplication are done in modulo q. As an example of the choice of parameters, the NTT implementation in NewHope [3], which our previous work on code generation is based on, uses $n = 1024$ and $q = 12289$.

Algorithm 1 shows the pseudocode of a textbook NTT algorithm. It uses the standard Cooley-Tukey algorithm [10] and all powers of ω_n, called twiddle factors, are precomputed and stored in an array Ω. Each iteration of the outermost loop is often called a *stage*.

Algorithm 1. The pseudocode for the iterative, in-place NTT

1: **procedure** NTT
    Input: $a = (a_0, a_1, ..., a_{n-1}) \in \mathbb{Z}_q^n$, precomputed constants table $\Omega \in \mathbb{Z}_q^n$
2:   **Output:** $y = \text{DFT}(a)$, in standard order
3:     bit-reverse(a)
4:     **for** $(s = 1; s \le \log_2(n); s = s + 1)$ **do**
5:         $m = 2^s$
6:         $o = 2^{s-1} - 1$
7:         **for** $(k = 0; k < m; k = k + m)$ **do**
8:             **for** $(j = 0; j < m/2; j = j + 1)$ **do**
9:                 $u = a[k + j]$
10:                 $t = (a[k + j + m/2] \cdot \Omega[o + j]) \bmod q$
11:                 $a[k + j] = (u + t) \bmod q$
12:                 $a[k + j + m/2] = (u - t) \bmod q$
13:             **end for**
14:         **end for**
15:     **end for**
16: **end procedure**

The innermost loop performs the Cooly-Tukey butterfly operation with modular arithmetic. Existing work [3,23] and our code-generation framework use specialized algorithms for modular reductions. We follow their choice of algorithms and use Barrett reduction [6] to reduce the results of addition and subtraction, and Montgomery multiplication [20] for multiplication followed by reduction. We also follow the setting in NewHope for the choice of parameters: The modulus parameter q is 12289, and the input size n is 1024. The input is an array of integers whose values fit in 14 bits. Modular-reduction algorithms take one or two 16-bit values and compute a 14-bit output.

2.2   NTT Code Generation in the Tagless-Final Style

In our previous work [19], we introduced a code-generation framework for NTT, based on the tagless-final style [9]. Since this work builds heavily on our code-generation framework, this section gives a brief introduction to that work.

The tagless-final style is a way to realize a typed DSL via embedding into a typed host language [9]. It uses abstraction facilities in host languages, such as Haskell type classes or the ML module system, to define the syntax of the DSL parameterized by an abstract type for the DSL semantics. Different type class instances or implementations of the module signature give distinct interpretations of a single DSL program[2].

Our code generator is parameterized in two ways: The first one is the semantics of DSL, which follows the standard practice of the tagless-final style. The second one is the semantics of the arithmetic domain the NTT program operates on. We call the first abstraction the **language abstraction** and the second one the **domain abstraction**. Both abstractions are represented in the ML-module system described below.

The language abstraction represents the DSL syntax by a module signature, and its semantics by a module structure. The following module signature C_lang represents the syntax of our DSL for generating code in the programming language C. The DSL has sufficient constructs for expressing the NTT algorithm in this paper.

```
module type C_lang = sig
  type 'a expr
  type 'a stmt = 'a expr
  val int_ : int -> int expr    (* constant *)
  val (%+) : int expr -> int expr -> int expr (* addition *)
  val for_ : int expr -> int expr -> int expr -> (int expr -> unit stmt)
             -> unit stmt
  ...
end
```

The domain abstraction is represented by the following signature:

```
module type Domain = sig
  type 'a expr
  type t
  val lift: t -> t expr
  val add: t expr -> t expr -> t expr
  val sub: t expr -> t expr -> t expr
  val mul: t expr -> t expr -> t expr
end
```

Using these signatures, we describe the innermost loop of Algorithm 1 as follows:

---

[2] In the module system of ML-family languages, a *signature* is an interface of a module, and a *structure* is its implementation.

```
for_ (int_ 0) m_half (int_ 1) (fun j ->
    let index = k %+ j in
    let omega = arr_get prim_root_powers (coeff_offset %+ j) in
    let2
      (arr_get input index)
      (D.mul (arr_get input (index %+ m_half)) omega)
      (fun u t ->
        seq
          (arr_set input index (D.add u t))
          (arr_set input (index %+ m_half) (D.sub u t))))
```

arr_get and arr_set are array access and assignment, respectively. let2 V1 V2 (fun t u -> V3) is syntactic sugar for the doubly-nested let binding: let t = V1 in let u = V2 in V3. The variable prim_root_powers stores precomputed twiddle factors in an array. All modular-arithmetic operations are performed by the module D which implements the Domain signature.

The meaning of this program depends on concrete instantiations of the two abstractions. For this work, we use the term **interpretation** to refer to a concrete instantiation of the language abstraction, and **domain implementation** to refer to a corresponding one for the domain abstraction.

The behavior of DSL programs is determined by giving an interpretation of the module signature C_lang including the type 'a expr. In our previous work, the type 'a expr is interpreted as an OCaml string, since their purpose was solely to generate C programs. For instance, a DSL term for_ is translated to the string representation of the for loop in the C language. In this work, we use another interpretation that evaluates DSL terms in OCaml by interpreting the type 'a expr as 'a as follows:

```
module R = struct
  type 'a expr = 'a
  let int_ n = n
  let (%+) x y = x + y
  ...
  let for_ low high step body =
    let index = ref low in
    for _ = 0 to (high - low) / step - 1 do
      body !index;
      index := !index + step
    done
  ...
end
```

When the NTT program is instantiated with this interpretation, we can directly *execute* the program under the normal semantics for OCaml. The output depends on the domain implementation. The most canonical one, also used in C-code generation, is the domain of integers modulo q with low-level implementations of modular reductions. But we can also use entirely different domains for analysis or verification purposes. For example, we can lift implementations of modular reductions to the domain of *intervals* of integers modulo q: This lets us analyze the NTT program to verify the absence of integer overflow, as we will discuss in Sect. 4. Similarly, by using a domain representing purely symbolic operations on a finite field, the NTT program would be able to compute a polynomial representation of the outputs with respect to symbolic inputs. Such a highly abstract representation of the NTT computation facilitates verification of functional correctness, as discussed in Sect. 5.

3   Verification Tasks and Strategy

Before going into our technical contributions, we summarize the verification tasks at hand and our strategy for tackling them.

To generate a highly efficient C program, our NTT program contains various low-level tricks that make it vulnerable to subtle errors. We highlight several issues that are particularly unique to our program, using the pseudocode of the innermost loop of the NTT program shown in Algorithm 2. The pseudocode differs from Algorithm 1 in that we use low-level modular reductions barrett_reduce and montgomery_multiply_reduce for Barrett reduction and Montgomery multiplication, respectively. We have also introduced an optimization technique called lazy reduction [3,19] for Barrett reduction.

Algorithm 2. The pseudocode for the innermost loop

---

for ($j = 0$; $j < m/2$; $j = j + 1$) do
    $u = a[k + j]$
    $t = $ montgomery_multiply_reduce($a[k + j + m/2], \Omega[o + j]$)
    if s mod $2 == 0$ then
        $a[k + j] = $ barrett_reduce($u + t$)   ▷ lazy reduction
    else
        $a[k + j] = u + t$
    end if
    $a[k + j + m/2] = $ barrett_reduce($u + 2q - t$)
end for

Highly Non-trivial Implementation of Modular Reductions. Given a 16-bit integer, barrett_reduce computes a value that is congruent to the input and fits in 14 bits[3]. montgomery_multiply_reduce multiplies 16-bit and 14-bit integers and reduces the product to fit in 14 bits. To be efficient and safe against timing attacks, these algorithms are implemented in a tricky way. Listing 1 shows a C implementation of Montgomery multiplication. They rely on the instructions mullo (and mulhi, resp.) to compute the lower 16 bits (and the upper 16 bits, resp.) of the 32-bit product, to keep all intermediate values within 16 bits[4]. The implementation is carefully constructed to make sure that an occasional carry bit is correctly accounted and the output is guaranteed to fit in 14 bits. The latter requirement is satisfied by inserting conditional subtraction csub, which

---

[3] We use 12289, which fits in 14 bits, as the modulus parameter q (See Sect. 2.1).

[4] This is for maximizing parallelism from vectorization.

subtracts the modulus parameter q from its argument if it is greater than or equal to q, and returns it otherwise. csub computes such a value in constant time[5].

```c
uint16_t csub(uint16_t arg0) {
  int16_t v_0 = ((int16_t)arg0 - Q);
  return (uint16_t)(v_0 + ((v_0 >> 15) & Q));
}

uint16_t montgomery_multiply_reduce(uint16_t x, uint16_t y) {
  uint16_t mlo = mullo(x, y);
  uint16_t mhi = mulhi(x, y);
  uint16_t mlo_qinv = mullo(mlo, Q_INV);
  uint16_t t = mulhi(mlo_qinv, Q);
  uint16_t has_carry = mlo != 0;
  return csub(mhi + t + has_carry);
}
```

Listing 1: Montgomery multiplication implemented in C (non-vectorized version)

Subtraction in Unsigned Integers. Since data values in our generated code are unsigned integers, we need to be careful with subtraction. to avoid underflow. We need to add to the first operand a multiple of q that is greater than the second operand. We must also ensure that this addition never causes overflow. For our choice of q, the correct multiple of q meeting these conditions turned out to be $2q$.

Lazy Reduction. As observed in the work on NewHope [3], we do not have to apply Barrett reduction after every addition: Since the result of adding two 14-bit values fits in 15 bits, in the next stage we can add two 15-bit values without the risk of 16-bit overflow. Therefore, Barrett reduction only has to be applied at every other stage. Sect. 4.3 will show that we can further eliminate Barrett reductions. A more aggressive optimization makes the generated code more vulnerable to integer overflow.

End-to-End Verification. We are not merely interested in verifying individual pieces of low-level code: The computation of the innermost loop shown in Algorithm 2 is executed $O(n \log n)$ times over an entire execution of NTT, where $n = 1024$ in our case. Our goal is to show that such an accumulated computation gives rise to the value that is equivalent (modulo q) to the one computed by the DFT formula (1).

In this work, we consider both safety and functional correctness. In particular, for the safety aspect, we consider the problem of verifying the absence of integer

---

[5] In cryptography implementations, being constant-time refers to having no data-dependent control flow, which can become a security hole for timing attacks.

overflow, and for the functional correctness, we consider the equivalence of the NTT program against DFT. We consider the safety aspect separately because (1) it simplifies the latter task and (2) interval analysis we develop for verifying the absence of integer overflow uncovers a new optimization opportunity. So we believe our safety verification is of independent interest.

For verifying functional correctness, we do not pursue an approach using an interactive proof assistant such as Coq, which can give us the highest level of correctness guarantee. Since we aim at generating and verifying highly efficient cryptographic code whose implementation strategy changes frequently, we stick to a lightweight approach that allows one to change the implementation and adapt the verification component quickly and easily.

Thus, we have developed a dedicated procedure for our verification problem. Our approach works on a DSL program, not on the generated C program. But the DSL program contains all low-level details that are present in the C program, so our verification procedure takes all of such details into account. Thus, correctness assurance we give to the DSL program directly translates to the generated C program[6]. We have found that an attempt to prove functional correctness of the whole program all at once is intractable: Instead, our overall strategy for end-to-end verification is based on decoupling low-level components in the NTT program from the high-level aspect of the NTT algorithm. Verification of low-level components can be done straightforwardly, while we developed a simple and effective verification procedure to show the equivalence of the NTT program and the DFT formula in a purely mathematical setting. The decision to do verification at the DSL level and the highly parameterized nature of our DSL program make such decoupling and subsequent verification possible.

4   Interval Analysis on the NTT Program

To verify the absence of integer overflow, we present a simple interval analysis as part of a program-generation framework for NTT programs. We have implemented our own analyzer, rather than using an off-the-shelf tool for C programs, to exploit domain-specific knowledge and compute more precise bounds than the ones computed by the latter tools such as Frame-C [7]. We will show that our analysis not only verifies the absence of integer overflow but also allows us to derive a new optimization that was not known previously.

4.1   Modular Arithmetic on Intervals

We have designed an abstract interpreter for our modular-arithmetic routines, building on the two abstractions we described in Sect. 2.2: We use the interpretation of DSL that evaluates DSL terms directly in OCaml, and the set of

---

[6] For simplicity, we do not consider the effect of vectorization for our verification purpose, although the generated program is fully vectorized with multiple SIMD instruction sets. All of the low-level issues that motivate our verification effort are manifested in the non-vectorized implementation.

intervals (low, high) as our domain implementation where low and high are integers representing the lower and upper bounds, respectively. The Domain module in Sect. 2.2 is instantiated to the following structure:

```
module IntegerModulo_interval : Domain = struct
  type t = int * int
  let add (x1, y1) (x2, y2) = ...
  let sub (x1, y1) (x2, y2) = barrett_reduce([x1 + 2q - y2, y1 + 2q - x2])
  let mul (x1, y1) (x2, y2) = ...
end
```

Simple operations such as addition can be directly lifted to the intervals, building on the standard definition of interval arithmetic. Montgomery multiplication, represented by mul above, is lifted to intervals by composing basic operations, such as mullo and mulhi, lifted to the interval domain.

Lifting Barrett reduction to interval domains requires more care. As shown below, Barrett reduction requires only three operations.

```
uint16_t barrett_reduce(uint16_t x) {
  uint16_t v = mulhi(x, 5);
  return x - mullo(v, Q);
}
```

We could have lifted Barrett reduction by composing the interval version of high product, low product, and subtraction. But this approach faces difficulty in the subtraction x - mullo(v, Q): Its second operand is the result of low product, which, when lifted to intervals, always results in the least precise range $[0, 65535]$. Even though the first operand x is always greater than the second one[7], it cannot be automatically inferred by applying interval analysis naively. To get maximally precise bounds, we lift Barrett reduction to intervals by applying the integer domain operation to all integers in the input interval, and taking the minimum and maximum of the results of these operations. This comes at the cost of higher runtime, but since the input to Barrett reduction is at most 16 bits, it does not significantly slow down the analysis[8].

4.2 Verifying Bounds

Each low-level modular-arithmetic operation has certain conditions on its inputs and output that need to be satisfied. We formulate these conditions as assertions to be checked during interval analysis, summarized in Table 1.

For example, the second operand of addition and subtraction has a tighter bound of max_uint14, because it is the result of modular multiplication which must fit in 14 bits where max_uint14 refers to the maximum of unsigned 14-bit integers, namely $(1 \ll 14) - 1$. Similarly for max_uint15 and max_uint16.

---

[7] mullo(mulhi(x,5),q) is not greater than $\left\lfloor x\frac{1}{q} \right\rfloor q$, since $5q < 65535$ for our choice of q.

[8] It took only a few seconds for the input of size 1024.

The bound of `max_uint15` on the first operand is due to lazy reduction. Bounds in Table 1 in turn depend on the validity of bounds on Barrett reduction and conditional subtraction, shown in Table 2.

Table 1. Pre/Post-conditions for input $[x_1, y_1], [x_2, y_2]$ and output $[x_3, y_3]$

Operations	Precondition	Postcondition
add	$y_1 \leq \mathtt{max\_uint15} \wedge y_2 \leq \mathtt{max\_uint14}$	$y_3 \leq \mathtt{max\_uint16}$
sub	$y_1 \leq \mathtt{max\_uint15} \wedge y_2 \leq \mathtt{max\_uint14}$	$y_3 \leq \mathtt{max\_uint14}$
mul	$y_1 \leq \mathtt{max\_uint15} \wedge y_2 < q$	$y_3 \leq \mathtt{max\_uint14}$

Table 2. Pre/Post-conditions for input $[x_1, y_1]$ and output $[x_2, y_2]$

Operations	Precondition	Postcondition
barrett_reduce	$y_1 \leq \mathtt{max\_uint16}$	$y_2 \leq \mathtt{max\_uint14}$
csub	$y_1 < 2q$	$y_2 < q$

For Barrett reduction, we need to verify an additional assertion saying that the first argument of the final subtraction is not smaller than the second argument. This is realized by inserting an assertion as follows:

```
let barrett_reduce x =
  ...
  let y = mullo(v, Q) in
  assert (x >= y);
  let res = x - y in
  ...
```

Note that the assertion is inserted in the structure `IntegerModulo_interval` only. We do not have to modify the DSL program, because it is parameterized with respect to domain interpretations.

We have confirmed that, given an array of intervals $[0, q - 1]$ as input, all of our assertions are not violated. Hence, there is no possibility for integer overflow for our code.

We have also conducted the same verification experiment on the generated C code using the Frama-C value analysis plugin [7]. For this purpose, we added the above assertions as ACSL specifications [1] to the generated C code. Frama-C was able to verify all but two assertions: the postcondition in Table 2 and the assertion on the bound before the final subtraction[9]. We suspect that this outcome arises from directly translating Barrett reduction on integers to intervals by composing interval operations, which, as we observed in Sect. 4.1, can lead to a loss in precision.

---

[9] We have chosen options that maximize the precision of the analysis.

4.3 Improving Lazy Reduction

During the course of interval analysis in the previous subsection, we found a way to optimize the generated code even further: Barrett reduction after addition, which we refer to as lazy Barrett reduction for brevity, needs to be applied only once in **three** stages, rather than every other stage as we adopted from NewHope. Realization of lazy reductions comes from the following observations:

- An operation that is most vulnerable to unsigned overflow is the addition of $2q$ in subtraction, $(x + 2q) - y$. Since x is an unsigned 16-bit integer, the maximum value that x can take without causing overflow in the addition is $65535 - 2q = 65535 - 2 * 12289 = 40957$, where 65535 is the maximum value of an unsigned 16-bit integer.
- Our analysis showed that the maximum value that an input to lazy Barrett reduction can take is 39319.

The first observation suggests that there is no need to apply Barrett reduction before the value reaches 40957, while from the second one we know that the input to lazy Barrett reduction is at most 39319. Therefore, we can omit one more reduction before we need to reduce the value to 14 bits. Since each stage has 512 additions, and we have reduced the number of stages where lazy Barrett reduction is applied from 5 to 3, in total we are able to remove $2 * 512$ Barrett reductions. The actual speedup over our previous work is summarized in Table 3. On AVX2, the improved lazy reduction brought good speedup (14%) compared to the baseline, while on AVX512 the speedup is modest (1.5%).

Table 3. Speedup by the improved lazy reduction (CPU: Intel Core i7-1065G7)

	Cycle counts	Speedup
AVX2 baseline	5398	
AVX2 backend + improved lazy reduction	4744	14%
AVX512 baseline	4381	
AVX512 backend + improved lazy reduction	4317	1.5%

The interval estimated by Frama-C is not precise enough to derive the same conclusion as above: Frama-C computed the maximum value an input to lazy Barrett reduction can take to be 40959, which is slightly bigger than the hard threshold of 40957 required for safely enabling the optimization above. This difference in bounds comes from the increased precision in our implementation of lifted Barrett reduction: Our analysis shows that the maximum value after interval subtraction is 14743, in contrast to 16383 computed by Frama-C. The difference in the precision, (16383–14743), is equal to (40959–39319), that is the difference in the maximum values an input to lazy Barrett reduction can take.

As a sanity check, we confirmed that our analysis fails to verify the assertions if we omit one more Barrett reduction from our code. We also tested the generated C program with the improved lazy reduction on 10000 randomly chosen concrete values as an input, and confirmed that all outputs were correct with respect to the DFT formula, and that each output belongs to the corresponding interval computed by our interval analysis.

5   Verifying Functional Correctness

The goal is to show that the output computed by the optimized NTT program is equivalent to the one computed by DFT. We first discuss the first attempt which did not work out, and then explain the final solution we developed.

5.1   Naive Approach

One straightforward but naive approach is to translate the entire NTT program into a formula in the bit-vector theory [16], and verify using an SMT solver the equivalence of the formula and the one obtained from the DFT formula. The translation to a formula is easily done by symbolically computing the NTT program in the bit-vector theory.

This approach did not work, since the resulting formulas were so large that Z3, the SMT solver we used, did not terminate after more than six hours and before it ran out of memory. We also tried replacing complicated implementations of modular reductions with the naive ones using the modulo operator (bv_urem in SMT-LIB), but the end-to-end verification was still not tractable.

5.2   Decomposition of Verification Task

A natural idea to overcome the difficulty of verifying a program like optimized NTT, which has both low-level details and a high-level algorithmic structure, is to decompose the original verification problem into several components, in a way that separate verification of each component would imply functional correctness of the whole program. We give an overview of the decomposition here; a more detailed account on the whole verification process is shown in Appendix A.

Recall the pseudocode in Algorithm 2. Our interval analysis in Section 4 has shown that, on an end-to-end execution of the NTT program, there will be no possibility of integer overflow. This means that, to verify program equivalence modulo q, we can replace lazy reduction by an eager one that always applies

```
u = a[k + j]
t = montgomery_multiply_reduce(...)
if s mod 2 == 0 then
    a[k + j] = barrett_reduce(u + t)
else
    a[k + j] = u + t
end if
a[k + j + m/2] = barrett_reduce(u + 2q − t)
```

```
u = a[k + j]
t = montgomery_multiply_reduce(...)
a[k + j] = barrett_reduce(u + t)
a[k + j + m/2] = barrett_reduce(u + 2q − t)
```

Fig. 1. Simplifying the lazy reduction (left) to the eager one (right)

Barrett reduction after addition. This simplifies the original psuedocode on the left of Fig. 1 to the one on the right.

The next step for simplification is to replace low-level implementations of modular arithmetic with much simpler operations. For this purpose, we need to prove correctness of Barrett reduction and Montgomery multiplication by (u + t) % q = csub(barrett_reduce(u + t)) for Barrett reduction and similarly for Montgomery multiplication[10]. We describe our verification procedure in Sect. 5.3. The simplified arithmetic operations, represented by $+'$, $-'$, and $*'$ in Fig. 2, are interpreted as symbolic operations on a finite field with built-in modular arithmetic.

$u = a[k+j]$
$t = a[k+j+m/2] *' \Omega[o+j]$
$a[k+j] = u +' t$
$a[k+j+m/2] = u -' t$

Fig. 2. Simplified butterfly computation on a finite field

Section 5.4 describes how such symbolic operations facilitate equivalence checking against the DFT formula. Since all low-level concerns have been resolved until this point, we can focus on the algorithmic aspect of the NTT program.

5.3   Verifying Modular-Reduction Algorithms

We have verified the equivalence of Barrett reduction and Montgomery multiplication implementations against the naive approach of using a built-in modulo operator (the % operator in C). We encode both approaches into Z3 formulas using the bit-vector theory, and check their equivalence. For example, Montgomery multiplication is implemented in the DSL as follows:

```
let montgomery_multiply_reduce x y =
  let mlo = mullo x y in
  let mhi = mulhi x y in
  let mlo_qinv = mullo mlo (const Param.qinv) in
  let t = mulhi mlo_qinv (const Param.q) in
  let carry = not_zero mlo in
  let res = mhi %+ t %+ carry in
  csub res
```

Listing 2: Montgomery multiplication implementation from [19]

---

[10] The symbol = represents the exact equality on integers. The additional conditional subtraction is necessary since the outputs of Barrett reduction can be larger than q.

We provide an implementation of the domain abstraction that, together with the direct evaluation of DSL terms by the host language, translates the DSL expression into a bit-vector formula. All DSL constructs required for Montgomery multiplication have a direct counterpart in the bit-vector theory, except for the high-product instruction `mulhi` which can be emulated easily[11].

By these ingredients, we can apply Z3 to verify Montgomery multiplication. More concretely, let `opt_formula` and `ref_formula` be the Z3 formulas for the implementation in Listing 2 and the naive multiplication followed by a modulo operation, respectively. We ran Z3 to check unsatisfiability of the formula `opt_formula ≠ ref_formula`, which has been successful. Similarly, correctness of the Barrett reduction has been proved using Z3.

5.4   Proving Correctness of the Simplified NTT Program

Our strategy for verifying the simplified NTT program is based on the following observation: Since DFT is a linear transformation, each output element can be represented as a linear polynomial on input variables. Since NTT also represents a linear transformation, we only have to prove that all coefficients on each variable in the two polynomials coincide up to congruence[12]. Therefore, we symbolically execute the simplified NTT program to compute such a linear polynomial for all output elements, and test if all coefficients are congruent to the corresponding rows of the DFT matrix. Thanks to the simplification stated before, the polynomial is truly linear in the sense that it consists of addition, subtraction, and multiplication by a constant (no explicit modulo operations) only. We can extract coefficients from the polynomials and compare them.

To make this idea concrete, we introduce a domain implementation that represents symbolic computations on polynomials:

```
module D_symbolic : Domain = struct
  type exp =
    | Const of int
    | Sym of string
    | Add of exp * exp
    | Sub of exp * exp
    | Mul of exp * exp
  type t = exp

  let add x y = Add(x, y)
  . . .
end
```

When we symbolically execute the NTT program using this domain, with an array of symbolic integers (represented by `Sym` constructor of `exp` type above) as an input, we end up with an output array whose i-th element represents all

---

[11] Refer to our source code for details on the translation from DSL to Z3 formulas.

[12] The coefficients computed by the NTT program may contain negative values due to subtraction in the butterfly operation.

computations that contribute to the i-th output. For each output, we simplify such a nested polynomial expression to obtain a linear polynomial, and compare the coefficients array with the corresponding row of the DFT matrix. We have confirmed that, for all output elements, our verification succeeded in establishing congruence of the NTT outputs and the DFT matrix.

Note how the two abstractions, the language and domain abstractions, simplified equivalence checking via symbolic computation: By composing the language interpretation that evaluates DSL terms directly in the host language, and the domain implementation representing symbolic operations, symbolic computation of NTT is naturally realized. Such a high degree of program abstraction would be nearly impossible if we would have operated on the low-level C program.

6 Discussion

Why a "unified" approach? In a traditional approach where generated code is verified directly, one has to reconstruct the original high-level structure in a DSL program from the generated low-level program, before doing any kind of analysis or verification. Even if such reconstruction was possible, we believe that the kind of program abstraction we rely on, such as the reinterpretation of the DSL program for symbolically computing polynomials, is extremely hard to accomplish automatically. In our unified approach, a verification procedure starts with a high-level DSL program. This makes the verification task simpler and paves a way for verifying more challenging properties than those handled by off-the-shelf automatic tools. At the same time, since program generation is based on the same DSL program, all interesting low-level concerns in the generated program are taken into account during verification.

The downsides of our approach are in (1) not verifying the generated code directly and (2) relying on unconventional trusted base[13]. Since we regard verification of the DSL program as a proxy for verification of the generated program, there is always a question on the gap between what is generated and what is verified. In addition, our approach assumes that our implementation of the two DSL interpretations, the program generator and the verifier, correctly respects the semantics of the original DSL program[14].

Despite the major disadvantages above, we believe that our approach is a promising step toward verifying functional correctness of a low-level, highly optimized program. We view the pros and cons of our approach as a trade-off between more possibilities for verification and larger trusted base.

---

[13] See Appendix A for our trusted base.

[14] However, note that both interpretations are based on the tagless-final style and thus they operate on DSL constructs at the most primitive level (such as translating the DSL for loop to that of OCaml or C). Therefore, we believe that their correctness is a reasonable assumption.

7   Related Work

Earlier work on verifying FFT focused on establishing equivalence of a textbook-style, recursive formulation of the FFT algorithm against DFT using a proof assistant [2,8,12]. Recently, Navas et al. [21] verified the absence of integer overflow in an implementation of NTT [17]. However, verification of functional correctness has been largely left open. To the best of our knowledge, there has been no prior work on verifying functional correctness of a highly optimized NTT implementation.

Verified implementations of low-level cryptographic primitives have been an active research topic [4,11,22,26]. Existing work targets those primitives that are already used widely, for example those in the Internet protocols, and proposes optimized implementations that are thoroughly verified using Coq or F*. We think that such full-scale verification is realistic only for primitives that are important today and whose implementations are more or less stable, due to its high cost: For bleeding-edge primitives such as NTT, more lightweight approaches like ours would be more accessible and useful for practitioners.

Outside of cryptography, the pioneering work by Amin et al. [5] considered correctness issues in the context of staging and generative programming. Their approach is based on generating C code together with correctness contracts as ACSL specifications, which can be verified by an external tool. Since they verify the generated code directly, they do not have to trust the code generator or a verifier for the DSL program. Although the approach of Amin et al. has a major advantage in this respect, what they can verify are fundamentally limited by the capability of external tools operating on the generated C program. For example, the case studies in [5] are limited to verifying safety properties such as memory safety of an HTTP parser or functional correctness of simple programs such as sorting. Our approach is complementary to theirs in the sense that we can verify more challenging properties in exchange for bigger trusted computing base.

8   Conclusion

We have proposed an approach for giving correctness assurance to the generated code in the context of generative programming. Integration of code generation and verification under one DSL framework enabled us to (1) incorporate an abstract interpretation to prove, for instance, the absence of integer overflow, and (2) decompose the end-to-end correctness verification problem into low-level and high-level parts, each of which can be verified separately. Our approach is lightweight in the sense that we make use of automation via abstract interpretation and symbolic computation. We have applied our approach to a highly optimized implementation of NTT, which is a key building block of next-generation cryptographic protocols, and successfully verified its functional correctness.

For future work, we plan to generalize our approach so that existing schemes other than NewHope or new ones can be similarly reimplemented and verified. We are also interested in exploring whether our unified approach is applicable to other domains, outside of NTT or cryptography.

Acknowledgements. We thank Hiroshi Unno for the helpful discussion. Feedback from anonymous reviewers helped improve this paper and is greatly appreciated. The second author is supported in part by JSPS Grant-in-Aid for Scientific Research (B) 18H03218.

Appendix A   Programs to be Verified and their Semantics

The verification procedure in Sect. 5 is a series of step-by-step simplifications of programs and their correctness proofs. The following table lists the programs and the domain interpretations in the procedure.

	Program	Domain	Arithmetic operation
P_0	DFT formula (1)	Z_q	Arithmetic operations in Z_q
P_1	DSL program in Sect. 2.2	Z_q	Arithmetic operations in Z_q
P_2	The same as P_1	Unsigned int	Arithmetic with modulo-q
P_3	The same as P_1	Unsigned int	Low-level operations
P_4	P_1 + lazy reduction	Unsigned int	Low-level operations
P_5	Generated C code	Unsigned int in C	Arithmetic operations in C

P_0 is the DFT formula (1) in Sect. 2.1. P_1, P_2, and P_3 are the DSL program whose inner-most loop was given in Sect. 2.2 with different domain interpretations. For the interpretation of DSL, we take the natural 'interpreter' semantics, which is essentially the same as the module R in Sect. 2.2.

P_1, P_2, and P_3 differ in the domain interpretations. For P_1, the domain is interpreted as Z_q. For P_2, the domain is interpreted as the set of 16 bit unsigned integers, and the arithmetic operations are those for unsigned integers followed by the modulo-q operation. To treat multiplication within 16 bits, we use mullo and mulhi in Sect. 3. For P_3, the domain remains the same as P_2, while the arithmetic operations are replaced by low-level operations such as Barrett reduction. The semantics of unsigned integers and their operations is specified by the bit-vector theory [16]. P_4 is the same as P_3 except that it employs lazy reduction in Sect. 3.

P_5 is the C code generated by interpreting the DSL constructs as generators for strings that represent the corresponding C code. This process (called *off-shoring* in the literature) is conceptually a trivial injection, however, formalizing it involves the semantics of the C language and is beyond the scope of this paper, and we put the equivalence of P_4 and P_5 into our trusted base.

Besides it, our trusted base includes correctness of our interval analysis, symbolic execution, and the implementations of helper functions such as mullo and mulhi. With this trusted base as well as the language and domain interpretations explained above, this paper has verified that, for $0 \leq k \leq 3$, P_k is extensionally equal (modulo q) to P_{k+1} (written $P_k =_{ext} P_{k+1}$): $P_3 =_{ext} P_4$ and $P_1 =_{ext} P_2$ in Sect. 4, $P_2 =_{ext} P_3$ in Sect. 5.3, and $P_0 =_{ext} P_1$ in Sect. 5.4.

References

1. ANSI/ISO C specification language. https://frama-c.com/html/acsl.html
2. Akbarpour, B., Tahar, S.: A methodology for the formal verification of FFT algorithms in HOL. In: Hu, A.J., Martin, A.K. (eds.) FMCAD 2004. LNCS, vol. 3312, pp. 37–51. Springer, Heidelberg (2004). https://doi.org/10.1007/978-3-540-30494-4_4
3. Alkim, E., Ducas, L., Pöppelmann, T., Schwabe, P.: Post-quantum key exchange: a new hope. In: Proceedings of the 25th USENIX Conference on Security Symposium, SEC 2016, pp. 327–343. USENIX Association, USA (2016)
4. Almeida, J.B., et al.: Jasmin: high-assurance and high-speed cryptography. In: Proceedings of the 2017 ACM SIGSAC Conference on Computer and Communications Security, CCS 2017, pp. 1807–1823. Association for Computing Machinery, New York (2017). https://doi.org/10.1145/3133956.3134078
5. Amin, N., Rompf, T.: LMS-Verify: abstraction without regret for verified systems programming. In: Castagna, G., Gordon, A.D. (eds.) Proceedings of the 44th ACM SIGPLAN Symposium on Principles of Programming Languages, POPL 2017, Paris, France, 18–20 January 2017. pp. 859–873. ACM (2017). https://doi.org/10.1145/3009837.3009867
6. Barrett, P.: Implementing the rivest shamir and adleman public key encryption algorithm on a standard digital signal processor. In: Odlyzko, A.M. (ed.) CRYPTO 1986. LNCS, vol. 263, pp. 311–323. Springer, Heidelberg (1987). https://doi.org/10.1007/3-540-47721-7_24
7. Bühler, D.: Structuring an abstract interpreter through value and state abstractions: EVA, an LC. (Structurer un interpréteur abstrait au moyen d'abstractions de valeurs et d'états: Eva, une analyse de valeur évoluée pour Frama-C). Ph.D. thesis, University of Rennes 1, France (2017), https://tel.archives-ouvertes.fr/tel-01664726
8. Capretta, V.: Certifying the fast fourier transform with Coq. In: Boulton, R.J., Jackson, P.B. (eds.) TPHOLs 2001. LNCS, vol. 2152, pp. 154–168. Springer, Heidelberg (2001). https://doi.org/10.1007/3-540-44755-5_12
9. Carette, J., Kiselyov, O., Shan, C.: Finally tagless, partially evaluated: tagless staged interpreters for simpler typed languages. J. Funct. Program. **19**(5), 509–543 (2009). https://doi.org/10.1017/S0956796809007205
10. Cormen, T.H., Leiserson, C.E., Rivest, R.L., Stein, C.: Introduction to Algorithms, 3rd edn. The MIT Press, Cambridge (2009)
11. Erbsen, A., Philipoom, J., Gross, J., Sloan, R., Chlipala, A.: Simple high-level code for cryptographic arithmetic - with proofs, without compromises. In: 2019 IEEE Symposium on Security and Privacy, SP 2019, San Francisco, CA, USA, 19–23 May 2019, pp. 1202–1219. IEEE (2019). https://doi.org/10.1109/SP.2019.00005
12. Gamboa, R.A.: The correctness of the fast fourier transform: a structured proof in ACL2. Form. Methods Syst. Des. **20**(1), 91–106 (2002). https://doi.org/10.1023/A:1012912614285
13. Güneysu, T., Oder, T., Pöppelmann, T., Schwabe, P.: Software speed records for lattice-based signatures. In: Gaborit, P. (ed.) PQCrypto 2013. LNCS, vol. 7932, pp. 67–82. Springer, Heidelberg (2013). https://doi.org/10.1007/978-3-642-38616-9_5
14. Kiselyov, O., Biboudis, A., Palladinos, N., Smaragdakis, Y.: Stream fusion, to completeness. In: Proceedings of the 44th ACM SIGPLAN Symposium on Principles of Programming Languages, POPL 2017, pp. 285–299. Association for Computing Machinery, New York (2017). https://doi.org/10.1145/3009837.3009880

15. Krishnaswami, N.R., Yallop, J.: A typed, algebraic approach to parsing. In: Proceedings of the 40th ACM SIGPLAN Conference on Programming Language Design and Implementation, PLDI 2019, pp. 379–393. Association for Computing Machinery, New York (2019). https://doi.org/10.1145/3314221.3314625

16. Kroening, D., Strichman, O.: Decision Procedures - An Algorithmic Point of View, Second Edition. Texts in Theoretical Computer Science. An EATCS Series. Springer, Heidelberg (2016). https://doi.org/10.1007/978-3-662-50497-0

17. Longa, P., Naehrig, M.: Speeding up the number theoretic transform for faster ideal lattice-based cryptography. In: Foresti, S., Persiano, G. (eds.) CANS 2016. LNCS, vol. 10052, pp. 124–139. Springer, Cham (2016). https://doi.org/10.1007/978-3-319-48965-0_8

18. Lyubashevsky, V., Peikert, C., Regev, O.: On ideal lattices and learning with errors over rings. In: Gilbert, H. (ed.) EUROCRYPT 2010. LNCS, vol. 6110, pp. 1–23. Springer, Heidelberg (2010). https://doi.org/10.1007/978-3-642-13190-5_1

19. Masuda, M., Kameyama, Y.: FFT program generation for ring LWE-based cryptography. In: Nakanishi, T., Nojima, R. (eds.) IWSEC 2021. LNCS, vol. 12835, pp. 151–171. Springer, Cham (2021). https://doi.org/10.1007/978-3-030-85987-9_9

20. Montgomery, P.L.: Modular multiplication without trial division. Math. Comput. **44**, 519–521 (1985)

21. Navas, J.A., Dutertre, B., Mason, I.A.: Verification of an optimized NTT algorithm. In: Christakis, M., Polikarpova, N., Duggirala, P.S., Schrammel, P. (eds.) NSV/VSTTE -2020. LNCS, vol. 12549, pp. 144–160. Springer, Cham (2020). https://doi.org/10.1007/978-3-030-63618-0_9

22. Protzenko, J., et al.: Evercrypt: a fast, verified, cross-platform cryptographic provider. In: 2020 IEEE Symposium on Security and Privacy (SP), pp. 983–1002 (2020). https://doi.org/10.1109/SP40000.2020.00114

23. Seiler, G.: Faster AVX2 optimized NTT multiplication for Ring-LWE lattice cryptography. IACR Cryptol. ePrint Arch. **2018**, 39 (2018)

24. Shaikhha, A., Klonatos, Y., Koch, C.: Building efficient query engines in a high-level language. ACM Trans. Database Syst. **43**(1) (2018). https://doi.org/10.1145/3183653

25. Wei, G., Chen, Y., Rompf, T.: Staged abstract interpreters: fast and modular whole-program analysis via meta-programming. Proc. ACM Program. Lang. **3**(OOPSLA), 126:1–126:32 (2019). https://doi.org/10.1145/3360552

26. Zinzindohoué, J.K., Bhargavan, K., Protzenko, J., Beurdouche, B.: HACL*: a verified modern cryptographic library. In: Proceedings of the 2017 ACM SIGSAC Conference on Computer and Communications Security, CCS 2017, pp. 1789–1806. Association for Computing Machinery, New York (2017). https://doi.org/10.1145/3133956.3134043

Scheduling Complexity of Interleaving Search

Dmitry Rozplokhas$^{(\boxtimes)}$ and Dmitry Boulytchev

St Petersburg University and JetBrains Research, Saint Petersburg, Russia
rozplokhas@gmail.com, dboulytchev@math.spbu.ru

Abstract. MINIKANREN is a lightweight embedded language for logic and relational programming. Many of its useful features come from a distinctive search strategy, called *interleaving search*. However, with interleaving search conventional ways of reasoning about the complexity and performance of logical programs become irrelevant. We identify an important key component—*scheduling*—which makes the reasoning for MINIKANREN so different, and present a semi-automatic technique to estimate the scheduling impact via symbolic execution for a reasonably wide class of programs.

Keywords: miniKanren · Interleaving search · Time complexity · Symbolic execution

1 Introduction

A family of embedded languages for logic and, more specifically, relational programming MINIKANREN [10] has demonstrated an interesting potential in various fields of program synthesis and declarative programming [5,6,14]. A distinctive feature of MINIKANREN is *interleaving search* [13] which, in particular, delivers such an important feature as completeness.

However, being a different search strategy than conventional BFS/DFS/iterative deepening, etc., interleaving search makes the conventional ways of reasoning about the complexity of logical programs not applicable. Moreover, some intrinsic properties of interleaving search can manifest themselves in a number of astounding and, at the first glance, unexplainable performance effects.

As an example, let's consider two implementations of list concatenation relation (Fig. 1, left side); we respect here a conventional tradition for MINIKANREN programming to superscript all relational names with "o". The only difference between the two is the position of the recursive call. The evaluation of these implementations on the same problem (Fig. 1, right side) shows that the first implementation works significantly slower, although it performs exactly the same number of unifications. As a matter of fact, these two implementations even have different *asymptotic* complexity under the assumption that occurs check is disabled.[1] Although the better performance of the append$^o_{opt}$ relation is expected

---

[1] The role of occurs check is discussed in Sect. 5.

M. Hanus and A. Igarashi (Eds.): FLOPS 2022, LNCS 13215, pp. 152–170, 2022.
https://doi.org/10.1007/978-3-030-99461-7_9

```
append° =λ a b ab .
   ((a ≡ Nil) ∧ (ab ≡ b)) ∨
   (fresh (h t tb)
       (a ≡ Cons(h, t)) ∧
       (append° t b tb) ∧
       (ab ≡ Cons(h, tb)))

append°_opt =λ a b ab .
   ((a ≡ Nil) ∧ (ab ≡ b)) ∨
   (fresh (h t tb)
       (a ≡ Cons(h, t)) ∧
       (ab ≡ Cons(h, tb) ∧
       (append°_opt t b tb)))
```

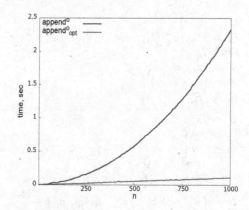

Fig. 1. Two implementations of list concatenation and their performance for $a = [1, \ldots, n]$, $b = [1, \ldots, 100]$, and ab left free.

even under conventional strategies due to tail recursion, the asymptotic difference is striking.

A careful analysis discovers that the difference is caused not by unifications, but by the process of *scheduling* goals during the search. In MINIKANREN a lazy structure is maintained to decompose the goals into unifications, perform these unifications in a certain order, and thread the results appropriately. For the $\mathtt{append}°_{opt}$ relation the size of this structure is constant, while for the $\mathtt{append}°$ this structure becomes linear in size, reducing the performance.

This paper presents a formal framework for scheduling cost complexity analysis for interleaving search in MINIKANREN. We use the reference operational semantics, reflecting the behaviour of actual implementations [15], and prove the soundness of our approach w.r.t. this semantics. The roadmap of the approach is as follows: we identify two complexity measures (one of which captures *scheduling complexity*) and give exact and approximate recursive formulae to calculate them (Sect. 3); then we present a procedure to automatically extract inequalities for the measures for a given goal using symbolic execution (Sect. 4). These inequalities have to be reformulated and solved manually in terms of a certain *metatheory*, which, on success, provides asymptotic bounds for the scheduling complexity of a goal evaluation. Our approach puts a number of restrictions on the goal being analyzed as well as on the relational program as a whole. We explicitly state these restrictions in Sect. 2 and discuss their impact in Sect. 7. The proofs of all lemmas and theorems can be found in the extended version of this paper.[2]

2   Background: Syntax and Semantics of miniKanren

In this section, we recollect some known formal descriptions for MINIKANREN language that will be used as a basis for our development. The descriptions here are

---
[2] https://arxiv.org/abs/2202.08511.

$$\mathcal{C} = \{C_i^{k_i}\}$$ constructors

$$\mathcal{T}_X = X \cup \{C_i^{k_i}(t_1, \ldots, t_{k_i}) \mid t_j \in \mathcal{T}_X\}$$ terms over the set of variables X

$$\mathcal{D} = \mathcal{T}_\varnothing$$ ground terms

$$\mathcal{X} = \{\mathbf{x}, \mathbf{y}, \mathbf{z}, \ldots\}$$ syntactic variables

$$\mathcal{A} = \{x, y, z \ldots\}$$ logic variables

$$\mathcal{R} = \{R_i^{k_i}\}$$ relational symbols with arities

$$\mathcal{G} = \mathcal{T}_X \equiv \mathcal{T}_X$$ equality

$$\mathcal{G} \wedge \mathcal{G}$$ conjunction

$$\mathcal{G} \vee \mathcal{G}$$ disjunction

fresh $\mathcal{X} . \mathcal{G}$ fresh variable introduction

$$R_i^{k_i}(t_1, \ldots, t_{k_i}), \ t_j \in \mathcal{T}_X$$ relational symbol invocation

$$\mathcal{S} = \{R_i^{k_i} = \lambda \, \mathbf{x}_1^i \ldots \mathbf{x}_{k_i}^i . g_i; \} \, g, \ g_i, g \in \mathcal{G}$$ specification

Fig. 2. The syntax of MINIKANREN

$$\Sigma = \mathcal{A} \to \mathcal{T}_\mathcal{A} \text{ substitutions} \qquad S = \langle \mathcal{G}, E \rangle \text{ task}$$

$$E = \Sigma \times \mathbb{N} \quad \text{environments} \qquad\qquad S \oplus S \text{ sum}$$

$$S \otimes \mathcal{G} \text{ product}$$

$$L = \circ \mid E \quad \text{labels} \qquad\qquad \hat{S} = \diamond \mid S \text{ states}$$

Fig. 3. States and labels in the LTS for MINIKANREN

taken from [15] (with a few non-essential adjustments for presentation purposes) to make the paper self-contained, more details and explanations can be found there.

The syntax of core MINIKANREN is shown in Fig. 2. All data is presented using terms $\mathcal{T}_X$ built from a fixed set of constructors $\mathcal{C}$ with known arities and variables from a given set X. We parameterize the terms with an alphabet of variables since in the semantic description we will need *two* kinds of variables: *syntactic* variables $\mathcal{X}$, used for bindings in the definitions, and *logic* variables $\mathcal{A}$, which are introduced and unified during the evaluation. We assume the set $\mathcal{A}$ is ordered and use the notation α_i to specify a position of a logical variable w.r.t. this order.

There are five types of goals: unification of two terms, conjunction and disjunction of goals, fresh logic variable introduction, and invocation of some relational definition. For the sake of brevity, in code snippets, we abbreviate immediately nested "**fresh**" constructs into the one, writing "**fresh** x y .... g" instead of "**fresh** x . **fresh** y . .... g". The *specification* $\mathcal{S}$ consists of a set of relational definitions and a top-level goal. A top-level goal represents a search procedure that returns a stream of substitutions for the free variables of the goal.

During the evaluation of MINIKANREN program an environment, consisting of a substitution for logic variables and a counter of allocated logic variables, is threaded through the computation and updated in every unification and fresh

$$\langle t_1 \equiv t_2, (\sigma, n) \rangle \xrightarrow{\circ} \Diamond, \ \not\exists \, mgu\,(t_1\sigma, t_2\sigma) \qquad \text{[UnifyFail]}$$

$$\langle t_1 \equiv t_2, (\sigma, n) \rangle \xrightarrow{(mgu\,(t_1\sigma, t_2\sigma)\circ\sigma),\, n)} \Diamond \qquad \text{[UnifySuccess]}$$

$$\langle\, \mathbf{fresh}\ \mathbf{x} \,.\, g,\, (\sigma, n) \rangle \xrightarrow{\circ} \langle g\,[\alpha_{n+1}/\mathbf{x}],\, (\sigma, n+1) \rangle \qquad \text{[Fresh]}$$

$$\frac{R_i^{k_i} = \lambda\, \mathbf{x}_1 \ldots \mathbf{x}_{k_i} \,.\, g}{\langle R_i^{k_i}\,(t_1, \ldots, t_{k_i}),\, e \rangle \xrightarrow{\circ} \langle g\,[{t_1}/{\mathbf{x}_1} \ldots {t_{k_i}}/{\mathbf{x}_{k_i}}],\, e \rangle} \qquad \text{[Invoke]}$$

$$\langle g_1 \vee g_2,\, e \rangle \xrightarrow{\circ} \langle g_1,\, e \rangle \oplus \langle g_2,\, e \rangle \quad \text{[Disj]} \qquad \langle g_1 \wedge g_2,\, e \rangle \xrightarrow{\circ} \langle g_1,\, e \rangle \otimes g_2 \qquad \text{[Conj]}$$

$$\frac{s_1 \xrightarrow{l} \Diamond}{(s_1 \oplus s_2) \xrightarrow{l} s_2} \quad \text{[DisjStop]} \qquad \frac{s_1 \xrightarrow{l} s_1'}{(s_1 \oplus s_2) \xrightarrow{l} (s_2 \oplus s_1')} \quad \text{[DisjStep]}$$

$$\frac{s \xrightarrow{\circ} \Diamond}{(s \otimes g) \xrightarrow{\circ} \Diamond} \quad \text{[ConjStop]} \qquad \frac{s \xrightarrow{e} \Diamond}{(s \otimes g) \xrightarrow{\circ} \langle g, e \rangle} \quad \text{[ConjStopAns]}$$

$$\frac{s \xrightarrow{\circ} s'}{(s \otimes g) \xrightarrow{\circ} (s' \otimes g)} \quad \text{[ConjStep]} \qquad \frac{s \xrightarrow{e} s'}{(s \otimes g) \xrightarrow{\circ} (\langle g, e \rangle \oplus (s' \otimes g))} \quad \text{[ConjStepAns]}$$

Fig. 4. Operational semantics of interleaving search

variable introduction. The substitution in the environment at a given point and given branch of evaluation contains all the information about relations between the logical variables at this point. Different branches are combined via *interleaving search* procedure [13]. The answers for a given goal are extracted from the final environments.

This search procedure is formally described by operational semantics in the form of a labeled transition system. This semantics corresponds to the canonical implementation of interleaving search.

The form of states and labels in the transition system is defined in Fig. 3. Non-terminal states S have a tree-like structure with intermediate nodes corresponding to partially evaluated conjunctions ("$\otimes$") or disjunctions ("$\oplus$"). A leaf in the form $\langle g, e \rangle$ determines a task to evaluate a goal g in an environment e. For a conjunction node, its right child is always a goal since it cannot be evaluated unless some result is provided by the left conjunct. We also need a terminal state $\Diamond$ to represent the end of the evaluation. The label "$\circ$" is used to mark those steps which do not provide an answer; otherwise, a transition is labeled by an updated environment.

The transition rules are shown in Fig. 4. The first six rules define the evaluation of leaf states. For the disjunction and conjunction, the corresponding node states are constructed. For other types of goals the environment and the evaluated goal are updated in accordance with the task given by the goal: for an equality the most general unifier of the terms is incorporated into the substitution (or execution halts if the terms are non-unifiable); for a fresh construction a new variable is introduced and the counter of allocated variables is incremented; for a relational call the body of the relation is taken as the next goal. The rest of the rules define composition of evaluation of substates for partial disjunctions and conjunctions. For a partial disjunction, the first constituent is evaluated for

$$
\begin{aligned}
B_{nf} &= \mathcal{T}_\mathcal{X} \equiv \mathcal{T}_\mathcal{X} \mid R^k\left(\mathcal{T}_\mathcal{X}, \ldots, \mathcal{T}_\mathcal{X}\right) \\
C_{nf} &= B_{nf} \mid C_{nf} \wedge B_{nf} \\
F_{nf} &= C_{nf} \mid \textbf{fresh } X \,.\, F_{nf} \\
D_{nf} &= F_{nf} \mid D_{nf} \vee F_{nf}
\end{aligned}
$$

Fig. 5. Disjunctive normal form for goals

one step, then the constituents are swapped (which constitutes the *interleaving*), and the label is propagated. When the evaluation of the first constituent of partial disjunction halts, the evaluation proceeds with the second constituent. For a partial conjunction, the first constituent is evaluated until the answer is obtained, then the evaluation of the second constituent with this answer as the environment is scheduled for evaluation together with the remaining partial conjunction (via partial disjunction node). When the evaluation of the first constituent of partial conjunction halts, the evaluation of the conjunction halts, too.

The introduced transition system is completely deterministic, therefore a derivation sequence for a state s determines a certain *trace*—a sequence of states and labeled transitions between them. It may be either finite (ending with the terminal state $\diamond$) or infinite. We will denote by $\mathcal{T}r^{st}(s)$ the sequence of states in the trace for initial state s and by $\mathcal{T}r^{ans}(s)$ the sequence of answers in the trace for initial state s. The sequence $\mathcal{T}r^{ans}(s)$ corresponds to the stream of answers in the reference MINIKANREN implementations.

In the following we rely on the following property of leaf states:

Definition 2.1. A leaf state $\langle g, (\sigma, n) \rangle$ is well-formed iff $\mathcal{FV}(g) \cup \mathcal{Dom}(\sigma) \cup \mathcal{VRan}(\sigma) \subseteq \{\alpha_1, \ldots, \alpha_n\}$, where $\mathcal{FV}(g)$ denotes the set of free variables in a goal g, $\mathcal{Dom}(\sigma)$ and $\mathcal{VRan}(\sigma)$—the domain of a substitution σ and a set of all free variables in its image respectively.

Informally, in a well-formed leaf state all free variables in goals and substitution respect the counter of free logical variables. This definition is in fact an instance of a more general definition of well-formedness for all states, introduced in [15], where it is proven that the initial state is well-formed and any transition from a well-formed state results in a well-formed one.

Besides operational semantics, we will make use of a denotational one analogous to the least Herbrand model. For a relation R^k, its denotational semantics $[\![R^k]\!]$ is treated as a k-ary relation on the set of all ground terms, where each "dimension" corresponds to a certain argument of R^k. For example, $[\![\texttt{append}^o]\!]$ is a set of all triplets of ground lists, in which the third component is a concatenation of the first two. The concrete description of the denotational semantics is given in [15] as well as the proof of the soundness and completeness of the operational semantics w.r.t. to the denotational one.

Finally, we explicitly enumerate all the restrictions required by our method to work:

- All relations have to be in DNF (set D_{nf} in Fig. 5).
- We only consider goals which converge with a finite number of answers.
- All answers have to be ground (*groundness* condition) for all relation invocations encountered during the evaluation.
- All answers have to be unique (*answer uniqueness* condition) for all relation invocations encountered during the evaluation.

3   Scheduling Complexity

We may notice that the operational semantics described in the previous section can be used to calculate the exact number of elementary scheduling steps. Our first idea is to take the number of states $d(s)$ in the finite trace for a given state s:

$$d(s) \overset{\text{def}}{=} |\mathcal{T}r^{st}(s)|$$

However, it turns out that this value alone does not provide an accurate scheduling complexity estimation. The reason is that some elementary steps in the semantics are not elementary in existing implementations. Namely, a careful analysis discovers that each semantic step involves navigation to the leftmost leaf of the state which in implementations corresponds to multiple elementary actions, whose number is proportional to the height of the leftmost branch of the state in question. Here we provide an *ad-hoc* definition for this value, $t(s)$, which we call the *scheduling factor*:

$$t(s) \overset{\text{def}}{=} \sum_{s_i \in \mathcal{T}r^{st}(s)} lh(s_i)$$

where $lh(s_i)$ is the height of the leftmost branch of the state.

In the rest of the section, we derive recurrent equations which would relate the scheduling complexity for states to the scheduling complexity for their (immediate) substates. It turns out that to come up with such equations both t and d values have to be estimated simultaneously.

The next lemma provides the equations for $\oplus$-states:

Lemma 3.1. *For any two states* s_1 *and* s_2

$$d(s_1 \oplus s_2) = d(s_1) + d(s_2)$$
$$t(s_1 \oplus s_2) = t(s_1) + t(s_2) + cost_\oplus(s_1 \oplus s_2)$$

where $cost_\oplus(s_1 \oplus s_2) = \min\{2 \cdot d(s_1) - 1, 2 \cdot d(s_2)\}$

Informally, for a state in the form $s_1 \oplus s_2$ the substates are evaluated separately, one step at a time for each substate, so the total number of semantic steps is the sum of those for the substates. However, for the scheduling factor, there is an extra summand $cost_\oplus(s_1 \oplus s_2)$ since the "leftmost heights" of the states in the trace are one node greater than those for the original substates due to the introduction of one additional $\oplus$-node on the top. This additional node persists in the trace until the evaluation of one of the substates comes to an end, so the scheduling factor is increased by the number of steps until that.

The next lemma provides the equations for $\otimes$-states:[3]

Lemma 3.2. *For any state s and any goal g*

$$d\left(s \otimes g\right) = d\left(s\right) + \sum_{a_i \in Trans(s)} d\left(\langle g, a_i\rangle\right) \qquad (\star)$$

$$t\left(s \otimes g\right) = t\left(s\right) + cost_\otimes(s \otimes g) + \sum_{a_i \in Trans(s)}\left(t\left(\langle g, a_i\rangle\right) + cost_\oplus(\langle g, a_i\rangle \oplus (s_i' \otimes g))\right) \qquad (\dagger)$$

where

$$cost_\otimes(s \otimes g) = d\left(s\right)$$
$$s_i' = \text{the first state in the trace for } s \text{ after}$$
$$\text{a transition delivering the answer } a_i$$

For the states of the form $s \otimes g$ the reasoning is the same, but the resulting equations are more complicated. In an $\otimes$-state the left substate is evaluated until an answer is found, which is then taken as *an environment* for the evaluation of the right subgoal. Thus, in the equations for $\otimes$-states the evaluation times of the second goal *for all the answers* generated for the first substate are summed up. The evaluation of the right subgoal in different environments is added to the evaluation of the left substate via creation of an $\oplus$-state, so for the scheduling factor there is an additional summand $cost_\oplus(\langle g, a_i\rangle \oplus s_i')$ for each answer with s_i' being the state after discovering the answer. There is also an extra summand $cost_\otimes(s \otimes g)$ for the scheduling factor because of the $\otimes$-node that increases the height in the trace, analogous to the one caused by $\oplus$-nodes. Note, a $\otimes$-node is always placed immediately over the left substate so this addition is exactly the number of steps for the left substate.

Unfolding costs definitions in ($\dagger$) gives us a cumbersome formula that includes some intermediate states s_i' encountered during the evaluation. However, as ultimately we are interested in asymptotic estimations, we can approximate these costs up to a multiplicative constant. We can notice that the value $d\left(s_i' \otimes g\right)$ occurring in the second argument of $cost_\oplus$ includes values $d\left(\langle g, a_j\rangle\right)$ (like in the first argument) for all answers a_j after this intermediate state. So in the sum of all $cost_\oplus$ values $d\left(\langle g, a_i\rangle\right)$ may be excluded for at most one answer, and in fact, if we take the maximal one of these values we will get a rather

---

[3] We assume $\Diamond \otimes g = \Diamond$.

precise approximation. Specifically, we can state the following approximation[4] for $t(s \otimes g)$.

Lemma 3.3.

$$t(s \otimes g) = t(s) + \left(\sum_{a_i \in \mathcal{T}^{rans}(s)} t(\langle g, a_i \rangle) \right) + \Theta \left(d(s) + \sum_{a_i \in \mathcal{T}^{rans}(s)} d(\langle g, a_i \rangle) - \overset{\bullet}{\max_{a_i \in \mathcal{T}^{rans}(s)}} d(\langle g, a_i \rangle) \right)$$

Hereafter we use the following notation: $\overset{\bullet}{\max} S = \max (S \cup \{0\})$. We can see that the part under Θ is very similar to the $(\star)$ except that here we exclude d value for one of the answers from the sum. This difference is essential and, as we will see later, it is in fact responsible for the difference in complexities for our motivating example.

4   Complexity Analysis via Symbolic Execution

Our approach to complexity analysis is based on a semi-automatic procedure involving symbolic execution. In the previous section, we presented formulae to compositionally estimate the complexity factors for *non-leaf states* of operational semantics under the assumption that corresponding estimations for *leaf states* are given. In order to obtain corresponding estimations for relations as a whole, we would need to take into account the effects of relational invocations, including the recursive ones.

Another observation is that as a rule we are interested in complexity estimations in terms of some *metatheory*. For example, dealing with relations on lists we would be interested in estimations in terms of list lengths, with trees—in terms of depth or number of nodes, with numbers—in terms of their values, etc. It is unlikely that a generic term-based framework would provide such specific information automatically. Thus, a viable approach would be to extract some inequalities involving the complexity factors of certain relational calls automatically and then let a human being solve these inequalities in terms of a relevant metatheory.

For the sake of clarity we will provide a demonstration of complexity analysis for a specific example—append^o relation from the introduction—throughout the section.

The extraction procedure utilizes a symbolic execution technique and is completely automatic. It turns out that the semantics we have is already abstract enough to be used for symbolic execution with minor adjustments. In this symbolic procedure, we mark some of the logic variables as "grounded" and at certain moments substitute them with ground terms. Informally, for some goal with

---

[4] We assume the following definition for $f(x) = g(x) + \Theta(h(x))$:

$$\exists C_1, C_2 \in \mathcal{R}^+, \forall x : g(x) + C_1 \cdot h(x) \leq f(x) \leq g(x) + C_2 \cdot h(x)$$

some free logic variables we consider the complexity of a search procedure which finds the bindings for all non-grounded variables based on the ground values substituted for the grounded ones. This search procedure is defined precisely by the operational semantics; however, as the concrete values of grounded variables are unknown (only the fact of their *groundness*), the whole procedure becomes symbolic. In particular, in unification the groundness can be propagated to some non-grounded free variables. Thus, the symbolic execution is determined by a set of grounded variables (hereafter denoted as $V \subset \mathcal{A}$). The initial choice of V determines the problem we analyze.

In our example the objective is to study the execution when we specialize the first two arguments with ground values and leave the last argument free. Thus, we start with the goal $\mathsf{append}^o \ a \ b \ ab$ (where a, b and ab are distinct free logic variables) and set the initial $V = \{a, b\}$.

We can make an important observation that both complexity factors (d and t) are stable w.r.t. the renaming of free variables; moreover, they are also stable w.r.t. the change of the fresh variables counter as long as it stays adequate, and change of current substitution, as long as it gives the same terms after application. Formally, the following lemma holds.

Lemma 4.1. *Let* $s = \langle g, (\sigma, n) \rangle$ *and* $s' = \langle g', (\sigma', n') \rangle$ *be two well-formed states. If there exists a bijective substitution* $\pi \colon FV(g\sigma) \to FV(g'\sigma')$ *such that* $g\sigma\pi = g'\sigma'$, *then* $d(s) = d(s')$ *and* $t(s) = t(s')$.

The lemma shows that the set of states for which a call to relation has to be analyzed can be narrowed down to a certain family of states.

Definition 4.1. Let g be a goal. An initial state for g is $init(g) = \langle g, (\varepsilon, n_{init}(g)) \rangle$ with $n_{init}(g) = \min\{n \mid FV(g) \subseteq \{\alpha_1 \ldots \alpha_n\}\}$.

Due to the Lemma 4.1 it is sufficient for analysis of a relational call to consider only the family of initial states since an arbitrary call state encountered throughout the execution can be transformed into an initial one while preserving both complexity factors. Thus, the analysis can be performed in a compositional manner where each call can be analyzed separately. For our example the family of initial states is $q^{app}(\mathbf{a}, \mathbf{b}) = init(\mathsf{append}^o \ \mathbf{a} \ \mathbf{b} \ ab)$ for arbitrary ground terms $\mathbf{a}$ and $\mathbf{b}$.

As we are aiming at the complexity estimation depending on specific ground values substituted for grounded variables, in general case extracted inequalities have to be parameterized by *valuations*—mappings from the set of grounded variables to ground terms. As the new variables are added to this set during the execution, the valuations need to be extended for these new variables. The following definition introduces this notion.

Definition 4.2. Let $V \subset U \subset \mathcal{A}$ and $\rho \colon V \to \mathcal{T}_{\varnothing}$ and $\rho' \colon U \to \mathcal{T}_{\varnothing}$ be two valuations. We say that ρ' extends ρ (denotation: $\rho' \succ \rho$) if $\rho'(x) = \rho(x)$ for all $x \in V$.

The main objective of the symbolic execution in our case is to find constraints on valuations for every leaf goal in the body of a relation that determine whether the execution will continue and how a valuation changes after this goal. For internal relational calls, we describe constraints in terms of denotational semantics (to be given some meaning in terms of metatheory later). We can do it because of a precise equivalence between the answers found by operational semantics and values described by denotational semantics thanks to soundness and completeness as well as our requirements of grounding and uniqueness of answers. Our symbolic treatment of equalities relies on the fact that substitutions of ground terms commute, in a certain sense, with unifications. More specifically, we can use the most general unifier for two terms to see how unification goes for two terms with some free variables substituted with ground terms. The most general unifier may contain bindings for both grounded and non-grounded variables. A potential most general unifier for terms after substitution contains the same bindings for non-grounding terms (with valuation applied to their rhs), while bindings for grounding variables turn into equations that should be satisfied by the unifier with ground value on the left and bound term on the right. In particular, this means that all variables in bindings for grounded variables become grounded, too. We can use this observation to define an iterative process that determines the updated set of grounded variables $\mathbf{upd}\,(U,\,\delta)$ for a current set U and a most general unifier δ and a set of equations $\mathbf{constr}\,(\delta,\,U)$ that should be respected by the valuation.

$$\mathbf{upd}\,(U,\,\delta) = \begin{cases} U & \forall x \in U : FV\,(\delta\,(x)) \subset U \\ \mathbf{upd}\,(U \cup \bigcup_{x \in U} FV\,(\delta\,(x)),\,\delta) & \text{otherwise} \end{cases}$$

$$\mathbf{constr}\,(\delta,\,U) = \{x = \delta\,(x) \mid x \in U \cap \mathcal{D}om\,(\delta)\}$$

Using these definitions we can describe symbolic unification by the following lemma.

Lemma 4.2. *Let t_1, t_2 be terms, $V \subset \mathcal{A}$ and $\rho \colon V \to \mathcal{T}_\varnothing$ be a valuation. If $mgu\,(t_1, t_2) = \delta$ and $U = \mathbf{upd}\,(V, \delta)$ then $t_1\rho$ and $t_2\rho$ are unifiable iff there is some $\rho' \colon U \to \mathcal{T}_\varnothing$ such that $\rho' \succ \rho$ and $\forall (y = t) \in \mathbf{constr}\,(\delta,\,U) : \rho'(y) = t\rho'$. In such case ρ' is unique and $\rho \circ mgu\,(t_1\rho, t_2\rho) = \delta \circ \rho'$ up to alpha-equivalence (e.g. there exists a bijective substitution $\pi \colon FV(t_1) \to FV(t_2)$, s.t. $\rho \circ mgu\,(t_1\rho, t_2\rho) = \delta \circ \rho' \circ \pi$).*

In our description of the extraction process, we use a visual representation of symbolic execution of a relation body for a given set of grounded variables in a form of a *symbolic scheme*. A symbolic scheme is a tree-like structure with different branches corresponding to execution of different disjuncts and nodes corresponding to equalities and relational calls in the body augmented with subsets of grounded variables at the point of execution.[5] Constraints for substituted

---

[5] Note the difference with conventional symbolic execution graphs with different branches representing mutually exclusive paths of evaluation, not the different parts within one evaluation.

$$\mathfrak{S}^{\varUpsilon} = \qquad \mathcal{T_A} \equiv \mathcal{T_A} \qquad\qquad R^k\left(\mathcal{T_A}, \ldots, \mathcal{T_A}\right)$$

$$\mathcal{T_A} \equiv \mathcal{T_A}$$

$$R^k\left(\mathcal{T_A}, \ldots, \mathcal{T_A}\right)$$

Fig. 6. Symbolic scheme forms

grounded variables that determine whether the execution continues are presented as labels on the edges of a scheme.

Each scheme is built as a composition of the five patterns, shown in Fig. 6 (all schemes are indexed by subsets of grounded variables with $\varUpsilon = 2^{\mathcal{A}}$ denoting such subsets).

Note, the constraints after nodes of different types differ: unification puts a constraint in a form of a set of equations on substituted ground values that should be respected while relational call puts a constraint in a form of a tuple of ground terms that should belong to the denotational semantics of a relation.

The construction of a scheme for a given goal (initially, the body of a relation) mimics a regular execution of a relational program. The derivation rules for scheme formation have the following form $\langle \varGamma, \sigma, n, V \rangle \vdash g \rightsquigarrow \mathfrak{S}^V$. Here g is a goal, $\varGamma$ is a list of *deferred* goals (these goals have to be executed after the execution of g in every branch in the same order, initially this list is empty; this resembles continuations, but the analogy is not complete), σ and n are substitution and counter from the current environment respectively, V is a set of grounded variables at the moment.

The rules are shown in Fig. 7. [CONJ$_\mathfrak{S}$] and [DISJ$_\mathfrak{S}$] are structural rules: when investigating conjunctions we defer the second conjunct by adding it to $\varGamma$ and continue with the first conjunct; disjunctions simply result in forks. [FRESH$_\mathfrak{S}$] introduces a fresh logic variable (not grounded) and updates the counter of occupied variables. When the investigated goal is equality or relational call it is added as a node to the scheme. If there are no deferred goals, then this node is a leaf (rules [UNIFYLEAF$_\mathfrak{S}$] and [INVOKELEAF$_\mathfrak{S}$]). Equality is also added as a leaf if there are some deferred goals, but the terms are non-unifiable and so the execution stops (rule [UNIFYFAIL$_\mathfrak{S}$]). If the terms in the equality are unifiable and there are deferred goals (rule [UNIFYSUCCESS$_\mathfrak{S}$]), the equality is added as a node and the execution continues for the deferred goals, starting from the leftmost one; also the set of grounded variables is updated and constraint labels are added for the edge in accordance with Lemma 4.2. For relational calls the

$$\frac{\langle g_2 : \Gamma, \sigma, n, V \rangle \vdash g_1 \rightsquigarrow \mathfrak{S}^V}{\langle \Gamma, \sigma, n, V \rangle \vdash g_1 \wedge g_2 \rightsquigarrow \mathfrak{S}^V} \qquad [\text{CONJ}_\mathfrak{S}]$$

$$\frac{\langle \Gamma, \sigma, n, V \rangle \vdash g_1 \rightsquigarrow \mathfrak{S_1}^V, \ \langle \Gamma, \sigma, n, V \rangle \vdash g_2 \rightsquigarrow \mathfrak{S_2}^V}{\langle \Gamma, \sigma, n, V \rangle \vdash g_1 \vee g_2 \rightsquigarrow \overset{\textstyle\frown}{\quad \mathfrak{S_1}^V \quad \mathfrak{S_2}^V}} \qquad [\text{DISJ}_\mathfrak{S}]$$

$$\frac{\langle \Gamma, \sigma, n+1, V \rangle \vdash g\,[{}^{\alpha_n}/_{\mathbf{x}}] \rightsquigarrow \mathfrak{S}^V}{\langle \Gamma, \sigma, n, V \rangle \vdash \mathbf{fresh}\ \mathbf{x} \,.\, g \rightsquigarrow \mathfrak{S}^V} \qquad [\text{FRESH}_\mathfrak{S}]$$

$$\langle \epsilon, \sigma, n, V \rangle \vdash t_1 \equiv t_2 \rightsquigarrow t_1\sigma \equiv t_2\sigma \qquad [\text{UNIFYLEAF}_\mathfrak{S}]$$

$$\langle \epsilon, \sigma, n, V \rangle \vdash R^k\,(t_1, \ldots, t_k) \rightsquigarrow R^k\,(t_1\sigma, \ldots, t_k\sigma) \qquad [\text{INVOKELEAF}_\mathfrak{S}]$$

$$\frac{\nexists mgu\,(t_1\sigma, t_2\sigma)}{\langle g : \Gamma, \sigma, n, V \rangle \vdash t_1 \equiv t_2 \rightsquigarrow t_1\sigma \equiv t_2\sigma} \qquad [\text{UNIFYFAIL}_\mathfrak{S}]$$

$$\frac{mgu\,(t_1\sigma, t_2\sigma) = \delta, \ U = \mathbf{upd}\,(V, \delta), \ \langle \Gamma, \sigma\delta, n, U \rangle \vdash g \rightsquigarrow \mathfrak{S}^U}{t_1\sigma \equiv t_2\sigma} \qquad [\text{UNIFYSUCCESS}_\mathfrak{S}]$$

$$\langle g : \Gamma, \sigma, n, V \rangle \vdash t_1 \equiv t_2 \rightsquigarrow \quad \Big\downarrow \mathrm{constr}\,(\delta,\,U) \atop \mathfrak{S}^U$$

$$\frac{U = V \cup \bigcup_i FV\,(t_i\sigma), \ \langle \Gamma, \sigma, n, U \rangle \vdash g \rightsquigarrow \mathfrak{S}^U}{R^k\,(t_1\sigma, \ldots, t_k\sigma)} \qquad [\text{INVOKE}_\mathfrak{S}]$$

$$\langle g : \Gamma, \sigma, n, V \rangle \vdash R^k\,(t_1, \ldots, t_k) \rightsquigarrow \quad \Big\downarrow {}_{(t_1\sigma, \ldots, t_k\sigma)\,\in\,[\![R^k]\!]} \atop \mathfrak{S}^U$$

Fig. 7. Scheme formation rules

proccess is similar: if there are some deferred goals (rule [INVOKE$_\mathfrak{S}$]), all variables occurring in a call become grounded (due to the grounding condition we imposed) and should satisfy the denotational semantics of the invoked relation.

The scheme constructed by these rules for our append^o example is shown in Fig. 8. For simplicity, we do not show the set of grounded variables for each node, but instead overline grounded variables in-place. Note, all variables that occur in constraints on the edges are grounded after parent node execution.

Now, we can use schemes to see how the information for leaf goals in relation body is combined with conjunctions and disjunctions. Then we can apply formulae from Sect. 3 to get recursive inequalities (providing lower and upper bounds simultaneously) for both complexity factors.

In these inequalities we need to sum up the values of d and t-factor for all leaf goals of a body and for all environments these goals are evaluated for. The leaf goals are the nodes of the scheme and evaluated environments can be derived from the constraints attached to the edges. So, for this summation we introduce the following notions: $\mathcal{D}$ is the sum of d-factor values and $\mathcal{T}$ is the sum of t-factor values for the execution of the body with specific valuation ρ.

Their definitions are shown in Fig. 9 (both formulas are given in the same figure as the definitions coincide modulo factor denotations). For nodes, we take the corresponding value (for equality it always equals 1). When going through an equality we sum up the rest with an updated valuation (by Lemma 4.2 this sum always has one or zero summands depending on whether the unification succeeds or not). When going through a relational call we take a sum of all valuations that satisfy the denotational

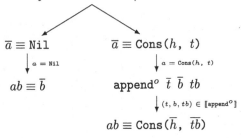

Fig. 8. Symbolic execution scheme for the goal $\mathtt{append}^o\ a\ b\ ab$ with initial set of grounded variables $V = \{a, b\}$. For each node, variables that are grounded at the point of execution of this node are overlined.

semantics (these valuations will correspond exactly to the set of all answers produced by the call since operational semantics is sound and complete w.r.t. the denotational one and because we require all answers to be unique). For disjunctions, we take the sum of both branches.

As we saw in Sect. 3 when computing the scheduling factors we need to exclude from the additional cost the value of d-factor for one of the environments (the largest one). This is true for the generalized formula for a whole scheme, too. This time we need to take all executed environments for all the leaves of a scheme and exclude the d-factor value for a maximal one (the formula for conjunction ensures that we make the exclusion for the leaf, and the formula for disjunction ensures that we make it for only one of the leaves). So, we will need additional notion $\mathcal{L}$, similar to $\mathcal{D}$ and $\mathcal{T}$ that will collect all the goals of the form $init\,(g_i\rho)$, where g_i is a leaf goal and ρ is a valuation corresponding to one of the environments this leaf is evaluated for. The definition of $\mathcal{L}$ is shown in Fig. 10.

Now we can formulate the following main theorem that provides the principal recursive inequalities, extracted from the scheme for a given goal.

Theorem 4.1. *Let g be a goal, and let $\langle \epsilon,\ \varepsilon,\ n_{init}(g),\ V\rangle \vdash g\ \leadsto \mathfrak{S}^V$. Then*

$$d\,(init\,(g\,\rho)) = \mathcal{D}\,(\mathfrak{S}^V)(\rho) + \Theta\,(1)$$
$$t\,(init\,(g\,\rho)) = \mathcal{T}\,(\mathfrak{S}^V)(\rho) + \Theta\,\Big(\mathcal{D}\,(\mathfrak{S}^V)(\rho) - \max_{\langle g_i,\,e_i\rangle \in \mathcal{L}(\mathfrak{S}^V)(\rho)} d\,(\langle g_i,\ e_i\rangle) + 1\Big)$$

being considered as functions on $\rho\colon V \to T_\varnothing$.

The theorem allows us to extract two inequalities (upper and lower bounds) for both factors with a multiplicative constant that is the same for all valuations.

$$\mathcal{D}/\mathcal{T}\left(\quad t_2 \equiv t_2 \quad\right)(\rho) = 1$$

$$\mathcal{D}/\mathcal{T}\left(\quad R^k\,(t_1, \ldots, t_k)\quad\right)(\rho) = \mathrm{d}/\mathrm{t}\,(init\,(R^k\,(t_1\rho, \ldots, t_k\rho)))$$

$$\mathcal{D}/\mathcal{T}\left(\begin{array}{c} t_1 \equiv t_2 \\ \Big\downarrow C_s \\ \mathfrak{S}^U \end{array}\quad\right)(\rho) = 1 + \sum_{\substack{\rho': V \to T_\varnothing \\ \rho' \succ \rho \\ \forall (y,t) \in Cs\,:\,\rho'\,(y) = t\,\rho'}} \mathcal{D}/\mathcal{T}\,(\mathfrak{S}^U)(\rho')$$

$$\mathcal{D}/\mathcal{T}\left(\begin{array}{c} R^k\,(t_1, \ldots, t_k) \\ \Big\downarrow {\scriptstyle (t_1, \ldots, t_k)\,\in\,[\![R^k]\!]} \\ \mathfrak{S}^U \end{array}\right)(\rho) = \mathrm{d}/\mathrm{t}\,(init\,(R^k\,(t_1\rho, \ldots, t_k\rho))) + \sum_{\substack{\rho': V \to T_\varnothing \\ \rho' \succ \rho \\ (t_1\rho', \ldots, t_k\rho')\in[\![R^k]\!]}} \mathcal{D}/\mathcal{T}\,(\mathfrak{S}^U)(\rho')$$

$$\mathcal{D}/\mathcal{T}\left(\begin{array}{cc} \diagup & \diagdown \\ \mathfrak{S}_1{}^V & \mathfrak{S}_2{}^V \end{array}\right)(\rho) = \mathcal{D}/\mathcal{T}\,(\mathfrak{S}_1{}^V)(\rho) + \mathcal{D}/\mathcal{T}\,(\mathfrak{S}_2{}^V)(\rho)$$

Fig. 9. Complexity factors extraction: $\mathcal{D}$ and $\mathcal{T}$

$$\mathcal{L}\left(\quad t_2 \equiv t_2 \quad\right)(\rho) = \{init\,(t_2 \equiv t_2)\}$$

$$\mathcal{L}\left(\quad R^k\,(t_1, \ldots, t_k)\quad\right)(\rho) = \{init\,(R^k\,(t_1\rho, \ldots, t_k\rho))\}$$

$$\mathcal{L}\left(\begin{array}{c} t_1 \equiv t_2 \\ \Big\downarrow C_s \\ \mathfrak{S}^U \end{array}\quad\right)(\rho) = \bigcup_{\substack{\rho': V \to T_\varnothing \\ \rho' \succ \rho \\ \forall (y,t) \in Cs\,:\,\rho'\,(y) = t\,\rho'}} \mathcal{L}\,(\mathfrak{S}^U)(\rho')$$

$$\mathcal{L}\left(\begin{array}{c} R^k\,(t_1, \ldots, t_k) \\ \Big\downarrow {\scriptstyle (t_1, \ldots, t_k)\,\in\,[\![R^k]\!]} \\ \mathfrak{S}^U \end{array}\right)(\rho) = \bigcup_{\substack{\rho': V \to T_\varnothing \\ \rho' \succ \rho \\ (t_1\rho', \ldots, t_k\rho')\in[\![R^k]\!]}} \mathcal{L}\,(\mathfrak{S}^U)(\rho')$$

$$\mathcal{L}\left(\begin{array}{cc} \diagup & \diagdown \\ \mathfrak{S}_1{}^V & \mathfrak{S}_2{}^V \end{array}\right)(\rho) = \mathcal{L}\,(\mathfrak{S}_1{}^V)(\rho) \cup \mathcal{L}\,(\mathfrak{S}_2{}^V)(\rho)$$

Fig. 10. Complexity factors extraction: $\mathcal{L}$

For our example, we can extract the following recursive inequalities from the scheme in Fig. 8. For presentation purposes, we will not show valuation in inequalities explicitly, but instead show the ground values of grounded variables (using variables in bold font) that determine each valuation. We can do such a simplification for any concrete relation.

$$d\,(q^{app}\,(\mathbf{a}, \mathbf{b})) = (1 + \sum_{\mathbf{a}=Nil} 1) + (1 + \sum_{\mathbf{h},\mathbf{t}:\mathbf{a}=Cons(\mathbf{h},\,\mathbf{t})}(d\,(q^{app}\,(\mathbf{t}, \mathbf{b})) + \sum_{\mathbf{tb}:(\mathbf{t},\mathbf{b},\mathbf{tb})\in[\![append^o]\!]} 1)) + \Theta\,(1)$$

$$t\left(q^{app}\left(\mathbf{a},\mathbf{b}\right)\right)=\left(1+\sum_{a=\mathtt{Nil}}1\right)+\left(1+\sum_{h,t:a=\mathtt{Cons}(h,\ t)}\left(t\left(q^{app}\left(\mathbf{t},\mathbf{b}\right)\right)+\sum_{tb:(t,b,tb)\in[\![append^o]\!]}1\right)\right)$$

$$+\,\Theta\Bigl(\bigl(1+\sum_{a=\mathtt{Nil}}1\bigr)+\bigl(1+\sum_{h,t:a=\mathtt{Cons}(h,\ t)}\bigl(d\left(q^{app}\left(\mathbf{t},\mathbf{b}\right)\right)+\sum_{tb:(t,b,tb)\in[\![append^o]\!]}1\bigr)\bigr)$$

$$-\overset{\bullet}{\max_{\substack{h,t,tb:a=\mathtt{Cons}(h,\ t)\wedge\\(t,b,tb)\in[\![append^o]\!]}}}\{d\left(init\left(ab\equiv\mathbf{b}\right)\right),d\left(init\left(ab\equiv\mathtt{Cons}\left(\mathbf{h},\ \mathbf{tb}\right)\right)\right)\}+1\Bigr)$$

Automatically extracted recursive inequalities, as a rule, are cumbersome, but they contain all the information on how scheduling affects the complexity. Often they can be drastically simplified by using metatheory-level reasoning.

For our example, we are only interested in the case when substituted values represent some lists. We thus perform the usual for lists case analysis considering the first list empty or non-empty. We can also notice that the excluded summand equals one. So we can rewrite the inequalities in the following way:

$$\begin{aligned}
d\left(q^{app}\left(\mathtt{Nil},\mathbf{b}\right)\right)&=\Theta\left(1\right)\\
d\left(q^{app}\left(\mathtt{Cons}\left(\mathbf{h},\ \mathbf{t}\right),\mathbf{b}\right)\right)&=d\left(q^{app}\left(\mathbf{t},\mathbf{b}\right)\right)+\Theta\left(1\right)\\
t\left(q^{app}\left(\mathtt{Nil},\mathbf{b}\right)\right)&=\Theta\left(1\right)\\
t\left(q^{app}\left(\mathtt{Cons}\left(\mathbf{h},\ \mathbf{t}\right),\mathbf{b}\right)\right)&=t\left(q^{app}\left(\mathbf{t},\mathbf{b}\right)\right)+\Theta\left(d\left(q^{app}\left(\mathbf{t},\mathbf{b}\right)\right)\right)
\end{aligned}$$

These trivial linear inequalities can be easily solved:

$$\begin{aligned}
d\left(q^{app}\left(\mathbf{a},\mathbf{b}\right)\right)&=\Theta\left(len\left(\mathbf{a}\right)\right)\\
t\left(q^{app}\left(\mathbf{a},\mathbf{b}\right)\right)&=\Theta\left(len^2\left(\mathbf{a}\right)\right)
\end{aligned}$$

In this case, scheduling makes a big difference and changes the asymptotics. Note, we expressed the result using notions from metatheory (*len* for the length of the list represented by a term).

In contrast, if we consider the optimal definition $\mathbf{append}^o_{opt}$ the analysis of the call $q^{app\text{-}opt}\left(\mathbf{a},\mathbf{b}\right)=init\left(\mathbf{append}^o_{opt}\,\mathbf{a}\,\mathbf{b}\,ab\right)$ is analogous, but among the candidates for exclusion there is the value $d\left(q^{app\text{-}opt}\left(\mathbf{t},\mathbf{b}\right)\right)$ since the recursive call is placed in a leaf. So the last simplified recursive approximation is the following (the rest is the same as in our main example):

$$t\left(q^{app\text{-}opt}\left(\mathtt{Cons}\left(\mathbf{h},\ \mathbf{t}\right),\mathbf{b}\right)\right)=t\left(q^{app\text{-}opt}\left(\mathbf{t},\mathbf{b}\right)\right)+\Theta\left(1\right)$$

So in this case the complexity of both factors is linear on $len\left(\mathbf{a}\right)$.

5 Evaluation

The theory we have built was so far applied to only one relation—$\mathbf{append}^o$— which we used as a motivating example. With our framework, it turned out to be possible to explain the difference in performance between two nearly identical implementations, and the difference—linear vs. quadratic asymptotic

	d	t		d	t
append° a b ab	$len\,(\mathrm{a})$	$len^2\,(\mathrm{a})$	plus° n m r	$\lvert \mathrm{n}\rvert$	$\lvert \mathrm{n}\rvert$
append°$_{opt}$ a b ab	$len\,(\mathrm{a})$	$len\,(\mathrm{a})$	plus° n m r	$\min\{\lvert \mathrm{n}\rvert, \lvert \mathrm{r}\rvert\}$	$\min\{\lvert \mathrm{n}\rvert, \lvert \mathrm{r}\rvert\}$
append°$_{opt}$ a b ab	$len\,(\mathrm{ab})$	$len\,(\mathrm{ab})$	plus° n m r	$\lvert \mathrm{r}\rvert$	$\lvert \mathrm{r}\rvert$
revers° a r	$len^2\,(\mathrm{a})$	$len^3\,(\mathrm{a})$	mult° n m r	$\lvert \mathrm{n}\rvert \cdot \lvert \mathrm{m}\rvert$	$\lvert \mathrm{n}\rvert^2 \cdot \lvert \mathrm{m}\rvert$
revers° a r	$len^2\,(\mathrm{r})$	$len^2\,(\mathrm{r})$	mult° (S n) (S m) r	$\lvert \mathrm{r}\rvert^2$	$\lvert \mathrm{r}\rvert^2$

Fig. 11. Derived d- and t-factors for some goals; $len\,(\bullet)$ stands for the length of a ground list, $\lvert \bullet \rvert$—for the value of a Peano number, represented as ground term.

complexity—was just as expected from the experimental performance evaluation. In this section, we present some other results of complexity estimations and discuss the adequacy of these estimations w.r.t. the real MINIKANREN implementations.

Derived complexity estimations for a few other relations are shown in Fig. 11. Besides concatenation, we deal with naive list reversing and Peano numbers addition and multiplication. We show both $d-$ and $t-$ factors since the difference between the two indicates the cases when scheduling strikes in. We expect that for simple relations like those presented the procedure of deriving estimations should be easy; however, for more complex ones the dealing with extracted inequalities may involve a non-trivial metatheory reasoning.

The justification of the adequacy of our complexity estimations w.r.t. the existing MINIKANREN implementations faces the following problem: it is not an easy task to separate the contribution of scheduling from other components of the search procedure—unification and occurs check. However, it is common knowledge among PROLOG users that in practice unification takes a constant time almost always; some theoretical basis for this is given in [1]. There are some specifics of unification implementation in MINIKANREN. First, for the simplicity of backtracking in a non-mutable fashion triangular substitution [3] is used instead of the idempotent one. It brings in an additional overhead which is analyzed in some detail in [4], but the experience shows that in the majority of practical cases this overhead is insignificant. Second, MINIKANREN by default performs the "occurs check", which contributes a significant overhead and often subsumes the complexity of all other search components. Meanwhile, it is known, that occurs checks are rarely violated [2]. Having said this, we expect that in the majority of the cases the performance of MINIKANREN programs with the occurs check disabled are described by scheduling complexity alone. In particular, this is true for all cases in Fig. 11. To confirm the adequacy of our model we evaluated the running time of these and some other goals (under the conditions we've mentioned) and found that it confirms the estimations derived using our framework. The details of implementation, evaluation, and results can be found in an accompanying repository.[6]

---

[6] https://www.dropbox.com/sh/ciceovnogkeeibz/AAAoclpTSDeY3OMagOBJHNiSa ?dl=0.

6   Related Work

To our knowledge, our work is the first attempt of comprehensive time complexity analysis for interleaving search in MINIKANREN. There is a number of separate observations on how certain patterns in relational programming affect performance and a number of "rules of thumb" based on these observations [4]. Some papers [9,12,16] tackle specific problems with relational programming using quantitative time measuring for evaluation. These approaches to performance analysis, being sufficient for specific relational problems, do not provide the general understanding of interleaving search and its cost.

At the same time complexity analysis was studied extensively in the broader context of logic programming (primarily, for PROLOG). As one important motivation for complexity analysis is granularity control in parallel execution, the main focus was set on the automated approaches.

Probably the best known among them is the framework [7] for cost analysis of logic programs (demonstrated on plain PROLOG), implemented in the system CASLOG. It uses data dependency information to estimate the sizes of the arguments and the number of solutions for executed atoms. These estimations are formulated as recursive inequalities (more precisely, as difference equations for upper bounds), which are then automatically solved with known methods. The time and space complexity are expressed using these estimations, the variations of this approach can provide both upper [7] and lower [8] bounds.

An alternative approach is suggested in [11] for symbolic analysis of logic programs (demonstrated in PROLOG with cuts). It constructs symbolic evaluation graphs capturing grounding propagation and reduction of recursive calls to previous ones, in the process of construction some heuristic approximations are used. These graphs may look similar to the symbolic schemes described in the Sect. 4 at first glance, but there is a principal difference: symbolic graphs capture the whole execution with all invoked calls (using inverse edges to represent cycles with recursive calls), while our schemes capture only the execution inside the body of a specific relation (representing the information about internal calls in terms of denotational semantics). The graphs are then transformed into term rewriting systems, for which the problem of the complexity analysis is well-studied (specifically, APROVE tool is used).

While these two approaches can be seen as partial bases for our technique, they are mainly focused on how the information about the arguments and results of the evaluated clauses can be derived automatically, since the calculation of time complexity of SLD-resolution is trivial when this information is available. In contrast, we are interested in the penalty of non-trivial scheduling of relational calls under interleaving search, so we delegate handling the information about calls to the reasoning in terms of a specific metatheory.

7   Discussion and Future Work

The formal framework presented in this paper analyzes the basic aspects of scheduling cost for interleaving search strategy from the theoretical viewpoint. As we have shown, it is sufficiently powerful to explain some surprising asymptotic behaviour for simple standard programs in MINIKANREN, but the applicability of this framework in practice for real implementations of MINIKANREN requires further investigation. Two key aspects that determine practical applicability are the admissibility of the imposed requirements and the correspondence of specific MINIKANREN implementations to the reference operational semantics, which should be studied individually for each application. We see our work as the ground for the future development of methods for analyzing the cost of interleaving search.

Our approach imposes three requirements on the analyzed programs: disjunctive normal form, uniqueness of answers, and grounding of relational calls. The first two are rather non-restrictive: DNF is equivalent to the description of relation as a set of Horn clauses in PROLOG, and the majority of well-known examples in MINIKANREN are written in this or very similar form. Repetition of answers is usually an indication of a mistake in a program [4]. The groundness condition is more serious: it prohibits program execution from presenting infinitely many individual ground solutions in one answer using free variables, which is a useful pattern. At the same time, this requirement is not unique for our work (the framework for CASLOG system mentioned above imposes exactly the same condition) and the experience shows that many important kinds of programs satisfy it (although it is hard to characterize the class of such programs precisely). Relaxing any of these restrictions will likely mess up the current relatively compact description of symbolic execution (for the conditions on relational calls) or the form of the extracted inequalities (for the DNF condition).

Also, for now, we confine ourselves to the problem of estimating the time of the full search for a given goal. Estimating the time before the first (or some specific) answer is believed to be an important and probably more practical task. Unfortunately, the technique we describe can not be easily adjusted for this case. The reason for this is that the reasoning about time (scheduling time in particular) in our terms becomes non-compositional for the case of interrupted search: if an answer is found in some branch, the search is cut short in other branches, too. Dealing with such a non-compositionality is a subject of future research.

References

1. Albert, L., Casas, R., Fages, F.: Average-case analysis of unification algorithms. Theor. Comput. Sci. **113**(1), 3–34 (1993). https://doi.org/10.1016/0304-3975(93)90208-B
2. Apt, K.R., Pellegrini, A.: Why the occur-check is not a problem. In: Bruynooghe, M., Wirsing, M. (eds.) PLILP 1992. LNCS, vol. 631, pp. 69–86. Springer, Heidelberg (1992). https://doi.org/10.1007/3-540-55844-6_128
3. Baader, F., Snyder, W.: Unification theory. In: Robinson, J.A., Voronkov, A. (eds.) Handbook of Automated Reasoning (in 2 volumes), pp. 445–532. Elsevier and MIT Press (2001). https://doi.org/10.1016/b978-044450813-3/50010-2
4. Byrd, W.E.: Relational Programming in Minikanren: techniques, applications, and implementations. Ph.D. thesis, USA (2009)

5. Byrd, W.E., Ballantyne, A., Rosenblatt, G., Might, M.: A unified approach to solving seven programming problems (functional pearl). Proc. ACM Program. Lang. 1(ICFP), 8:1–8:26 (2017). https://doi.org/10.1145/3110252

6. Byrd, W.E., Holk, E., Friedman, D.P.: miniKanren, live and untagged: quine generation via relational interpreters (programming pearl). In: Danvy, O. (ed.) Proceedings of the 2012 Annual Workshop on Scheme and Functional Programming, Scheme 2012, Copenhagen, Denmark, 9–15 September 2012, pp. 8–29. ACM (2012). https://doi.org/10.1145/2661103.2661105

7. Debray, S.K., Lin, N.: Cost analysis of logic programs. ACM Trans. Program. Lang. Syst. 15(5), 826–875 (1993). https://doi.org/10.1145/161468.161472

8. Debray, S.K., López-García, P., Hermenegildo, M.V., Lin, N.: Lower bound cost estimation for logic programs. In: Maluszynski, J. (ed.) Logic Programming, Proceedings of the 1997 International Symposium, Port Jefferson, Long Island, NY, USA, 13–16 October 1997, pp. 291–305. MIT Press (1997)

9. Donahue, E.: Guarded fresh goals: dependency-directed introduction of fresh logic variables. In: third miniKanren and Relational Programming Workshop (2021)

10. Friedman, D.P., Byrd, W.E., Kiselyov, O.: The Reasoned Schemer. MIT Press, Cambridge (2005)

11. Giesl, J., Ströder, T., Schneider-Kamp, P., Emmes, F., Fuhs, C.: Symbolic evaluation graphs and term rewriting: a general methodology for analyzing logic programs. In: Schreye, D.D., Janssens, G., King, A. (eds.) Principles and Practice of Declarative Programming, PPDP 2012, Leuven, Belgium - 19–21 September 2012, pp. 1–12. ACM (2012). https://doi.org/10.1145/2370776.2370778

12. Jin, E., Rosenblatt, G., Might, M., Zhang, L.: Universal quantification and implication in miniKanren. In: Third miniKanren and Relational Programming Workshop (2021)

13. Kiselyov, O., Shan, C., Friedman, D.P., Sabry, A.: Backtracking, interleaving, and terminating monad transformers: (functional pearl). In: Danvy, O., Pierce, B.C. (eds.) Proceedings of the 10th ACM SIGPLAN International Conference on Functional Programming, ICFP 2005, Tallinn, Estonia, 26–28 September 2005, pp. 192–203. ACM (2005). https://doi.org/10.1145/1086365.1086390

14. Kosarev, D., Lozov, P., Boulytchev, D.: Relational synthesis for pattern matching. In: Oliveira, B.C.S. (ed.) APLAS 2020. LNCS, vol. 12470, pp. 293–310. Springer, Cham (2020). https://doi.org/10.1007/978-3-030-64437-6_15

15. Rozplokhas, D., Vyatkin, A., Boulytchev, D.: Certified semantics for relational programming. In: Oliveira, B.C.S. (ed.) APLAS 2020. LNCS, vol. 12470, pp. 167–185. Springer, Cham (2020). https://doi.org/10.1007/978-3-030-64437-6_9

16. Sandre, L., Zaidi, M., Zhang, L.: Relational floating-point arithmetic. In: Third miniKanren and Relational Programming Workshop (2021)

Automated Generation of Control Concepts Annotation Rules Using Inductive Logic Programming

System Description

Basel Shbita[1](✉) and Abha Moitra[2](✉)

[1] University of Southern California, Los Angeles, CA, USA
`shbita@usc.edu`
[2] General Electric Research, Niskayuna, NY, USA
`moitraa@ge.com`

Abstract. Capturing domain knowledge is a time-consuming procedure that usually requires the collaboration of a Subject Matter Expert (SME) and a modeling expert to encode the knowledge. This situation is further exacerbated in some domains and applications. The SME may find it challenging to articulate the domain knowledge as a procedure or a set of rules but may find it easier to classify instance data. In the cyber-physical domain, inferring the implemented mathematical concepts in the source code or a different form of representation, such as the Resource Description Framework (RDF), is difficult for the SME, requiring particular expertise in low-level programming or knowledge in Semantic Web technologies. To facilitate this knowledge elicitation from SMEs, we developed a system that automatically generates classification and annotation rules for control concepts in cyber-physical systems (CPS). Our proposed approach leverages the RDF representation of CPS source code and generates the rules using Inductive Logic Programming and semantic technologies. The resulting rules require a small set of labeled instance data that is provided interactively by the SME through a user interface within our system. The generated rules can be inspected, iterated and manually refined.

Keywords: Knowledge capture · Semantic model · Knowledge graphs · Rules · Rule annotation · Cyber-physical systems

1 Introduction

Capturing domain knowledge is a critical task in many domains and applications. This process may involve knowledge elicitation followed by knowledge representation to facilitate inferencing, reasoning, or integration in some decision support systems. Knowledge capture frequently poses a roadblock in developing and

---

B. Shbita—This work was done while the author was at GE Global Research.

M. Hanus and A. Igarashi (Eds.): FLOPS 2022, LNCS 13215, pp. 171–185, 2022.
https://doi.org/10.1007/978-3-030-99461-7_10

deploying systems that automate processing or reasoning tasks. For instance, a Subject Matter Expert (SME) might have deep domain knowledge but may not be able to describe it in terms of concepts and relationships that can be used to represent the knowledge. Also, at times, the SME may not describe the knowledge at the right level of detail that may be needed for making automated decisions. For example, in the cyber-physical domain, we are often required to analyze a legacy product without an adequate description of its software, imposing a challenge on the system operator. In the same domain, we frequently require the recovery of mathematical structures implemented without having the required software proficiency. Considering the vast amount of code presently used in such systems, the problem becomes intractable and tedious even for an SME and is often susceptible to human error.

To overcome such issues, we use an Inductive Logic Programming (ILP) based approach wherein the SME identifies positive and negative examples for describing a concept in the code. The ILP system uses these examples to derive logic programming rules (i.e., annotation or classification rules) for formally defining those concepts. This allows the SME to quickly detect the desired software modules in his task and route the software's relevant components to designated experts. Our approach is iterative in that the SME can refine the rules learned by adding more positive and negative examples.

Our approach is based on a semantic model (consisting of an ontology and rules), which first describes the basic concepts and relationships of the domain. In order to learn the definition of more complex concepts, the SME provides positive and negative examples that are automatically translated into a formal representation using the basic semantic concepts and relationships.

Our approach tackles both issues described above. Since we automatically translate the example data provided by the SME into a logical representation, the SME does not need to have an understanding of the concepts and relationships in the ontology. In addition, since the SME only identifies positive and negative examples and repeats the learning approach until the acquired knowledge is satisfactory, it provides a way to derive complete and accurate descriptions of the concepts in the domain.

1.1 Inductive Logic Programming

Inductive Logic Programming (ILP) [8] is a branch of Machine Learning that deals with learning theories in logic programs where there is a uniform representation for examples, background knowledge, and hypotheses.

Given background knowledge (B) in the form of a logic program, and positive and negative examples as conjunctions $E+$ and $E-$ of positive and negative literals respectively, an ILP system derives a logic program H such that:

- All the examples in $E+$ can be logically derived from $B \wedge H$, and
- No negative example in $E-$ can be logically derived from $B \wedge H$.

ILP has been successfully used in applications such as Bioinformatics and Natural Language Processing [1,2,5]. A number of ILP implementations are available. In our work we use Aleph [10] and run it using SWI-Prolog [11]. Aleph bounds the hypothesis space from the most general hypothesis to the most specific one. It starts the search from the most general hypothesis and specialises it by adding literals from the bottom clause until it finds the best hypothesis.

Aleph requires three files to construct theories:

- Text file with a .b extension containing background knowledge in the form of logic clauses that encode information relevant to the domain and the instance data.
- Text file with a .f extension that includes the positive ground facts of the concept to be learned.
- Text file with a .n extension that includes the negative ground facts of the concept to be learned.

As an example, consider an ILP task with the following sets of background knowledge, positive examples, and negative examples:

$$B = \left\{ \begin{array}{l} \texttt{builder(alice).} \\ \texttt{builder(bob).} \\ \texttt{enjoys\_lego(alice).} \\ \texttt{enjoys\_lego(claire).} \end{array} \right\} E^+ = \{\texttt{happy(alice).}\} \ E^- = \left\{ \begin{array}{l} \texttt{happy(bob).} \\ \texttt{happy(claire).} \end{array} \right\}$$

Given these three sets, ILP induces the following hypothesis (written in reverse implication form, as usually done in logic programs):

$$H = \{\texttt{happy(X) :- builder(X),enjoys\_lego(X).}\}$$

This hypothesis contains one rule that says: if `builder(X)` and `enjoys_lego(X)` are true, then `happy(X)` must also be true for all X. In other words, this rule says that if persons are builders and enjoy lego then they are happy. Having induced a rule, we can deduce knowledge from it. Cropper et al. [4] provides a comprehensive survey of ILP along with various applications.

1.2 Cyber-Physical Systems

Cyber-Physical System (CPS) is a term describing a broad range of complex, multi-disciplinary, physically-aware engineered systems that integrate embedded computing technologies and software into the physical world. The control aspect of the physical phenomena and the theory behind control systems are the basis for all state-of-the-art continuous time dynamical systems and thus have a crucial role in CPS design. In control theory, SMEs describe a system using a set of primitive and higher-level concepts that represent and govern the system's signals and enforce its desired behavior. Table 1 presents several math primitives and higher-level control concepts that are widely used in industrial control systems and a variety of other applications requiring continuously modulated control (e.g., water systems, robotics systems).

Table 1. A partial list of control concepts and math primitives employed in control mechanisms in cyber-physical systems and their description

Concept	Description and associated properties
Constant	Variables that are initialized and not updated
Reference signal	Variable/signal that represent desired behavior or setpoint
Output signal	Variable/signal that goes as output from a control block
Difference	Control block generating a subtraction of two signals
Sum	Control block generating an addition of two signals
Error signal	Variable/signal that is an output of a difference operation with a reference and measured (output) signal
Gain	Control block generating a multiplication between signals and/or scalars
Division	Control block generating a division between signals and/or scalars (often includes some divide by zero protection)
Switch	Control block that selects an input to be an output based on a condition or discrete/boolean input
Magnitude saturation	Control block that limits the input signal to the upper and lower saturation values, where the limit values are pre-defined constants
PI controller	Control block that continuously calculates an error signal and applies a correction based on proportional and integral terms
PID controller	Control block that continuously calculates an error signal and applies a correction based on proportional, integral, and derivative terms

Conventionally, control-policy software are completely separate from the system infrastructure and implemented after manufacturing the system prototype. This presents a challenge for SMEs who are proficient with the required mathematical knowledge and control theory background but are not equipped with a sufficient knowledge in low-level programming or software design. Locating the appropriate code blocks that correspond to a specific control concept (e.g., an integrator) that is of interest to the SME, either for the purpose of validation or reverse engineering, imposes a significant challenge. It is extremely difficult for the SME to recover mathematical structures implemented in the software. Further, the SME can find it challenging to articulate their domain knowledge in a form of code or the formalism required to address their task.

1.3   From Source Code to a Knowledge Graph

Knowledge Graphs (KGs), in the form of RDF statements, are the appropriate representations to store and link complex data. KGs combine expressivity, interoperability, and standardization in the Semantic Web stack, thus providing a strong foundation for querying and analysis.

The RDF representation of the desired CPS system source code is obtained in two steps. First, from the source code a JSON file is extracted with the method of Pyarelal et al. [9] to describe the function networks and expression trees (i.e., representations of arithmetic expressions). Next, the RDF data is produced by generating RDF triples following a pre-defined semantic model using the materialized JSON instance data. Listing 1.1 shows a portion of the pre-defined semantic model that is used to model the instance data into RDF, expressed in SADL [3] (Semantic Application Design Language). SADL is an open-sourced domain-independent language that provides a formal yet easily understandable representation of models. The SADL tool, which is available as a plugin to Eclipse[1], automatically translates statements in SADL to a Web Ontology Language (OWL) [6] file, which contains the RDF statements (i.e., triples). For example, in our model (as shown in Listing 1.1), a HyperEdge is related to a single Function via the property function, and has multiple input and output of type Variable. It is important to note that this pre-defined model does not vary and is similar for any given code input; it is merely required to define the ontological elements needed to describe code in an RDF form.

Finally, the resulting RDF contains representations of basic code elements found in a given source code. Listing 1.2 shows an excerpt from the resulting knowledge graph of the file simple_PI_controller.c shown in Appendix A, expressed in SADL as well.

```
1   HyperEdge is a type of Node
2       described by inputs with values of type Variable
3       described by function with a single value of type Function
4       described by outputs with values of type Variable.
5   Function is a type of Node
6       described by ftype with a single value of type string
7       described by lambda with a single value of type string
8       described by expression_tree with a single value of type ExpressionTree.
9   Variable is a type of ExpNode
10      described by object_ref with a single value of type string
11      described by data_type with a single value of type string.
```

Listing 1.1. A portion of the semantic model used to model the data (written in SADL). A Function is a Node with the relations ftype (function type) and lambda with a range of type string and an expression_tree of type ExpressionTree

```
1   _21df3f15-1763-9632-e936-8aca2281a699 is a grfnem:Function,
2       has grfnem:metadata (a grfnem:Metadata with grfnem:line_begin 12),
3       has grfnem:ftype "ASSIGN",
4       has grfnem:lambda "lambda error,Kp_M,Ki_M,integrator_state: ((error * Kp_M) + (Ki_M *
              ↪ integrator_state))".
5   d4000e07-fe4a-aa23-b882-1030d655eee0 is a grfnem:Variable,
6       has grfnem:metadata (a grfnem:Metadata with grfnem:line_begin 27, with grfnem:from_source true),
7       has grfnem:identifier "simple_PI_controller::simple_PI_controller.main::Kp_M::0".
```

Listing 1.2. An excerpt from the resulting knowledge graph representation (written in SADL) of the file simple_PI_controller.c (see Appendix A). The Function shown above is of type ASSIGN and starts at line 12. This is the resulting instance data that is automatically generated from the c source code

---

[1] https://www.eclipse.org/.

2   Integrated Control-Concept Induction Platform

The question we are addressing is *how can we streamline and leverage the CPS program knowledge graph data to capture domain-knowledge and assist the SME with additional knowledge discovery?* Knowledge discovery in data is the non-trivial extraction of implicit, previously unknown, and potentially useful information from data.

As we mentioned earlier, and in order to overcome this challenge, we use an ILP-based approach wherein the SME essentially identifies positive and negative examples for describing a concept. The ILP system uses them to derive logic programming rules for formally defining that concept.

2.1   Problem Definition

The task we address here is as follows: Given an input in the form of an OWL file containing RDF triples that represent basic code elements found in the source code (as seen in Listing 1.2 in SADL format), we want to generate logic programming rules for formally defining control concepts and math primitives (e.g., a Constant, see Table 1) that are provided as example instances interactively by the SME. The rules should be expressed with Horn logic clauses, similarly to the example we have shown in Sect. 1.1. We require the solution to be iterative in the sense that the SME can refine the learned rules by adding more positive and negative examples.

2.2   Overview of Our Approach: An ILP Platform

As described in Sect. 1.3, the knowledge graph, constructed from the function networks and expression trees, is materialized in an OWL format. Our suggested platform and approach consists of several steps and components, as illustrated in Fig. 1. The platform consists of a module (`owl2aleph`) that automatically translates the OWL data into background knowledge (clauses and instances), namely B, in a format required by Aleph, the ILP system. The module then invokes an interactive user interface in which the SME selects positive and negative instances, namely $E+$ and $E-$ respectively. Lastly, Aleph is invoked using SWI-Prolog to produce a hypothesized clause H (i.e., the learned rule) and provide a list of new positive instances that adhere to H, so that the SME can evaluate the accuracy of the learned rule and select new examples to refine it.

Since we automatically translate the example data provided by the SME into a logical representation (i.e., "Aleph format"), the SME is not required to have knowledge of the concepts and relationships in the ontology. Also, since the SME only identifies positive and negative examples and repeats the learning approach until the knowledge learned is satisfactory, it provides a convenient and fast way for deriving complete and accurate descriptions of the concepts in the domain. The iterative nature of the approach is illustrated via the loop seen in the lower right side of Fig. 1. The loop runs through the SME (i.e., User), the Examples Selection UI (producing $E+$ and $E-$), then through Aleph to produce a new learned rule (i.e., H) then back to the SME.

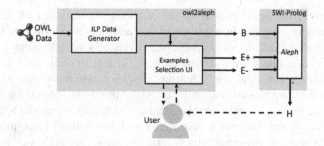

Fig. 1. The integrated control-concept induction platform for deriving math primitives and control concepts classification rules

2.3   Generating the ILP Data

The `owl2aleph` module, which generates the ILP data, consists of two main components (as seen previously in Fig. 1). The architecture of the module is detailed in Fig. 2. We construct the ILP instances based on hyperedges, function nodes, variable nodes, and expression trees based on the semantic model that describes the basic concepts and relationships of the domain (Listing 1.1) and executed over the instance data (Listing 1.2).

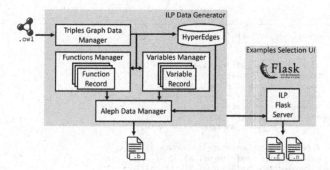

Fig. 2. Architecture of the `owl2aleph` module, generator of the ILP data files

As seen in Fig. 2, there are several sub-components, each one is designed to tackle a different task:

- **Triples Graph Data Manager** reads the OWL data and provides an easy serialization functionality over the given RDF statements. The manager classifies each statement by their functionality to serve other components (i.e., Functions Manager, Variables Manager, HyperEdges).
- **Variables Manager** performs variables disambiguation to enable linking variable nodes (explicit and implicit variables in the source code) and is also responsible for generating attributes regarding their usage (assignments, updates, usage inside other blocks, etc...).

- **Functions Manager** generates the relevant information about the code statement (hyperedge) functionality, the arithmetic operations (expression tree attributes such as multiplication, division, etc...) present in the code statement, and block level attributes (e.g., in a loop call).
- **HyperEdges** is a database of hyperedges, each one represents a code statement. Each hyperedge corresponds to zero or more variable nodes and a single function node. Hyperedges are the primary instances we use to aggregate the information about the math primitives and the control concepts we would like to form logic programs about. In the final pre-inference stage (upon selection of the positive and negative examples), a hyperedge is named as "newfeature" for each example, so that the same process and structure can be used for generating rules for any given concept.
- **Aleph Data Manager** generates the background knowledge in an Aleph format (.b file). This also includes the construction of definite clauses and additional constraints (rules about predicates and their inputs and outputs) from the source code and materializes the instance data.
- **ILP Flask Server** Runs a Flask[2] application (local HTTP server) to enable an interaction with the SME (User) via a web browser. The application provides a user-friendly interface to inspect and select the hyperedge instances that are positive and negative and to generate them in the required Aleph format (.f and .n files).

```
10 :- modeh(1,newfeature(+hyperedge)).
11
30 :- modeb(*,outputs_of(+xvariable,-hyperedge)).
31 :- modeb(*,xfunction(+hyperedge,-xnode)).
32 :- modeb(*,has_operator_mult(+xnode)).
33 :- modeb(*,has_operator_ifexpr(+xnode)).
34 :- modeb(*,xinterface(+xnode)).
35 :- modeb(*,var_assigned_once(+xvariable)).
36 :- modeb(*,var_multi_assigned(+xvariable)).

50 :- determination(newfeature/1,outputs/2).
51 :- determination(newfeature/1,xliteral/1).
52 :- determination(newfeature/1,xfunction/2).
53 :- determination(newfeature/1,inputs/2).
54 :- determination(newfeature/1,xassign/1).

86 hyperedge(xa1f96097abb845469e519fb7f237f9f9).
87 outputs(xa1f96097abb845469e519fb7f237f9f9,variable3).
88 xnode(node2).
89 xassign(node2).
90 has_operator_div(node2).
91 xfunction(xa1f96097abb845469e519fb7f237f9f9,node2).
```

Fig. 3. An excerpt of a resulting background knowledge (.b) file

In Fig. 3, we show an excerpt from a background knowledge (.b) file. The file includes four different sections of encoded knowledge. First, the modeh clause

---

[2] https://flask.palletsprojects.com/.

defines the hypothesis and takes a **hyperedge** as an input (highlighted with yellow). Second, the **modeb** clauses define the signatures of the predicate functions. Third, the **determination** clauses specify what concepts can be used in rules and how many arguments each one takes. The last section includes the instance data describing the entire CPS program in a logic formalism. All of the above is generated automatically from the RDF data.

The example files (.f/.n) we provide as input to Aleph simply list a collection of positive or negative **hyperedges** that correspond to the desired concept we want to learn. These files are generated automatically using the Examples Selection User Interface by simply inspecting their attributes and then adding them either as positives or negatives.

A snapshot of the user interface (UI) is shown in Fig. 4. It is fairly straight-forward to operate the UI. The system lists all available **hyperedges** with their relevant information (line numbers, functionality types, etc...). The user can add a **hyperedge** as a positive or negative example or simply ignore it. Once ready, the user can generate the example files to trigger the next step in the pipeline.

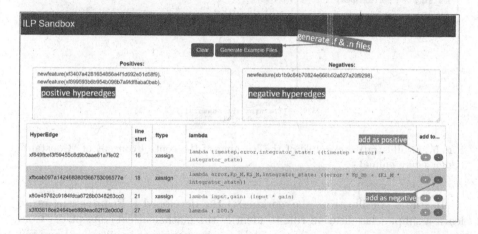

Fig. 4. The examples selection user interface for generating Aleph example files

By automating the translation and modeling of the semantic data into ILP rules, clauses, and instances, and by enabling a straightforward process of example files creation, we can quickly generate classification rules for formally identifying math primitives and control concepts in an iterative, fast, and interactive fashion.

2.4 Rule Generation from ILP Data via an Illustrative Example

Given the ILP data (B, $E+$, $E-$) in Aleph format, we can now trigger the execution of the ILP platform using SWI-Prolog to induce the learned rule, i.e., the hypothesis (H). The outcome is classification rules, expressed in domain

terms, for formally identifying math primitives and control concepts. The SME
identifies positive and negative examples and repeats the learning approach until
the knowledge learned rule is satisfactory.

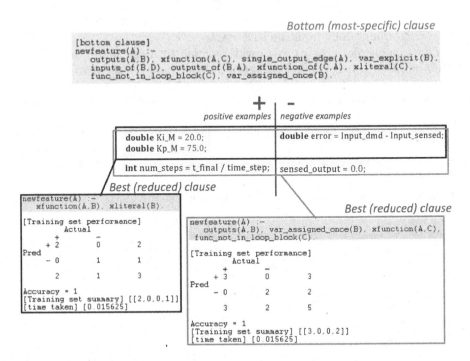

Fig. 5. An illustrative example of the learning of the control concept of "Constant"
(Color figure online)

In Fig. 5, we illustrate the working of the developed ILP infrastructure to
learn a simple classification rule to identify the mathematical concept of "Constant" (i.e., an expression with a variable assignment that is initialized and not
updated in the code). The selected examples in Fig. 5, and the ones discussed in
this section, correspond to code statements in the file `simple_PI_controller.c`
shown in Appendix A. In the first iteration in this scenario, the SME selects two
positive examples and a single negative example (upper orange box in Fig. 5)
corresponding to the code statements in lines 26 and 27 as positives, and line
8 as a negative. As explained in Sect. 1.1, the ILP system constructs the most
specific clause (given B and entailing $E+$), which is shown highlighted in blue.
The generated rule in this execution produces the rule (also seen highlighted in
yellow inside the lower orange box):

```
newfeature(A) :- xfunction(A,B), xliteral(B).
```

Which basically means that `hyperedge A` corresponds to a "Constant" (the
`newfeature`) if A has a function B that is an assignment to a literal.

Upon query of the instances that adhere to the generated rule, the SME can add more examples, either as a positive or a negative. The SME then selects an additional positive and negative example in a second iteration (upper green box in Fig. 5) corresponding to the code statement in line 29 as a positive, and line 38 as a negative. The generated rule in this execution produces the rule (also seen highlighted in yellow inside the lower green box):

```
newfeature(A) :- outputs(A,B), var_assigned_once(B),
        xfunction(A,C), func_not_in_loop_block(C).
```

Which means that hyperedge A corresponds to a "Constant" if A has a variable B that is assigned only once and the hyperedge A has a function C in which the assignment is not inside any loop, as we would have expected.

The ILP infrastructure enables an automatic, iterative, and fast process for capturing domain knowledge for math primitives and control concepts in the form of classification rules. The resulting rules are used as feedback for the SME and can be further utilized to learn additional levels of knowledge.

3   Evaluation and Discussion

We evaluate the ILP-based approach for learning classification rules for control and math primitives on a dataset consisting of three OWL files originating from three source code files driving proportional-integral (PI) controllers with a simple plant model. The dataset consists of 8974 triples pertaining to 61 different instances of math and control concepts.

We have been successful in generating classification rules for simple math primitives and several control concepts. Table 2 shows a summary of the results. For each concept, we show the size of the training data (number of positive and negative examples provided), the number of bottom clause literals before the learning, the total number of reduced clause literals after the learning, the learning time, number of true positives, number of false positives, number of false negatives, precision, recall, and the F1 score. We note that the concepts of "Switch", "Magnitude saturation", and "PID controller" could not be learned due to an insufficient number of positive examples. We require at least two positive examples per concept to generate the most specific clause that initiates the ILP process.

As seen in Table 2, for 7 out of the applicable 9 concepts, the resulting generated rules had a perfect F1 score (maximum precision and recall) and a significant reduction in the number of literals in the generated rule (from bottom clause, pre-learning, to reduced clause, post-learning). Additionally, the process took less than a second to complete for all concepts shown in the table, which is a crucial and important ability to have in such a problem setting. Further, it required no more than two positive examples (and no more than 5 negatives, depending on the complexity of the concept in our data) to generate the final rule for all concepts.

Table 2. Results summary for the ILP generated rules for our targeted math and control concepts

Concept	(E+, E−)	Bottom clause size	Reduced clause size	Time [seconds]	True posi-tives	False posi-tives	False nega-tives	Precision	Recall	F1
Difference	(2, 1)	24	3	0.063	4	0	0	1.0	1.0	**1.0**
Sum	(2, 2)	29	3	0.063	9	0	0	1.0	1.0	**1.0**
Gain	(2, 1)	23	3	0.047	9	0	0	1.0	1.0	**1.0**
Division	(2, 2)	24	3	0.094	3	0	0	1.0	1.0	**1.0**
Constant	(2, 5)	11	6	0.125	23	0	0	1.0	1.0	**1.0**
Error signal	(2, 5)	24	6	0.859	2	0	0	1.0	1.0	**1.0**
PI controller	(2, 5)	45	5	0.453	3	0	0	1.0	1.0	**1.0**
Output signal	(2, 3)	12	12	0.859	3	3	0	0.50	1.0	0.67
Reference signal	(2, 2)	11	11	0.375	3	17	0	0.15	1.0	0.26
Switch	Not enough positives (E+)									
Magnitude saturation										
PID controller										

One must note that the number of iterations needed is dependent on how many and which positive and negative examples are selected by the SME. For example, suppose a user chooses similar positive or negative examples. In that case, it could be not very meaningful in converging towards a more reduced clause, requiring the user to pick additional and substantially different examples.

The remaining two concepts out of the applicable 9 concepts ("Output Signal" and "Reference Signal") did not achieve a high F1 score (or any reduction in the size of the clause literals) since there is not enough data to separate the positive examples from the negative examples in these concepts. The training data must have a sufficient number of positive examples with a certain amount of "richness" (diversity in implementation and usage) to enable the separation of the examples to generate an accurate and satisfying rule. This is an expected requirement, as there are some concepts that can be coded in different approaches (logic vs. arithmetic). Further, the code can have several mutations even if implemented using the same "approach". For example, the code could include pointers that get allocated dynamically, imposing a difficulty in our approach, which relies on a static semantic analysis.

One must note that these scores reflect the accuracy of the rules within our dataset. The same rules, if executed on a different dataset, may not necessarily produce similar results. We inspected the generated rules with the prefect F1 scores. We noticed that some of the rules are aligned with our expectations. For example, the generated rule for the concept of "Gain" was:

```
gain(A) :- xfunction(A,B), has_operator_mult(B).
```

Which means the **hyperedge** A has a function B that includes the multiplication operator, as expected.

Other rules were not completely aligned to what we would expect the SME to define. For example, the generated rule for the concept of "PI Controller" was:

```
picontroller(A) :- outputs(A,B), var_implicit(B),
        xfunction(A,C), has_operator_add(C).
```

Which is not sufficient to capture the two control terms of proportional and integral operations of addition and multiplication that are required to define a PI controller, but it was sufficient to capture the 3 instances that exist in our dataset accurately.

The quality of the ILP generated rules is dependent on the supplied input. Sub-par rules result from inadequate input data that does not hold sufficient information about the targeted concept. By providing additional code examples and richer data, we provide better coverage and generate more accurate rules.

4   Related Work and Conclusions

Since a vast amount of domain knowledge has already been captured in text, considerable effort has been made in extracting this written knowledge into formal models. Wong et al. [12] provides a survey of various approaches. Most of this effort has been in extracting concepts and relationships between the concepts and representing it in a semantic model. We have also previously used ILP in the domain of Design for Manufacturability (DFM) where the goal was to design products that are easier to manufacture by providing early manufacturability feedback in Moitra et al. [7].

In this work we have considered how we can automate the capture of Cyber-Physical Systems (CPS) domain knowledge by applying Inductive Logic Programming (ILP) to positive and negative instance data in RDF format, originating from a CPS program source code. We have shown this by developing an Integrated Control-Concept Induction Platform for generating annotation and classification rules for control concepts and math primitives. Our approach is feasible and effective in terms of time, completeness, and robustness. These early results we have shown are encouraging and provide promising opportunities and applications.

Acknowledgements. Distribution Statement "A" (Approved for Public Release, Distribution Unlimited). This material is based upon work supported by the Defense Advanced Research Projects Agency (DARPA) under the Agreement No. HR00112190017. The views, opinions and/or findings expressed are those of the authors and should not be interpreted as representing the official views or policies of the Department of Defense or the U.S. Government.

A   simple_PI_controller.c

A PI controller simple_PI_controller.c used in Sect. 2.4 is shown below. The
selected examples in Fig. 5 correspond to code statements in this file.

```c
1   #include <stdio.h>
2
3   double integrator_state = 0.0;
4
5   /* Simple PI controller */
6   double PI_calc(double Input_dmd, double Input_sensed, double Kp_M, double Ki_M, double
          ↪ timestep)
7   {
8       double error = Input_dmd - Input_sensed; // negative example for ILP (iteration 1)
9
10      integrator_state = integrator_state + timestep*error;
11
12      return error*Kp_M + integrator_state*Ki_M;
13  }
14
15  /* Proportional plant! */
16  double plant_model(double input, double gain)
17  {
18      return input*gain;
19  }
20
21  int main(int argc, char **argv)
22  {
23      double t_final = 100.5;
24      double time_step = 0.015;
25
26      double Ki_M = 20.0; // positive example for ILP (iteration 1)
27      double Kp_M = 75.0; // positive example for ILP (iteration 1)
28
29      int num_steps = t_final / time_step; // positive example for ILP (iteration 2)
30
31      double desired_output = 10.0;
32
33      double plant_command;
34      double sensed_output;
35
36      double plant_gain = 0.01;
37
38      sensed_output = 0.0; // negative example for ILP (iteration 2)
39
40      for (int i = 0; i < num_steps; i++)
41      {
42          plant_command = PI_calc(desired_output, sensed_output, Kp_M, Ki_M, time_step);
43
44          sensed_output = plant_model(plant_command, plant_gain);
45
46          printf("%f, %f, %f", (double)i*time_step, plant_command, sensed_output);
47      }
48
49      return 0;
50  }
```

Listing 1.3. simple_PI_controller.c

References

1. Bratko, I., Muggleton, S.: Applications of inductive logic programming. Commun. ACM **38**(11), 65–70 (1995)
2. Chen, D., Mooney, R.: Learning to interpret natural language navigation instructions from observations. In: Proceedings of the AAAI Conference on Artificial Intelligence, vol. 25 (2011)
3. Crapo, A., Moitra, A.: Toward a unified English-like representation of semantic models, data, and graph patterns for subject matter experts. Int. J. Semant. Comput. **7**(03), 215–236 (2013)
4. Cropper, A., Dumančić, S., Evans, R., Muggleton, S.H.: Inductive logic programming at 30. Mach. Learn. **111**(1), 147–172 (2022). Springer
5. Faruquie, T.A., Srinivasan, A., King, R.D.: Topic models with relational features for drug design. In: Riguzzi, F., Železný, F. (eds.) ILP 2012. LNCS (LNAI), vol. 7842, pp. 45–57. Springer, Heidelberg (2013). https://doi.org/10.1007/978-3-642-38812-5_4
6. McGuinness, D.L., Van Harmelen, F., et al.: Owl web ontology language overview. W3C Recommend. **10**(10), 2004 (2004)
7. Moitra, A., Palla, R., Rangarajan, A.: Automated capture and execution of manufacturability rules using inductive logic programming. In: Twenty-Eighth IAAI Conference (2016)
8. Muggleton, S.: Inductive logic programming. New Gener. Comput. **8**(4), 295–318 (1991)
9. Pyarelal, A., et al.: Automates: automated model assembly from text, equations, and software. arXiv preprint arXiv:2001.07295 (2020)
10. Srinivasan, A.: The aleph manual (2001)
11. Wielemaker, J., Schrijvers, T., Triska, M., Lager, T.: SWI-prolog. Theory Pract. Logic Program. **12**(1–2), 67–96 (2012)
12. Wong, W., Liu, W., Bennamoun, M.: Ontology learning from text: a look back and into the future. ACM Comput. Surv. (CSUR) **44**(4), 1–36 (2012)

A Functional Account of Probabilistic Programming with Possible Worlds
Declarative Pearl

Birthe van den Berg$^{(\boxtimes)}$ and Tom Schrijvers

KU Leuven, Leuven, Belgium
{birthe.vandenberg,tom.schrijvers}@kuleuven.be

Abstract. While there has been much cross-fertilization between functional and logic programming—e.g., leading to functional models of many Prolog features—this appears to be much less the case regarding probabilistic programming, even though this is an area of mutual interest. Whereas functional programming often focuses on modeling probabilistic processes, logic programming typically focuses on modeling possible worlds. These worlds are made up of facts that each carry a probability and together give rise to a distribution semantics. The latter approach appears to be little-known in the functional programming community. This paper aims to remedy this situation by presenting a functional account of the distribution semantics of probabilistic logic programming that is based on possible worlds. We present a term monad for the monadic syntax of queries together with a natural interpretation in terms of boolean algebras. Then we explain that, because probabilities do not form a boolean algebra, they—and other interpretations in terms of commutative semirings—can only be computed after query normalisation to deterministic, decomposable negation normal form (d-DNNF). While computing the possible worlds readily gives such a normal form, it suffers from exponential blow-up. Using heuristic algorithms yields much better results in practice.

Keywords: Possible worlds · Monad · Functional programming · Probabilistic programming · Logic programming

1 Introduction

Thanks to the FLOPS conference and related venues, there is a large body of research at the crossroads between Functional (FP) and Logic Programming (LP), which has lead to much cross-fertilization between the two communities.

Although many programming-related aspects are of common interest, both communities have a somewhat different focus, with FP tending more towards processes ("doing") and LP more towards probabilistic models ("being"). This is quite prominent in the FP view of logic programming, which mostly focuses on the operational aspects such as backtracking search [21,23,29,38], least fixed-points of non-deterministic computations [41] and unification algorithms [6,36].

© Springer Nature Switzerland AG 2022
M. Hanus and A. Igarashi (Eds.): FLOPS 2022, LNCS 13215, pp. 186–204, 2022.
https://doi.org/10.1007/978-3-030-99461-7_11

In contrast, non-operational matters, such as well-founded semantics [39] and stable model semantics [16], have received less attention from the FP community.

Of particular interest here is the subarea of probabilistic programming, which, under the aegis of Artificial Intelligence, is receiving much attention. Again, both communities have developed a somewhat different focus on the matter: probabilistic processes for FP, probabilistic models for LP. This difference in focus is not always very pronounced and of course there is still much overlap. Yet, there are also subtle differences that may be overlooked or misunderstood.

In this paper we aim to raise awareness for probabilistic LP aspects that are less well-known in the FP community. In particular, we provide a functional programming incarnation of probabilistic logic programming based on Sato's *distribution semantics* [35]. This distribution semantics is derived from intensionally modeling *possible worlds* in terms of formulas over facts and associating probability distributions with those facts. This approach underlies most contemporary probabilistic LP languages (Probabilistic Logic Programs [8], Probabilistic Horn Abduction [31], Independent Choice Logic [32], PRISM [35], LPADs [42], ProbLog [15], and PITA [34]) and lends itself well to declarative modeling of complex systems, even ones that have a cyclic structure (e.g., graphs or networks). Computing probabilities in these models gives rise to problems that simply do not arise in typical FP approaches.

Our specific contributions are as follows.

- We present a term monad for queries over possible worlds, and assign a general and quite natural semantics in terms of boolean algebras to those queries. This semantics has the typical models judgment ($\models$) and possible worlds interpretation as special cases.
- We explain that the probabilistic interpretation does not fit in the boolean algebra representation. However, it can be admitted by means of normalisation. In fact, after normalisation the interpretation of queries can be further generalized from boolean algebras to arbitrary commutative semirings.
- We show how a least fixed-point operator enables cyclic models, e.g., of networks.

The code presented in this paper is available at https://github.com/birthevdb/functional-possible-worlds.

2 Background: Possible Worlds

In logic programming the subsets W of a finite set B (usually called the Herbrand base) of possible facts $A_1, \ldots, A_n$ are known as *worlds*. The notation $A_i \in W$ means that A_i is true in that world; otherwise it is false. Thus, for n facts, there are 2^n worlds. Other ways to characterize worlds are as partitions of B into true and false facts, or as sets with both positive occurrences (written just A_i) and negative occurrences (write $\bar{A}_i$) where all facts must be accounted for and no fact can appear both positively and negatively.

For example, there could be two facts A_1 and A_2 where A_1 means that the sky is blue and A_2 that Hyppolyta is a queen. Two facts give rise to four different worlds,

$$W_1 = \{\} \qquad\qquad W_2 = \{A_1\}$$
$$W_3 = \{A_2\} \qquad\qquad W_4 = \{A_1, A_2\}$$

For example, the world W_4 has a blue sky and Hyppolyta as a queen.

Among all the worlds, only some may be possible. The possible worlds are typically expressed intentionally, by means of a logical formula Q (often called *query*) over the facts. A formula expresses those worlds in which the formula holds; this is captured in the judgement $W \models Q$. Usually, formulas are made of positive and negative occurrences of facts, the literals *true* and *false*, and the logical connectives $\wedge$, $\vee$, and $\neg$. In fact, negation is often omitted and then the formula is known as *definite*. The $W \models Q$ relation is then defined as follows:

$$\frac{A \in W}{W \models A} \qquad \frac{A \notin W}{W \models \bar{A}}$$

$$\frac{W \models Q_1}{W \models Q_1 \vee Q_2} \qquad \frac{W \models Q_2}{W \models Q_1 \vee Q_2} \qquad \frac{W \models Q_1 \quad W \models Q_2}{W \models Q_1 \wedge Q_2}$$

For example, the possible worlds of formula $A_1 \vee \bar{A}_2$ are W_1, W_2 and W_4 because they do model the formula and W_3 does not.

Often (parts) of formulas are abstracted over by Horn clauses. When these clauses are circularly defined, a more sophisticated semantics is needed. We return to this matter in Sect. 5.

Probabilities are introduced at the level of facts. An *interpretation* function $I : B \rightarrow [0, 1]$ associates each fact with a probability. Then the probability $P(W)$ of a world W follows from its facts.

$$P(W) = \prod_{A_i \in W} I(A_i) \times \prod_{A_i \notin W} (1 - I(A_i))$$

Likewise, the probability of a query is the sum of the probabilities of the worlds in which it holds.

$$P(Q) = \sum_{W \models Q} P(W)$$

Example. Consider the following example. "Toss a coin and draw a ball from each of two urns. The two urns contain both red and blue balls. You win if you toss heads and draw a red ball or if you draw two balls of the same color. What are the odds of that if the probability of tossing heads is 0.4, that of drawing a red ball form the first urn 0.3 and from the second urn 0.2?"

The facts in this example are H (heads), R_1 (the first ball is red) and R_2 (the second ball is red). We give them an interpretation in terms of their probability.

$$I(H) = 0.4 \qquad I(R_1) = 0.3 \qquad I(R_2) = 0.2$$

We compute the probabilities of the worlds.

$$
\begin{aligned}
P(W_1) &= I(\bar{H}) \times I(\bar{R}_1) \times I(\bar{R}_2) = (1 - 0.4) \times (1 - 0.3) \times (1 - 0.2) = 0.336 \\
P(W_2) &= I(\bar{H}) \times I(\bar{R}_1) \times I(R_2) = (1 - 0.4) \times (1 - 0.3) \times 0.2 \quad\;\; = 0.084 \\
P(W_3) &= I(\bar{H}) \times I(R_1) \times I(\bar{R}_2) = (1 - 0.4) \times 0.3 \quad\;\;\; \times (1 - 0.2) = 0.144 \\
P(W_4) &= I(\bar{H}) \times I(R_1) \times I(R_2) = (1 - 0.4) \times 0.3 \quad\;\;\; \times 0.2 \quad\;\; = 0.036 \\
P(W_5) &= I(H) \times I(\bar{R}_1) \times I(\bar{R}_2) = 0.4 \quad\;\;\; \times (1 - 0.3) \times (1 - 0.2) = 0.224 \\
P(W_6) &= I(H) \times I(\bar{R}_1) \times I(R_2) = 0.4 \quad\;\;\; \times (1 - 0.3) \times 0.2 \quad\;\; = 0.056 \\
P(W_7) &= I(H) \times I(R_1) \times I(\bar{R}_2) = 0.4 \quad\;\;\; \times 0.3 \quad\;\;\; \times (1 - 0.2) = 0.096 \\
P(W_8) &= I(H) \times I(R_1) \times I(R_2) = 0.4 \quad\;\;\; \times 0.3 \quad\;\;\; \times 0.2 \quad\;\; = 0.024
\end{aligned}
$$

You win the game when you toss heads and draw a red ball, or when you draw two red balls or two blue balls. This is expressed by the following query:

$$
\text{Win} = (H \wedge (R_1 \vee R_2)) \vee (R_1 \wedge R_2) \vee (\bar{R}_1 \wedge \bar{R}_2)
$$

The worlds that model this query are W_1, W_4, W_5, W_6, W_7 and W_8. The probability to win is then computed as follows:

$$
\begin{aligned}
P(\text{Win}) &= P(W_1) + P(W_4) + P(W_5) + P(W_6) + P(W_7) + P(W_8) \\
&= 0.336 + 0.036 + 0.224 + 0.056 + 0.096 + 0.024 \\
&= 0.772
\end{aligned}
$$

3   The Possible Worlds Monad

This section presents our functional model of many-worlds logic programming. It represents queries with a term monad and interprets them with boolean algebras.

3.1   Facts and Worlds

We use designated types, which we name *fact types*, to denote the different available facts. For example, fact type F_{Ex} provides two possible facts F_1 and F_2.

  data $F_{Ex} = F_1 \mid F_2$

We require that fact types provide a finite number of facts and instantiate a type class with a method *facts* that enumerates them.

  class $Ord\; f \Rightarrow Fact\; f$ **where**   **instance** $Fact\; F_{Ex}$ **where**
  $facts :: [f]$ $facts = [F_1, F_2]$

A world over these facts is then a (sub)set of values of the fact type.

  type $World\; f = Set\; f$

For example, the world where F_1 is true and F_2 is not, is represented by

  $w_{F_1} :: World\; F_{Ex}$
  $w_{F_1} = Set.fromList\; [F_1]$

The universe is the list of all possible worlds. We compute all the subsequences of the facts, convert them to sets and collect them in a list.

$$universe :: Fact\ f \Rightarrow [\,World\ f\,]$$
$$universe = [\,Set.fromList\ l \mid l \leftarrow subsequences\ facts\,]$$

3.2   The Monad

Finally, we have the possible worlds monad $Q\ f$ which captures formulas or queries over the facts f. We realise this monad through the algebraic effects and handlers methodology [30]. Its representation is a *term monad*[1], which allows to construct syntactic structures in the functional programming context, similar to terms in Prolog. Its interpretations—the handlers—are expressed in terms of the structural recursion scheme over this representation.

Term Monad. To define the *term monad* $Q\ f$, which is parameterized in the fact type f, we adopt the approach of Wu et al. [45] to model the free nondeterminism monad with a free monad. Its definition is as follows:

data $Q\ f\ a$ **where**
$\quad Var :: a \rightarrow Q\ f\ a$
$\quad Fail :: Q\ f\ a$
$\quad Or\ :: Q\ f\ a \rightarrow Q\ f\ a \rightarrow Q\ f\ a$

This has the typical term monad structure where the *Var* constructor is the *return* method of the monad and denotes a non-terminal. The remaining constructors denote algebraic operations that have distribute with the monadic bind operator ($\gg\!=$), which recursively descends into the terms and fills in the non-terminal variables. Moreover, *Or* and *Fail* provide *Alternative* structure.

instance *Monad* $(Q\ f)$ **where**
$\quad return = Var$
$\quad Var\ x\ \gg\!= k = k\ x$
$\quad Fail\ \quad \gg\!= k = Fail$
$\quad Or\ p\ q \gg\!= k = Or\ (p \gg\!= k)\ (q \gg\!= k)$

instance *Alternative* $(Q\ f)$
$\quad$ **where**
$\quad\quad empty = Fail$
$\quad\quad (\Diamond)\quad = Or$

The type $Q\ f\ ()$, where the result type a is the unit type $()$, corresponds to the syntax of boolean formulas.

$true :: Q\ f\ ()$
$true\ = return\ ()$
$(\wedge)\ :: Q\ f\ () \rightarrow Q\ f\ () \rightarrow Q\ f\ ()$
$p \wedge q = p \gg q$

$false :: Q\ f\ ()$
$false = empty$
$(\vee)\ :: Q\ f\ () \rightarrow Q\ f\ () \rightarrow Q\ f\ ()$
$p \vee q = p \Diamond q$

Indeed, the monadic structure of the term monad aligns with the conjunctive structure of formulas, while the *Fail* and *Or* constructors align with their disjunctive structure.

---

[1] Also called *free monad*.

Adding Literals. Finally, formula literals are captured in the *Lit* constructor. We extend our term monad with literals as follows:

data $Q\ f\ a$ **where**

...

$Lit :: Lit\ f \to Q\ f\ a \to Q\ f\ a$

The *Lit* constructor has two fields: a literal ($Lit\ f$) and, to distribute with $\gg\!=$, another formula. As $\gg\!=$ means conjunction, $Lit\ l\ p$ represents the conjunction of the the literal l with the query p; the *lit* function conveniently fills in the trivial query *true*. The literal l itself is a positive or negative occurrence of a fact.

$lit\ \ :: Lit\ f \to Q\ f\ ()$
$lit\ l = Lit\ l\ true$

data $Lit\ f = Pos\ f\ |\ Neg\ f$

For example, we can capture the example formula $F_1 \vee \bar{F}_2$ as

$query :: Q\ F_{Ex}\ ()$
$query = lit\ (Pos\ F_1) \vee lit\ (Neg\ F_2)$

Compositional Programming. Although most of our examples consider the syntax of boolean formulas (using $Q\ f\ ()$), we can use type $Q\ f\ a$ to construct programs from program fragments. The return values of those fragments can influence the remainder of the program. For example, consider the following three booleans, which encode the possible outcomes of rolling a dice.

$F_{dice} = B_1\ |\ B_2\ |\ B_3$

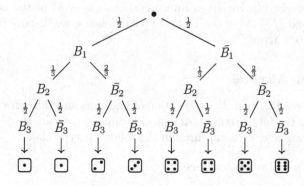

Consequently, we represent the six sides of a dice as follows:

$one = lit\ (Pos\ B_1) \wedge lit\ (Pos\ B_2)$ $\hspace{2cm} \gg return\ 1$
$two = lit\ (Pos\ B_1) \wedge lit\ (Neg\ B_2) \wedge lit\ (Pos\ B_3) \gg return\ 2$
...
$six = lit\ (Neg\ B_1) \wedge lit\ (Neg\ B_2) \wedge lit\ (Neg\ B_3) \gg return\ 6$

We can define two independent dice as follows:

$$dice_1 = one_1 \Diamond \ ... \ \Diamond \ six_1$$
$$dice_2 = one_2 \Diamond \ ... \ \Diamond \ six_2$$

A winning condition of throwing these dice can be defined in terms of their returned values. The *guard* function comes in handy to transform the boolean condition into a query of type $Q \ f \ ()$.

$guard :: Bool \rightarrow Q \ f \ ()$
$guard \ True \ = true$
$guard \ False = false$

$win = \textbf{do} \ x \leftarrow dice_1; y \leftarrow dice_2; guard \ (x + y > 10)$

Handlers and Laws. As usual with the algebraic effects approach, $Q \ f \ a$ programs do not respect any particular laws other than the monad laws on the nose. Instead, the interpretation functions, known as *handlers*, must ensure that the interpretations they produce respect further laws. To enable this we provide a structural recursion scheme, the *fold*.

$fold :: BooleanAlgebra \ b \Rightarrow (a \rightarrow b) \rightarrow (f \rightarrow b) \rightarrow Q \ f \ a \rightarrow b$
$fold \ gen \ inj \ (Var \ x) \qquad = gen \ x$
$fold \ gen \ inj \ Fail \qquad\quad = \perp$
$fold \ gen \ inj \ (Or \ p \ q) \qquad = fold \ gen \ inj \ p \lor fold \ gen \ inj \ q$
$fold \ gen \ inj \ (Lit \ (Pos \ f) \ p) = inj \ f \land fold \ gen \ inj \ p$
$fold \ gen \ inj \ (Lit \ (Neg \ f) \ p) = \neg \ (inj \ f) \land fold \ gen \ inj \ p$

This recursion scheme enforces that programs are interpreted compositionally in terms of a *boolean algebra* given interpretations $(a \rightarrow b)$ of the non-terminals or variables and $(f \rightarrow b)$ of the facts. In what follows, we discuss these boolean algebras in more detail.

3.3 Boolean Algebras

Boolean algebras [3] generalize the notion of booleans and thus provide a natural framework for the interpretation of logical formulas; they are subject to Fig. 1's laws. A boolean algebra is captured in the following type class.

class *BooleanAlgebra b* **where**
$\perp \ :: b$
$\top \ :: b$
$\neg \ :: b \rightarrow b$
$(\land) :: b \rightarrow b \rightarrow b$
$(\lor) :: b \rightarrow b \rightarrow b$

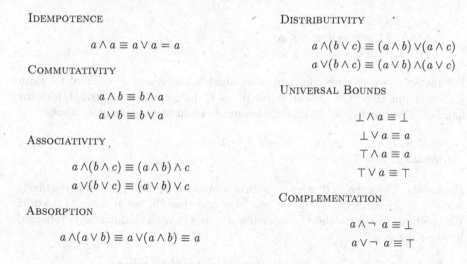

Fig. 1. Laws of boolean algebras.

We give three well-known examples of boolean algebras with their implementation using the *BooleanAlgebra* class and with their application to our many-worlds semantics: booleans, the pointwise construction and powersets.

Booleans. The standard instance for boolean algebras is of course that of *Bool*.

```
instance BooleanAlgebra Bool where
  ⊤  = True
  ⊥  = False
  ¬  = not
  (∧) = (&&)
  (∨) = (||)
```

For example, we can evaluate the truth of a formula of type $Q\ f\ ()$ with *fold* by interpreting it in terms of *Bool* and by supplying the truth of the facts.

$$truth :: (f \to Bool) \to Q\ f\ () \to Bool$$
$$truth\ truth_f = fold\ (\lambda() \to True)\ truth_f$$

This interpretation maps the variable () to *True*, indicating effectively that *Var* () means *True*.

The Pointwise Construction. The function type $w \to b$ is a boolean algebra provided that b is a boolean algebra:

```
instance BooleanAlgebra b ⇒ BooleanAlgebra (w → b) where
  ⊤  = const ⊤
  ⊥  = const ⊥
```

$$\neg \quad = \lambda f \ w \to \neg \ (f \ w)$$
$$(\wedge) = \lambda f \ g \ w \to f \ w \wedge g \ w$$
$$(\vee) = \lambda f \ g \ w \to f \ w \vee g \ w$$

For instance, we can use the pointwise algebra for $World \ f \to Bool$ to write a *models* function that captures the $W \models Q$ judgement as a straightforward handler. The function *elem* checks the membership of an element in a set.

$$models :: Eq \ f \Rightarrow Q \ f \ a \to World \ f \to Bool$$
$$models = fold \ \top \ elem$$

Powersets. The subsets of a set also form a boolean algebra. This is particularly relevant if the elements of the set are facts and thus the set represents a world. We use functions from the Data.Set library, of which the behaviour is reflected by their name.

instance $Fact \ f \Rightarrow BooleanAlgebra \ (Set \ (World \ f))$ **where**
$$\top \quad = Set.fromList \ universe$$
$$\bot \quad = Set.empty$$
$$\neg \quad = Set.difference \ \top$$
$$(\wedge) = Set.intersection$$
$$(\vee) = Set.union$$

With this boolean algebra we can compute the possible worlds of a query:

$$possibleWorlds :: Fact \ f \Rightarrow Q \ f \ a \to Set \ (World \ f)$$
$$possibleWorlds = fold \ \top \ lit \ \textbf{where}$$
$$\quad lit \ f = Set.filter \ (elem \ f) \ \top$$

This implementation of the possible worlds is naive; we present an optimized version using heuristics in Sect. 4.3.

3.4   Example: A Bit of Gambling

Let us revisit the example in Sect. 2 and express it in terms of our possible worlds monad. We model the three relevant facts with the F_{Gmb} fact type.

data $F_{Gmb} = Heads \mid Red_1 \mid Red_2$ **instance** $Fact \ F_{Gmb}$ **where**
$$facts = [Heads, Red_1, Red_2]$$

The *win* query models the winning condition.

$$win :: Q \ F_{Gmb} \ ()$$
$$win = (heads \wedge (red_1 \vee red_2)) \vee ((red_1 \wedge red_2) \vee (blue_1 \wedge blue_2))$$
$$\quad \textbf{where}$$
$$\quad\quad heads = lit \ (Pos \ Heads)$$
$$\quad\quad red_1 \ = lit \ (Pos \ Red_1)$$
$$\quad\quad blue_1 = lit \ (Neg \ Red_1)$$

$$red_2 = lit\ (Pos\ Red_2)$$
$$blue_2 = lit\ (Neg\ Red_2)$$

For example,

```
> possible Worlds win
fromList [fromList [],                      -- W_1
          fromList [Heads],                 -- W_5
          fromList [Heads, Red_1],          -- W_6
          fromList [Heads, Red_1, Red_2],   -- W_8
          fromList [Heads, Red_2],.         -- W_6
          fromList [Red_1, Red_2]]          -- W_4
```

With this example, we have shown that the possible worlds interpretation in terms of boolean algebras is straightforward and intuitive. In what follows, we propose a more expressive and efficient form of interpretation in terms of commutative semirings, which are enabled by prior normalization of the query.

4   Commutative Semiring Interpretation

The typical interpretation of queries in probabilistic logic programming is their probability, given the independent probabilities of the facts.

newtype $Prob = P\ Float$ **deriving** $(Eq, Ord, Num, Fractional)$

Unfortunately, probabilities do not form a boolean algebra with $(*)$ for $(\wedge)$ and $(+)$ for $(\vee)$. Indeed, several of the boolean algebra laws are not satisfied: idempotence, absorption, $\top \vee a \equiv \top$, and $a \wedge \neg\ a \equiv \bot$.

Hence, the probability of queries cannot be expressed compositionally in terms of a *fold*. This makes sense at a conceptual level where we know, for example, that in general it holds that $P(Q_1 \vee Q_2) = P(Q_1) + P(Q_2) - P(Q_1 \wedge Q_2)$ which contains the non-compositional summand $-P(Q_1 \wedge Q_2)$. Also, in general we compute $P(Q_1 \wedge Q_2) = P(Q_1) \times P(Q_2|Q_1)$ where we read $P(Q_2|Q_1)$ as the probability of Q_2 given Q_1.

4.1   Commutative Semirings

Restricted forms of queries do admit compositional computation of probabilities:

Determinism: Two queries Q_1 and Q_2 are *mutually exclusive* when no world makes both queries true. This means, we get the compositional form

$$P(Q_1 \vee Q_2) = P(Q_1) + P(Q_2)$$

Here, indeed, $P(Q_1 \wedge Q_2)$ equals zero. A query in which all branches of or-nodes are mutually exclusive is known as *deterministic*.

COMMUTATIVITY

$$a \otimes b \equiv b \otimes a$$
$$a \oplus b \equiv b \oplus a$$

DISTRIBUTIVITY

$$a \otimes (b \oplus c) \equiv (a \otimes b) \oplus (a \otimes c)$$
$$a \oplus (b \otimes c) \equiv (a \oplus b) \otimes (a \oplus c)$$

ASSOCIATIVITY

$$a \otimes (b \otimes c) \equiv (a \otimes b) \otimes c$$
$$a \oplus (b \oplus c) \equiv (a \oplus b) \oplus c$$

IDENTITIES

$$zero \oplus a \equiv a$$
$$one \otimes a \equiv a$$

ANNIHILATION

$$zero \otimes a \equiv zero$$

Fig. 2. Laws of commutative semirings.

Decomposability. Similarly, the probability of the conjunction of two queries Q_1 and Q_2 is compositional if they are independent. Then

$$P(Q_1 \wedge Q_2) = P(Q_1) \times P(Q_2)$$

Thus, in this case, $P(Q_2|Q_1) = P(Q_2)$, making Q_2 independent of Q_1. A query in which this is true for all children of and-nodes is known as *decomposable*.

Queries that are deterministic, decomposable and also only feature negations on facts are said to be in *deterministic, decomposable negation normal form (d-DNNF)* [9,10]. For example, the query q is equivalent to its deterministic, decomposable negation normal form $q_{\text{d-DNNF}}$:

$$q \qquad = (heads \wedge red_1) \vee (red_1 \wedge red_2)$$
$$q_{\text{d-DNNF}} = ((tails \wedge red_2) \vee heads) \vee red_1$$

where $heads = lit\ (Pos\ Heads)$
$\quad\ tails\ \ = lit\ (Neg\ Heads)$
$\quad\ red_1\ \ = lit\ (Pos\ Red_1)$
$\quad\ red_2\ \ = lit\ (Pos\ Red_2)$

Such d-DNNF queries do have a well-defined mapping from possible worlds to probabilities, and, more generally, to any other interpretation that satisfies the remaining laws (see Fig. 2), which are those of *commutative semirings*. Probabilities are indeed a special case of commutative semirings.

class *Semiring* r **where**
$\quad zero :: r$
$\quad one\ :: r$
$\quad (\oplus) :: r \to r \to r$
$\quad (\otimes) :: r \to r \to r$

instance *Semiring Prob* **where**
$\quad zero = 0$
$\quad one\ = 1$
$\quad (\oplus) = (+)$
$\quad (\otimes) = (*)$

The main advantage of the d-DNNF is that we can interpret queries in linear time. For example, the interpretation of the above query q in terms of a commutative semiring, yields the following:

$$I(q_{\text{d-DNNF}}) = (I(tails) \otimes I(red_2) \oplus I(heads)) \otimes I(red_1)$$
$$= (0.6 * 0.2 + 0.4) * 0.3 = 0.156$$

4.2 The Possible Worlds as d-DNNF

We need not look far for a d-DNNF: the possible worlds representation, which is essentially isomorphic to a query with the d-DNNF structure. That is, it corresponds to a disjunction of mutually exclusive worlds. Each world is a conjunction of independent facts. In this form, $\top$ and $\bot$ are absent, and negations are in normal form: they only appear on facts.

We can define a valuation val function, which interprets possible worlds in terms of a commutative semiring. Given an interpretation of the literals in terms of a commutative semiring, it valuates a set of possible worlds over those literals.

```
val :: (Fact f, Semiring r) ⇒ (Lit f → r) → (Set (World f) → r)
val gen_lit = sum ∘ map (prod ∘ lits) ∘ Set.toList where
    prod = foldr     (⊗) one
    sum  = foldr     (⊕) zero
    lits s = map lit facts where
      lit f. | Set.member f s = gen_lit (Pos f)
             | otherwise      = gen_lit (Neg f)
```

Interpreting a query means computing its possible worlds and valuating these worlds. For example, we capture the probability for each fact in our gambling example in the function $gmbProb$.

```
gmbProb :: Lit F_Gmb → Prob
gmbProb (Pos Heads) = 0.4
gmbProb (Pos Red_1) = 0.3
gmbProb (Pos Red_2) = 0.2
gmbProb (Neg f) = 1 − gmbProb (Pos f)
```

From that we can derive the probability of winning.

```
> val gmbProb (possibleWorlds win)
0.7720001
```

Note that the val function allows additional interpretations beyond probabilities.

Dual Numbers. A useful commutative semiring is that of the so-called *dual numbers* [7]. Dual number have applications in physics [43], robotics [20] and automatic differentiation algorithms [44]. In the latter context, a dual number $D\ x\ dx$ represents a number x together with its derivative dx.

data $Dual\ d = D\ d\ d$
instance $Semiring\ d \Rightarrow Semiring\ (Dual\ d)$ **where**
   $zero = D\ zero\ zero$
   $one = D\ one\ zero$
   $D\ x\ dx \oplus D\ y\ dy = D\ (x \oplus y)\ (dx \oplus dy)$
   $D\ x\ dx \otimes D\ y\ dy = D\ (x \otimes y)\ (x \otimes dy \oplus y \otimes dx)$

This can be used to perform gradient-descent style learning of the facts' probabilities based on the observed probability of a query.

Tropical Semiring. The tropical max-semiring selects the maximum among disjuncts and adds conjuncts. It is an example of a commutative semirings without a notion of an additive inverse.

data $Max\ n = Max\ n$
instance $(Num\ n,\ Ord\ n) \Rightarrow Semiring\ (Max\ n)$ **where**
   $zero = Max\ 0$ -- for positive numbers only
   $one = Max\ 0$
   $Max\ n \oplus Max\ m = Max\ (max\ n\ m)$
   $Max\ n \otimes Max\ m = Max\ (n + m)$

With this semiring, we can for example find the highest cost if we interpret positive facts as carrying a cost and negative facts as the absence of that cost.

4.3 Optimized d-DNNF Representations

The above way of interpreting a query in terms of the possible worlds is correct but highly expensive due to its $\mathcal{O}(2^n)$ time complexity (with n the number of facts). Fortunately, the possible worlds representation is not the only d-DNNF. For example, $q_{\text{d-DNNF}}$ (Sect. 4.1) represents a more compact d-DNNF query:

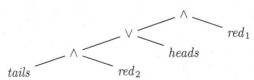

Several compilers exist that use heuristics to efficiently compute compact d-DNNFs for a query, e.g., c2d [11], dsharp [27] and d4 [24]. All three compilers improve efficiency with orders of magnitude compared to state-of-the-art model counters, with d4 the most efficient one, substantially saving computational power in terms of time and size over the other two [24]. We have created an alternative for *val* that interprets a query into a commutative semiring by way of the d4 compiler.

$$val_{d4} :: (Fact\ f,\ Semiring\ r,\ Eq\ a) \Rightarrow (Lit\ f \to r) \to Q\ f\ a \to r$$

This function turns the query first into conjunctive normal form (CNF), which is the expected input of d4, and afterwards interprets d4's output format using the commutative semiring operations.

For example, *win* is transformed and interpreted, yielding the same result as ProbLog does.

> val_{d4} *gmbProb win*
0.772

Note that, while the boolean algebra interpretation is naturally compositional, that is not the case with the commutative semiring interpretation. Indeed, the normalization procedure is a whole program transformation. This means that there is no room for variables as non-terminals with arbitrary interpretations. Therefore, we consider variables *Var* to denote the terminal *true* or *one* in case of a positive occurrence and *false* or *zero* in case of a negative occurrence.

In summary, although the interpretation of a query in terms of a commutative semiring is more expressive and efficient than that in terms of a boolean algebra, it also requires an additional normalization step, which forces us to use a trivial implementation for interpreting variables. Ongoing research, especially on so-called lifted inference techniques [4], develops additional optimization heuristics to exploit common structure in subqueries.

5   Circular Queries

An advanced but key feature of probabilistic logic programming are circular queries, which is often illustrated by the *social smokers* problem. This problem models a group of people that may or may not smoke. If a person p smokes that may be either due to stress or due to being influenced by another smoker q. This can be modelled by the query:

smokes p = *stress p* $\vee$ (*exists person* ($\lambda q \rightarrow$ *influences q p* $\wedge$ *smokes q*))

where auxiliary definitions are given in Fig. 3. The problem with this definition is that it is circular. *Alice* may smoke because she is influenced by *Bob* who may smoke because he is influenced by *Alice* who may smoke because...

5.1   Least Fixed-Points

Fortunately, cyclic queries readily have a least fixed-point interpretation. This is a consequence of the Kleene fixed-point theorem: Monotone functions ϕ over a directed-complete partial order $\langle L, \sqsubseteq \rangle$ with a least element $\bot$ have a least fixed point that is the supremum of the ascending Kleene chain

$$\bot \sqsubseteq \phi(\bot) \sqsubseteq \phi(\phi(\bot)) \sqsubseteq \ldots$$

Finite Boolean algebras are indeed a directed-complete partial orders, where $a \sqsubseteq b$ is defined as $a \wedge b = a$. Also, since the queries do not involve circularity through negation, they can indeed be expressed as fixed-points of monotone functions. For instance, we can see *smokes* as the fixed point of the monotone function *smokesF* over a finite pointwise boolean algebra.

People:

    data *Person = Alice | Bob*

    person = [Alice, Bob]

Auxiliary Functions:

    exists l f = foldr Or Fail (map f l)

    stress p   = lit (Pos (Stress p))

    influences p_1 p_2 = lit (Pos (Influences p_1 p_2))

Facts:

    data *FSS = Stress Person | Influences Person Person*

    instance *Fact FSS* **where**

      facts = [Stress p | p ← person] ++ [Influences p_1 p_2 | p_1 ← person, p_2 ← person]

Fig. 3. Auxiliary definitions for the social smokers problem.

smokesF smk p = stress p ∨ (exists person (λq → influences q p ∧ smk q))

With a "top-down" tabulation-based strategy, the fixed-point for pointwise boolean algebras can be obtained. We proceed with an approach based on that of Vandenbroucke et al. [41]. For this purpose, we extend the query type Q with two additional type parameters i and o and a constructor *Rec*. All former uses of Q can have $i = Void$ and $o = Void$.

    data Q *i o f a* **where**

      ...

      Rec :: i → (o → Q i o f a) → Q i o f a

    rec :: i → Q i o f o

    rec i = Rec i Var

The *Rec* constructor is used by the fixed-point combinator *fix* to mark the recursive function invocations. The i type is the parameter type of the recursive function, e.g., $i = Person$ in the social smokers example. Similarly, o is the output type of the recursion function, e.g., $o =$ () in the social smokers example.

    Our approach simplifies that of Vandenbroucke et al. [41], which detects cycles in the call graph and then iteratively computes ascending chains based on those cycles. Because, following the logician Charles Sanders Peirce [12], monotone functions over a boolean algebra reach a least fixed-point in one step (i.e., $\phi(\phi(\bot)) = \phi(\bot)$), we do not need to iterate and inspect intermediate results to see whether a fixed-point has been reached. Instead, we know that one step is sufficient and thus can perform it syntactically at the level of queries, rather than semantically in a boolean algebra domain. Having the result as a syntactic query is convenient for the subsequent efficient interpretation of Sect. 4.3.

    fix :: Ord i ⇒ ((i → Q i o f o) → (i → Q i o f o)) → (i → Q Void Void f o)

    fix f x = go'(f rec x) (Set.singleton x) **where**

      go (Var x) h = Var x

      go Fail   h = Fail

      go (Or p q) h = Or (go p h) (go q h)

      go (Lit l p) h = Lit l (go p h)

      go (Rec i p) h | Set.member i h = Fail

                | otherwise   = go (f rec i ⋙ p) (Set.insert i h)*

The fixed-point strategy traverses the query structure and copies all query constructors except for *Rec*. When a *Rec* is encountered, the recursive call is unfolded and its parameter added to the history. Yet, in case the *Rec*'s parameter appears in the history and thus closes a cycle, the bottom element *Fail* is returned instead. With this fixed-point operator, we have that *smokes* = *fix smokesF*. Using the following probabilities of the facts:

$$smkProb :: Lit\ FSS \rightarrow Prob$$
$$smkProb\ (Pos\ (Stress\ p)) \qquad = 0.3$$
$$smkProb\ (Pos\ (Influences\ x\ y)) = 0.2$$
$$smkProb\ (Neg\ f) \qquad\qquad\quad = 1 - smkProb\ (Pos\ f)$$

We can now compute the probability that *Alice* smokes.

$$> val_{d4}\ smkProb\ (smokes\ Alice)$$
$$0.34200004$$

6   Related Work

There is much literature that studies either logic programming or probabilistic programming from the point of view of functional programming.

Many works focus on functional models of logic programming. Most focus on monads to model the backtracking search aspects of Prolog [21,23,29,38] and some on logical variables [6,36]. Moreover, there is a range of languages that combine functional and logic programming, such as Curry [13], DataFun [1], Mercury [37], miniKanren [5], and Toy [26]. Probabilistic programming has been based on the monadic structure of probability distributions [14,18,33]. Again, there are many languages that combine elements of both functional and probabilistic programming, such as Anglican [25], Church [19], and Hakaru [28]. As far as we know, there is very little work that combines all three and studies, e.g., functional models of probabilistic logic programming. Gibbons [17] studies the possible interactions between nondeterministic and probabilistic choice. More closely related is the applicative-functor model of ProbLog of Vandenbroucke and Schrijvers [40] which corresponds to our naive exponential enumeration of possible worlds. Kimmig et al. [22] have argued that weighted model counting should be generalized to arbitrary commutative semirings, and Belle and De Raedt [2] have argued that commutative semirings have many artificial intelligence applications.

7   Conclusion

In summary, this paper has presented a functional account of probabilistic logic programming in terms of possible worlds. We believe that this account is of interest, not only because it makes functional programmers aware of this alternative flavor of probabilistic programming, but also because it involves many typical functional programming concepts: We represent queries using a *term monad* and interpret these queries with a *structural recursion scheme* and boolean *algebras*. Computing the probability of a query requires *normalisation* into deterministic, decomposable negation normal form before interpretation in terms of a *commutative semiring*. While the possible world semantics are in this normal form, they take exponential time to compute. Heuristic compilers, such as d4, are more efficient in practice. To support circular queries, a key feature of probabilistic logic programming languages, we employ a custom *fixed-point combinator*. We hope that this bridging development enables further cross-fertilization.

References

1. Arntzenius, M., Krishnaswami, N.R.: Datafun: a functional datalog. In: Garrigue, J., Keller, G., Sumii, E. (eds.) Proceedings of the 21st ACM SIGPLAN International Conference on Functional Programming, ICFP 2016, Nara, Japan, 18–22 September 2016, pp. 214–227. ACM (2016). https://doi.org/10.1145/2951913.2951948
2. Belle, V., Raedt, L.D.: Semiring programming: a framework for search, inference and learning. CoRR abs/1609.06954 (2016). http://arxiv.org/abs/1609.06954
3. Birkhoff, G., Mac Lane, S.: A Survey of Modern Algebra. Taylor & Francis (1997)
4. Van den Broeck, G., Kersting, K., Natarajan, S., Poole, D.: An Introduction to Lifted Probabilistic Inference. MIT Press, Cambridge (2021)
5. Byrd, W.E.: Relational programming in miniKanren: techniques, applications, and implementations. Ph.D. thesis, Indiana University (2009)
6. Claessen, K., Ljunglöf, P.: Typed logical variables in haskell. Electron. Notes Theor. Comput. Sci. **41**(1), 37 (2000). https://doi.org/10.1016/S1571-0661(05)80544-4
7. Clifford: Preliminary Sketch of Biquaternions. Proc. London Math. Soc. **s1-4**(1), 381–395 (1871). https://doi.org/10.1112/plms/s1-4.1.381
8. Dantsin, E.: Probabilistic logic programs and their semantics. In: Voronkov, A. (ed.) RCLP -1990. LNCS, vol. 592, pp. 152–164. Springer, Heidelberg (1992). https://doi.org/10.1007/3-540-55460-2_11
9. Darwiche, A.: On the tractable counting of theory models and its application to belief revision and truth maintenance. CoRR cs.AI/0003044 (2000). https://arxiv.org/abs/cs/0003044
10. Darwiche, A.: A compiler for deterministic, decomposable negation normal form. In: Eighteenth National Conference on Artificial Intelligence, pp. 627–634. American Association for Artificial Intelligence, USA (2002)
11. Darwiche, A.: New advances in compiling CNF to decomposable negation normal form. In: Proceedings of the 16th European Conference on Artificial Intelligence, ECAI 2004, pp. 318–322. IOS Press, NLD (2004)
12. Dau, F.: Some Notes on proofs with alpha graphs. In: Schärfe, H., Hitzler, P., Øhrstrøm, P. (eds.) ICCS-ConceptStruct 2006. LNCS (LNAI), vol. 4068, pp. 172–188. Springer, Heidelberg (2006). https://doi.org/10.1007/11787181_13
13. Dylus, S., Christiansen, J., Teegen, F.: Implementing a library for probabilistic programming using non-strict non-determinism. Theory Pract. Logic Program. **20**(1), 147–175 (2020). https://doi.org/10.1017/S1471068419000085
14. Erwig, M., Kollmansberger, S.: Functional pearls: probabilistic functional programming in haskell. J. Funct. Program. **16**(1), 21–34 (2006). https://doi.org/10.1017/S0956796805005721

15. Fierens, D., et al.: Inference and learning in probabilistic logic programs using weighted boolean formulas. Theory Pract. Logic Program. **15**(3), 358–401 (2015)
16. Gelfond, M., Lifschitz, V.: The stable model semantics for logic programming. In: Kowalski, R.A., Bowen, K.A. (eds.) Logic Programming, Proceedings of the Fifth International Conference and Symposium, Seattle, Washington, USA, 15–19 August 1988, vol. 2, pp. 1070–1080. MIT Press (1988)
17. Gibbons, J.: Unifying theories of programming with monads. In: Wolff, B., Gaudel, M.-C., Feliachi, A. (eds.) UTP 2012. LNCS, vol. 7681, pp. 23–67. Springer, Heidelberg (2013). https://doi.org/10.1007/978-3-642-35705-3_2
18. Giry, M.: A categorical approach to probability theory. In: Banaschewski, B. (ed.) Categorical Aspects of Topology and Analysis. LNM, vol. 915, pp. 68–85. Springer, Heidelberg (1982). https://doi.org/10.1007/BFb0092872
19. Goodman, N.D., Mansinghka, V.K., Roy, D., Bonawitz, K., Tenenbaum, J.B.: Church: a language for generative models. In: Proceedings of the Twenty-Fourth Conference on Uncertainty in Artificial Intelligence, UAI 2008, pp. 220–229. AUAI Press, Arlington (2008)
20. Gu, Y.L., Luh, J.: Dual-number transformation and its applications to robotics. IEEE J. Robot. Autom. **3**(6), 615–623 (1987). https://doi.org/10.1109/JRA.1987.1087138
21. Hinze, R.: Prological features in a functional setting axioms and implementation. In: Sato, M., Toyama, Y. (eds.) Third Fuji International Symposium on Functional and Logic Programming, FLOPS 1998, Kyoto, Japan, 2–4 April 1998, pp. 98–122. World Scientific, Singapore (1998)
22. Kimmig, A., Van den Broeck, G., De Raedt, L.: An algebraic prolog for reasoning about possible worlds, vol. 1, pp. 209–214. AAAI Press, Burgard (2011). http://www.informatik.uni-trier.de/~ley/db/conf/aaai/aaai2011.html
23. Kiselyov, O., Shan, C., Friedman, D.P., Sabry, A.: Backtracking, interleaving, and terminating monad transformers: (functional pearl). In: Danvy, O., Pierce, B.C. (eds.) Proceedings of the 10th ACM SIGPLAN International Conference on Functional Programming, ICFP 2005, Tallinn, Estonia, 26–28 September 2005, pp. 192–203. ACM (2005). https://doi.org/10.1145/1086365.1086390
24. Lagniez, J.M., Marquis, P.: An improved decision-DNNF compiler. In: Proceedings of the 26th International Joint Conference on Artificial Intelligence, IJCAI 2017, pp. 667–673. AAAI Press (2017)
25. Le, T.A., Baydin, A.G., Wood, F.: Inference compilation and universal probabilistic programming. In: 20th International Conference on Artificial Intelligence and Statistics, 20–22 April 2017, Fort Lauderdale, FL, USA (2017)
26. López Fraguas, F.J., Sánchez Hernández, J.: TOY: a multiparadigm declarative system. In: Narendran, P., Rusinowitch, M. (eds.) RTA 1999. LNCS, vol. 1631, pp. 244–247. Springer, Heidelberg (1999). https://doi.org/10.1007/3-540-48685-2_19
27. Muise, C., McIlraith, S.A., Beck, J.C., Hsu, E.I.: DSHARP: fast d-DNNF compilation with sharpSAT. In: Kosseim, L., Inkpen, D. (eds.) AI 2012. LNCS (LNAI), vol. 7310, pp. 356–361. Springer, Heidelberg (2012). https://doi.org/10.1007/978-3-642-30353-1_36
28. Narayanan, P., Carette, J., Romano, W., Shan, C., Zinkov, R.: Probabilistic inference by program transformation in Hakaru (system description). In: Kiselyov, O., King, A. (eds.) FLOPS 2016. LNCS, vol. 9613, pp. 62–79. Springer, Cham (2016). https://doi.org/10.1007/978-3-319-29604-3_5
29. Piróg, M., Staton, S.: Backtracking with cut via a distributive law and left-zero monoids. J. Funct. Program. **27**, e17 (2017). https://doi.org/10.1017/S0956796817000077

30. Plotkin, G., Pretnar, M.: Handlers of algebraic effects. In: Castagna, G. (ed.) ESOP 2009. LNCS, vol. 5502, pp. 80–94. Springer, Heidelberg (2009). https://doi.org/10.1007/978-3-642-00590-9_7

31. Poole, D.: Logic programming, abduction and probability: a top-down anytime algorithm for estimating prior and posterior probabilities. In: Selected Papers of International Conference on Fifth Generation Computer Systems, vol. 92, pp. 377–400. Springer, Heidelberg (1993)

32. Poole, D.: The independent choice logic for modelling multiple agents under uncertainty. Artif. Intell. **94**(1–2), 7–56 (1997). https://doi.org/10.1016/S0004-3702(97)00027-1

33. Ramsey, N., Pfeffer, A.: Stochastic lambda calculus and monads of probability distributions. In: Launchbury, J., Mitchell, J.C. (eds.) Conference Record of POPL 2002: The 29th SIGPLAN-SIGACT Symposium on Principles of Programming Languages, Portland, OR, USA, 16–18 January 2002, pp. 154–165. ACM (2002). https://doi.org/10.1145/503272.503288

34. Riguzzi, F., Swift, T.: The PITA system: tabling and answer subsumption for reasoning under uncertainty. Theory Pract. Log. Program. **11**(4–5), 433–449 (2011). https://doi.org/10.1017/S147106841100010X

35. Sato, T.: A statistical learning method for logic programs with distribution semantics. In: Sterling, L. (ed.) Logic Programming, Proceedings of the Twelfth International Conference on Logic Programming, Tokyo, Japan, 13–16 June 1995, pp. 715–729. MIT Press (1995)

36. Seres, S., Spivey, J.M., Hoare, C.A.R.: Algebra of logic programming. In: Schreye, D.D. (ed.) Logic Programming: The 1999 International Conference, Las Cruces, New Mexico, USA, 29 November–4 December 1999, pp. 184–199. MIT Press (1999)

37. Somogyi, Z., Henderson, F.J., Conway, T.C.: Mercury, an efficient purely declarative logic programming language. Austral. Comput. Sci. Commun. **17**, 499–512 (1995)

38. Spivey, J.M.: Algebras for combinatorial search. J. Funct. Program. **19**(3–4), 469–487 (2009). https://doi.org/10.1017/S0956796809007321

39. Van Gelder, A., Ross, K.A., Schlipf, J.S.: The well-founded semantics for general logic programs. J. ACM **38**(3), 619–649 (1991). https://doi.org/10.1145/116825.116838

40. Vandenbroucke, A., Schrijvers, T.: ProbLog and applicative probabilistic programming, January 2017. https://lirias.kuleuven.be/1656686. Workshop on Probabilistic Programming Semantics (PPS), Paris, France, 17 January 2017

41. Vandenbroucke, A., Schrijvers, T., Piessens, F.: Fixing non-determinism. In: Lämmel, R. (ed.) Proceedings of the 27th Symposium on the Implementation and Application of Functional Programming Languages, IFL 2015, Koblenz, Germany, 14–16 September 2015, pp. 5:1–5:12. ACM (2015). https://doi.org/10.1145/2897336.2897342

42. Vennekens, J., Verbaeten, S., Bruynooghe, M.: Logic programs with annotated disjunctions. In: Demoen, B., Lifschitz, V. (eds.) ICLP 2004. LNCS, vol. 3132, pp. 431–445. Springer, Heidelberg (2004). https://doi.org/10.1007/978-3-540-27775-0_30

43. Walker, M.W., Shao, L., Volz, R.A.: Estimating 3-D location parameters using dual number quaternions. CVGIP Image Underst. **54**(3), 358–367 (1991). https://doi.org/10.1016/1049-9660(91)90036-O

44. Wengert, R.E.: A simple automatic derivative evaluation program. Commun. ACM **7**(8), 463–464 (1964). https://doi.org/10.1145/355586.364791

45. Wu, N., Schrijvers, T., Hinze, R.: Effect handlers in scope. In: Proceedings of the 2014 ACM SIGPLAN Symposium on Haskell, pp. 1–12 (2014)

Explanations as Programs in Probabilistic Logic Programming

Germán Vidal[(✉)]

VRAIN, Universitat Politècnica de València, Valencia, Spain
gvidal@dsic.upv.es

Abstract. The generation of comprehensible explanations is an essential feature of modern artificial intelligence systems. In this work, we consider *probabilistic logic programming*, an extension of logic programming which can be useful to model domains with relational structure and uncertainty. Essentially, a program specifies a probability distribution over possible *worlds* (i.e., sets of facts). The notion of *explanation* is typically associated with that of a world, so that one often looks for the *most probable world* as well as for the worlds where the query is true. Unfortunately, such explanations exhibit no causal structure. In particular, the chain of inferences required for a specific prediction (represented by a query) is not shown. In this paper, we propose a novel approach where explanations are represented as programs that are generated from a given query by a number of unfolding-like transformations. Here, the chain of inferences that proves a given query is made explicit. Furthermore, the generated explanations are minimal (i.e., contain no irrelevant information) and can be parameterized w.r.t. a specification of *visible* predicates, so that the user may hide uninteresting details from explanations.

1 Introduction

Artificial intelligence (AI) and, especially, machine learning systems are becoming ubiquitous in many areas, like medical diagnosis [9], intelligent transportation [33], or different types of recommendation systems [26], to name a few. While prediction errors are sometimes acceptable, there are areas where blindly following the assessment of an AI system is not desirable (e.g., medical diagnosis). In these cases, generating *explanations* that are comprehensible by non-expert users would allow them to verify the reliability of the prediction as well as to improve the system when the prediction is not correct. Furthermore, the last regulation on data protection in the European Union [10] has introduced

This work has been partially supported by the EU (FEDER) and the Spanish MCI under grant PID2019-104735RB-C41/ AEI/10.13039/501100011033 (SAFER), by the *Generalitat Valenciana* under grant Prometeo/2019/098 (DeepTrust), and by TAILOR, a project funded by EU Horizon 2020 research and innovation programme under GA No. 952215.

M. Hanus and A. Igarashi (Eds.): FLOPS 2022, LNCS 13215, pp. 205–223, 2022.
https://doi.org/10.1007/978-3-030-99461-7_12

a "right to explanation" for algorithmic decisions. All in all, the generation of comprehensible explanations is an essential feature of modern AI systems.

Currently, there exist many approaches to *explainable AI* (XAI) [3], which greatly differ depending on the considered application. In particular, so-called *interpretable machine learning* [18] puts the emphasis on the interpretability of the models and their predictions. In this work, we consider *probabilistic logic programming* (PLP) [24], which can be useful to model domains with relational structure and uncertainty. PLP has been used for both inference—e.g., computing the marginal probability of a set of random variables given some evidence—and learning [11,30]. Among the different approaches to PLP, we consider those that are based on Sato's *distribution semantics* [29]. This is the case of several proposals that combine logic programming and probability, like Logic Programs with Annotated Disjunctions (LPADs) [32], ProbLog [25], Probabilistic Horn Abduction (PHA) [22], Independent Choice Logic (ICL) [23], and PRISM [30].

In particular, we consider the ProbLog approach for its simplicity, but we note that the expressive power of all languages mentioned above is the same (see, e.g., [27, Chapter 2]). A ProbLog program extends a logic program with a set of *probabilistic facts*. A probabilistic fact has the form $p :: a$ and denotes a random variable which is true with probability p and false with probability $1 - p$. Here, a program defines a probability distribution over *worlds*, i.e., sets of (possibly negated) atoms corresponding to the probabilistic facts of the program. Essentially, the probability of a world is equal to the product of the probabilities of its true and false facts, while the probability of a query is computed by *marginalization*, i.e., by summing up the probabilities of the worlds where the query is true.

The notion of *explanation* of a query is often associated with that of a world. For instance, the MPE task [31], which stands for *Most Probable Explanation*, consists in finding the world with the highest probability. However, a world exhibits no causal structure and, thus, it is up to the user to understand *why* the given collection of facts actually allow one to infer a particular prediction (it might even be counterintuitive; see Example 4). Moreover, a world typically contains facts whose truth value is irrelevant for the query, which might be an additional source of confusion. Alternatively, one could consider a *proof tree* of a query as an explanation. While the chain of inferences and the links to the query are now explicit, proof trees are typically very large and can be complex to understand by non-experts.

In this paper, we propose a novel approach where explanations are represented as programs that are generated from a given query by a number of unfolding-like transformations. In this way, we have the same advantages of using proof trees as explanations (the chain of inferences and the link to the query are explicit), but they are often easier to understand by non-experts because of the following reasons: first, an explanation is associated with a *single* proof, so it is conceptually simpler than a proof tree (that might comprise several proofs); second, facts and rules have a more intuitive reading than a proof tree (and could easily be represented using natural language); finally, the generated explanations can be parameterized w.r.t. a set of *visible* predicates. If no predicate is visible, our explanations are not very different from a (partial) world, since they just contain the probabilistic facts that make a query true in a particular proof. On the other hand, if all predicates are visible, the computation of an explanation essentially boils down to computing the (relevant) grounding of a program for a given proof of the query. It is thus up to the user to determine the appropriate level of detail in the explanation so that only the most interesting relations are shown.

In this work, we present a constructive algorithm for generating the explanations of a query such that the following essential properties hold: i) the probability of each proof is preserved in the corresponding explanation, ii) explanations do not contain facts that are irrelevant for the given query, and iii) the (marginal) probability of the query in the original program is equivalent to that in the union of the computed explanations. In order to check the viability of the approach, we have developed a proof-of-concept implementation, xgen,[1] that takes a ProbLog program and a query and produces a set of explanations for this query, together with their associated probabilities.

2   Probabilistic Logic Programming (PLP)

In this section, we briefly introduce PLP following the ProbLog approach (see, e.g., [11,14,24,25,27] for a detailed account).

Let us first recall some basic terminology from logic programming [1,15]. We consider a first-order language with a fixed vocabulary of predicate symbols, constants, and variables denoted by Π, $\mathcal{C}$ and $\mathcal{V}$, respectively.[2] An *atom* has the form $f(t_1, \ldots, t_n)$ with $f/n \in \Pi$ and $t_i \in (\mathcal{C} \cup \mathcal{V})$ for $i = 1, \ldots, n$. A *definite clause* has the form $h \leftarrow B$, where h (the *head*) is an atom and B (the *body*) is a conjunction of atoms, typically denoted by a sequence $a_1, \ldots, a_n$, $n \geq 0$; if $n = 0$, the clause is called a *fact* and denoted by h; otherwise $(n > 0)$, it is called a *rule*. A *query* is a clause with no head, and is denoted by a sequence of atoms. $\mathrm{var}(s)$ denotes the set of variables in the syntactic object s, where s can be an atom, a query or a clause. A syntactic object s is *ground* if $\mathrm{var}(s) = \emptyset$. Substitutions and their operations are defined as usual; the application of a substitution θ to a syntactic object s is denoted by juxtaposition, i.e., we write $s\theta$ rather than $\theta(s)$.

In the following, we consider that $\Pi = \Pi_p \uplus \Pi_d$, where Π_p are the *probabilistic predicates* and Π_d are the *derived predicates*, which are disjoint. An atom $f(t_1, \ldots, t_n)$ is called a *probabilistic atom* if $f \in \Pi_p$ and a *derived atom* if $f \in \Pi_d$. A *probabilistic logic program* (or just *program* when no confusion can arise) $\mathcal{P} = \mathcal{P}_p \uplus \mathcal{P}_d$ consists of a set of ground probabilistic facts $\mathcal{P}_p$ and a set of definite clauses $\mathcal{P}_d$. A *probabilistic fact* has the form $p :: a$, where a is a ground atom and $p \in [0, 1]$ is a probability such that a is true with probability p and false with probability $1 - p$. These ground facts represent the Boolean random variables of the model, which we assume mutually independent.

---

[1] Publicly available from https://github.com/mistupv/xgen.
[2] We do not consider function symbols in this work.

In this paper, we also allow *nonground* probabilistic facts, that are replaced by their finite groundings using the Herbrand universe, i.e., using the constants from $\mathcal{C}$. More generally, we consider *intensional* probabilistic facts defined by (probabilistic) clauses of the form $p :: f(x_1, \ldots, x_n) \leftarrow B$, where B only contains derived atoms. Such a rule represents the set of ground probabilistic facts $p ::$ $f(x_1, \ldots, x_n)\theta$ such that $B\theta$ is true in the underlying model.

Example 1. Consider the following program (a variation of an example in [11]):[3]

```
0.8::stress(X) :- person(X).        person(ann).
0.3::influences(bob,carl).          person(bob).
smokes(X) :- stress(X).
smokes(X) :- influences(Y,X),smokes(Y).
```

Here, we have two probabilistic predicates, stress/1 and influences/2, and a logic program that defines the relation smokes/1. Basically, the program states that a person (either ann or bob) is stressed with probability 0.8, bob influences carl with probability 0.3, and that a person smokes either if (s)he is stressed or is influenced by someone who smokes.

Observe that the first probabilistic clause is equivalent to the following set of ground probabilistic facts: 0.8::stress(ann), 0.8::stress(bob).

We note that probabilistic clauses can always be rewritten to a combination of probabilistic facts and non-probabilistic clauses [11]. For instance, the probabilistic clause in the example above could be replaced by

```
0.8::p(X).        stress(X) :- person(X),p(X).
```

In this work, we assume that the Herbrand universe is finite (and coincides with the domain $\mathcal{C}$ of constants) and, thus, the set of ground instances of each probabilistic fact is finite.[4] Given a program $\mathcal{P}$, we let $G(\mathcal{P})$ denote the set of its *ground* probabilistic facts (after grounding nonground probabilistic and intensional facts, if any). An *atomic choice* determines whether a ground probabilistic fact is chosen or not. A *total choice* makes a selection for *all* ground probabilistic facts; it is typically represented as a set of ground probabilistic atoms (the ones that are true). Note that, given n ground probabilistic atoms, we have 2^n possible total choices.

A program $\mathcal{P}$ then defines a probability distribution over the total choices. Moreover, since the random variables associated with the ground probabilistic facts are mutually independent, the probability of a total choice $L \subseteq G(\mathcal{P})$ can be obtained from the product of the probabilities of its atomic choices:

$$P(L) = \prod_{a\theta \in L} \pi(a) \cdot \prod_{a\theta \in G(\mathcal{P}) \setminus L} 1 - \pi(a)$$

---

[3] We follow Prolog's notation in examples: variables start with an uppercase letter and the implication "←" is denoted by ":-".

[4] See Sato's seminal paper [29] for the distribution semantics in the infinite case.

		$P(w_i)$
w_1	{stress(ann),stress(bob),influences(bob, carl)}	$0.8 \cdot 0.8 \cdot 0.3 = 0.192$
w_2	{stress(ann),stress(bob) }	$0.8 \cdot 0.8 \cdot 0.7 = 0.448$
w_3	{stress(ann), influences(bob, carl)}	$0.8 \cdot 0.2 \cdot 0.3 = 0.048$
w_4	{stress(ann) }	$0.8 \cdot 0.2 \cdot 0.7 = 0.112$
w_5	{ stress(bob),influences(bob, carl)}	$0.2 \cdot 0.8 \cdot 0.3 = 0.048$
w_6	{ stress(bob) }	$0.2 \cdot 0.8 \cdot 0.7 = 0.112$
w_7	{ influences(bob, carl)}	$0.2 \cdot 0.2 \cdot 0.3 = 0.012$
w_8	{ }	$0.2 \cdot 0.2 \cdot 0.7 = 0.028$

Fig. 1. Possible worlds for Example 1

where $\pi(a)$ denotes the probability of the fact, i.e., $\pi(a) = p$ if $p :: a \in \mathcal{P}_p$. A possible *world* is then defined as the least Herbrand model of $L \cup \mathcal{P}_d$, which is unique. Typically, we denote a world by a total choice, omitting the (uniquely determined) truth values for derived atoms. By definition, the sum of the probabilities of all possible worlds is equal to 1.

In the following, we only consider *atomic* queries. Nevertheless, note that an arbitrary query B could be encoded using an additional clause of the form $q \leftarrow B$. The probability of a query q in a program $\mathcal{P}$, called the *success probability* of q in $\mathcal{P}$, in symbols $P(q)$, is defined as the marginal of $P(L)$ w.r.t. query q:

$$P(q) = \sum_{L \subseteq G(\mathcal{P})} P(q|L) \cdot P(L)$$

where $P(q|L) = 1$ if there exists a substitution θ such that $L \cup \mathcal{P}_d \models q\theta$ and $P(q|L) = 0$ otherwise. Intuitively speaking, the success probability of a query is the sum of the probabilities of all the worlds where this query is provable.[5]

Example 2. Consider again the program in Example 1. Here, we have eight possible worlds, which are shown in Fig. 1. Observe that the sum of the probabilities of all worlds is 1. Here, the query smokes(carl) is true in worlds w_1 and w_5. Thus, its probability is $0.192 + 0.048 = 0.24$.

Since the number of worlds is finite, one could compute the success probability of a query by enumerating all worlds and, then, checking whether the query is true in each of them. Unfortunately, this approach is generally unfeasible in practice due to the large number of possible worlds. Instead, a combination of inference and a conversion to a Boolean formula is often used (see, e.g., [11]).

3   Explanations as Programs

In this section, we focus on the notion of explanation in the context of PLP. Here, we advocate that a *good* explanation should have the following properties:

---

[5] Equivalently, has a successful SLD derivation; see Sect. 3.1 for a precise definition of SLD (*Selective Linear Definite clause*) resolution.

– *Causal structure.* An explanation should include the chain of inferences that supports a given prediction. It is not sufficient to just show a collection of facts. It should answer *why* a given query is true, so that the user can follow the reasoning from the query back to the considered probabilistic facts.
– *Minimality.* An explanation should not include irrelevant information. In particular, those facts whose truth value is indifferent for a given query should not be part of the explanation.
– *Understandable.* The explanation should be easy to follow by non-experts in PLP. Moreover, it is also desirable for explanations to be parametric w.r.t. the information that is considered relevant by the user.

In the following, we briefly review some possible notions of an explanation and, then, introduce our new proposal.

3.1 Explanations in PLP

Typically, *explanations* have been associated with *worlds*. For instance, the MPE (*Most Probable Explanation*) task [31] consists in finding the world with the highest probability given some *evidence* (in our context, given that some query is true). However, a world does not show the chain of inferences of a given query and, moreover, it is not minimal by definition, since it usually includes a (possibly large) number of probabilistic facts whose truth value is irrelevant for the query.

Alternatively, one can consider a probabilistic logic program itself as an explanation. Here, the causal structure is explicit (given by the program clauses). Moreover, derived rules are easy to understand or can easily be explained using natural language. However, the program explains the complete *model* but it is not so useful to explain a particular query: the chain of inferences is not obvious and, moreover, programs are not usually minimal since they often contain a (possibly large) number of facts and rules which are not relevant for a particular query.

Another alternative consists in using the *proof of a query* as an explanation. Following [14], one can associate a *proof* of a query with a (minimal) *partial world* w' such that for all worlds $w \supseteq w'$, the query is true in w. In this case, one can easily ensure minimality (e.g., by using SLD resolution to determine the ground probabilistic atoms that are needed to prove the query). However, even if the partial world contains no irrelevant facts, it is still not useful to determine the chain of inferences behind a given query. In order to avoid this shortcoming, one could represent the proofs of a query by means of an SLD tree. Let us further explore this possibility.

First, we recall some background from logic programming [15]. Given a logic program $\mathcal{P}$, we say that $B_1, a, B_2 \leadsto_\theta (B_1, B, B_2)\theta$ is an *SLD resolution step* if $h \leftarrow B$ is a renamed apart clause (i.e., with fresh variables) of program $\mathcal{P}$, in symbols, $h \leftarrow B \ll \mathcal{P}$, and $\theta = \mathsf{mgu}(a, h)$ is the *most general unifier* of atoms a and h. An *SLD derivation* is a (finite or infinite) sequence of SLD resolution steps. As is common, $\leadsto^*$ denotes the reflexive and transitive closure of $\leadsto$. In particular, we denote by $A_0 \leadsto^*_\theta A_n$ a derivation $A_0 \leadsto_{\theta_1} A_1 \leadsto_{\theta_2} \ldots \leadsto_{\theta_n} A_n$, where $\theta = \theta_1 \ldots \theta_n$ if $n > 0$ (and $\theta = id$ otherwise). An SLD derivation is called *successful* if it ends with the query *true* (an empty conjunction), and it is called *failed* if there is an atom that does not unify with the head of any clause. Given a successful SLD derivation $A \rightsquigarrow_\theta^* true$, the associated *computed answer*, $\theta\!\restriction_{var(A)}$, is the restriction of θ to the variables of the initial query A. SLD derivations are represented by a (possibly infinite) finitely branching tree called *SLD tree*.

All the previous notions (SLD step, derivation and tree, successful derivation, computed answer, etc.) can be naturally extended to deal with probabilistic logic programs by simply ignoring the probabilities in probabilistic clauses.

Following [14], the probability of a single proof is the marginal over all programs where such a proof holds. Thus, it can be obtained from the product of the probabilities of the ground probabilistic facts used in the corresponding SLD derivation.[6] In principle, one could first apply a grounding stage—where all non-ground and intensional probabilistic facts are replaced by ground probabilistic facts—and, then, apply the above definition. Often, only a partial grounding is required (see, e.g., [11]). Since grounding is orthogonal to the topics of this paper, in the following we assume that the following property holds: for each considered successful SLD derivation $q \rightsquigarrow_\theta^* true$ that uses probabilistic clauses (i.e., probabilistic facts and rules) $p_1 :: c_1, \ldots, p_n :: c_n$, we have that $c_1\theta, \ldots, c_n\theta$ are ground, i.e., it suffices if the probabilistic clauses used in the derivation *become eventually* ground.

In practice, *range-restrictedness* is often required for ensuring that all probabilistic facts become eventually ground in an SLD derivation, where a program is range-restricted if all variables in the head of a clause also appear in some atom of the body [28]. Moreover, one can still allow some probabilistic facts with non-ground arguments (which are not range-restricted) as long as they are called with a ground term in these arguments; see [4, Theorem 1]. A similar condition is required in ProbLog, where a program containing a probabilistic fact of the form `0.6::p(X)` is only acceptable if the query bounds variable X, e.g., `p(a)`. However, if the query is also non-ground, e.g., `p(X)`, then ProbLog outputs an error: "Encountered a non-ground probabilistic clause".[7]

In the following, given a successful SLD derivation $D = (q \rightsquigarrow_\theta^* true)$, we let *prob_facts*$(D)$ be the set of ground probabilistic clauses used in D, i.e., $c\theta$ for each probabilistic clause c used in D. The probability of a proof (represented by a successful SLD derivation) can then be formalized as follows:

Definition 1 (probability of a proof). *Let $\mathcal{P}$ be a program and D a successful SLD derivation for some (atomic) query q in $\mathcal{P}$. The probability of the proof represented by D is obtained as follows: $P(D) = \Pi_{c\theta \in prob\_facts(D)}\, \pi(c)$.*

Let us illustrate this definition with an example:

---

[6] Observe that each fact should only be considered once. E.g., given a successful SLD derivation that uses the ground probabilistic fact $0.4 ::$ `person(ann)` twice, the associated probability is 0.4 rather than $0.4 \cdot 0.4 = 0.16$.

[7] The interested reader can try the online ProbLog interpreter at https://dtai.cs.kuleuven.be/problog/editor.html.

Example 3. Consider again our running example. Here, we have the following successful SLD derivation D for the query smokes(carl):[8]

$$\begin{array}{ll} \text{smokes(carl)} \rightsquigarrow & \text{influences(Y, carl), smokes(Y)} \\ \rightsquigarrow_{\{Y/\text{bob}\}} & \text{smokes(bob)} \\ \rightsquigarrow & \text{stress(bob)} \\ \rightsquigarrow & true \end{array}$$

Here, $prob\_facts(D) = \{\text{influence(bob, carl)}, \text{ stress(bob) :- person(bob)}\}$, whose probabilities are 0.3 and 0.8, respectively. Hence, $P(D) = 0.3 \cdot 0.8 = 0.24$.

One might think that the probability of a query can then be computed as the sum of the probabilities of its successful derivations. This is not generally true though, since the successful derivations may *overlap* (e.g., two successful derivations may use some common probabilistic facts). Nevertheless, several techniques use the SLD tree as a first stage to compute the success probability (see, e.g., [11,14]).

Computing the most likely proof of a query attracted considerable interest in the PLP field (where it is also called *Viterbi proof* [14]). Here, one aims at finding the most probable partial world that entails the query (which can be obtained from the proof with the highest probability). Note that, although it may seem counterintuitive, the MPE cannot always be obtained by extending the most likely proof of a query, as the following example illustrates:

Example 4. Consider the following program from [31, Example 6]:

```
0.4::red.    0.9::green.    win :- red, green.
0.5::blue.   0.6::yellow.   win :- blue, yellow.
```

Here, win has two proofs: one uses the probabilistic facts red and green, with probability $0.4 \cdot 0.9 = 0.36$, and another one uses the probabilistic facts blue and yellow, with probability $0.5 \cdot 0.6 = 0.30$. Hence, the most likely proof is the first one, represented by the partial world {red, green}. However, the MPE is the world {green, blue, yellow}, with probability $(1 - 0.4) \cdot 0.9 \cdot 0.5 \cdot 0.6 = 0.162$, which does not extend the partial world {red, green}. This counterintuitive result can be seen as a drawback of representing explanations as worlds.

Considering proofs or SLD trees as explanations has obvious advantages: they allows one to follow the chain of inferences from the query back to the considered probabilistic facts and, moreover, can be considered minimal. However, their main weaknesses are their complexity and size, which might be a problem for non-experts.

3.2   Explanations as Programs

In this section, we propose to represent explanations as programs. In principle, we consider that rules and facts are easier to understand than proof trees for

---

[8] We only show the relevant bindings of the computed mgu's in the examples.

non-experts (and could more easily be translated into natural language).[9] Each program thus represents a minimal and more understandable explanation of a proof. Moreover, the generation of explanations is now parametric w.r.t. a set of *visible* predicates, thus hiding unnecessary information. We will then prove that the probability of a query in an explanation is equivalent to that of the associated proof in the original program, and that the marginal probability of a query is preserved when considering the union of all generated explanations.

The explanations of a query are essentially obtained using *unfolding*, a well-known transformation in the area of logic programming [21]. Let $h \leftarrow B, a, B'$ be a clause and $h_1 \leftarrow B_1, \ldots, h_n \leftarrow B_n$ be *all* the (renamed apart) clauses whose head unifies with a. Then, unfolding replaces

$$h \leftarrow B, a, B'$$

with the clauses

$$(h \leftarrow B, B_1, B')\theta_1, \ \ldots, \ (h \leftarrow B, B_n, B')\theta_n$$

where $\mathsf{mgu}(a, h_i) = \theta_i$, $i = 1, \ldots, n$. In the following, we assume that derived predicates are split into *visible* and *hidden* predicates. In practice, both predicates will be unfolded, but we introduce a special treatment for visible atoms so that their calls are kept in the unfolded clause, and a separate definition is added. Intuitively speaking, visible predicates represent information that the user considers relevant, while hidden predicates represent intermediate or less relevant relations that the user prefers not to see in an explanation.

Given an atom a, we let $visible(a)$ be true if a is rooted by a visible predicate and false otherwise. The list of visible predicates should be given by the user, though a default specification can be considered (e.g., our tool xgen assumes that all predicates are hidden unless otherwise specified).

The generation of explanations is modeled by a number of transition rules. Given a query q, the initial explanation has the form $\{\mathsf{query}(q) \leftarrow q\}$, where we assume that query is a fresh predicate that does not appear in the considered probabilistic program. Then, we aim at unfolding this clause as much as possible. However, there are some relevant differences with the standard unfolding transformation (as in, e.g., [21]):

- First, we do not unfold the clauses of the original program but consider a new program (i.e., the initial explanation). This is sensible in our context since we are only interested in those clauses of the original program that are necessary for proving the query q.
- Second, we keep every nondeterministic unfolding separated in different explanations. This is due to the fact that our explanations represent a *single* proof rather than a complete proof tree.
- Finally, as mentioned above, we distinguish *visible* and *hidden* predicates. While unfolding a hidden predicate follows a standard unfolding, the case of visible predicates is slightly different (see Example 5 below).

---

[9] The use of rule-based models to explain the predictions of AI systems is not new in the field of XAI (see, e.g., [3]).

During unfolding, we might find four different cases depending on whether the considered clause is probabilistic or not, and whether the considered atom is a derived or a probabilistic atom. In the following, we consider each case separately.

Unfolding of Derived Atoms in Derived Clauses. This is the simplest case. Here, unfolding can be performed using the following transition rules, depending on whether the atom is visible or not:

$$\frac{\neg visible(a) \wedge h' \leftarrow B \ll \mathcal{P} \wedge \mathsf{mgu}(a, h') = \theta}{E \cup \{h \leftarrow B_1, a, B_2\} \rightarrowtail (E \cup \{h \leftarrow B_1, B, B_2\})\theta} \quad (\text{unf1})$$

$$\frac{visible(a) \wedge h' \leftarrow B \ll \mathcal{P} \wedge \mathsf{mgu}(a, h') = \theta \wedge \rho(a\theta) = a'}{E \cup \{h \leftarrow B_1, a, B_2\} \rightarrowtail E\theta \cup \{a' \leftarrow B\theta, h\theta \leftarrow B_1\theta, \underline{a'}, B_2\theta\}} \quad (\text{unf2})$$

where atoms marked with an underscore (e.g., atom $\underline{a'}$ in rule unf2 above) cannot be selected for unfolding anymore, and ρ is a simple renaming function that takes an atom and returns a new atom with a fresh predicate name and the same arguments (e.g., by adding a suffix to the original predicate name in order to keep its original meaning). For instance, $\rho(\mathsf{smokes(carl)}) = \mathsf{smokes}_1(\mathsf{carl})$. While rule (unf1) denotes a standard unfolding rule (unf2) is a bit more involved. The fact that an atom is visible does not mean that the atom should not be unfolded. It only means that the call should be kept in the unfolded clause in order to preserve the visible components of the inference chain. Indeed, observe that the computed mgu is applied to *all* clauses in the current explanation. This is sensible since all clauses in an explanation actually represent one single proof (i.e., a successful SLD derivation).

Example 5. Consider the following logic program:

```
p(X) :- r(X,Y).        r(X,Y) :- s(Y).        s(b).
```

and the query p(a). A successful SLD derivation for this query is as follows:

$$\mathsf{p(a)} \rightsquigarrow \mathsf{r(a, Y)} \rightsquigarrow \mathsf{s(Y)} \rightsquigarrow_{\{Y \mapsto b\}} \mathtt{true}$$

Given the initial explanation $E_0 = \{\mathsf{query(p(a))} \mathrel{:-} \mathsf{p(a)}\}$, and assuming that no predicate is visible, the (repeated) unfolding of E_0 using rule (unf1) would eventually produce the explanation $E' = \{\mathsf{query(p(a))}\}$, which can be read as "the query q(a) is true". In contrast, if we consider that r/2 is visible, we get the following unfolding sequence:

$E_0 = \{\mathsf{query(p(a))} \mathrel{:-} \mathsf{p(a)}\}$
$E_1 = \{\mathsf{query(p(a))} \mathrel{:-} \mathsf{r(a, Y)}\}$ //*using rule* $\mathsf{p(X)} \mathrel{:-} \mathsf{r(X, Y)}$
$E_2 = \{\mathsf{r}_1(\mathsf{a, Y}) \mathrel{:-} \mathsf{s(Y)}, \mathsf{query(p(a))} \mathrel{:-} \underline{\mathsf{r}_1(\mathsf{a, Y})}\}$ //*using rule* $\mathsf{r(X, Y)} \mathrel{:-} \mathsf{s(Y)}$
$E_3 = \{\mathsf{r}_1(\mathsf{a, b}), \mathsf{query(p(a))} \mathrel{:-} \underline{\mathsf{r}_1(\mathsf{a, b})}\}$ //*using fact* $\mathsf{s(b)}$

The generated explanation (E_3) is a bit more informative than E' above: "the query p(a) is true because r(a, b) is true", where r/2 is renamed as $\mathsf{r}_1/2$ in E_3.

In the example above, renaming r/2 is not really needed. However, in general, the renaming of visible atoms is necessary to avoid confusion when unfolding nondeterministic predicates, since we want each explanation to represent one, *and only one*, proof. Consider, e.g., the following program:

```
p :- q,q.     q :- a.     q :- b.     a.     b.
```

ant the query q. Assume that predicate q/0 is visible and that the first call to q is unfolded using clause q :- a and the second one using clause q :- b. Without predicate renaming, we will produce an explanation including a clause of the form query(p) :- q, q, together with the two clauses defining q. Unfortunately, this explanation does not represent a single proof (as intended) since every call to q could be unfolded with either clause. Renaming is then needed to ensure that only one unfolding is possible: query(p) :- q_1, q_2, together with the clauses q_1 :- a and q_2 :- b.

Unfolding of Derived Atoms in Probabilistic Clauses. As mentioned before, probabilistic rules are used to provide an intensional representation of a set of ground probabilistic facts. One could think that the unfolding a derived atom in such a clause will always preserve the probability of a query. However, some caution is required:

Example 6. Consider the following program:

```
q(a,a).     q(a,b).     0.8::p(X) :- q(X,Y).
```

By unfolding clause 0.8::p(X) :- q(X,Y), we would get the following program:

```
q(a,a).     q(a,b).     0.8::p(a).     0.8::p(a).
```

Here, $P(p(a)) = 0.8$ in the first program but $P(p(a)) = 0.8 \cdot 0.2 + 0.2 \cdot 0.8 + 0.8 \cdot 0.8 = 0.96$ in the second one.

The problem with the above example is related to the interpretation of intensional facts. Observe that *prob_facts* in Definition 1 returns a *set*. This is essential to compute the right probability and to avoid duplicates when there are several successful derivations computing the same ground answer.

Therefore, if we want to preserve the probability of a query, we can only unfold derived atoms when they do not have several proofs computing the same ground answer. Since we are assuming that derivations are finite, this property could be dynamically checked. In the following, for simplicity, we assume instead that programs cannot contain several occurrences of the same (ground) probabilistic fact.[10] The new unfolding rule is thus as follows:

$$\frac{h' \leftarrow B \ll \mathcal{P} \wedge \mathsf{mgu}(a, h') = \theta}{E \cup \{p :: h \leftarrow B_1, a, B_2\} \rightarrowtail (E \cup \{p :: h \leftarrow B_1, B, B_2\})\theta} \quad \text{(unf3)}$$

---

[10] Nevertheless, our tool xgen considers more general programs by requiring the specification of those predicates that may violate the above condition (see Sect. 4).

Unfolding of a Probabilistic Atom in a Derived Clause. In this case, one might be tempted to define the unfolding of clause $h \leftarrow B_1, a, B_2$ using clause $p :: h' \leftarrow B$ and $\mathsf{mgu}(a, h) = \theta$ as the clause $p :: (h \leftarrow B_1, B, B_2)\theta$. However, such a transformation would generally change the success probability of a query, as illustrated in the following example:

Example 7. Consider the following program

$$p \text{ :- } a,b. \qquad p \text{ :- } b,c. \qquad 0.6::a. \qquad 0.7::b. \qquad 0.8::c.$$

where p holds either because a and b are true or because b and c are true. By unfolding b in the first clause of p using the strategy above, we would get

$$0.7::p \text{ :- } a. \qquad p \text{ :- } b,c. \qquad 0.6::a. \qquad 0.7::b. \qquad 0.8::c.$$

However, $P(\mathsf{p}) = P(\mathsf{a}, \mathsf{b}) + P(\mathsf{b}, \mathsf{c}) - P(\mathsf{a}, \mathsf{b}, \mathsf{c}) = 0.6 \cdot 0.7 + 0.7 \cdot 0.8 - 0.6 \cdot 0.7 \cdot 0.8 = 0.644$ in the original program but $P(\mathsf{p}) = 0.7448$ in the unfolded one. Intuitively speaking, the issue is that, by embedding the probability of b into the unfolded clause of p, the worlds associated with the two proofs of p no longer overlap. To be precise, the clause $0.7\text{: } \text{:p} \text{ :- } a.$ is equivalent to $\mathsf{p} \text{ :- } \mathsf{a}, \mathsf{pp}$ with $0.7\text{: } \text{:pp}$. Thus, we now have $P(\mathsf{p}) = P(\mathsf{a}, \mathsf{pp}) + P(\mathsf{b}, \mathsf{c}) - P(\mathsf{a}, \mathsf{pp}, \mathsf{b}, \mathsf{c}) = 0.6 \cdot 0.7 + 0.7 \cdot 0.8 - 0.6 \cdot 0.7 \cdot 0.7 \cdot 0.8 = 0.7448$.

Therefore, in the following, probabilistic atoms are always (implicitly) considered as *visible* atoms:

$$\frac{p :: h' \leftarrow B \ll \mathcal{P} \wedge \mathsf{mgu}(a, h') = \theta}{E \cup \{h \leftarrow B_1, a, B_2\} \rightarrowtail (E \cup \{p :: h' \leftarrow B, h \leftarrow B_1, \underline{a}, B_2\})\theta} \qquad \text{(unf4)}$$

Note that the probabilistic atom is not renamed, in contrast to the renaming of visible atoms in rule (unf2) above. Renaming would be required only if a program could have several probabilistic atoms with different probabilities, thus introducing some undesired nondeterminism (but we ruled out this possibility, as mentioned before).

Unfolding of a Probabilistic Atom in a Probabilistic Rule. Although this situation cannot happen in the original program (we required intensional facts to have only derived atoms in their bodies), such a situation may show up after a number of unfolding steps. This case is similar to unfolding a probabilistic atom in a derived clause:

$$\frac{p' :: h' \leftarrow B \ll \mathcal{P} \wedge \mathsf{mgu}(a, h') = \theta}{E \cup \{p :: h \leftarrow B_1, a, B_2\} \rightarrowtail (E \cup \{p' :: h' \leftarrow B, p :: h \leftarrow B_1, \underline{a}, B_2\})\theta} \qquad \text{(unf5)}$$

In the following, given some initial explanation E_0, we refer to a sequence $E_0 \rightarrowtail E_1 \rightarrowtail \ldots \rightarrowtail E_n$, $n \geq 0$, as an *unfolding sequence*. If further unfolding steps are possible, we say that E_n is a *partial explanation*. Otherwise, if $E_n \not\rightarrowtail$, we have two possibilities:

- If the clauses in E_n contain no selectable atom (i.e., all atoms in the bodies of the clauses are either *true* or have the form $\underline{a}$), then E_n is called a *successful explanation* and we refer to $E_0 \rightarrowtail \ldots \rightarrowtail E_n$ as a *successful unfolding sequence*. The *probability of a successful explanation*, $P(E_n)$, can be simply obtained as the product of the probabilities of the probabilistic clauses in this explanation.
- If the clauses in E_n contain some selectable atom which does not unify with the head of any program clause, then E_n is called a *failing explanation* and it is discarded from the generation process.

By construction, there exists one successful unfolding sequence associated with each successful SLD derivation of a query.

Example 8. Consider again the program in Example 1, where we now add one additional ground probabilistic fact: 0.1: :influences(ann,bob). Moreover, assume that predicate smokes/1 is visible. Then, we have the following successful explanation sequence:

$E_0 = \{$ query(smokes(carl)) :- smokes(carl) $\}$
$E_1 = \{$ query(smokes(carl)) :- $\underline{\text{influences(bob, carl)}}$, smokes(bob) $\}$
$E_2 = \{$ query(smokes(carl)) :- $\underline{\text{influences(bob, carl)}}$, smokes(bob),
              0.3 :: influences(bob, carl) $\}$
$E_3 = \{$ query(smokes(carl)) :- $\underline{\text{influences(bob, carl)}}$, smokes_1(bob),
              0.3 :: influences(bob, carl), smokes_1(bob) :- stress(bob) $\}$
$E_4 = \{$ query(smokes(carl)) :- $\underline{\text{influences(bob, carl)}}$, smokes_1(bob),
              0.3 :: influences(bob, carl), smokes_1(bob) :- $\underline{\text{stress(bob)}}$,
              0.8 :: stress(bob) $\}$

Therefore, E_4 is a successful explanation for the query with probability $P(E_4) = 0.24$, and can be read as "carl smokes because bob influences carl (with probability 0.3) and bob smokes, and bob smokes because he is stressed (with probability 0.8)". There exists another (less likely) explanation E' as follows:

$E' = \{$ smokes(carl) :- $\underline{\text{influences(bob, carl)}}$, smokes_1(bob),
           smokes_1(bob) :- $\underline{\text{influences(ann, bob)}}$, $\underline{\text{smokes}_2\text{(ann)}}$,
           smokes_2(ann) :- $\underline{\text{stress(ann)}}$,   0.1 :: influences(ann, bob),
           0.3 :: influences(bob, carl),   0.8 :: stress(ann) $\}$

with probability $P(E') = 0.024$. Note that the probability of the query in $E_4 \cup E'$ is the same as in the original program: 0.2448 (and different from $P(E_4)+P(E')$).

Correctness. Our main result states the soundness and completeness of successful explanations:[11]

---

[11] Proofs of technical results can be found in [35].

Theorem 1. *Let $\mathcal{P}$ be a program and q a query. Then, q has a successful SLD derivation in $\mathcal{P}$ with (ground) computed answer θ iff there exists a successful explanation E such that* query(q) *has one, and only one, successful SLD derivation in E computing the same answer θ and using the same probabilistic clauses.*

As a consequence, we have the following property that states that the probability of a successful derivation can be obtained from the product of the probabilistic clauses in the associated explanation:

Corollary 1. *Let $\mathcal{P}$ be a program and q a query. Then, there is a successful derivation D for q in $\mathcal{P}$ iff there is a successful explanation E with $P(D) = P(E)$. Moreover, $P(E) = P(\text{query}(q))$ in E.*

The above result is an easy consequence of Theorem 1 and the fact that E contains all, and only, the probabilistic facts required for the considered derivation. Note that the success probability of a query and that of a proof trivially coincide in successful explanations since only one proof per explanation exists.

Finally, we consider the preservation of the success probability of a query in the union of generated explanations:

Theorem 2. *Let $\mathcal{P}$ be a program and q a query. Let $E_1, \ldots, E_n$ be all an only the successful explanations for q in $\mathcal{P}$. Then, $P(q)$ in $\mathcal{P}$ is equal to $P(\text{query}(q))$ in $E_1 \cup \ldots \cup E_n$, $n \geq 0$.*

4   The Explanation Generator **xgen**

In order to put into practice the ideas introduced so far, we have developed a proof-of-concept implementation of the explanation generator, called xgen. The tool has been implemented in SWI Prolog and includes four modules and approximately one thousand lines of code. The main module implementing the transition rules of the previous section has some 300 lines of Prolog code. This module also implements an unfolding *strategy* that ensures termination in many cases (see the discussion below). The remaining modules implement some utility predicates as well as the parser of ProbLog files with visibility annotations. The tool can be downloaded from https://github.com/mistupv/xgen.

The tool accepts ProbLog programs containing probabilistic facts defined by (not necessarily ground) facts and rules (i.e., intensional facts). The user can also (optionally) specify which predicates are *visible* (if any) by means of annotations. Furthermore, xgen accepts duplicated probabilistic facts as long as the corresponding predicates are declared *unsafe* using an annotation. Unsafe atoms are dealt with similarly to visible atoms when they occur in probabilistic clauses, but can be unfolded freely when they appear in a derived clause (this is why a new annotation is required). An example specifying an unsafe predicate can be found in the above URL.

As in ProbLog, a query q is added to the program as a fact of the form query(q). Let us consider, for instance, the program from Example 8, where we

```
$ swipl                                     smokes0(ann) :- stress(ann).
Welcome to SWI-Prolog (version 8.2.4)       query(smokes(carl)).
[...]                                       % Success probability: 0.024
?- [xgen].
true.                                       % No more explanations...
?- xgen('examples/smokes_paper.pl').
% Explanation #1:                           % Combined explanations:
0.3::infl(bob,carl).                        0.1::infl(ann,bob).
0.8::stress(bob).                           0.3::infl(bob,carl).
smokes(bob) :- stress(bob).                 0.8::stress(ann).
smokes(carl) :- infl(bob,carl),smokes(bob). 0.8::stress(bob).
query(smokes(carl)).                        smokes(bob) :- stress(bob).
% Success probability: 0.24                 smokes(bob) :- infl(ann,bob),smokes0(ann).
                                            smokes(carl) :- infl(bob,carl),smokes(bob).
% Explanation #2:                           smokes0(ann) :- stress(ann).
0.1::infl(ann,bob).                         query(smokes(carl)).
0.3::infl(bob,carl).                        % Success probability: 0.2448
0.8::stress(ann).
smokes(bob) :- infl(ann,bob),smokes0(ann).  Output files can be found in folder
smokes(carl) :- infl(bob,carl),smokes(bob). "explanations".
```

Fig. 2. A typical session with xgen

now add the query as the fact query(smokes(carl)). If the program is stored in
file smokes_paper.pl, a typical session proceeds as shown in Fig. 2, where the
predicate influences/2 is abbreviated to infl/2.

In order to deal with cyclic definitions, we have implemented the following
unfolding strategy in xgen: we select the leftmost atom in the body of a clause
that is not underlined nor a *variant* of any of its (instantiated) *ancestors*.[12] For
instance, our tool can deal with programs containing cyclic definitions like

```
path(X,Y) :- edge(X,Y).
path(X,Y) :- path(Z,Y), edge(X,Z).
```

(together with a set of probabilistic facts defining edge/2). Similar strategies
have been used, e.g., in partial deduction [5]. Although this strategy is clearly
sound—an infinite derivation must necessarily select the same atom once and
again, since the Herbrand universe is finite—completeness does not generally
hold (a counterexample can be found in [6]). As a consequence, our unfolding
strategy could prune some derivations despite the fact that they can eventually
give rise to a successful SLD derivation. Nevertheless, completeness can still be
guaranteed for certain classes of programs, like the *restricted* programs of [6]
that, intuitively speaking, only allow one recursive call in the bodies of recursive
predicates (as in the definition of predicate path/2 above), so that no infinitely
growing queries can be obtained. The class of restricted programs is similar to
that of *B-stratifiable* logic programs [12] and its generalization, *strongly regular*
logic programs [34], both used in the context of partial deduction [16]. As an
alternative to using a terminating unfolding strategy as we do in xgen, one could

---

[12] Let $B_1, a, B_2 \leadsto_\theta (B_1, B, B_2)\theta$ an SLD resolution step using clause $h \leftarrow B$ and
$mgu(a, h) = \theta$. Then, a is the direct ancestor of the atoms in B. The notion of
ancestor is the transitive closure of this relation.

also consider an implementation of *tabled* SLD resolution (as in [11]) or an iterative deepening strategy (as in [17]). Nevertheless, termination is not decidable for general logic programs no matter the considered strategy.

5 Related Work

An obvious related work is the definition of fold/unfold transformations for logic programs (see [21] and references herein). Indeed, rules (unf1) and (unf3) can be seen as standard unfolding transformations (except for the differences already mentioned in Sect. 3.2). In general, given a program $\mathcal{P}$ and an initial explanation $E_0 = \{\text{query}(q) \leftarrow q\}$, a standard unfolding transformation on $\mathcal{P} \cup E_0$ would return $\mathcal{P} \cup E_1 \cup \ldots \cup E_n$, where $E_0 \rightarrowtail E_1, \ldots, E_0 \rightarrowtail E_n$ are all the possible unfolding steps using rules (unf1) and (unf3). Rules for visible or probabilistic atoms, i.e., rules (unf2), (unf4) and (unf5), resemble a combination of definition introduction and folding, followed by unfolding. Nevertheless, a distinctive feature of our approach is that the computed bindings are shared by all the clauses in the explanation. Indeed, applying the computed mgu's to *all* clauses in the current explanation is sensible in our context since all clauses together represent a *single* proof.

To the best of our knowledge, the only previous approach to defining an unfolding transformation in the context of a probabilistic logic formalism is that in [20]. However, this work considers *stochastic logic programs* (SLPs) [19], a generalization of stochastic grammars and hidden Markov models. SLPs do not follow the distribution semantics (as PLP does). Actually, the unfolding transformation in [20] is the standard one for logic programs [21]. Here, the probability is always preserved by the unfolding transformation because of the way the probability of SLPs is computed (i.e., the probability of a query is obtained directly from the successful SLD derivations of the query).

In the context of PLP with a distribution semantics, we are not aware of any previous work focused on unfolding transformations or on the generation of explanations other than computing the MPE [31] or Viturbi proof [14]. Actually, we find more similarities between our approach and the technique called *knowledge-based model construction* [13] used to compute the grounding of the program clauses which are relevant for a given query (see also [11]). However, both the aim and the technique are different from ours.

Finally, let us mention some recent advances to improve the quality of explanations in a closely related field: *Answer Set Programming* (ASP) [7]. First, [8] presents a tool, xclingo, for generating explanations from annotated ASP programs. Annotations are then used to construct derivation trees containing textual explanations. Moreover, the language allows the user to select *which* atoms or rules should be included in the explanations. And, second, [2] presents so-called *justifications* for ASP programs with constraints, now based on a goal-directed semantics. As in the previous work, the user can decide the level of detail required in a justification tree, as well as add annotations to produce justifications using natural language. Obviously, our work shares the aim of these papers regarding the generation of minimal and understandable explanations. However, the considered language and the applied techniques are different. Nevertheless, we find it very interesting to extend our work with some of the ideas in [2,8], e.g., the use of annotations to produce explanations using natural language.

6 Concluding Remarks and Future Work

In this paper, we have presented a novel approach to generate explanations in the context of PLP languages like ProbLog [25]. In particular, and in contrast to previous approaches, we have proposed explanations to be represented as programs, one for each proof of a given query. In this way, the user can analyze each (minimal) proof separately, understand *why* the considered prediction (query) is true following the chain of inferences (an intuitive process) and using a familiar control structure, that of conditional rules. We have formally proved that explanations preserve the probability of the original proofs, and that the success probability of a query can also be computed from the union of the generated explanations. A proof-of-concept tool for generating explanations, xgen, has been implemented, demonstrating the viability of the approach.

We consider several avenues for future work. On the one hand, we plan to extend the features of the considered language in order to include negation,[13] disjunctive probabilistic clauses, evidences, some Prolog built-in's, etc. This will surely improve the applicability of our approach and will allow us to carry on an experimental evaluation of the technique. In particular, we plan to study both the scalability of the approach as well as the usefulness of the generated explanations w.r.t. some selected case studies.

Another interesting research line consists in allowing the addition of annotations in program clauses so that natural language explanations can be generated (as in [2,8]). Finally, we would also like to explore the use of our unfolding transformation as a pre-processing stage for computing the probability of a query. In particular, when no predicate is declared as visible, our transformation produces a number of explanations of the form $\{p_1 :: a_1, \ldots, p_n :: a_n, \mathsf{query}(q) \leftarrow a_1, \ldots, a_n\}$, where $p_1 :: a_1, \ldots, p_n :: a_n$ are ground probabilistic facts. Apparently, computing the probability of a query from the union of the generated explanations seems much simpler than computing it for an arbitrary program.

Acknowledgements. I would like to thank the anonymous reviewers for their suggestions to improve this paper.

References

1. Apt, K.R.: From Logic Programming to Prolog. Prentice Hall, Hoboken (1997)
2. Arias, J., Carro, M., Chen, Z., Gupta, G.: Justifications for goal-directed constraint answer set programming. In: Ricca, F., et al. (eds.) Proceedings of the 36th International Conference on Logic Programming (ICLP Technical Communications 2020). EPTCS, vol. 325, pp. 59–72 (2020). https://doi.org/10.4204/EPTCS.325.12

---

[13] Considering negated *ground* probabilistic facts is straightforward, but dealing with negated derived atoms is much more challenging.

3. Arrieta, A.B., et al.: Explainable artificial intelligence (XAI): concepts, taxonomies, opportunities and challenges toward responsible AI. Inf. Fusion **58**, 82–115 (2020). https://doi.org/10.1016/j.inffus.2019.12.012

4. Azzolini, D., Riguzzi, F.: Syntactic requirements for well-defined hybrid probabilistic logic programs. In: Formisano, A., et al. (eds.) Proceedings of the 37th International Conference on Logic Programming (Technical Communications) (ICLP Technical Communications 2021). EPTCS, vol. 345, pp. 14–26 (2021). https://doi.org/10.4204/EPTCS.345.12

5. Bol, R.N.: Loop checking in partial deduction. J. Log. Program. **16**(1), 25–46 (1993). https://doi.org/10.1016/0743-1066(93)90022-9

6. Bol, R.N., Apt, K.R., Klop, J.W.: An analysis of loop checking mechanisms for logic programs. Theor. Comput. Sci. **86**(1), 35–79 (1991)

7. Brewka, G., Eiter, T., Truszczynski, M.: Answer set programming at a glance. Commun. ACM **54**(12), 92–103 (2011). https://doi.org/10.1145/2043174.2043195

8. Cabalar, P., Fandinno, J., Muñiz, B.: A system for explainable answer set programming. In: Ricca, F., et al. (eds.) Proceedings of the 36th International Conference on Logic Programming (ICLP Technical Communications 2020). EPTCS, vol. 325, pp. 124–136 (2020). https://doi.org/10.4204/EPTCS.325.19

9. Choudhury, A., Gupta, D.: A survey on medical diagnosis of diabetes using machine learning techniques. In: Kalita, J., Balas, V.E., Borah, S., Pradhan, R. (eds.) Recent Developments in Machine Learning and Data Analytics. AISC, vol. 740, pp. 67–78. Springer, Singapore (2019). https://doi.org/10.1007/978-981-13-1280-9_6

10. EU, EEA: Regulation (EU) 2016/679 on the protection of natural persons with regard to the processing of personal data and on the free movement of such data. https://eur-lex.europa.eu/eli/reg/2016/679/oj

11. Fierens, D., et al.: Inference and learning in probabilistic logic programs using weighted boolean formulas. Theory Pract. Log. Program. **15**(3), 358–401 (2015). https://doi.org/10.1017/S1471068414000076

12. Hruza, J., Stepánek, P.: Speedup of logic programs by binarization and partial deduction. Theory Pract. Log. Program. **4**(3), 355–380 (2004). https://doi.org/10.1017/S147106840300190X

13. Kersting, K., Raedt, L.D.: Bayesian logic programs. CoRR cs.AI/0111058 (2001). https://arxiv.org/abs/cs/0111058

14. Kimmig, A., Demoen, B., Raedt, L.D., Costa, V.S., Rocha, R.: On the implementation of the probabilistic logic programming language ProbLog. Theory Pract. Log. Program. **11**(2–3), 235–262 (2011). https://doi.org/10.1017/S1471068410000566

15. Lloyd, J.W.: Foundations of Logic Programming, 2nd edn. Springer, Heidelberg (1987). https://doi.org/10.1007/978-3-642-83189-8

16. Lloyd, J.W., Shepherdson, J.C.: Partial evaluation in logic programming. J. Log. Program. **11**(3&4), 217–242 (1991). https://doi.org/10.1016/0743-1066(91)90027-M

17. Mantadelis, T., Rocha, R.: Using iterative deepening for probabilistic logic inference. In: Lierler, Y., Taha, W. (eds.) PADL 2017. LNCS, vol. 10137, pp. 198–213. Springer, Cham (2017). https://doi.org/10.1007/978-3-319-51676-9_14

18. Molnar, C., Casalicchio, G., Bischl, B.: Interpretable machine learning – a brief history, state-of-the-art and challenges. In: Koprinska, I., et al. (eds.) ECML PKDD 2020. CCIS, vol. 1323, pp. 417–431. Springer, Cham (2020). https://doi.org/10.1007/978-3-030-65965-3_28

19. Muggleton, S.: Stochastic logic programs. In: de Raedt, L. (ed.) Advances in Inductive Logic Programming, pp. 254–264. IOS Press (1996)

20. Muggleton, S.: Semantics and derivation for stochastic logic programs. In: Proceedings of the UAI-2000 Workshop on Fusion of Domain Knowledge with Data for Decision Support (2000)

21. Pettorossi, A., Proietti, M.: Transformation of logic programs: foundations and techniques. J. Log. Program. **19**(20), 261–320 (1994). https://doi.org/10.1016/0743-1066(94)90028-0

22. Poole, D.: Probabilistic horn abduction and Bayesian networks. Artif. Intell. **64**(1), 81–129 (1993). https://doi.org/10.1016/0004-3702(93)90061-F

23. Poole, D.: The independent choice logic for modelling multiple agents under uncertainty. Artif. Intell. **94**(1–2), 7–56 (1997). https://doi.org/10.1016/S0004-3702(97)00027-1

24. De Raedt, L., Kimmig, A.: Probabilistic (logic) programming concepts. Mach. Learn. **100**(1), 5–47 (2015). https://doi.org/10.1007/s10994-015-5494-z

25. Raedt, L.D., Kimmig, A., Toivonen, H.: ProbLog: a probabilistic Prolog and its application in link discovery. In: Veloso, M.M. (ed.) Proceedings of the 20th International Joint Conference on Artificial Intelligence (IJCAI 2007), pp. 2462–2467 (2007). http://ijcai.org/Proceedings/07/Papers/396.pdf

26. Ricci, F., Rokach, L., Shapira, B. (eds.): Recommender Systems Handbook. Springer, Boston (2015). https://doi.org/10.1007/978-1-4899-7637-6

27. Riguzzi, F.: Foundations of Probabilistic Logic Programming: Languages, Semantics, Inference and Learning. River Publishers (2018)

28. Riguzzi, F., Swift, T.: Well-definedness and efficient inference for probabilistic logic programming under the distribution semantics. Theory Pract. Log. Program. **13**(2), 279–302 (2013)

29. Sato, T.: A statistical learning method for logic programs with distribution semantics. In: Sterling, L. (ed.) Logic Programming, Proceedings of the Twelfth International Conference on Logic Programming, Tokyo, Japan, 13–16 June 1995, pp. 715–729. MIT Press (1995)

30. Sato, T., Kameya, Y.: PRISM: a language for symbolic-statistical modeling. In: Proceedings of the Fifteenth International Joint Conference on Artificial Intelligence, IJCAI 1997, Nagoya, Japan, 23–29 August 1997, vol. 2, pp. 1330–1339. Morgan Kaufmann (1997). http://ijcai.org/Proceedings/97-2/Papers/078.pdf

31. Shterionov, D., Renkens, J., Vlasselaer, J., Kimmig, A., Meert, W., Janssens, G.: The most probable explanation for probabilistic logic programs with annotated disjunctions. In: Davis, J., Ramon, J. (eds.) ILP 2014. LNCS (LNAI), vol. 9046, pp. 139–153. Springer, Cham (2015). https://doi.org/10.1007/978-3-319-23708-4_10

32. Vennekens, J., Verbaeten, S., Bruynooghe, M.: Logic programs with annotated disjunctions. In: Demoen, B., Lifschitz, V. (eds.) ICLP 2004. LNCS, vol. 3132, pp. 431–445. Springer, Heidelberg (2004). https://doi.org/10.1007/978-3-540-27775-0_30

33. Veres, M., Moussa, M.: Deep learning for intelligent transportation systems: a survey of emerging trends. IEEE Trans. Intell. Transp. Syst. **21**(8), 3152–3168 (2020). https://doi.org/10.1109/TITS.2019.2929020

34. Vidal, G.: A hybrid approach to conjunctive partial evaluation of logic programs. In: Alpuente, M. (ed.) LOPSTR 2010. LNCS, vol. 6564, pp. 200–214. Springer, Heidelberg (2011). https://doi.org/10.1007/978-3-642-20551-4_13

35. Vidal, G.: Explanations as programs in probabilistic logic programming (2022). http://personales.upv.es/gvidal/german/flops22/tr.pdf

FOLD-R++: A Scalable Toolset for Automated Inductive Learning of Default Theories from Mixed Data

Huaduo Wang[(⊠)] and Gopal Gupta[(⊠)]

Department of Computer Science, The University of Texas at Dallas, Richardson, TX, USA
{huaduo.wang,gupta}@utdallas.edu

Abstract. FOLD-R is an automated inductive learning algorithm for learning default rules for mixed (numerical and categorical) data. It generates an (explainable) normal logic program (NLP) rule set for classification tasks. We present an improved FOLD-R algorithm, called FOLD-R++, that significantly increases the efficiency and scalability of FOLD-R by orders of magnitude. FOLD-R++ improves upon FOLD-R without compromising or losing information in the input training data during the encoding or feature selection phase. The FOLD-R++ algorithm is competitive in performance with the widely-used XGBoost algorithm, however, unlike XGBoost, the FOLD-R++ algorithm produces an explainable model. FOLD-R++ is also competitive in performance with the RIPPER system, however, on large datasets FOLD-R++ outperforms RIPPER. We also create a powerful tool-set by combining FOLD-R++ with s(CASP)—a goal-directed *answer set programming (ASP)* execution engine—to make predictions on new data samples using the normal logic program generated by FOLD-R++. The s(CASP) system also produces a justification for the prediction. Experiments presented in this paper show that our improved FOLD-R++ algorithm is a significant improvement over the original design and that the s(CASP) system can make predictions in an efficient manner as well.

Keywords: Inductive logic programming · Machine learning · Explainable AI · Negation as failure · Normal logic programs · Data mining

1 Introduction

Dramatic success of machine learning has led to a torrent of Artificial Intelligence (AI) applications. However, the effectiveness of these systems is limited by the machines' current inability to explain their decisions and actions to human users. That's mainly because the statistical machine learning methods produce models that are complex algebraic solutions to optimization problems such as risk minimization or geometric margin maximization. Lack of intuitive descriptions makes it hard for users to understand and verify the underlying rules that govern the

© Springer Nature Switzerland AG 2022
M. Hanus and A. Igarashi (Eds.): FLOPS 2022, LNCS 13215, pp. 224–242, 2022.
https://doi.org/10.1007/978-3-030-99461-7_13

model. Also, these methods cannot produce a justification for a prediction they arrive at for a new data sample. The Explainable AI program [8] aims to create a suite of machine learning techniques that: a) Produce more explainable models, while maintaining a high level of prediction accuracy; and b) Enable human users to understand, appropriately trust, and effectively manage the emerging generation of artificially intelligent systems. Inductive Logic Programming (ILP) [14] is one Machine Learning technique where the learned model is in the form of logic programming rules that are comprehensible to humans. It allows the background knowledge to be incrementally extended without requiring the entire model to be re-learned. Meanwhile, the comprehensibility of symbolic rules makes it easier for users to understand and verify induced models and even refine them.

The ILP learning problem can be regarded as a search problem for a set of clauses that deduce the training examples. The search is performed either top down or bottom-up. A bottom-up approach builds most-specific clauses from the training examples and searches the hypothesis space by using generalization. This approach is not applicable to large-scale datasets, nor it can incorporate *negation-as-failure* into the hypotheses. A survey of bottom-up ILP systems and their shortcomings can be found at [22]. In contrast, the top-down approach starts with the most general clause and then specializes it. A top-down algorithm guided by heuristics is better suited for large-scale and/or noisy datasets [28].

The FOIL algorithm [19] by Quinlan is a popular top-down inductive logic programming algorithm that generates logic programs. FOIL uses weighted information gain (IG) as the heuristics to guide the search for best literals. The FOLD algorithm by Shakerin [23,24] is a new top-down algorithm inspired by the FOIL algorithm. It generalizes the FOIL algorithm by learning *default rules with exceptions*. It does so by first learning the default predicate that covers positive examples while avoiding negative examples, then next it swaps the positive and negative examples and calls itself recursively to learn the exception to the default. Both FOIL and FOLD cannot deal with numeric features directly; an encoding process is needed in the preparation phase of the training data that discretizes the continuous numbers into intervals. However, this process not only adds a huge computational overhead to the algorithm but also leads to loss of information in the training data.

To deal with the above problems, Shakerin developed an extension of the FOLD algorithm, called FOLD-R, to handle mixed (i.e., both numerical and categorical) features which avoids the discretization process for numerical data [23,24]. However, FOLD-R still suffers from efficiency and scalability issues when compared to other popular machine learning systems for classification. In this paper we report on a novel implementation method we have developed to improve the design of the FOLD-R system. In particular, we use the prefix sum technique [27] to optimize the process of calculation of information gain, the most time consuming component of the FOLD family of algorithms [23]. Our optimization, in fact, reduces the time complexity of the algorithm. If N is the number of unique values from a specific feature and M is the number of training examples, then the complexity of computing information gain for all the possible literals of a feature is reduced from $O(M * N)$ for FOLD-R to $O(M)$ in FOLD-R++.

In addition to using prefix sum, we also improved the FOLD-R algorithm by allowing negated literals in the default portion of the learned rules (explained later). Finally, a hyper-parameter, called *exception ratio*, which controls the training process that learns exception rules, is also introduced. This hyper-parameter helps improve efficiency and classification performance. These three changes make FOLD-R++ significantly better than FOLD-R and competitive with well-known algorithms such as XGBoost and RIPPER.

Our experimental results indicate that the FOLD-R++ algorithm is comparable to popular machine learning algorithms such as XGBoost [3] and RIPPER [4] wrt various metrics (accuracy, recall, precision, and F1-score) as well as in efficiency and scalability. However, in addition, FOLD-R++ produces an explainable and interpretable model in the form of a normal logic program. A normal logic program is a logic program extended with negation-as-failure [13]. Note that RIPPER also generates a set of CNF formulas to explain the model, however, as we will see later, FOLD-R++ outperforms RIPPER on large datasets.

This paper makes the following novel contribution: it presents the FOLD-R++ algorithm that significantly improves the efficiency and scalability of the FOLD-R ILP algorithm without adding overhead during pre-processing or losing information in the training data. As mentioned, the new approach is competitive with popular classification models such as the XGBoost classifier [3] and the RIPPER system [4]. The FOLD-R++ algorithm outputs a normal logic program (NLP) [7,13] that serves as an explainable/interpretable model. This generated normal logic program is compatible with s(CASP) [2], a goal-directed ASP solver, that can efficiently justify the prediction generated by the ASP model.[1]

2 Background

2.1 Inductive Logic Programming

Inductive Logic Programming (ILP) [14] is a subfield of machine learning that learns models in the form of logic programming rules that are comprehensible to humans. This problem is formally defined as:

Given

1. A background theory B, in the form of an extended logic program, i.e., clauses of the form $h \leftarrow l_1, ..., l_m$, *not* $l_{m+1}, ...,$ *not* l_n, where $l_1, ..., l_n$ are positive literals and *not* denotes *negation-as-failure* (NAF) [7,13]. We require that B has no loops through negation, i.e., it is stratified [13].
2. Two disjoint sets of ground target predicates E^+, E^- known as *positive* and *negative* examples, respectively
3. A hypothesis language of function free predicates L, and a refinement operator ρ under θ-subsumption [18] that would disallow loops over negation.

---

[1] The s(CASP) system is freely available at https://gitlab.software.imdea.org/ciao-lang/sCASP.

Find a set of clauses H such that:

- $\forall e \in E^+$, $B \cup H \models e$
- $\forall e \in E^-$, $B \cup H \not\models e$
- $B \wedge H$ is consistent.

2.2   Default Rules

Default Logic [7,21] is a non-monotonic logic to formalize commonsense reasoning. A default D is an expression of the form

$$\frac{A : \mathbf{M}B}{\Gamma}$$

which states that the conclusion Γ can be inferred if pre-requisite A holds and B is justified. $\mathbf{M}B$ stands for "it is consistent to believe B" [7]. Normal logic programs can encode a default quite elegantly. A default of the form:

$$\frac{\alpha_1 \wedge \alpha_2 \wedge \cdots \wedge \alpha_n : \mathbf{M}\neg\beta_1, \mathbf{M}\neg\beta_2 \ldots \mathbf{M}\neg\beta_m}{\gamma}$$

can be formalized as the following normal logic program rule:

$$\gamma :\text{-} \alpha_1, \alpha_2, \ldots, \alpha_n, \text{not } \beta_1, \text{not } \beta_2, \ldots, \text{not } \beta_m.$$

where α's and β's are positive predicates and **not** represents negation-as-failure. We call such rules *default rules*. Thus, the default $\frac{bird(X):M\neg penguin(X)}{fly(X)}$ will be represented as the following default rule in normal logic programming:

    fly(X) :- bird(X), not penguin(X).

We call `bird(X)`, the condition that allows us to jump to the default conclusion that X can fly, the *default part* of the rule, and **not** `penguin(X)` the *exception part* of the rule.

Default rules closely represent the human thought process (commonsense reasoning). FOLD-R and FOLD-R++ learn default rules represented as normal logic programs. An advantage of learning default rules is that we can distinguish between exceptions and noise [23,24]. Note that the programs currently generated by the FOLD-R++ system are stratified normal logic programs [13].

3   The FOLD-R Algorithm

The FOLD algorithm [23,24] is a top-down ILP algorithm that searches for best literals to add to the body of the clauses for hypothesis, H, with the guidance of an information gain-based heuristic. The FOLD-R algorithm is a numeric extension of the FOLD algorithm that adopts the approach of the well-known C4.5 algorithm [20] for finding literals. Algorithm 1 gives an overview of the FOLD-R algorithm. The extended algorithm will directly select the best numerical literal, in addition to selecting the categorical literals. Thus, the best_numerical function (line 37 in Algorithm 1) finds the best numerical literal and adds it to

---

Algorithm 1. FOLD-R Algorithm

Input: B: background knowledge, E^+: positive example, E^-: negative example
Output: $D = \{c_1, ..., c_n\}$: a set of defaults rules with exceptions
 1: **function** FOLD(E^+, E^-)   ▷ *target, B*: global vars
 2:     $D \leftarrow \varnothing$
 3:     **while** $|E^+| > 0$ **do**
 4:         $c \leftarrow$ SPECIALIZE(*target* :- *true*, E^+, E^-)
 5:         $E^+ \leftarrow E^+ \setminus covers(c, E^+)$ ▷ rule out already covered examples
 6:         $D \leftarrow D \cup \{c\}$
 7:     **end while**
 8:     **return** D
 9: **end function**
10: **function** SPECIALIZE(c, E^+, E^-)
11:     **while** $|E^-| > 0$ **do**
12:         $c', ig \leftarrow$ ADD_BEST_LITERAL(c, E^+, E^-)
13:         **if** $ig > 0$ **then**
14:             $c \leftarrow c'$
15:         **else**
16:             $c \leftarrow$ EXCEPTION(c, E^+, E^-)
17:             **if** c is *null* **then**
18:                 $c \leftarrow enumerate(c, E^+)$ ▷ generate clause to maximally cover E^+
19:             **end if**
20:         **end if**
21:         $E^+ \leftarrow covers(c, E^+)$
22:         $E^- \leftarrow covers(c, E^-)$
23:     **end while**
24:     **return** c
25: **end function**
26: **function** EXCEPTION(c, E^+, E^-)
27:     $AB \leftarrow$ FOLD(E^-, E^+)   ▷ recursively call FOLD after swapping E^+ and E^-
28:     **if** AB is $\varnothing$ **then**
29:         $c \leftarrow null$
30:     **else**
31:         $c \leftarrow set\_exception(c, AB)$ ▷ set exception part of clause c as AB
32:     **end if**
33:     **return** c
34: **end function**
35: **function** ADD_BEST_LITERAL(c, E^+, E^-)
         ▷ return the clause with the best literal added and its corresponding info gain
36:     $c_1, ig_1 \leftarrow best\_categorical(c, E^+, E^-)$
37:     $c_2, ig_2 \leftarrow best\_numerical(c, E^+, E^-)$ ▷ FOLD-R extension
38:     **if** $c_1 > c_2$ **then**
39:         **return** c_1, ig_1
40:     **else**
41:         **return** c_2, ig_2
42:     **end if**
43: **end function**

---

the clause after classifying all the training examples for each numerical split on all the features. The other functions remain the same as the FOLD algorithm [23,24]. We illustrate the FOLD-R algorithm through an example.

Example 1. *In the FOLD-R algorithm, the target is to learn rules for* $fly(X)$. B, E^+, E^- *are background knowledge, positive and negative examples, respectively.*

```
B:   bird(X) :- penguin(X).
     bird(tweety).    bird(et).
     cat(kitty).      penguin(polly).
E+: fly(tweety).      fly(et).
E-: fly(kitty).       fly(polly).
```

The target predicate {fly(X) :- true.} is specified when calling the specialize function at line 4 in Algorithm 1. The add_best_literal function selects the literal bird(X) as a result and adds it to the clause r = fly(X) :- bird(X) because it has the best information gain among {bird,penguin,cat} at line 12. Then, the training set gets updated to E^+ = {tweety, et}, E^- = {polly} at line 21–22 in SPECIALIZE function. The negative example polly is still falsely implied by the generated clause. The default learning of SPECIALIZE function is finished because the information gain of candidate literal c' is zero. Therefore, the exception learning starts by calling FOLD function recursively with swapped positive and negative examples, E^+ = {polly}, E^- = {tweety, et} at line 27. In this case, an abnormal predicate {ab0(X) :- penguin(X)} is generated and returned as the only exception to the previous learned clause as r = fly(X) :- bird(X), not ab0(X). The abnormal rule {ab0(X) :- penguin(X)} is added to the final rule set producing the program below:

```
fly(X) :- bird(X), not ab0(X).
ab0(X) :- penguin(X).
```

4   The FOLD-R++ Algorithm

The FOLD-R++ algorithm refactors the FOLD-R algorithm. FOLD-R++ makes three main improvements to FOLD-R: (i) it can learn and add negated literals to the default (positive) part of the rule; in the FOLD-R algorithm negated literals can only be in the exception part, (ii) prefix sum algorithm is used to speed up computation, and (iii) a hyper parameter called *ratio* is introduced to control the level of nesting of exceptions. These three improvements make FOLD-R significantly more efficient.

The FOLD-R++ algorithm is summarized in Algorithm 2. The output of the FOLD-R++ algorithm is a set of default rules [7] coded as a normal logic program. An example implied by any rule in the set would be classified as positive. Therefore, the FOLD-R++ algorithm rules out the already covered positive examples at line 9 after learning a new rule. To learn a particular rule, the best literal would be repeatedly selected—and added to the default part of the rule's body—based on information gain using the remaining training examples (line 17). Next, only the examples that can be covered by learned default literals would be used for further learning (specializing) of the current rule (line 20–21). When the information gain becomes zero or the number of negative examples drops below the *ratio* threshold, the learning of the default part is done. FOLD-R++ next learns exceptions after first learning default literals. This is done by swapping the residual positive and negative examples and calling itself recursively in line 26. The remaining positive and negative examples can be swapped again and exceptions to exceptions learned (and then swapped further to learn exceptions to exceptions of exceptions, and so on). The *ratio* parameter in Algorithm 2 represents the ratio of training examples that are part of the exception to the examples implied by only the default conclusion part of the rule. It allows users to control the nesting level of exceptions.

Generally, avoiding falsely covering negative examples by adding literals to the default part of a rule will reduce the number of positive examples the rule can imply. Explicitly activating the exception learning procedure (line 26) could increase the number of positive examples a rule can cover while reducing the total number of rules generated. As a result, the interpretability is increased due to fewer rules and literals being generated. For the Adult Income Census dataset, for example, without the hyper-parameter exception *ratio* (equivalent to setting the *ratio* to 0), the FOLD-R++ algorithm would take around 10 min to finish the training and generate hundreds of rules. With the *ratio* parameter set to 0.5, only 13 rules are generated in around 10 s.

Additionally, The FOLD and FOLD-R algorithms disabled the negated literals in the default theories to make the generated rules look more elegant (only exceptions included negated literals). However, a negated literal sometimes is the optimal literal with the most useful information gain. FOLD-R++ allows for negated literals in the default part of the generated rules. We cannot make sure that FOLD-R++ generates optimal combination of literals because it is a greedy algorithm, however, it is an improvement over FOLD and FOLD-R.

4.1   Literal Selection

The literal selection process for Shakerin's FOLD-R algorithm can be summarized as function SPECIALIZE in Algorithm 1. The FOLD-R algorithm [23,24] selects the best literal based on the weighted information gain for learning defaults, similar to the original FOLD algorithm described in [24]. For numeric features, the FOLD-R algorithm would enumerate all the possible splits. Then, it classifies the data and computes information gain for literals for each split. The literal with the best information gain would be selected as a result. In contrast, the FOLD-R++ algorithm uses a new, more efficient method employing *prefix sums* to calculate the information gain based on the classification categories. The FOLD-R++ algorithm divides features into two categories: *categorical* and *numerical*. All the values in a categorical feature would be considered as categorical values even if some of them are numbers. Only equality and inequality

Algorithm 2. FOLD-R++ Algorithm

Input: E^+: positive examples, E^-: negative examples
   ▷ Global Parameters: *target*, B: background knowledge, *ratio*: exception ratio
Output: $R = \{r_1, ..., r_n\}$: a set of defaults rules with exceptions

1: **function** FOLD_RPP(E^+, E^-, L_{used})   ▷ L_{used}: used literals, initially empty
2:     $R \leftarrow \varnothing$
3:     **while** $|E^+| > 0$ **do**
4:         $r \leftarrow$ LEARN_RULE(E^+, E^-, L_{used})
5:         $E_{tp} \leftarrow covers(r, E^+)$ ▷ E_{tp}: true positive examples implied by rule r
6:         **if** $|E_{tp}| = 0$ **then**
7:             **break**
8:         **end if**
9:         $E^+ \leftarrow E^+ \setminus E_{tp}$ ▷ rule out the already covered examples
10:       $R \leftarrow R \cup \{r\}$
11:     **end while**
12:     **return** R
13: **end function**
14: **function** LEARN_RULE(E^+, E^-, L_{used})
15:     $L \leftarrow \varnothing$ ▷ L: default literals for the result rule r
16:     **while** *true* **do**
17:         $l \leftarrow$ FIND_BEST_LITERAL(E^+, E^-, L_{used})
18:         $L \leftarrow L \cup \{l\}$
19:         $r \leftarrow set\_default(r, L)$ ▷ set default part of rule r as L
20:         $E^+ \leftarrow covers(r, E^+)$
21:         $E^- \leftarrow covers(r, E^-)$
22:         **if** l is invalid or $|E^-| \leq |E^+| * ratio$ **then**
23:             **if** l is invalid **then**
24:                $r \leftarrow set\_default(r, L \setminus \{l\})$ ▷ remove the invalid literal l from rule r
25:             **else**
26:                $AB \leftarrow$ FOLD_RPP($E^-, E^+, L_{used} + L$) ▷ learn exception rules for r
27:                $r \leftarrow set\_exception(r, AB)$ ▷ set exception part of rule r as AB
28:             **end if**
29:             **break**
30:         **end if**
31:     **end while**
32:     **return** r ▷ the head of rule r is *target*
33: **end function**

---

literals would be generated for categorical features. For numerical features, the FOLD-R++ algorithm would try to read each value as a number, converting it to a categorical value if the conversion fails. Additional numerical comparison ($\leq$ and $>$) literal candidates would be generated for numerical features. A mixed type feature that contains both categorical and numerical values would be treated as a numerical feature.

In FOLD-R++, information gain for a given literal is calculated as shown in Algorithm 3. The variables tp, fn, tn, fp for finding the information gain represent the numbers of true positive, false negative, true negative, and false positive examples, respectively. With the simplified information gain function *IG* in Algorithm 3, the new approach employs the *prefix sum technique* to speed up the calculation. Only one round of classification is needed for a single feature, even with mixed types of values.

Algorithm 3. FOLD-R++ Algorithm, Information Gain function

Input: tp, fn, tn, fp: the number of E_{tp}, E_{fn}, E_{tn}, E_{fp} implied by literal
Output: information gain
1: **function** IG(tp, fn, tn, fp) ▷ IG is the function that computes information gain
2:     **if** $fp + fn > tp + tn$ **then**
3:         **return** $-\infty$
4:     **end if**
5:     **return** $\frac{1}{tp+fp+tn+fn} \cdot (F(tp, fp) + F(fp, tp) + F(tn, fn) + F(fn, tn))$
6: **end function**
7: **function** F(a, b)
8:     **if** $a = 0$ **then**
9:         **return** 0
10:    **end if**
11:    **return** $a \cdot \log_2(\frac{a}{a+b})$
12: **end function**

In the FOLD-R++ algorithm, two types of literals would be generated: *equality comparison* literals and *numerical comparison* literals. The equality (*resp.* inequality) comparison is straightforward in FOLD-R++: two values are equal if they are same type and identical, else they are unequal. However, a different assumption is made for comparisons between a numerical value and categorical value in FOLD-R++. Numerical comparisons ($\leq$ and $>$) between a numerical value and a categorical value is always false. A comparison example is shown in Table 1 (Left), while an evaluation example for a given literal, $literal(i, \leq, 3)$, based on the comparison assumption is shown in Table 1 (Right). Given $E^+ = \{1, 2, 3, 3, 5, 6, 6, 6, b\}$, $E^- = \{2, 4, 6, 7, a\}$, and $literal(i, \leq, 3)$, the true positive example E_{tp}, false negative examples E_{fn}, true negative examples E_{tn}, and false positive examples E_{fp} implied by the literal are $\{1, 2, 3, 3\}$, $\{5, 6, 6, b\}$, $\{4, 6, 7, a\}$, $\{2\}$ respectively. Then, the information gain of $literal(i, \leq, 3)$ is calculated $IG_{(i, \leq, 3)}(4, 4, 4, 1) = -0.619$ through Algorithm 3.

The new approach to find the best literal that provides most useful information is summarized in Algorithm 4. In line 12, *pos* (*neg*) is the dictionary that holds the numbers of positive (negative) examples for each unique value. In line 13, *xs* (*cs*) is the list that holds the unique numerical (categorical) values. In line 14, *xp* (*xn*) is the total number of positive (negative) examples with numerical values; *cp* (*cn*) is the total number of positive (negative) examples with categorical values. After computing the prefix sum at line 16, *pos*[x] (*neg*[x]) holds the total number of positive (negative) examples that have a value less than or equal to x. Therefore, $xp - pos[x]$ ($xn - neg[x]$) represents the total number of positive

Algorithm 4. FOLD-R++ Algorithm, Find Best Literal function

Input: E^+: positive examples, E^-: negative examples, L_{used}: used literals
Output: $best\_lit$: the best literal that provides the most information

1: **function** FIND_BEST_LITERAL(E^+, E^-, L_{used})
2:   $best\_ig, best\_lit \leftarrow -\infty, invalid$
3:   **for** $i \leftarrow 1$ to N **do**   ▷ N is the number of features
4:     $ig, lit \leftarrow$ BEST_INFO_GAIN(E^+, E^-, i, L_{used})
5:     **if** $best\_ig < ig$ **then**
6:       $best\_ig, best\_lit \leftarrow ig, lit$
7:     **end if**
8:   **end for**
9:   **return** $best\_lit$
10: **end function**
11: **function** BEST_INFO_GAIN(E^+, E^-, i, L_{used})   ▷ i: feature index
12:   $pos, neg \leftarrow count\_classification(E^+, E^-, i)$
        ▷ pos (neg): dicts that holds the numbers of E^+ (E^-) for each unique value
13:   $xs, cs \leftarrow collect\_unique\_values(E^+, E^-, i)$
        ▷ xs (cs): lists that holds the unique numerical (categorical) values
14:   $xp, xn, cp, cn \leftarrow count\_total(E+, E-, i)$
        ▷ xp (xn): the total number of E^+ (E^-) with numerical value.
        ▷ cp (cn): the total number of E^+ (E^-) with categorical value.
15:   $xs \leftarrow couting\_sort(xs)$
16:   **for** $j \leftarrow 1$ to $size(xs)$ **do** ▷ compute prefix sum for E^+ & E^- numerical values
17:     $pos[xs_i] \leftarrow pos[xs_i] + pos[xs_{i-1}]$
18:     $neg[xs_i] \leftarrow neg[xs_i] + neg[xs_{i-1}]$
19:   **end for**
20:   **for** $x \in xs$ **do**   ▷ compute info gain for numerical comparison literals
21:     $lit\_dict[literal(i, \leq, x)] \leftarrow$ IG($pos[x], xp-pos[x]+cp, xn-neg[x]+cn, neg[x]$)
22:     $lit\_dict[literal(i, >, x)] \leftarrow$ IG($xp-pos[x], pos[x]+cp, neg[x]+cn, xn-neg[x]$)
23:   **end for**
24:   **for** $c \in cs$ **do**   ▷ compute info gain for equality comparison literals
25:     $lit\_dict[literal(i, =, x)] \leftarrow$ IG($pos[c], cp-pos[c]+xp, cn-neg[c]+xn, neg[c]$)
26:     $lit\_dict[literal(i, \neq, x)] \leftarrow$ IG($cp-pos[c]+xp, pos[c], neg[c], cn-neg[c]+xn$)
27:   **end for**
28:   $best\_ig, lit \leftarrow best\_pair(lit\_dict, L_{used})$
29:   **return** $best\_ig, lit$ ▷ return the best info gain and its corresponding literal
30: **end function**

(negative) examples that have a value greater than x. In line 21, the information gain of literal $(i, \leq, x)$ is calculated by calling Algorithm 3. Note that $pos[x]$ ($neg[x]$) is the actual value for the formal parameter tp (fp) of function IG in Algorithm 3. Likewise, $xp - pos[x] + cp$ ($xn - neg[x] + cn$) substitute for formal parameter fn (tn) of the function IG. cp (cn) is included in the actual parameter for formal parameter fn (tn) of function IG because of the assumption that any numerical comparison between a numerical value and a categorical value is false. The information gain calculation processes of other literals also follow the comparison assumption mentioned above. Finally, the best_info_gain function

Table 1. Left: Comparisons between a numerical value and a categorical value. Right: Evaluation and count for literal $(i, \leq, 3)$.

comparison	evaluation
3 = 'a'	False
3 ≠ 'a'	True
3 ≤ 'a'	False
3 > 'a'	False

	i^{th} feature values	count
E^+	1 2 3 3 5 6 6 b	8
E^-	2 4 6 7 a	5
$E_{tp(i, \leq, 3)}$	1 2 3 3	4
$E_{fn(i, \leq, 3)}$	5 6 6 b	4
$E_{tn(i, \leq, 3)}$	4 6 7 a	4
$E_{fp(i, \leq, 3)}$	2	1

(Algorithm 4) returns the best score on information gain and the corresponding literal except the literals that have been used in current rule-learning process. For each feature, we compute the best literal, then the find_best_literal function returns the best literal among this set of best literals. FOLD-R algorithm selects only positive literals in default part of rules during literal selection even if a negative literal provides better information gain. Unlike FOLD-R, the FOLD-R++ algorithm can also select negated literals for the default part of a rule at line 26 in Algorithm 4.

It is easy to justify the $O(M)$ complexity of information gain calculation in FOLD-R++ mentioned earlier. The time complexity of Algorithm 3 is obviously $O(1)$. Algorithm 3 is called in line 21, 22, 25, and 26 of Algorithm 4. Line 12–15 in Algorithm 4 can be considered as the preparation process for calculating information gain and has complexity $O(M)$, assuming that we use counting sort (complexity $O(M)$) with a pre-sorted list in line 15; it is easy to see that lines 16–29 take time $O(N)$.

Example 2. *Given positive and negative examples, E^+, E^-, with mixed type of values on feature i, the target is to find the literal with the best information gain on the given feature. There are 8 positive examples, their values on feature i are $[1, 2, 3, 3, 5, 6, 6, b]$. And, the values on feature i of the 5 negative examples are $[2, 4, 6, 7, a]$.*

With the given examples and specified feature, the numbers of positive examples and negative examples for each unique value are counted first, which are shown as *pos, neg* at right side of Table 2. Then, the prefix sum arrays are calculated for computing the heuristic as psum$^+$, psum$^-$. Table 3 shows the information gain for each literal, the *literal*$(i, \neq, a)$ has been selected with the highest score.

4.2 Explainability

Explainability is very important for some tasks like loan approval, credit card approval, and disease diagnosis system. Inductive logic programming provides explicit rules for how a prediction is generated compared to black box models like those based on neural networks. To efficiently justify the prediction, the FOLD-R++ system outputs normal logic programs that are compatible with the s(CASP) goal-directed answer set programming system [2]. The s(CASP)

Table 2. Left: Examples and values on i^{th} feature. Right: positive/negative count and prefix sum on each value

i^{th} feature values	
E^+	1 2 3 3 5 6 6 b
E^-	2 4 6 7 a

value	1	2	3	4	5	6	7	a	b
pos	1	1	2	0	1	2	0	0	1
psum$^+$	1	2	4	4	5	7	7	na	na
neg	0	1	0	1	0	1	1	1	0
psum$^-$	0	1	1	2	2	3	4	na	na

Table 3. The info gain on i^{th} feature with given examples

	Info Gain								
value	1	2	3	4	5	6	7	a	b
$\leq$ value	$-\infty$	$-\infty$	-0.619	-0.661	-0.642	-0.616	-0.661	na	na
$>$ value	-0.664	-0.666	$-\infty$	$-\infty$	$-\infty$	$-\infty$	$-\infty$	na	na
$=$ value	na	na	na	na	na	na	na	$-\infty$	$-\infty$
$\neq$ value	na	na	na	na	na	na	na	**-0.588**	-0.627

system executes answer set programs in a goal-directed manner [2]. Stratified normal logic programs output by FOLD-R++ are a special case of answer set programs.

Example 3. *The "Adult Census Income" is a classical classification task that contains 32561 records. We treat 80% of the data as training examples and 20% as testing examples. The task is to learn the income status of individuals (more/less than 50K/year) based on features such as gender, age, education, marital status, etc. FOLD-R++ generates the following program that contains only 13 rules:*

```
(1)  income(X,'=<50k') :- not marital_status(X,'married-civ-spouse'), not ab4(X), not ab5(X).
(2)  income(X,'=<50k') :- education_num(X,N4), N4=<12.0, capital_gain(X,N10), N10=<5013.0,
                          not ab6(X), not ab8(X).
(3)  income(X,'=<50k') :- occupation(X,'farming-fishing'), age(X,N0), N0>62.0, N0=<63.0,
                          education_num(X,N4), N4>12.0, capital_gain(X,N10), N10>5013.0.
(4)  income(X,'=<50k') :- age(X,N0), N0>65.0, education_num(X,N4), N4>12.0,
                          capital_gain(X,N10), N10>9386.0, N10=<10566.0.
(5)  income(X,'=<50k') :- age(X,N0), N0>35.0, fnlwgt(X,N2), N2>199136.0, education_num(X,N4),
                          N4>12.0, capital_gain(X,N10), N10>5013.0, hours_per_week(X,N12),
                          N12=<20.0.
(6)  ab1(X) :- age(X,N0), N0=<20.0.
(7)  ab2(X) :- education_num(X,N4), N4=<10.0, capital_gain(X,N10), N10=<7978.0.
(8)  ab3(X) :- capital_gain(X,N10), N10>27828.0, N10=<34095.0.
(9)  ab4(X) :- capital_gain(X,N10), N10>6849.0, not ab1(X), not ab2(X), not ab3(X).
(10) ab5(X) :- age(X,N0), N0=<27.0, education_num(X,N4), N4>12.0, capital_loss(X,N11),
               N11>1974.0, N11=<2258.0.
(11) ab6(X) :- not marital_status(X,'married-civ-spouse').
(12) ab7(X) :- occupation(X,'transport-moving'), age(X,N0), N0>39.0.
(13) ab8(X) :- education_num(X,N4), N4=<8.0, capital_loss(X,N11), N11>1672.0, N11=<1977.0,
               not ab7(X).
```

The above program achieves 0.86 accuracy, 0.88 precision, 0.95 recall, and 0.91 F_1 score. Given a new data sample, the predicted answer for this data sample

using the above logic program can be efficiently produced by the s(CASP) system
[2]. Since s(CASP) is query driven, an example query such as ?- income(30,
Y) which checks the income status of the person with ID 30, will succeed if the
income is indeed predicted as less than or equal to 50K by the model represented
by the logic program above.

The s(CASP) system will also produce a justification (a proof tree) for this
prediction query. It can even generate this proof tree in English, i.e., in a more
human understandable form [1]. The justification tree generated for the person
with ID 30 is shown below:

```
?- income(30,Y).
% QUERY:I would like to know if
       'income' holds (for 30, and Y).
ANSWER: 1 (in 2.246 ms)
JUSTIFICATION_TREE:
'income' holds (for 30, and '=<50k'), because
       there is no evidence that 'marital_status' holds (for 30, and married-civ-spouse), and
       there is no evidence that 'ab4' holds (for 30), because
             there is no evidence that 'capital_gain' holds (for 30, and Var1),
             with Var1 not equal 0.0, and 'capital_gain' holds (for 30, and 0.0).
       there is no evidence that 'ab5' holds (for 30), because
             there is no evidence that 'age' holds (for 30, and Var2), with Var2 not equal 18.0,
             and 'age' holds (for 30, and 18.0), and
             there is no evidence that 'education_num' holds (for 30, and Var3),
             with Var3 not equal 7.0, and 'age' holds (for 30, and 18.0), justified above, and
             'education_num' holds (for 30, and 7.0).
The global constraints hold.
BINDINGS:
Y equal '=<50k'
```

With the justification tree, the reason for the prediction can be easily understood by human beings. The generated NLP rule-set can also be understood by
a human. If there is any unreasonable logic generated in the rule set, it can also
be modified directly by the human without retraining. Thus, any bias in the
data that is captured in the generated NLP rules can be corrected by the human
user, and the updated NLP rule-set used for making new predictions.

The RIPPER system [4] is a well-known rule-induction algorithm that generates formulas in conjunctive normal form (CNF) as an explanation of the model.
RIPPER generates 53 formulas for Example 3 and achieves 0.61 accuracy, 0.98
precision, 0.50 recall, and 0.66 F_1 score. A few of the fifty three rules generated
by RIPPER for this dataset are shown below.

```
(1)  marital_status=Never-married & education_num=7.0-9.0 & workclass=Private &
     hours_per_week=35.0-40.0 & capital_gain=<9999.9 & sex=Female
(2)  marital_status=Never-married & capital_gain=<9999.9 & education_num=7.0-9.0 &
     hours_per_week=35.0-40.0 & relationship=Own-child
(3)  marital_status=Never-married & capital_gain=<9999.9 & education_num=7.0-9.0 &
     hours_per_week=35.0-40.0 & race=White & age=22.0-26.0
(4)  marital_status=Never-married & capital_gain=<9999.9 & education_num=7.0-9.0 &
     hours_per_week=24.0-35.0
     ... ...
(50) education_num=7.0-9.0 & age=26.0-30.0 & fnlwgt=177927.0-196123.0 & workclass=Private
(51) relationship=Not-in-family & capital_gain=<9999.9 & hours_per_week=35.0-40.0 &
     sex=Female & education=Assoc-voc
(52) education_num=<7.0 & workclass=Private & fnlwgt=260549.8-329055.0
(53) relationship=Not-in-family & capital_gain=<9999.9 & hours_per_week=35.0-40.0 &
     education_num=11.0-13.0 & occupation=Adm-clerical
```

Generally, a set of default rules is a more succinct description of a given concept compared to a set of CNFs, especially when nested (multiple) exceptions are allowed. For this reason, we believe that FOLD-R++ performs better than RIPPER on large datasets, as shown later. For similar reasons, FOLD-R++ can provide more intuitive and more succinct explanations than decision tree based methods.

5   Experiments

In this section, we present our experiments on UCI standard benchmarks [12].[2] The XGBoost Classifier is a popular classification model and used as a baseline in our experiment. We used simple settings for XGBoost classifier without limiting its performance. However, XGBoost cannot deal with mixed type (numerical and categorical) of examples directly. One-hot encoding has been used for data preparation. We use precision, recall, accuracy, F_1 score, and execution time to compare the results.

FOLD-R++ does not require any encoding before training. We implemented FOLD-R++ with Python (the original FOLD-R implementation is in Java). To make inferences using the generated rules, we developed a simple logic program-ming interpreter for our application that is part of the FOLD-R++ system. Note that the generated programs are stratified, so implementing an interpreter for such a restricted class in Python is relatively easy. However, for obtaining the justification/proof tree, or for translating the NLP rules into equivalent English text, one must use the s(CASP) system.

The time complexity for computing information gain on a feature is sig-nificantly reduced in FOLD-R++ due to the use of prefix-sum, resulting in rather large improvements in efficiency. For the credit-a dataset with only 690 instances, the new FOLD-R++ algorithm is a hundred times faster than the original FOLD-R. The hyper-parameter ratio is simply set as 0.5 for all the experiments. All the learning experiments have been conducted on a desktop with Intel i5-10400 CPU @ 2.9 GHz and 32 GB ram. To measure performance metrics, we conducted 10-fold cross-validation on each dataset and the average of accuracy, precision, recall, F_1 score and execution time are presented (See Table 4, Table 5, and Table 6). The best performer is highlighted in boldface.

Experiments reported in Table 4 are based on our re-implementation of FOLD-R in Python. The Python re-implementation is 6 to 10 times faster than Shakerin's original Java implementation according to the common tested datasets. However, the re-implementation still lacks efficiency on large datasets due to the original design. The FOLD-R experiments on the Adult Census Income and the Credit Card Approval datasets are performed with improvements in heuristic calculation while for other datasets the method of calculation remains as in Shakerin's original design. In these two cases, the efficiency improves sig-nificantly but the output is identical to original FOLD-R. The average execution

---

[2] The FOLD-R++ system is available at https://github.com/hwd404/FOLD-R-PP.

Table 4. Comparison of FOLD-R and FOLD-R++ on various datasets

| Data set | | | FOLD-R | | | | | | FOLD-R++ | | | | | |
Name	#Rows	#Cols	Acc.	Prec.	Rec.	F1	T(ms)	#Rules	Acc.	Prec.	Rec.	F1	T(ms)	#Rules
acute	120	7	0.99	1	0.98	0.99	12	**2.0**	0.99	1	**0.99**	0.99	**2.3**	2.6
autism	704	18	**0.95**	**0.97**	**0.97**	**0.96**	321	18.4	0.93	0.96	0.95	0.95	62	24.3
breast-w	699	10	0.95	0.96	**0.96**	0.96	373	11.2	0.95	**0.97**	0.95	0.96	32	10.2
cars	1728	7	**0.99**	0.99	1	**0.99**	134	17.9	0.97	1	0.97	0.98	50	**12.2**
credit-a	690	16	0.82	0.83	**0.85**	0.84	11,316	33.4	**0.85**	**0.92**	0.79	**0.85**	111	10.0
ecoli	336	9	0.93	0.92	0.92	0.91	686	**7.7**	0.94	**0.95**	0.92	0.93	34	11.4
heart	270	14	0.74	0.75	0.80	0.77	888	15.9	**0.79**	**0.80**	**0.83**	**0.80**	40	11.7
ionosphere	351	35	0.89	0.90	0.93	0.91	9,297	**5.9**	**0.91**	**0.93**	0.93	**0.93**	385	12.0
kidney	400	25	0.98	0.99	0.98	0.99	451	5.7	**0.99**	**1**	0.98	0.99	28	**5.0**
kr vs. kp	3196	37	0.99	0.99	0.99	0.99	1,259	**16.8**	0.99	0.99	0.99	0.99	319	18.4
mushroom	8124	23	1	1	1	1	1,556	8.6	1	1	1	1	523	**8.0**
voting	435	17	0.95	**0.93**	0.94	0.93	96	13.7	0.95	0.92	**0.95**	**0.93**	16	10.5
adult	32561	15	0.77	**0.94**	0.74	0.83	4+ days	595.5	**0.84**	0.86	**0.95**	**0.90**	10,066	**16.7**
credit card	30000	24	0.64	0.87	0.63	0.73	24+ days	514.9	**0.82**	**0.83**	**0.96**	**0.89**	21,349	**19.1**

time of these two datasets is still quite large, however, we use polynomial regression to estimate it. The estimated average execution time of the Adult Census Income dataset ranges from 4 to 7 days, and a random single test took 4.5 days. The estimated execution time of the Credit Card Approval dataset ranges from 24 to 55 days. For small datasets, the classification performance are similar, however, wrt execution time, the FOLD-R++ algorithm is order of magnitude faster than (the re-implemented Python version of) FOLD-R. For large datasets, FOLD-R++ significantly improves the efficiency, classification performance, and explainability over FOLD-R. For the Adult Census Income and the Credit Card Approval datasets, the average number of rules generated by FOLD-R are over 500 while the number for FOLD-R++ is less than 20.

Table 5. Comparison of RIPPER and FOLD-R++ on various datasets

| Data set | | | RIPPER | | | | | | FOLD-R++ | | | | | |
Name	#Rows	#Cols	Acc.	Prec.	Rec.	F1	T(ms)	#Rules	Acc.	Prec.	Rec.	F1	T(ms)	#Rules
acute	120	7	0.93	1	0.84	0.91	73	**2.0**	0.99	1	**0.99**	0.99	**2.3**	2.6
autism	704	18	0.93	0.96	0.95	0.95	444	**9.6**	0.93	0.96	0.95	0.95	62	24.3
breast-w	699	10	0.91	0.97	0.89	0.93	267	**7.7**	0.95	0.97	**0.95**	**0.96**	32	10.2
cars	1728	7	**0.99**	0.99	**0.99**	**0.99**	379	15.4	0.97	1	0.97	0.98	50	**12.2**
credit-a	690	16	**0.89**	**0.94**	**0.86**	**0.90**	972	11.1	0.85	0.92	0.79	0.85	111	**10.0**
ecoli	336	9	0.90	0.91	0.86	0.88	494	**8.0**	0.94	0.95	0.92	0.93	34	11.4
heart	270	14	0.73	**0.82**	0.69	0.72	338	**6.2**	0.79	0.80	**0.83**	**0.80**	40	11.7
ionosphere	351	35	0.81	0.85	0.86	0.85	1,431	9.9	0.91	0.93	0.93	0.93	385	12.0
kidney	400	25	0.98	0.99	0.98	0.99	451	5.7	0.99	1	0.98	0.99	28	**5.0**
kr vs. kp	3196	37	0.99	0.99	0.99	0.99	553	**8.1**	0.99	0.99	0.99	0.99	319	18.4
mushroom	8124	23	1	1	1	1	795	8.0	1	1	1	1	523	8.0
voting	435	17	0.94	0.92	0.92	0.92	146	**4.3**	0.95	0.92	0.95	0.93	16	10.5
adult	32561	15	0.70	**0.96**	0.63	0.76	59,505	46.9	**0.84**	0.86	**0.95**	**0.90**	10,066	**16.7**
credit card	30000	24	0.77	**0.87**	0.83	0.85	47,422	38.4	**0.82**	0.83	**0.96**	**0.89**	21,349	**19.1**
rain in aus	145460	24	0.65	**0.93**	0.57	0.71	2,850,997	175.4	**0.78**	0.87	**0.84**	**0.85**	223,116	**40.5**

The RIPPER system is another rule-induction algorithm that generates formulas in conjunctive normal form as an explanation of the model. As Table 5 shows, FOLD-R++ system's performance is comparable to RIPPER, however, it significantly outperforms RIPPER on large datasets (Rain in Australia [taken from Kaggle], Adult Census Income, Credit Card Approval). FOLD-R++ generates much smaller numbers of rules for these large datasets. Additionally, default rules capture more semantic information than CNF formulas.

Performance of the XGBoost system and FOLD-R++ is compared in Table 6. The XGBoost Classifier employs a decision tree ensemble method for classification tasks and provides quite good performance. FOLD-R++ almost always spends less time to finish learning compared to XGBoost classifier, especially for the (large) Adult Census Income dataset where numerical features have many unique values. For most datasets, FOLD-R++ can achieve equivalent scores. FOLD-R++ achieves higher scores on ecoli dataset. For the credit card dataset, the baseline XGBoost model failed training due to 32 GB memory limitation, but FOLD-R++ performed well.

Table 6. Comparison of XGBoost and FOLD-R++ on various datasets

Data set			XGBoost.Classifier					FOLD-R++				
Name	#Rows	#Cols	Acc.	Prec.	Rec.	F1	T(ms)	Acc.	Prec.	Rec.	F1	T(ms)
acute	120	7	1	1	1	1	35	0.99	1	0.99	0.99	**2.5**
autism	704	18	**0.97**	**0.98**	**0.98**	0.97	76	0.95	0.96	0.97	0.97	**47**
breast-w	699	10	0.95	0.97	0.96	0.96	78	**0.96**	0.97	0.96	**0.97**	**28**
cars	1728	7	1	1	1	1	77	0.98	1	0.97	0.98	**48**
credit-a	690	16	**0.85**	0.83	**0.83**	0.83	368	0.84	**0.92**	0.79	**0.84**	**100**
ecoli	336	9	0.76	0.76	0.62	0.68	165	**0.96**	**0.95**	**0.94**	**0.95**	**28**
heart	270	14	**0.80**	**0.81**	0.83	0.81	112	0.79	0.79	0.83	0.81	**44**
ionosphere	351	35	0.88	0.86	**0.96**	0.90	1,126	**0.92**	**0.93**	0.94	**0.93**	**392**
kidney	400	25	0.98	0.98	0.98	0.98	126	**0.99**	1	0.98	**0.99**	**27**
kr vs. kp	3196	37	0.99	0.99	0.99	0.99	**210**	0.99	0.99	0.99	0.99	361
mushroom	8124	23	1	1	1	1	**378**	1	1	1	1	476
voting	435	17	0.95	0.94	**0.95**	0.94	49	0.95	0.94	0.94	0.94	**16**
adult	32561	15	**0.86**	**0.88**	0.94	**0.91**	274,655	0.84	0.86	**0.95**	0.90	**10,069**
credit card	30000	24	–	–	–	–	–	0.82	0.83	**0.96**	0.89	**21,349**
rain in aus	145460	24	**0.83**	0.84	**0.95**	**0.89**	285,307	0.78	**0.87**	0.84	0.85	**279,320**

6 Related Work and Conclusion

ALEPH [25] is one of the most popular ILP system, which induces theories by using bottom-up generalization search. However, it cannot deal with numeric features and its specialization step is manual, there is no automation option. Takemura and Inoue's method [26] relies on tree-ensembles to generate explainable rule sets with pattern mining techniques. Its performance depends on the tree-ensemble model. While their algorithm advances the state of the art, it may not be scalable as it is exponential in the number of valid rules.

A survey of ILP can be found in [16]. Rule extraction from statistical Machine Learning models has been a long-standing goal of the community. These algorithms are classified into two categories: 1) Pedagogical (i.e., learning symbolic rules from black-box classifiers without opening them); and 2) Decompositional (i.e., to open the classifier and look into the internals). TREPAN [5] is a successful pedagogical algorithm that learns decision trees from neural networks. SVM+Prototypes [17] is a decompositional rule extraction algorithm that makes use of KMeans clustering to extract rules from SVM classifiers by focusing on support vectors. Another rule extraction technique that is gaining attention recently is "RuleFit" [6]. RuleFit learns a set of weighted rules from ensemble of shallow decision trees combined with original features. In the ILP community also, researchers have tried to combine statistical methods with ILP techniques. Support Vector ILP [15] uses ILP hypotheses as the kernel in dual form of the SVM algorithm. kFOIL [10] learns an incremental kernel for the SVM algorithm using a FOIL-style specialization. nFOIL [9] integrates the Naive-Bayes algorithm with FOIL. The advantage of our research over these is that we generate logic programs containing negation-as-failure that correspond closely to the human thought process. Thus, the descriptions are more concise. Second, the greedy nature of our clause search guarantees scalability. ILASP [11] is another novel ILP system that learns answer set programs. ILASP can learn non-stratified programs, however, *it requires a set of rules to describe the hypothesis space*. In contrast, the FOLD-R++ algorithm only needs the target predicate's name.

In this paper we presented an efficient and highly scalable algorithm, FOLD-R++, to induce default theories represented as a normal logic program. The resulting normal logic program has good performance wrt prediction and justification for the predicted classification. In this new approach, unlike other machine learning methods, the encoding of data is not needed anymore and no information from training data is discarded. Compared with the popular classification system XGBoost, our new approach has similar performance in terms of accuracy, precision, recall, and F1-score, but better training efficiency. In addition, the FOLD-R++ algorithm produces an explainable model. Predictions made by this model can be computed efficiently and their justification automatically produced using the s(CASP) system.

The main advantage of the FOLD-R++ system is that it is an ILP system that is competitive with main-stream machine learning algorithms (such as XGBoost). Almost all ILP systems (except RIPPER) are not competitive with mainstream machine learning systems. However, as we showed in Sect. 5, FOLD-R++ significantly outperforms the RIPPER system on large datasets. Compared to known existing ILP systems in its class, FOLD-R++ produces the most succinct set of rules, especially for larger datasets.

Acknowledgement. Authors gratefully acknowledge support from NSF grants IIS 1718945, IIS 1910131, IIP 1916206, and from Amazon Corp, Atos Corp and US DoD. We are grateful to Joaquin Arias and the s(CASP) team for their work on providing facilities for generating the justification tree and English encoding of rules in s(CASP).

References

1. Arias, J., Carro, M., Chen, Z., Gupta, G.: Justifications for goal-directed constraint answer set programming. In: Proceedings 36th International Conference on Logic Programming (Technical Communications). EPTCS, vol. 325, pp. 59–72 (2020)
2. Arias, J., Carro, M., Salazar, E., Marple, K., Gupta, G.: Constraint answer set programming without grounding. Theory Pract. Logic Program. 18(3–4), 337–354 (2018)
3. Chen, T., Guestrin, C.: XGBoost: a scalable tree boosting system. In: Proceedings of the 22nd ACM SIGKDD, KDD 2016, pp. 785–794 (2016)
4. Cohen, W.W.: Fast effective rule induction. In: Proceedings of the 12th ICML, ICML 1995, pp. 115–123. Morgan Kaufmann Publishers Inc., San Francisco (1995). http://dl.acm.org/citation.cfm?id=3091622.3091637
5. Craven, M.W., Shavlik, J.W.: Extracting tree-structured representations of trained networks. In: Proceedings of the 8th International Conference on Neural Information Processing Systems, NIPS 1995, pp. 24–30. MIT Press, Cambridge (1995)
6. Friedman, J.H., Popescu, B.E., et al.: Predictive learning via rule ensembles. Ann. Appl. Stat. 2(3), 916–954 (2008)
7. Gelfond, M., Kahl, Y.: Knowledge Representation, Reasoning, and the Design of Intelligent Agents: The Answer-Set Programming Approach. Cambridge University Press (2014)
8. Gunning, D.: Explainable Artificial Intelligence (XAI) (2015). https://www.darpa.mil/program/explainable-artificial-intelligence
9. Landwehr, N., Kersting, K., Raedt, L.D.: nFOIL: integrating Naïve Bayes and FOIL. In: Proceedings of the Twentieth National Conference on Artificial Intelligence and the Seventeenth Innovative Applications of Artificial Intelligence Conference, Pittsburgh, Pennsylvania, USA, 9–13 July 2005, pp. 795–800 (2005)
10. Landwehr, N., Passerini, A., Raedt, L.D., Frasconi, P.: kFOIL: learning simple relational kernels. In: Proceedings of the Twenty-First National Conference on Artificial Intelligence and the Eighteenth Innovative Applications of Artificial Intelligence Conference, MA, USA, 16–20 July 2006, pp. 389–394 (2006)
11. Law, M.: Inductive learning of answer set programs. Ph.D. thesis, Imperial College London, UK (2018)
12. Lichman, M.: UCI, Machine Learning Repository (2013). http://archive.ics.uci.edu/ml
13. Lloyd, J.: Foundations of Logic Programming, 2nd Ext. edn. Springer, Heidelberg (1987)
14. Muggleton, S.: Inductive logic programming. New Gen. Comput. 8(4) (1991)
15. Muggleton, S., Lodhi, H., Amini, A., Sternberg, M.J.E.: Support vector inductive logic programming. In: Hoffmann, A., Motoda, H., Scheffer, T. (eds.) DS 2005. LNCS (LNAI), vol. 3735, pp. 163–175. Springer, Heidelberg (2005). https://doi.org/10.1007/11563983_15
16. Muggleton, S., et al.: ILP turns 20. Mach. Learn. 86(1), 3–23 (2011). https://doi.org/10.1007/s10994-011-5259-2
17. Núñez, H., Angulo, C., Catalá, A.: Rule extraction from support vector machines. In: Proceedings of European Symposium on Artificial Neural Networks, pp. 107–112 (2002)
18. Plotkin, G.D.: A further note on inductive generalization. Mach. Intell. 6, 101–124 (1971)

19. Quinlan, J.R.: Learning logical definitions from relations. Mach. Learn. **5**, 239–266 (1990)
20. Quinlan, J.R.: C4.5: Programs for Machine Learning. Morgan Kaufmann Publishers Inc., San Francisco (1993)
21. Reiter, R.: A logic for default reasoning. Artif. Intell. **13**(1–2), 81–132 (1980)
22. Sakama, C.: Induction from answer sets in nonmonotonic logic programs. ACM Trans. Comput. Log. **6**(2), 203–231 (2005)
23. Shakerin, F.: Logic programming-based approaches in explainable AI and natural language processing. Ph.D. thesis, Department of Computer Science, The University of Texas at Dallas (2020)
24. Shakerin, F., Salazar, E., Gupta, G.: A new algorithm to automate inductive learning of default theories. TPLP **17**(5–6), 1010–1026 (2017)
25. Srinivasan, A.: The Aleph Manual (2001). https://www.cs.ox.ac.uk/activities/programinduction/Aleph/aleph.html
26. Takemura, A., Inoue, K.: Generating explainable rule sets from tree-ensemble learning methods by answer set programming. Electron. Proc. Theor. Comput. Sci. **345**, 127–140 (2021)
27. Wikipedia contributors: Prefix sum Wikipedia, the free encyclopedia (2021). https://en.wikipedia.org/wiki/Prefix_sum. Accessed 5 Oct 2021
28. Zeng, Q., Patel, J.M., Page, D.: QuickFOIL: scalable inductive logic programming. Proc. VLDB Endow. **8**(3), 197–208 (2014)

A Lazy Desugaring System for Evaluating Programs with Sugars

Ziyi Yang[1], Yushuo Xiao[2,3], Zhichao Guan[2,3], and Zhenjiang Hu[2,3(✉)]

[1] School of Computing, National University of Singapore, Singapore, Singapore
yangziyi@u.nus.edu
[2] Key Lab of High Confidence Software Technologies, Ministry of Education, Beijing, China
[3] School of Computer Science, Peking University, Beijing, China
{xiaoyushuo,guanzhichao,huzj}@pku.edu.cn

Abstract. Extending a programming language with syntactic sugars is common practice in language design. Given a core language, one can define a surface language on top of it with sugars. We propose a lazy desugaring system, which can generate the evaluation sequences of sugar programs in the syntax of the surface language. Specifically, we define an evaluation strategy on a mixed language which combines syntactic sugars with the core language. We formulate two properties, *emulation* and *laziness*, and prove that the evaluation strategy produces correct evaluation sequences. Besides, we have implemented a system based on this novel method and demonstrate its usefulness with several examples.

1 Introduction

Syntactic sugar, first coined by Landin [13] in 1964, was introduced to describe the surface syntax of a simple ALGOL-like programming language which was defined semantically in terms of the applicative expressions of the core lambda calculus. It has been proved to be very useful for defining domain-specific languages (DSLs) and extending existing languages [4,6]. Unfortunately, when syntactic sugar is eliminated by transformation, it obscures the relationship between the user's source program and the transformed program. As a result, a programmer who only knows the surface language cannot understand the execution of programs in the core language, which makes the debugging of programs with sugars hard.

Resugaring [14,15] is a powerful existing method to resolve this problem. It reverses the application of the desugaring transformation. As a typical example of resugaring, consider the sugars Or1 and Not, defined by the following desugaring rules[1].

---

[1] Throughout the paper, we use #t and #f to represent the Boolean constants true and false, respectively.

Z. Yang and Y. Xiao—Co-first authors, contributing equally to this work.

This work was partly supported by the National Key Research and Development Program of China (No. 2021ZD0110202).

M. Hanus and A. Igarashi (Eds.): FLOPS 2022, LNCS 13215, pp. 243–261, 2022.
https://doi.org/10.1007/978-3-030-99461-7_14

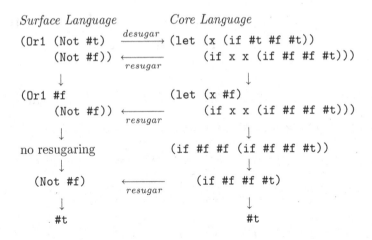

Fig. 1. A resugaring example.

$$(\text{Or1 } t_1 \ t_2) \overset{def}{=\!=} (\text{let } (\text{x } t_1) \ (\text{if x x } t_2))$$
$$(\text{Not } t_1) \overset{def}{=\!=} (\text{if } t_1 \ \#f \ \#t)$$

The resugaring process for

(Or1 (Not #t) (Not #f))

is shown in Fig. 1. The sequence of terms on the left shows the evaluation steps in the surface language, which is obtained from the evaluation sequence of the desugared program (in the core language) on the right by repeated attempts of reverse expansion of each sugar.

While this approach is natural, there are two practical problems. First, as the reverse expansion of sugars needs to match the desugared terms against the desugaring rules to check whether they can be resugared, it would be very expensive if the surface program uses a large number of syntactic sugars, or some syntactic sugars are desugared to complex core terms. Second, in the resugaring process, many core programs cannot be reverted to surface programs, which means that many attempts at reverse application of desugaring rules fail and introduce lots of useless work.

In this paper, we propose a lazy desugaring system, which *produces the evaluation sequence in the surface language without reverse desugaring.* Our key observation is that if we consider desugaring rules as reduction rules like those in the core language, then the evaluation sequence of a surface program should exist in the reduction sequence by these reduction rules. To see this, recalling the example in Fig. 1, we can see from Fig. 2 that the reduction sequence can be generated by the given desugaring rules and the reduction rules of the core language; the underlined part is the same as the resugaring sequence on the left of Fig. 1.

$$
\begin{array}{l}
\underline{\text{(Or1 (Not \#t) (Not \#f))}} \\
\xrightarrow{desugar} \text{(Or1 (if \#t \#f \#t) (Not \#f))} \\
\xrightarrow{core} \underline{\text{(Or1 \#f (Not \#f))}} \\
\xrightarrow{desugar} \text{(let (x \#f) (if x x (Not \#f)))} \\
\xrightarrow{core} \text{(if \#f \#f (Not \#f))} \\
\xrightarrow{core} \underline{\text{(Not \#f)}} \\
\xrightarrow{desugar} \text{(if \#f \#f \#t)} \\
\xrightarrow{core} \underline{\text{\#t}}
\end{array}
$$

Fig. 2. Proper desugaring for resugaring.

Attention should be paid here. There could be many possible reduction sequences if we do not restrict how to apply desugaring rules. For instance, Fig. 3 gives another possible evaluation sequence. Here, from this sequence, we could not extract the sequence we want, because the term (Or1 #f (Not #f)) is lost. How can we make sure that a sequence which contains all the evaluation steps wanted is produced?

$$
\begin{array}{l}
\underline{\text{(Or1 (Not \#t) (Not \#f))}} \\
\xrightarrow{desugar} \text{(let (x (Not \#t)) (if x x (Not \#f)))} \\
\xrightarrow{desugar} \text{(let (x (if \#t \#f \#t)) (if x x (Not \#f)))} \\
\xrightarrow{core} \text{(let (x \#f) (if x x (Not \#f)))} \\
\xrightarrow{core} \text{(if \#f \#f (Not \#f))} \\
\xrightarrow{core} \underline{\text{(Not \#f)}} \\
\xrightarrow{desugar} \text{(if \#f \#f \#t)} \\
\xrightarrow{core} \underline{\text{\#t}}
\end{array}
$$

Fig. 3. Improper desugaring.

The key insight of our approach is that we can delay the application of desugaring rules (sugar expansion) until it becomes necessary so that later reverse expansion in the original resugaring becomes unnecessary. To do so, we treat the surface language and the core language as one mixed language, regard desugaring rules as reduction rules of the mixed language, and derive the context rules of the mixed language to indicate when desugaring should take place. Our main technical contributions can be summarized as follows.

- We propose a lazy desugaring method, which evaluates sugar programs on the surface level. It guarantees that the evaluation sequence of a program in the mixed language is *correct* in the sense that it corresponds to the evaluation sequence of the fully desugared program in the core language, and that it is *sufficient* (*complete*) in the sense that it contains all evaluation steps we want in the surface language.
- We present a novel algorithm to calculate the context rules and the reduction rules for syntactic sugars to achieve lazy desugaring. Using the algorithm, we can get a new reduction strategy for the mixed language, based on which the evaluation sequence in the syntax of the surface language can be obtained.
- We have implemented a system based on this approach, and tested it with many non-trivial examples, which shows the promise of the system.

The rest of our paper is organized as follows. We start with an overview of our approach in Sect. 2. We give the template for language definition in Sect. 3, which makes clear what languages are supported. We then present the algorithm of lazy desugaring with its properties in Sect. 4. We briefly discuss the implementation of the system, and give some examples in Sect. 5. We discuss related work in Sect. 6 and conclude the paper in Sect. 7.

2   Overview

In this section, we give a brief overview of our approach. Given a very tiny core language and a surface language defined by a set of syntactic sugars, we shall demonstrate how we can obtain the evaluation sequence of a program with sugars in the syntax of the surface language by lazy desugaring.

Consider the following simple core language, which contains Boolean expressions using the `if` construct.

$$t ::= (\text{if } t\ t\ t)$$
$$\mid \text{\#t}$$
$$\mid \text{\#f}$$

The semantics of the language is given by reduction semantics: we have two reduction rules:

$$(\text{if \#t } t_1\ t_2) \rightarrow t_1$$
$$(\text{if \#f } t_1\ t_2) \rightarrow t_2$$

together with the following context rules specifying the reduction order.

$$C := (\text{if } C\ t\ t)$$
$$\mid \bullet \qquad \triangleright \ context\ hole$$

The surface language is defined by two syntactic sugars:

$$(\text{And } t_1\ t_2) \overset{def}{=\!=} (\text{if } t_1\ t_2\ \text{\#f})$$
$$(\text{Or } t_1\ t_2) \overset{def}{=\!=} (\text{if } t_1\ \text{\#t } t_2)$$

Now let us demonstrate how to evaluate (And (Or #t #f) (And #f #t)) by lazy desugaring to obtain the evaluation sequence on the surface level as follows.

$$\begin{aligned}
&\texttt{(And (Or \#t \#f) (And \#f \#t))}\\
\longrightarrow\ &\texttt{(And \#t (And \#f \#t))}\\
\longrightarrow\ &\texttt{(And \#f \#t)}\\
\longrightarrow\ &\texttt{\#f}
\end{aligned}$$

Step 1: Calculating Context Rules and Reduction Rules for Sugars

In lazy desugaring, we first decide when a sugar should be desugared. To this end, from the context rules of the core language, we automatically derive the following context rules for the sugars.

$$\begin{aligned}
C ::=\ &(\texttt{And}\ C\ t_2)\\
|\ &(\texttt{Or}\ C\ t_2)\\
|\ &\bullet
\end{aligned}$$

The idea of derivation will be discussed in Sect. 4. Intuitively, from the context rules of (if $t_1\ t_2$ #f), we can see that the condition, t_1, is always evaluated first, so (And $t_1\ t_2$) should also have t_1 evaluated first. This is indicated by the context rule of And. Similarly, we can calculate the context rule for Or.

Step 2: Forming Mixed Language with Mixed Reduction Rules

To treat desugaring rules and the reduction rules (of the core language) in one reduction system, we mix the surface language with the core language as in Fig. 4, and define $\rightarrow_m$, a one-step reduction for the mixed language (the letter m stands for "mixed"). It is derived from the reduction rules of the core language and the desugaring rules of the surface language. Note that the desugaring rules are a bit different from the initial definition. For instance, the desugaring rule (And $t_1\ t_2$) $\overset{def}{=\!=}$ (if $t_1\ t_2$ #f) has been changed to the reduction rule (And $v_1\ t_2$) $\rightarrow$ (if $v_1\ t_2$ #f) in Fig. 4, indicating that this reduction rule can be applied only when the first argument of Add has been reduced to a value. This change in fact follows from the context rules ontained at step 1.

Now, by using $\rightarrow_m$, we can get the evaluation sequence in the mixed language for the program

$$\texttt{(And (Or \#t \#f) (And \#f \#t))}$$

based on the computation order determined by the context rules obtained at step 1. The evaluation sequence in the mixed language is shown below.

$$\begin{aligned}
&\texttt{(And (Or \#t \#f) (And \#f \#t))}\\
\rightarrow_m\ &\texttt{(And (if \#t \#t \#f) (And \#f \#t))}\\
\rightarrow_m\ &\texttt{(And \#t (And \#f \#t))}\\
\rightarrow_m\ &\texttt{(if \#t (And \#f \#t) \#f)}\\
\rightarrow_m\ &\texttt{(And \#f \#t)}\\
\rightarrow_m\ &\texttt{(if \#f \#t \#f)}\\
\rightarrow_m\ &\texttt{\#f}
\end{aligned}$$

$$t ::= (\text{if } t_1\ t_2\ t_3) \qquad C ::= (\text{if } C\ t_2\ t_3) \qquad (\text{And } v_1\ t_2) \rightarrow (\text{if } v_1\ t_2\ \#\text{f})$$

$t ::=$	$(\text{if } t_1\ t_2\ t_3)$	$C ::=$	$(\text{if } C\ t_2\ t_3)$	$(\text{And } v_1\ t_2) \rightarrow (\text{if } v_1\ t_2\ \#\text{f})$
$\mid$	$(\text{And } t_1\ t_2)$	$\mid$	$(\text{And } C\ t_2)$	$(\text{Or } v_1\ t_2) \rightarrow (\text{if } v_1\ \#\text{t}\ t_2)$
$\mid$	$(\text{Or } t_1\ t_2)$	$\mid$	$(\text{Or } C\ t_2)$	$(\text{if } \#\text{t}\ t_1\ t_2) \rightarrow t_1$
$\mid$	$\#\text{t}$	$\mid$	$\bullet$	$(\text{if } \#\text{f}\ t_1\ t_2) \rightarrow t_2$
$\mid$	$\#\text{f}$			

(a) Syntax.   (b) Context rules.   (c) Reduction rules.

Fig. 4. A small mixed language.

Step 3: Removing Unnecessary Terms

As seen above, our evaluation sequence in the mixed language may contain constructs in the core language (e.g. (if #t (And #f #t) #f)). Since our goal is to show the evaluation sequence of sugar programs, we give a flexible method to clearly specify a *filter* showing which terms should be displayed. (A default filter can be generated automatically.) For example, we may define the following subset of the mixed language as a filter for displaying:

$$
\begin{aligned}
dt ::= &\ (\text{And } dt\ dt) \\
\mid &\ (\text{Or } dt\ dt) \\
\mid &\ \#\text{t} \\
\mid &\ \#\text{f}
\end{aligned}
$$

With this filter, the sugars And and Or, together with Boolean constants #t and #f, will be displayed. Notice that we make Boolean values displayable even if they are in the core language. By clearly specifying what should be displayed, we can always get the evaluation sequences we need. This practical step is not essential to our system, so we will not go into detail in the rest of the paper.

In short, given a core language and a surface language defined by syntactic sugars, the major effort to build an evaluator of the surface language is to derive context rules and reduction rules from sugar definitions, which can be done automatically by our method and will be explained in detail in the rest of this paper.

3 Defining Languages and Sugars

As seen in previous sections, by introducing sugars we construct a language hierarchy, which contains a "core language", and "surface languages" extended by sugars. Since our approach needs to inspect and manipulate context rules and reduction rules explicitly, we give a language template for the definition of the core language and sugars, which stipulates what languages are allowed in our setting. These definitions and notations will be used when discussing the algorithm and its properties in Sect. 4.

Syntax

$t ::= (\underline{\text{head}}\ t_1\ \cdots\ t_n)$ ▷ language constructs

$v ::= (\underline{\text{head}}\ t_1/v_1\ \cdots\ t_n/v_n)$ ▷ values

Context

$C ::= (\underline{\text{head}}\ t/v\ \cdots\ C\ t/v\ \cdots)*$ ▷ zero or more context rules

    $\mid\ \bullet$ ▷ context hole

Notion of reduction

$\mathcal{R}((\underline{\text{head}}\ t/v\ \cdots))$ ▷ one-step reduction without context

Fig. 5. Basic template for core language definition.

3.1 Core Language

We follow the syntax convention of Lisp for a core language, using S-expressions to represent programs, and we use reduction semantics to formalize the semantics of the core language.

The basic *template* for defining syntax, contexts, and reduction rules is shown in Fig. 5. This is merely a template for language definitions, with which we can encode more complex languages. In the template, all elements that are underlined will be replaced with some language-specific constructs. For example, $\underline{\text{head}}$ should be chosen from a set of language constructs specified by the user, such as `lambda`, `if`, `let`, etc. So the production of t may become $t ::= (\text{if } t_1\ t_2\ t_3)$. In addition, a language also needs to specify a set of *values*, which is the set of terms that can not be further reduced. Values must be defined in the format of v in Fig. 5. Here t/v means either t or v, and whether it is t or v is fixed in a given language. To encode the reduction semantics of the language, the user also needs to specify a set of context rules, in the form of the right-hand side of the production of C. Finally, the *notion of reduction* (as described in the literature [5]) needs to be defined, which is the one-step reduction without context. For simplicity, we define it using a partial function, $\mathcal{R}$, which yields the reduced term if the input is reducible, and $\bot$ if the input is not reducible. The notion of reduction should be *extensible*, in the sense that it can be extended to any mixed language. The exact meaning of "extensible" will be made clear in Sect. 3.2.

The languages defined using this template, while having a restricted form of syntax, can be arbitrarily complex, since the notion of reduction, $\mathcal{R}$, can be any partial function as long as it is extensible. We encode the language in the running example, the Boolean language, using our template, in Fig. 6. Note that constants can be encoded as language constructs with zero arguments, such as (`true`). And `#t` is merely a shorthand of (`true`). In Sect. 4, we use C_c to denote contexts generated by the non-terminal C of any given core language. In this example, one valid context is

$$(\text{if (if } \bullet\ \text{\#t \#f) \#f \#t}).$$

Syntax

$t ::=$ (if t_1 t_2 t_3)   ▷ language constructs
    | (true) | (false)   ▷ constants
$v ::=$ (true) | (false)   ▷ constants are values

Context

$C ::=$ (if C t_1 t_2)   ▷ evaluating the condition first
    | •   ▷ context hole

Notion of reduction

$\mathcal{R}($(if (true) t_2 t_3)$) = t_2$ ▷ one-step reduction without context (true branch)
$\mathcal{R}($(if (false) t_2 t_3)$) = t_3$ (false branch)

Fig. 6. Core language example: Boolean expressions.

Sugar definition

$$(\underline{\text{Sg}} \ t_1/v_1 \ \cdots \ t_n/v_n) \overset{def}{=\!=\!=} t$$

Fig. 7. Sugar definition.

Given a language definition, we can describe a small-step reduction of the core language with a partial function as follows.

$$\mathcal{R}_c(t) = \begin{cases} C_c[t'] & \text{▷ if } t = C_c[t_0] \text{ and } \mathcal{R}(t_0) = t' \\ \bot & \text{▷ otherwise} \end{cases} \quad (1)$$

And we naturally require that the reduction of any term t is deterministic, i.e., there does not exist more than one term t' such that t can be reduced to.

3.2   Mixed Language

Given a core language, we can define syntactic sugars on top of it. In the theoretical discussion, we assume for simplicity that only one sugar is defined based on the given language. The sugar definition follows a strict pattern, as illustrated in Fig. 7. We use $\underline{\text{Sg}}$ to denote a new sugar name, and use t_i's and v_i's as metavariables (for terms and values), which appear on the right-hand side (RHS). To distinguish the constructs from the core language and the names of sugars, we make the head of the core language constructs in lowercase and the first letter of sugar names in uppercase. Below is an example of a sugar definition based on pre-defined sugars And, Or and core language's construct not.

$$(\text{Sg}_1 \ t_1 \ t_2 \ mt_3) \overset{def}{=\!=\!=} (\text{And (Or } t_1 \ t_3) \ (\text{not } t_2))$$

To simplify later discussion of our algorithm, we assume that any metavariable on the left-hand side (LHS) of a sugar definition appears only once on the

Syntax

$$t ::= \ldots \qquad\qquad\qquad\qquad\qquad \triangleright \text{ terms in the core language form}$$
$$\mid (\underline{\text{Sg}} \; t_1 \; \cdots \; t_n) \qquad\qquad\qquad\qquad \triangleright \text{ sugars}$$
$$v ::= \ldots \qquad\qquad\qquad\qquad\qquad \triangleright \text{ values in the core language}$$

Context

$$C ::= \ldots \qquad\qquad\qquad\qquad \triangleright \text{ context rules of the core language and hole}$$
$$\mid (\underline{\text{Sg}} \; t/v \; \cdots \; C \; t/v \; \cdots)* \qquad \triangleright \text{ zero or more Sg's context rules}$$

Notion of reduction

$$(\underline{\text{head}} \; t/v \; \cdots) \rightarrow_{m_1} t \qquad \triangleright \text{ remained reduction rules of core language}$$
$$(\underline{\text{Sg}} \; t/v \; \cdots) \rightarrow_{m_1} t \qquad \triangleright \text{ reduction rule derived from desugaring rules}$$

Fig. 8. Template for the mixed language.

RHS (*linear expansion*). (The restriction can be lifted with a simple extension.) Given a sugar definition, we now define the mixed language. The mixed language simply allows the sugar to appear as any part of a term. Formally, the syntax of the mixed language is defined in Fig. 8. Notice that the arguments of a core language's head can also be a sugar now, like in

$$(\text{if} \; (\text{And} \; \#t \; \#f) \; \#f \; \#t).$$

We use $\mathcal{D}$ to denote the outermost desugaring function induced by the sugar definition. For example, we have

$$\mathcal{D}((\text{And} \; (\text{And} \; \#t \; \#f) \; \#t)) = (\text{if} \; (\text{And} \; \#t \; \#f) \; \#t \; \#f)$$

for the And sugar above. Then we can naturally define the fully desugaring function, $\mathcal{D}_F$, which works as traditional desugaring, recursively expanding all sugars of the input term. Formally, $\mathcal{D}_F$ is defined as follows.

$$\mathcal{D}_F((\text{Sg} \; t_1 \; \cdots \; t_n)) = \mathcal{D}_F(\mathcal{D}((\text{Sg} \; t_1 \; \cdots \; t_n)))$$
$$\mathcal{D}_F((\text{head} \; t_1 \; \cdots \; t_n)) = (\text{head} \; \mathcal{D}_F(t_1) \; \cdots \; \mathcal{D}_F(t_n))$$

With the definition of $\mathcal{D}_F$, we can now make the meaning of the extensible property of the core language clear.

Definition 1 (Extensible). *The notion of reduction $\mathcal{R}$ of a core language is extensible, if for any possible sugar, and for any term t in the mixed language,*

$$\mathcal{D}_F(\mathcal{R}(t)) = \mathcal{R}(\mathcal{D}_F(t)), \; \text{if } \mathcal{R}(t) \neq \bot.$$

It is saying that, for any term t that is reducible by the notion of reduction, reducing it first and then fully desugaring it will be the same as fully desugaring it first and then reducing it. One can easily check that reductions of our familiar language constructs are usually extensible. For example, the reduction rules of if is extensible, since it treats t_2 and t_3 as a whole, and thus the order of the reduction and the desugaring does not matter.

4 Lazy Desugaring Algorithm

As shown in Sect. 2, given *a core language, sugar definition* and *any term with sugars*, we can get the *evaluation sequence* of the term as the output. To obtain the sequence, the first step is to generate the reduction semantics for the mixed language, which is non-trivial. Then the sequence can be obtained easily by recursively applying the one-step reduction on the term in the mixed language. In this section, we start by describing a procedure that generates the reduction semantics of the mixed language in Sect. 4.1, and then show that the semantics gives the correct evaluation sequence in Sect. 4.2.

4.1 Algorithm Desciption

Supposing that we have a core language, we use the following function `getRules` to generate the reduction semantics for a given desugaring rule (i.e., a sugar definition):

$$D_{\text{LHS}} \stackrel{def}{=\!=} t_{\text{RHS}}, \quad \text{where } D_{\text{LHS}} = (\text{Sg } t_1/v_1 \ \cdots \ t_n/v_n),$$

and the generated semantics consist of zero or more *context rules* of the sugar, and exactly one *reduction rule* corresponding to the original desugaring rule. These rules, together with the context rules and reduction rules of the core language, form the semantics of the mixed language. The following function `getRules` calculates the context rules and the reduction rule of `Sg`, which are put in a set.

$$\text{getRules}(D_{\text{LHS}} \stackrel{def}{=\!=} t_{\text{RHS}}) = \begin{cases} \{[t_i := C] \, D_{\text{LHS}}\} \cup \\ \text{getRules}\left([t_i := v_i]\left(D_{\text{LHS}} \stackrel{def}{=\!=} t_{\text{RHS}}\right)\right) \\ \quad \triangleright \text{ if } \exists \, i, C_c, \text{ s.t. } t_{\text{RHS}} = C_c[t_i] \\ \{D_{\text{LHS}} \rightarrow_{m_1} t_{\text{RHS}}\} \\ \quad \triangleright \text{ otherwise} \end{cases}$$

The substitutions are on the metalanguage level. For example, $[t_i := C]$ means substituting a context hole C for metavariable t_i. Metavariables t_i and v_i are implicitly replaced with symbols t_i and v_i, respectively (because our sugar definition and context rules use different notations). The substitution produces a new *rule*. Rules need to be interpreted properly to represent actual contexts. Intuitively, the function tries to match the RHS of sugar definition with context rules of the core language, and calculates the context rules of the sugar accordingly. When the expansion cannot be matched with any core context rules, we acquire the last item of the returned list, $D_{\text{LHS}} \rightarrow_{m_1} t_{\text{RHS}}$, which is the reduction rule (notion of reduction) of the sugar in the mixed language.

To demonstrate how `getRules` runs, we explain how the following invocation executes.

$$\text{getRules}((\text{And } t_1 \ t_2) \stackrel{def}{=\!=} (\text{if } t_1 \ t_2 \ \#\text{f}))$$

In the first step, t_{RHS} is $C_c[t_1]$, where C_c is (if $\bullet$ t_2 #f). The metavariable t_1 is matched with the hole, so the first rule to be output is the context rule (And C t_2), indicating that the first operand of And sugar should be evaluated first. Then the algorithm runs recursively, calling

$$\text{getRules}((\text{And } v_1\ t_2) \overset{def}{=\!=} (\text{if } v_1\ t_2\ \text{\#f})).$$

This time there does not exist i, C_c, such that $t_{\text{RHS}} = C_c[t_i]$, so the second rule output is the reduction rule

$$(\text{And } v_1\ t_2) \rightarrow_{m_1} (\text{if } v_1\ t_2\ \text{\#f}).$$

Finally, with the context rule and the reduction rule, the reduction semantics of the mixed language can be formed (as partly seen in Fig. 4), following the template in Fig. 8.

Based on the setting in the previous section, we can generate the semantics of the mixed language by the rules of the core language and the calculated rules. Following the definition of C_c and $\mathcal{R}_c$ in Sect. 3.1, we define the contexts of the mixed language, C_m, and the partial reduction function, $\mathcal{R}_m$, based on the mixed language's semantics as well. If there are more than one sugar definition, we calculate their rules and add them to the mixed language one by one. With the first sugar's rules calculated, the language mixed by the core and the first sugar becomes the new core language of the second sugar, and so on. If one desugaring rule's RHS depends on another syntactic sugar, the previous one's rules should be obtained first. Therefore, the context rules of sugars derived by the algorithm must not be cyclically dependent for mutual recursive sugars.[2] Finally, given any term in the mixed language, we can evaluate it by the mixed semantics.

4.2 Properties

What will the semantics of the mixed language do? It is important to answer the question because the evaluation sequences produced by lazy desugaring should be meaningful enough to have a practical use. In this section, we state and prove two important properties about the mixed semantics: *emulation* and *laziness*.

Emulation. The first property, *emulation*, adapted from the original resugaring work by [14], is described as follows (a diagram illustrating the property graphically is shown in Fig. 9). It says that, a one-step reduction of any t in the mixed language either (1) corresponds to a reduction of the desugared program in the core language, or (2) corresponds to a single-step expansion of the sugar.

Property 4.1 (Emulation). For any term $t = (H\ t_1\ \cdots\ t_n)$ where H is a core construct head or a sugar name Sg, either $\mathcal{R}_m(t)$ is not defined, or one of

---

[2] The sugars with cyclic dependence on evaluation contexts are ill-formed for general desugaring.

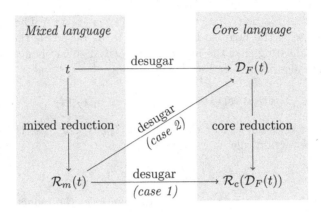

Fig. 9. Illustration of emulation.

the following statements holds: (Case 1) $\mathcal{D}_F(\mathcal{R}_m(t)) = \mathcal{R}_c(\mathcal{D}_F(t))$; and (Case 2) $\mathcal{D}_F(\mathcal{R}_m(t)) = \mathcal{D}_F(t)$.

Proof. By structural induction on the term t.

- BASE CASE. If t is a normal form, $\mathcal{R}_m(t) = \bot$, which clearly satisfies the property.
- INDUCTION HYPOTHESIS. Every sub-term of t, namely t_i, follows the emulation property.
- INDUCTION STEP. If t is not a normal form, we conduct the proof with a case analysis.
  1. $H = \mathsf{Sg}$, and $\mathcal{R}_m(t)$ expands the outermost Sg in t. Thus, we have

  $$\mathcal{D}_F(\mathcal{R}_m(t)) = \mathcal{D}_F(t).$$

  It turns out that the equation of *case 2* holds.
  2. $H = \mathsf{Sg}$, and $\mathcal{R}_m(t)$ reduces t_i, i.e.,

  $$\mathcal{R}_m(t) = (\mathsf{Sg}\ t_1\ \cdots\ \mathcal{R}_m(t_i)\ \cdots\ t_n).$$

In this case,

$$\mathcal{D}_F(\mathcal{R}_m(t)) = \mathcal{D}((\mathsf{Sg}\ \mathcal{D}_F(t_1)\ \cdots\ \mathcal{D}_F(\mathcal{R}_m(t_i))\ \cdots\ \mathcal{D}_F(t_n))).$$

On the other hand,

$$\mathcal{D}_F(t) = \mathcal{D}((\mathsf{Sg}\ \mathcal{D}_F(t_1)\ \cdots\ \mathcal{D}_F(t_i)\ \cdots\ \mathcal{D}_F(t_n))).$$

If $\mathcal{D}_F(\mathcal{R}_m(t_i)) = \mathcal{D}_F(t_i)$, *case 2* holds. Otherwise, if $\mathcal{D}_F(\mathcal{R}_m(t_i)) = \mathcal{R}_c(\mathcal{D}_F(t_i))$, with Lemma 4.1 (which we state and prove later), we have

$$\mathcal{R}_c(\mathcal{D}_F(t)) = \mathcal{D}((\mathsf{Sg}\ \mathcal{D}_F(t_1)\ \cdots\ \mathcal{R}_c(\mathcal{D}_F(t_i))\ \cdots\ \mathcal{D}_F(t_n))).$$

Thus, we conclude that either $\mathcal{D}_F(\mathcal{R}_m(t)) = \mathcal{D}_F(t)$ or $\mathcal{D}_F(\mathcal{R}_m(t)) = \mathcal{R}_c(\mathcal{D}_F(t))$ holds.

3. $H =$ head, and $\mathcal{R}_m(t)$ is an application of the notion of reduction to t itself (the outermost head). In this case, we are going to prove that the equation of *case 1* holds. That is,

$$\mathcal{D}_F(\mathcal{R}((\text{head } t_1 \cdots t_n))) = \mathcal{R}((\text{head } \mathcal{D}_F(t_1) \cdots \mathcal{D}_F(t_n))).$$

This is exactly the definition of the extensible requirement of the notion of reduction in the core language.

4. $H =$ head, and $\mathcal{R}_m(t)$ reduces t_i. First, $\mathcal{R}_m$ and $\mathcal{R}_c$ will reduce a term with the same index in

$$(\text{head } t_1 \cdots t_n)$$

and

$$(\text{head } \mathcal{D}_F(t_1) \cdots \mathcal{D}_F(t_n)),$$

respectively. The left-hand-side

$$\mathcal{D}_F(\mathcal{R}_c(t)) = (\text{head } \mathcal{D}_F(t_1) \cdots \mathcal{D}_F(\mathcal{R}_m(t_i)) \cdots \mathcal{D}_F(t_n)).$$

As for the RHS of *case 1* and *2*, we have

$$\mathcal{D}_F(t) = (\text{head } \mathcal{D}_F(t_1) \cdots \mathcal{D}_F(t_i) \cdots \mathcal{D}_F(t_n))$$

and

$$\mathcal{R}_c(\mathcal{D}_F(t)) = (\text{head } \mathcal{D}_F(t_1) \cdots \mathcal{R}_c(\mathcal{D}_F(t_i)) \cdots \mathcal{D}_F(t_n)).$$

By induction hypothesis, we can conclude that either $\mathcal{D}_F(\mathcal{R}_m(t)) = \mathcal{D}_F(t)$ or $\mathcal{D}_F(\mathcal{R}_m(t)) = \mathcal{R}_c(\mathcal{D}_F(t))$ holds.

□

In the above proof, we use Lemma 4.1 (for the second case at the induction step), which is stated and proved as follows.

Lemma 4.1. *For a term*

$$t = (Sg\ t_1 \cdots t_n),$$

if

$$\mathcal{R}_m(t) = (Sg\ t_1 \cdots \mathcal{R}_m(t_i) \cdots t_n), \tag{2}$$

and $\mathcal{D}_F(\mathcal{R}_m(t_i)) \neq \mathcal{D}_F(t_i)$, *then*

$$\mathcal{R}_c(\mathcal{D}_F(t)) = \mathcal{D}((Sg\ \mathcal{D}_F(t_1) \cdots \mathcal{R}_c(\mathcal{D}_F(t_i)) \cdots \mathcal{D}_F(t_n))).$$

Proof. Equation (2) suggests that the sugar Sg is given a context rule like

$$(Sg\ \underline{t/v} \cdots C_i \cdots \underline{t/v})$$

in the mixed semantics by the getRules algorithm. According to the algorithm, $\mathcal{D}(t)$ will also reduce at t_i's location for core context rule. Because $\mathcal{D}_F(\mathcal{R}_m(t_i)) \neq \mathcal{D}_F(t_i)$, $\mathcal{R}_m(t_i)$ reduces t_i by core language's reduction rule (as opposed to desugaring), so $\mathcal{D}_F(t_i)$ can be reduced by core language's reduction. Thus, the lemma holds. □

Laziness. Another property is *laziness*, which guarantees that desugaring acts as "lazy" as possible. In other words, the algorithm exposes as many terms in the surface level as possible. This property is crucial to the usefulness of lazy desugaring.

With the desugaring rule of a sugar $\mathtt{Sg}$, we can define a $\mathbf{term}^n \to \mathbf{term}$ function $\mathcal{DSG}$ (the terms can be natually extended to metavariables) such that

$$\mathcal{DSG}(t_1, \cdots, t_n) = \mathcal{D}((\mathtt{Sg}\ t_1 \cdots t_n)).$$

Then it is obvious that

$$\mathcal{D}_F((\mathtt{Sg}\ t_1 \cdots t_n)) = \mathcal{DSG}(\mathcal{D}_F(t_1), \cdots, \mathcal{D}_F(t_n)). \tag{3}$$

Property 4.2 (Laziness). For any term $t = (\mathtt{Sg}\ t_1 \cdots t_n)$, if

$$\mathcal{R}_c(\mathcal{D}_F(t)) = \mathcal{DSG}(\mathcal{D}_F(t_1), \cdots, \mathcal{R}_c(\mathcal{D}_F(t_i)), \cdots, \mathcal{D}_F(t_n)) \tag{4}$$

then there exists j, such that

$$\mathcal{R}_m(t) = (\mathtt{Sg}\ t_1 \cdots \mathcal{R}_m(t_j) \cdots t_n).$$

That is to say, the sugar $\mathtt{Sg}$ will not be expanded in the mixed language, if the reduction occurs at one of the expanded $\mathcal{D}_F(t_i)$ in $\mathcal{D}_F(t)$.

Proof. Equations 3 and 4 imply

$$\mathcal{DSG}(t_1/v_1, \cdots, t_n/v_n) = C_c[t_i]$$

where the j-th sub-metavariable is v_k when $\mathcal{D}_F(t_k)$ is a value, or t_k otherwise.

Then according to the first branch of function $\mathtt{getRules}$, the context rule $[t_i := C]\, D_{\mathrm{LHS}}$ will be obtained, where $D_{\mathrm{LHS}} = (\mathtt{Sg}\ t_1/v_1\ cdots\ t_n/v_n)$. Then for any k, such that $\mathcal{D}_F(t_k)$ is a value,

– if all t_k are also values, then based on the context rule above, equation $j = i$ holds;
– otherwise, simply assume that t_h is the only sub-term which is not a value, when $\mathcal{D}_F(t_k)$ is. Based on the function $\mathtt{getRules}$, one of the context rule before computing $[t_i := C]\, D_{\mathrm{LHS}}$ will make t_h be a context hole, equation $j = h$ holds. (If t_h is not the only one, there must be one of t_h corresponding to the former context hole.)   □

5   Case Studies

We have implemented our lazy desugaring system in PLT Redex [5], a semantic engineering tool based on reduction semantics [7]. It provides a useful environment for combining the core language's semantics with rules from our algorithm.

We have successfully tested a bunch of syntactic sugars with our system. In this paper, for the lack of space, we only describe the core algorithm of our method in Sect. 4, but other features like hygienic, (mutual) recursive, pattern based can be handled by simple extensions of our basic algorithm.

5.1 Simple Examples

We have seen several simple sugars in our running example, and we will give other examples to demonstrate some interesting observations.

It is not hard to convert from SKI combinator to call-by-need lambda calculus. Consider the S combinator as an example, which can be defined as a sugar below.

$$\text{S} \stackrel{def}{=\!=} (\lambda_N \ (\text{x}_1 \ \text{x}_2 \ \text{x}_3) \ (\text{x}_1 \ \text{x}_3 \ (\text{x}_2 \ \text{x}_3)))$$

The interesting point is that we can use the call-by-need lambda calculus to force an expansion of a sugar in case we need it. For example, we may consider defining S in another form:

$$(\text{S} \ t_1 \ t_2 \ t_3) \stackrel{def}{=\!=} (\text{let} \ (\text{x} \ t_3) \ (t_1 \ \text{x} \ (t_2 \ \text{x}))).$$

In this case, the expansion of S will not happen until enough sub-terms have been normal-formed, which is different from the original combinator.

Similarly, recall the *And* sugar defined before. We may redefine it with call-by-need lambda calculus as follows.

$$\text{ForceAnd} \stackrel{def}{=\!=} (\lambda_N \ (\text{x}_1 \ \text{x}_2) \ (\text{if} \ \text{x}_1 \ \text{x}_2 \ \#\text{f}))$$

Given any program with $(\text{ForceAnd} \ t_1 \ t_2)$ as its sub-term, when $(\text{ForceAnd} \ t_1 \ t_2)$ should be reduced, the evaluation sequence will look like this.

$$(\ldots \ (\text{ForceAnd} \ t_1 \ t_2) \ \ldots)$$
$$\longrightarrow (\ldots \ ((\lambda_N \ (\text{x}_1 \ \text{x}_2) \ (\text{if} \ \text{x}_1 \ \text{x}_2 \ \#\text{f})) \ t_1 \ t_2) \ \ldots)$$
$$\longrightarrow (\ldots \ (\text{if} \ t_1 \ t_2 \ \#\text{f}) \ \ldots)$$
$$\longrightarrow \ldots$$

5.2 More Examples

Since the essential idea of our approach is not complex, it is possible to extend the basic algorithm to handle many kinds of complex sugar features. In this section, we give two examples of hygienic sugar and higher-order sugar.

Given a typical hygienic sugar

$$(\text{HygienicAdd} \ t_1 \ t_2) \stackrel{def}{=\!=} (\text{let} \ (\text{x} \ t_1) \ (+ \ \text{x} \ t_2)),$$

for the program

$$(\text{let} \ (\text{x} \ 2) \ (\text{HygienicAdd} \ 1 \ \text{x})),$$

the existing resugaring approach [15] uses an abstract syntax DAG to distinguish different variables x in the desugared term

$$(\text{let} \ (\text{x} \ 2) \ (\text{let} \ (\text{x} \ 1) \ (+ \ \text{x} \ \text{x}))).$$

But in our lazy desugaring setting, the `HygienicAdd` sugar is not expanded until necessary. The sequence will be as follows.

$$(\text{let } (x\ 2)\ (\text{HygienicAdd } 1\ x))$$
$$\longrightarrow (\text{HygienicAdd } 1\ 2)$$
$$\longrightarrow (+\ 1\ 2)$$
$$\longrightarrow 3$$

Higher-order functions from the functional language are introduced to many other programming languages as important features. We attempt to process the higher-order sugar with our method, for example, with the sugar[3]

```
(Filter t (list v₁ v₂ ...))  ≝  (let (f t)
                                    (if (f v₁)
                                        (cons v₁ (Filter f (list v₂ ...)))
                                        (Filter f (list v₂ ...)))))
            (Filter t (list))  ≝  (list)
```

and we obtain the following sequence with the example.

```
      (Filter (λ (x) (and (> x 1) (< x 4))) (list 1 2 3 4))
  ⟶  (Filter (λ (x) (and (> x 1) (< x 4))) (list 2 3 4))
  ⟶  (cons 2 (Filter (λ (x) (and (> x 1) (< x 4))) (list 3 4)))
  ⟶  (cons 2 (cons 3 (Filter (λ (x) (and (> x 1) (< x 4))) (list 4))))
  ⟶  (cons 2 (cons 3 (Filter (λ (x) (and (> x 1) (< x 4))) (list))))
  ⟶  (cons 2 (cons 3 (list)))
  ⟶  (cons 2 (list 3))
  ⟶  (list 2 3)
```

6   Related Work

As we discussed before, our work is closely related to the pioneering work of *resugaring* [14]. The idea of "tagging" and "reverse desugaring" is a clear explanation of "resugaring", but it becomes very complex when the RHS of the desugaring rule becomes complex. Our approach does not need reverse desugaring, which is both more powerful and efficient. For hygienic sugar, compared with the approach of using DAG to solve the variable binding problem [15], our approach of "lazy desugaring" can achieve natural hygiene with a hygienic expansion.

Macros as multi-stage computations [10] is a work related to our lazy expansion of sugars. Some other work [16] on multi-stage programming [18] indicates that it is useful for implementing domain-specific languages. However, multi-stage programming is a meta-programming method, which mainly aims for run-time code generation and optimization. In contrast, our lazy desugaring method treats sugars as part of a mixed language, rather than separating them by staging. Moreover, lazy desugaring gives us a chance to derive evaluation rules of sugars, which is an advantage over multi-stage programming.

---

[3] The expression 't ...' means zero or more t as a pattern.

The lazy desugaring used to be explored [3]. They model the expansion with explicit substitutions [1] and delay the expansion by subtle rules. They also declare the benefit to avoid unnecessary expansions. While their main contribution is a formal semantics of macro expansion, the macros in a program do not preserve their original formats. In contrast, our lazy desugaring can preserve the sugars as long as they do not have to be expanded.

There is a long history of hygienic macro expansion [12], and a formal specific hygiene definition was given by specifying the binding scopes of macros [11]. Another formal definition of the hygienic macro [2] is based on nominal logic [9]. Instead of designing something special for the hygienic sugar as by [15], our method can be easily combined with the existing hygienic method, because the reverse desugaring is not needed.

Our implementation is built upon PLT Redex [5], a semantics engineering tool, but it is possible to implement our approach with other semantics engineering tools [17,19] which aim to test or verify the semantics of languages. Their methods can be easily combined with our approach to implementing more general rule derivation. *Ziggurat* [8] is a semantics extension framework, also allowing defining new macros with semantics based on existing terms of a language. It should be useful for static analysis of the mixed language in our approach.

7   Conclusion

In this paper, we propose a novel lazy desugaring method which smartly evaluates the programs with sugar. Our algorithm automatically generates the mixed language semantics from the core language and the sugar definition, and achieves "resugaring" by outputting the evaluation sequence of a program with sugars based on the mixed language semantics. In our method, the most important point is delaying the expansion of syntactic sugars by deriving suitable context rules, which decide whether the mixed language should reduce the sub-term by reduction rules of the core language or expand a sugar term. Our approach is flexible for more extensions.

There are some interesting future works. One is to extend the framework from evaluation to other language components such as type system, analyzer, and optimizer. Also, we find it possible to derive stand-alone evaluation rules for the surface language by means similar to how we calculate context rules. This would make it more convenient to develop domain-specific languages. The usefulness of lazy desugaring's expressiveness is also worth exploring, since some ill-formed sugar definitions[4] for the general desugaring can be handled by lazy desugaring.

---

[4] For example, $(\text{Odd } t) \overset{def}{=\!=} (\text{let } (\text{x } t) \ (\text{if } (> \text{x } 0) \ (\text{not } (\text{Odd } (- \text{x } 1))) \ \text{\#f}))$ is ill-formed because of expansion without termination, but can be avoided by lazy desugaring.

References

1. Abadi, M., Cardelli, L., Curien, P.L., Levy, J.J.: Explicit substitutions. In: Proceedings of the 17th ACM SIGPLAN-SIGACT Symposium on Principles of Programming Languages, POPL 1990, pp. 31–46. Association for Computing Machinery, New York (1989). https://doi.org/10.1145/96709.96712
2. Adams, M.D.: Towards the essence of hygiene. SIGPLAN Not. **50**(1), 457–469 (2015). https://doi.org/10.1145/2775051.2677013
3. Bove, A., Arbilla, L.: A confluent calculus of macro expansion and evaluation. In: Proceedings of the 1992 ACM Conference on LISP and Functional Programming, LFP 1992, pp. 278–287. Association for Computing Machinery, New York (1992). https://doi.org/10.1145/141471.141562
4. Culpepper, R., Felleisen, M., Flatt, M., Krishnamurthi, S.: From Macros to DSLs: the evolution of racket. In: Lerner, B.S., Bodík, R., Krishnamurthi, S. (eds.) 3rd Summit on Advances in Programming Languages, SNAPL 2019, Providence, RI, USA, 16–17 May 2019. LIPIcs, vol. 136, pp. 5:1–5:19. Schloss Dagstuhl - Leibniz-Zentrum für Informatik (2019)
5. Felleisen, M., Findler, R.B., Flatt, M.: Semantics Engineering with PLT Redex, 1st edn. The MIT Press (2009)
6. Felleisen, M., et al.: A programmable programming language. Commun. ACM **61**(3), 62–71 (2018)
7. Felleisen, M., Hieb, R.: The revised report on the syntactic theories of sequential control and state. Theor. Comput. Sci. **103**(2), 235–271 (1992). https://doi.org/10.1016/0304-3975(92)90014-7
8. Fisher, D., Shivers, O.: Static analysis for syntax objects. In: Proceedings of the Eleventh ACM SIGPLAN International Conference on Functional Programming, ICFP 2006, pp. 111–121. Association for Computing Machinery, New York (2006). https://doi.org/10.1145/1159803.1159817
9. Gabbay, M.J., Pitts, A.M.: A new approach to abstract syntax with variable binding. Form. Asp. Comput. **13**(3–5), 341–363 (2002). https://doi.org/10.1007/s001650200016
10. Ganz, S.E., Sabry, A., Taha, W.: Macros as multi-stage computations: type-safe, generative, binding macros in MacroML. In: Proceedings of the Sixth ACM SIGPLAN International Conference on Functional Programming, ICFP 2001, pp. 74–85. Association for Computing Machinery, New York (2001). https://doi.org/10.1145/507635.507646
11. Herman, D., Wand, M.: A theory of hygienic macros. In: Drossopoulou, S. (ed.) ESOP 2008. LNCS, vol. 4960, pp. 48–62. Springer, Heidelberg (2008). https://doi.org/10.1007/978-3-540-78739-6_4
12. Kohlbecker, E., Friedman, D.P., Felleisen, M., Duba, B.: Hygienic macro expansion. In: Proceedings of the 1986 ACM Conference on LISP and Functional Programming, LFP 1986, pp. 151–161. Association for Computing Machinery, New York (1986). https://doi.org/10.1145/319838.319859
13. Landin, P.J.: The mechanical evaluation of expressions. Comput. J. **6**(4), 308–320 (1964). https://doi.org/10.1093/comjnl/6.4.308
14. Pombrio, J., Krishnamurthi, S.: Resugaring: lifting evaluation sequences through syntactic sugar. SIGPLAN Not. **49**(6), 361–371 (2014). https://doi.org/10.1145/2666356.2594319
15. Pombrio, J., Krishnamurthi, S.: Hygienic resugaring of compositional desugaring. IGPLAN Not. **50**(9), 75–87 (2015). https://doi.org/10.1145/2858949.2784755

16. Rompf, T., Odersky, M.: Lightweight modular staging: a pragmatic approach to runtime code generation and compiled DSLs. SIGPLAN Not. **46**(2), 127–136 (2010). https://doi.org/10.1145/1942788.1868314
17. Roşu, G., Şerbănuţă, T.F.: An overview of the K semantic framework. J. Logic Algebraic Program. **79**(6), 397–434 (2010)
18. Taha, W.: A Gentle Introduction to Multi-stage Programming, pp. 30–50, January 2003
19. Vergu, V., Neron, P., Visser, E.: DynSem: a DSL for dynamic semantics specification. In: Fernández, M. (ed.) 26th International Conference on Rewriting Techniques and Applications (RTA 2015). Leibniz International Proceedings in Informatics (LIPIcs), vol. 36, pp. 365–378. Schloss Dagstuhl-Leibniz-Zentrum fuer Informatik, Dagstuhl (2015). https://doi.org/10.4230/LIPIcs.RTA.2015.365. http://drops.dagstuhl.de/opus/volltexte/2015/5208

On Transforming Cut- and Quantifier-Free Cyclic Proofs into Rewriting-Induction Proofs

Shujun Zhang[(⊠)] and Naoki Nishida[(⊠)]

Graduate School of Informatics, Nagoya University, Nagoya 4648601, Japan
shujun@trs.css.i.nagoya-u.ac.jp, nishida@i.nagoya-u.ac.jp

Abstract. An inductive definition set (IDS, for short) of first-order predicate logic can be transformed into a many-sorted term rewrite system (TRS, for short) such that a quantifier-free sequent is valid w.r.t. the IDS if and only if a term equation representing the sequent is an inductive theorem of the TRS. In this paper, to compare rewriting induction (RI, for short) with cyclic proof systems, under certain assumptions, we show that if a sequent has a cut- and quantifier-free cyclic proof, then there exists an RI proof for a term equation of the sequent. To this end, we propose a transformation of a cut- and quantifier-free cyclic proof of the sequent into an RI proof for the corresponding equation.

Keywords: Term rewriting · Rewriting induction · Cyclic proof · Inductive theorem proving · Sequent calculus

1 Introduction

Inductive theorem proving is well investigated in functional programming and term rewriting. In the field of term rewriting, *rewriting induction* [16] (RI, for short) is one of the most powerful principles to prove equations to be *inductive theorems*. Here, an equation $s \approx t$ of terms is called an *inductive theorem* of a given (many-sorted) *term rewrite system* (TRS, for short) if the equation is inductively valid w.r.t. the reduction of the TRS. RI has been extended to several kinds of rewrite systems, e.g., *logically constrained term rewrite systems* [11] (LCTRS, for short) that are models of not only functional but also imperative programs [8].

RI consists of inference rules that are applied to RI processes $(\mathcal{E}, \mathcal{H})$, where $\mathcal{E}$ is a finite set of term equations and $\mathcal{H}$ is a TRS. The application of rewrite rules in $\mathcal{H}$ corresponds to the application of induction hypotheses to subsequent RI processes. Given a TRS $\mathcal{R}$ and a finite set $\mathcal{E}_0$ of term equations, we start with the initial RI process $(\mathcal{E}_0, \emptyset)$, and succeed in proving all equations in $\mathcal{E}_0$ to be inductive theorems of $\mathcal{R}$ if the initial process is reduced to $(\emptyset, \mathcal{H}')$ for some

This work was partially supported by JSPS KAKENHI Grant Number 18K11160. The first author was partially supported by *Aichi Scholarship Program*.

M. Hanus and A. Igarashi (Eds.): FLOPS 2022, LNCS 13215, pp. 262–281, 2022.
https://doi.org/10.1007/978-3-030-99461-7_15

TRS $\mathcal{H}'$, i.e., we find an *RI proof* $(\mathcal{E}_0, \emptyset) \Rightarrow \cdots \Rightarrow (\emptyset, \mathcal{H}')$, where $\Rightarrow$ denotes the application of RI inference rules.

A *cyclic proof system* [6] is a proof system in sequent-calculus style for first-order logics with *inductive predicates* which are defined by productions. In contrast to structural proofs which are (possibly infinite) derivation trees, cyclic proofs are finite derivation trees with back-links from *bud* nodes to inner nodes which are called *companions*. Such back-links allow explicit induction rules, making trees finite. For the last decade, cyclic proof systems have been well investigated for several logics, e.g., *separation logic* [17].

RI and cyclic proof systems have similar inference rules: Case analysis, the application of rules in given systems, generalization, and so on. RI is based on *implicit induction* by means of the application of rewrite rules representing induction hypotheses; the measure of the induction is the terminating reduction of the combined system of a given system and the induction hypotheses such as $\mathcal{R} \cup \mathcal{H}'$ above. Cyclic proofs have bud nodes that are connected with their companion, and the back-link corresponding to induction; the measure of the induction is that every (possibly infinite) path from the root passes infinitely many times through the application of the *case* rule which is based on the inductive definition of predicates.

From the above observation, RI and cyclic proof systems seem very similar and we are interested in differences between RI and cyclic proof systems. If RI and cyclic proof systems have the same proof power, then it would be easy to apply several developed techniques for one to the other; otherwise, we must be able to know something new for inductive theorem proving, e.g., one of them could be improved by the advantage of the other. For this reason, it is worth comparing RI and cyclic proof systems.

For the comparison, we need a common setting for target systems: RI proves given equations to be inductive theorems of a given TRS; cyclic proof systems prove validity of given sequents w.r.t. a given *inductive definition set* (IDS, for short) which is a set of productions of the form $\frac{A_1 \;\; \cdots \;\; A_m}{A}$. For a common setting, it has been shown in [26,27] that a (A1) *GSC-terminating* and (A2) *orthogonal* IDS Φ such that

(A3) there is no *ordinary* predicate in Φ, and
(A4) any variable in $A_1, \ldots, A_m$ appears in A for any production $\frac{A_1 \;\; \cdots \;\; A_m}{A} \in \Phi$,

can be transformed into a GSC-terminating confluent TRS $\mathcal{R}_\Phi$ such that a quantifier-free sequent $\Gamma \vdash \Delta$ is valid w.r.t. Φ if and only if the corresponding equation $\mathsf{seq}(\widehat{\Gamma}, \widecheck{\Delta}) \approx \top$ is an inductive theorem of $\mathcal{R}_\Phi \cup \mathcal{R}_{seq}$. Here, $\widehat{\Gamma}$ and $\widecheck{\Delta}$ are terms representing the conjunction and disjunction of formulas in Γ and Δ, respectively, $\mathcal{R}_{seq}$ is a TRS for seq, a TRS is called *GSC-terminating* if its termination is proved by the *generalized subterm criterion* [25, Theorem 33], and Φ is called *orthogonal* (*GSC-terminating*) if $\{A \to A_i \mid \frac{A_1 \;\; \cdots \;\; A_n}{A} \in \Phi, \; 1 \le i \le n\}$ is orthogonal (GSC-terminating) [27].

To compare RI with cyclic proof systems, we would like to show that a sequent $\Gamma \vdash \Delta$ has a cyclic proof if and only if there exists an RI proof for $\mathsf{seq}(\widehat{\Gamma}, \widecheck{\Delta}) \approx \top$.

To be more precise, we would like to transform cyclic proofs and RI proofs into each other. For a common setting of cyclic proof systems and RI, we employ the above transformation in [26, 27]. In the following, we use Φ and $\mathcal{R}_\Phi$ as an IDS with (A1)–(A4) and the TRS obtained from Φ by the transformation in [26, 27], respectively, without notice.

In this paper, for the goal above, we transform a quantifier-free cyclic proof into an RI proof. As in [26, 27], we assume (A1)–(A4). RI does not deal with quantifiers directly, while every variable is universally quantified. For this reason, we consider (A5) quantifier-free sequents and cyclic proofs. As the first step of the transformation, we assume all of the following in addition to (A1)–(A5):

(A6) Cyclic proofs are *cut-free*,

(A7) each inductive definition has at most one premise,

(A8) for any sequent $\Gamma \vdash \Delta$ in a cyclic proof, the multiset Γ is empty or singleton and the multiset Δ is singleton,[1]

(A9) cyclic proofs do not include the application of $(\wedge L_1)$, $(\wedge L_2)$, $(\vee R_1)$, $(\vee R_2)$, and (WL), and

(A10) any companion in cyclic proofs is the conclusion of an instance of the *case* rule which corresponds to a case distinction depending on rules in Φ.

Note that (A8) implies (A7), but we explicitly assume (A7) to emphasize it.

The application of some sequent-calculus rules replaces a sequent by two sequents. To simulate such a replacement by an RI inference step, we need rewrite rules because RI inference rules replace equations with others by referring to rewrite rules. Sequent-calculus rules (Axiom), $(\vee L)$, and $(\wedge R)$ are represented by rewrite rules that are inductive theorems of $\mathcal{R}_\Phi \cup \mathcal{R}_{seq}$. For this reason, from (Axiom), $(\vee L)$, and $(\wedge R)$, we generate a GSC-terminating TRS $\mathcal{R}_{scr}$ such that an equation is an inductive theorem of $\mathcal{R}_\Phi \cup \mathcal{R}_{seq} \cup \mathcal{R}_{scr}$ if and only if the equation is an inductive theorem of $\mathcal{R}_\Phi \cup \mathcal{R}_{seq}$ (Sect. 3.2). This enables us to use $\mathcal{R}_\Phi \cup \mathcal{R}_{seq} \cup \mathcal{R}_{scr}$ instead of $\mathcal{R}_\Phi \cup \mathcal{R}_{seq}$ to prove equations to be inductive theorems. On the other hand, none of rewrite rules for $(\wedge L_1)$, $(\wedge L_2)$, $(\vee R_1)$, $(\vee R_2)$, and (WL) is an inductive theorem of $\mathcal{R}_\Phi \cup \mathcal{R}_{seq}$. For this reason, we assume (A9). Rewrite rules representing the *cut* rule and some other inference rules for sequent calculus may violate termination of $\mathcal{R}_\Phi \cup \mathcal{R}_{seq} \cup \mathcal{R}_{scr}$. For this reason, we assume (A6) and (A8), while (A8) sets a limit to the use of inference rules of sequent calculus in cyclic proofs.

As our main result, we transform a cyclic proof for a sequent $F \vdash F'$ into an RI proof $(\{\,\mathsf{seq}(\widetilde{F}, \widetilde{F'}) \approx \top\,\}, \emptyset) \Rightarrow^* (\emptyset, \mathcal{H}')$ for some TRS $\mathcal{H}'$ (Sect. 4), where $\widetilde{F}, \widetilde{F'}$ are terms representing formulas F, F', respectively. The transformation starts with the root of the cyclic proof, and proceeds step-by-step. We transform a *bud* node into two continuous RI steps of rules SIMPLIFY and DELETE. For the step of SIMPLIFY at $(\mathcal{E}, \mathcal{H})$, the *companion* has to be included in $\mathcal{H}$ as a rewrite rule. To add the companion to $\mathcal{H}$, EXPAND has been applied in advance in order to transform the companion into an RI step. For this reason, we assume (A10).

---

[1] This assumption indirectly implies that none of $(\neg L)$, $(\neg R)$, (CL), (CR), (WR), (PL), and (PR) is used in cyclic proofs.

We have technical reasons of the assumptions (A1)–(A10), and we will discuss the possibility of relaxing them in the conclusion of this paper (Sect. 5).

The contribution of this paper is the first step to compare RI with cyclic proof systems. To the best of our knowledge, this is the first work for the comparison. RI and cyclic proof systems have similar inference rules, but transformations between RI proofs and cyclic proofs are not so trivial.

Related Work. A related work is a comparison between RI and Hoare-triple proofs [13]: A proof of Hoare triples for a simple imperative program is equivalent to an RI proof w.r.t. the LCTRS obtained from the imperative program. Proofs of Hoare triples are not based on induction, while they often rely on loop invariants. The other related work is the comparison between structural proofs and cyclic induction [21]. This work may help us in the sense to compare RI and structural proofs; instead of comparing RI and cyclic proof systems, we may compare RI and structural proofs and then we may be able to indirectly compare RI and cyclic proof systems. In [20], the relationship between term- and formula-based induction principles has been discussed. This work would help us e.g., drop the assumptions in this paper.

2   Preliminaries

In this section, we briefly recall basic notions and notations of many-sorted term rewriting [22], RI [2,16], and cyclic proofs [6]. Basic familiarity with term rewriting is assumed [3,15].

2.1   Many-Sorted Term Rewriting

Let S be a set of *sorts*. Throughout the paper, we use $\mathcal{X}$ as a family of S-sorted sets of variables: $\mathcal{X} = \biguplus_{s \in S} \mathcal{X}_s$. Each *function symbol* f in a *signature* Σ is equipped with its sort declaration $\alpha_1 \times \cdots \times \alpha_n \to \alpha$, written as $f :$ $\alpha_1 \times \cdots \times \alpha_n \to \alpha$, where $\alpha_1, \ldots, \alpha_n, \alpha \in S$ and $n \geq 0$. The set of (well-sorted) *terms* is denoted by $T(\Sigma, \mathcal{X})$. The set of *ground* terms, $T(\Sigma, \emptyset)$, is abbreviated to $T(\Sigma)$. The set of variables appearing in any of terms $t_1, \ldots, t_n$ is denoted by $Var(t_1, \ldots, t_n)$. Let t be a term. The set of positions of t is denoted by $\mathcal{P}os(t)$. The function symbol at the *root* position ε of t is denoted by $root(t)$. The *subterm* of t at a position $p \in \mathcal{P}os(t)$ is denoted by $t|_p$; we write $t \trianglerighteq t|_p$, and $t \rhd t|_p$ if $p \neq \varepsilon$. Given a term s, we denote by $t[s]_p$ the term obtained from t by replacing the subterm $t|_p$ at $p \in \mathcal{P}os(t)$ by s.

A *substitution* σ is a sort-preserving mapping from variables to terms such that the number of variables x with $\sigma(x) \neq x$ is finite, which is naturally extended over terms. The *domain* and *range* of σ are denoted by $\mathcal{D}om(\sigma)$ and $\mathcal{R}an(\sigma)$, respectively. We may denote σ by $\{x_1 \mapsto t_1, \ldots, x_n \mapsto t_n\}$ if $\mathcal{D}om(\sigma) = \{x_1, \ldots, x_n\}$ and $\sigma(x_i) = t_i$ for all $1 \leq i \leq n$. The application of a substitution σ to a term t, $\sigma(t)$, is abbreviated to $t\sigma$, and $t\sigma$ is called an *instance* of t. A *most general unifier* of terms s, t is denoted by $mgu(s, t)$.

An S-sorted *term rewrite system* (TRS, for short) is a set of rewrite rules of the form $\ell \to r$ such that the sorts of the LHS ℓ and the RHS r coincide, ℓ is not a variable, and $Var(\ell) \supseteq Var(r)$. The *reduction relation* $\to_{\mathcal{R}}$ of a TRS $\mathcal{R}$ is defined as follows: $s \to_{\mathcal{R}} t$ if and only if there exist a rewrite rule $\ell \to r \in \mathcal{R}$, a position $p \in \mathcal{P}os(s)$, and a substitution θ such that $s|_p = \ell\theta$ and $t = s[r\theta]_p$.

The sets of *defined symbols* and *constructors* of $\mathcal{R}$ are denoted by $\mathcal{D}_{\mathcal{R}}$ and $\mathcal{C}_{\mathcal{R}}$, respectively: $\mathcal{D}_{\mathcal{R}} = \{root(\ell) \mid \ell \to r \in \mathcal{R}\}$ and $\mathcal{C}_{\mathcal{R}} = \Sigma \setminus \mathcal{D}_{\mathcal{R}}$. Terms in $T(\mathcal{C}_{\mathcal{R}}, \mathcal{X})$ are called *constructor terms* (of $\mathcal{R}$). A substitution σ is called *ground constructor* if $\mathcal{R}an(\sigma) \subseteq T(\mathcal{C}_{\mathcal{R}})$. A term t is called *basic* if t is of the form $f(t_1, \ldots, t_n)$ such that $f \in \mathcal{D}_{\mathcal{R}}$ and $t_1, \ldots, t_n \in T(\mathcal{C}_{\mathcal{R}}, \mathcal{X})$. A position p of a term t is called *basic* if $t|_p$ is basic. The set of basic positions of t is denoted by $\mathcal{B}(t)$. $\mathcal{R}$ is called *quasi-reductive* if every ground basic term is reducible.

We denote the set of *dependency pairs* of $\mathcal{R}$ by $DP(\mathcal{R})$, and the *estimated dependency graph* of $\mathcal{R}$ by $EDG(\mathcal{R})$ (cf. [15, Section 5.4.1]). As a termination criterion, we use a simplified variant of the *generalized subterm criterion* [25]. A *multi-projection* π for a set $\mathcal{F}$ of function symbols is a mapping that assigns every symbol $f \in \mathcal{F}$ a non-empty multiset of its argument positions. We extend π for terms as follows:

- $\pi(t) = \pi(t_{i_1}) \oplus \cdots \oplus \pi(t_{i_m})$ if $t = f(t_1, \ldots, t_n)$, $f \in \mathcal{F}$, and $\pi(f) = \{i_1, \ldots, i_m\} \neq \emptyset$, and
- $\pi(t) = \{t\}$, otherwise,

where $\oplus$ is the union of multisets. For a binary relation $\sqsupseteq$ on terms, we denote the multiset extension of $\sqsupseteq$ by $\sqsupseteq^{mul}$, and we write $s \sqsupseteq^\pi t$ if $\pi(s) \sqsupseteq^{mul} \pi(t)$. $\mathcal{R}$ is said to be *GSC-terminating* if for every cycle $\mathcal{P}$ in $EDG(\mathcal{R})$ there exists a multi-projection π for $\mathcal{D}_{\mathcal{R}}^{\#}$ such that $\mathcal{P} \subseteq \unrhd^\pi$ and $\mathcal{P} \cap \rhd^\pi \neq \emptyset$ [27]. Note that GSC-termination of $\mathcal{R}$ implies termination of $\mathcal{R}$.

2.2   Rewriting Induction

Our formulation of RI [4,16] with the *generalization* (cf. [8]) follows [1,19]. In the RI setting below, $\mathcal{R}$ is assumed to be terminating and quasi-reductive.

An *equation* (over a signature Σ) is a pair of terms, written as $s \approx t$, such that $s, t \in T(\Sigma, \mathcal{X})$. We write $s \simeq t$ to denote either $s \approx t$ or $t \approx s$. An equation $s \approx t$ is called an *inductive theorem* (of $\mathcal{R}$) if $s\theta \leftrightarrow^*_{\mathcal{R}} t\theta$ for all ground constructor substitutions θ with $Var(s, t) \subseteq \mathcal{D}om(\theta)$.

A pair $(\mathcal{E}, \mathcal{H})$ consisting of an equation set $\mathcal{E}$ and a TRS $\mathcal{H}$ is called an *RI process*. Inference rules of RI defined below replace an equation by some equations, drop an equation, and insert some equations. From viewpoint of the replacement, to explicitly show descendant/ancestor relationships between equations, we attach to each equation $s \approx t$ a unique label ρ, written $(\rho)\, s \approx t$, that is a sequence of non-zero integers such as positions of terms;[2] We may use nega-

---

[2] $\mathcal{E}$ of an RI process $(\mathcal{E}, \mathcal{H})$ is a set, but due to attached labels, $\mathcal{E}$ may contain an equation $s \approx t$ as $\rho_1 : s \approx t$ and $\rho_2 : s \approx t$ such that $\rho_1 \neq \rho_2$. This is not a problem because we can apply the same inference rules to both equations in order.

tive integers for freshly introduced labels. For case distinctions based on rewrite rules, we assume some fixed order of rewrite rules for each function symbol f.

The basic inference rules of *rewriting induction* are defined over RI processes as follows:

SIMPLIFY $(\mathcal{E} \uplus \{(\rho)\ s \simeq t\}, \mathcal{H}) \Rightarrow_s (\mathcal{E} \cup \{(\rho.1)\ s' \approx t\}, \mathcal{H}),$[3] where $s \rightarrow_{\mathcal{R} \cup \mathcal{H}} s'$.

DELETE $(\mathcal{E} \uplus \{(\rho)\ s \approx t\}, \mathcal{H}) \Rightarrow_d (\mathcal{E}, \mathcal{H}),$ where $s \leftrightarrow^*_{\mathcal{R} \cup \mathcal{E}} t$.[4]

EXPAND $(\mathcal{E} \uplus \{(\rho)\ s \simeq t\}, \mathcal{H}) \Rightarrow_e (\mathcal{E} \cup Expd_p(s, t), \mathcal{H} \cup \{s \rightarrow t\}),$ where $p \in \mathcal{B}(s)$, $\mathcal{R} \cup \mathcal{H} \cup \{s \rightarrow t\}$ is terminating, and $Expd_p(s, t) = \{(\rho.i)\ (s[r]_p)\sigma \approx t\sigma \mid \sigma = mgu(s|_p, \ell),\ \ell \rightarrow r \in \mathcal{R}$ is the i-th rule of $root(s|_p)\}$.

GENERALIZE $(\mathcal{E} \uplus \{(\rho)\ s\theta \simeq t\theta\}, \mathcal{H}) \Rightarrow_g (\mathcal{E} \cup \{(\rho.1)\ s \approx t\}, \mathcal{H})$.

POSTULATE $(\mathcal{E}, \mathcal{H}) \Rightarrow_p (\mathcal{E} \cup \{(\delta.i)\ s_i \approx t_i \mid 1 \le i \le n\}, \mathcal{H}),$ where δ is a fresh negative integer to indicate that $s_1 \approx t_1, \ldots, s_n \approx t_n$ are newly introduced.[5]

We denote $\Rightarrow_s \cup \Rightarrow_d \cup \Rightarrow_e \cup \Rightarrow_g \cup \Rightarrow_p$ by $\Rightarrow$. In addition, $\Rightarrow_s$ with $\rightarrow_{\mathcal{R}}$ and $\rightarrow_{\mathcal{H}}$ for side condition $\rightarrow_{\mathcal{R} \cup \mathcal{H}}$ are denoted by $\Rightarrow_{sR}$ and $\Rightarrow_{sH}$, respectively. The proof based on RI starts with the initial RI process $(\mathcal{E}, \emptyset)$ and proceeds by applying the inference rules above to RI processes. We attach labels to equations in $\mathcal{E}$ as follows: If $\mathcal{E}$ is singleton, then $\mathcal{E} = \{(\varepsilon)\ s \approx t\}$, and otherwise, $\mathcal{E} = \{(1)\ s_1 \approx t_1, (2)\ s_2 \approx t_2, \ldots\}$. A sequence $(\mathcal{E}, \emptyset) = (\mathcal{E}_0, \mathcal{H}_0) \Rightarrow (\mathcal{E}_1, \mathcal{H}_1) \Rightarrow \cdots \Rightarrow (\mathcal{E}_n, \mathcal{H}_n) = (\emptyset, \mathcal{H})$ is called an *RI proof* (of $\mathcal{E}$).

Theorem 2.1 ([1,16]). *For a finite set $\mathcal{E}$ of equations, if $(\mathcal{E}, \emptyset) \Rightarrow^* (\emptyset, \mathcal{H})$ for some TRS $\mathcal{H}$, then every equation in $\mathcal{E}$ is an inductive theorem of $\mathcal{R}$.*

Example 2.2. Let us consider the signature $\Sigma_1 = \{+ : nat \times nat \rightarrow nat,\ s : nat \rightarrow nat,\ 0 : nat\}$ and the TRS $\mathcal{R}_1 = \{0 + y \rightarrow y,\ s(x) + y \rightarrow s(x + y)\}$ representing addition over natural numbers. Using RI, we can prove that $x + 0 \approx x$ is an inductive theorem of $\mathcal{R}_1$ as follows:

$$(\{(\varepsilon)\ x + 0 \approx x\}, \emptyset) \Rightarrow_e (\{(1)\ 0 \approx 0, (2)\ s(x_1 + 0) \approx s(x_1)\}, \{(\varepsilon)\ x + 0 \rightarrow x\})$$
$$\Rightarrow_d (\{(2)\ s(x_1 + 0) \approx s(x_1)\}, \qquad \{(\varepsilon)\ x + 0 \rightarrow x\})$$
$$\Rightarrow_{sH} (\{(2.1)\ s(x_1) \approx s(x_1)\}, \qquad \{(\varepsilon)\ x + 0 \rightarrow x\})$$
$$\Rightarrow_d (\ \emptyset, \qquad\qquad\qquad \{(\varepsilon)\ x + 0 \rightarrow x\})$$

2.3 First-Order Formulas with Inductive Definition Sets

In the rest of this paper, we consider a signature Σ with sorts $\mathcal{S} \supseteq \{bool\}$ such that true, false : $bool \in \Sigma$. A symbol $P : \alpha_1 \times \cdots \times \alpha_n \rightarrow bool \in \Sigma$ is called a *predicate symbol*. A term $P(t_1, \ldots, t_n)$ with predicate symbol $P : \alpha_1 \times \cdots \times \alpha_n \rightarrow bool$ is called an *atomic formula*. For brevity, we assume that $\mathcal{S} = \{\alpha, bool\}$, and every predicate symbol P has sort $\alpha \times \cdots \times \alpha \rightarrow bool$. In addition, we do not deal with *ordinary* predicates but *inductive* predicates as in [26,27].

---

[3] We may reuse (ρ) instead of $(\rho.1)$.

[4] We use a simplified side condition, which is enough for our purpose.

[5] We may use (1)–(n) instead of $(\delta.1)$–$(\delta.n)$ if none of (1)–(n) is used in $\mathcal{E}$.

An *inductive definition set* (IDS, for short) Φ over Σ is a finite set of *productions* of the form $\dfrac{A_1 \quad \cdots \quad A_m}{A}$, where $A, A_1, \ldots, A_m$ are atomic formulas over Σ. We denote the set of productions for a predicate symbol P by $\Phi|_P$: $\Phi|_P = \{\frac{A_1 \cdots A_m}{A} \in \Phi \mid root(A) = P\}$. We say that Φ is *orthogonal* (*GSC-terminating*, resp.) if $\{A \to A_i \mid \frac{A_1 \cdots A_n}{A} \in \Phi,\ 1 \leq i \leq n\}$ is orthogonal (GSC-terminating, resp.). In the rest of this paper, we assume that (A4) and (A7), i.e., every production in Φ is of the form either $\frac{}{A}$ or $\frac{A'}{A}$ such that $\mathcal{V}ar(A) \supseteq \mathcal{V}ar(A')$. For brevity, we allow A' to be true, writing both $\frac{}{A}$ as $\frac{A'}{A}$.

Example 2.3 ([6]). Let us consider the signature $\Sigma_2 = \{\ 0 : nat,\ s : nat \to nat,\ \text{true}, \text{false} : bool,\ \text{E}, \text{O}, \text{N} : nat \to bool\ \}$ and the following inductive definition set:

$$\Phi_2 = \left\{ \quad \frac{}{\text{N}(0)} \quad \frac{\text{N}(x)}{\text{N}(\text{s}(x))} \quad \frac{}{\text{E}(0)} \quad \frac{\text{O}(x)}{\text{E}(\text{s}(x))} \quad \frac{\text{E}(x)}{\text{O}(\text{s}(x))} \quad \right\}$$

Note that the symbols E, O, and N stand for predicates *Even*, *Odd*, and *Nat*, respectively. This IDS is orthogonal and GSC-terminating.

We now consider standard first-order quantifier-free formulas over Σ. Structures for Σ are irrelevant because we do not deal with any *ordinary predicate*. For this reason, we do not deal with any structure for Σ, and define the semantics of formulas over the term structure for Σ in the syntactic way as usual: For an IDS Φ and a ground formula F, we write $\Phi \models F$ if F holds w.r.t. Φ (cf. [26,27]). We say that a formula F' is *valid w.r.t.* Φ if $\Phi \models F'\theta$ for all ground substitutions θ with $\mathcal{D}om(\theta) \supseteq \mathcal{V}ar(F')$.

A sequent is a pair $\Gamma \vdash \Delta$ such that Γ, Δ are finite multisets of formulas, which can be written like lists of formulas. Recall that we assume (A8), i.e., both Γ and Δ are singleton. A sequent $F \vdash F'$ is said to be *valid* (w.r.t. Φ) if $\neg F \lor F'$ is valid w.r.t. Φ.

Example 2.4. For Φ_2 in Example 2.3, the sequent $\text{E}(x) \lor \text{O}(x) \vdash \text{N}(x)$ is valid w.r.t. Φ_2 because $\neg(\text{E}(x) \lor \text{O}(x)) \lor \text{N}(x)$ is valid w.r.t. Φ_2.

2.4   Cyclic Proofs

In this section, we consider proofs in the sequent-calculus style. We follow the formulation in [6] to define cyclic proofs. Thanks to our assumptions (A8) and (A10), we do not have to consider *infinitely progressing traces* and simplify the definition of cyclic proofs: Every infinite path of cyclic proofs we deal with has exactly one trace, and every companion goes through a *progressing point* which is the conclusion of (Case P) below.

Due to (A8), we consider simplified rules for sequent calculus illustrated in Fig. 1, while none of (WL), ($\land$L$_1$), ($\land$L$_2$), ($\lor$R$_1$), and ($\lor$R$_2$) is used in cyclic proofs due to (A9). For example, we do not consider the following full version of ($\lor$L):

$$\frac{\Gamma, F_1 \vdash \Delta \quad \Gamma', F_2 \vdash \Delta'}{\Gamma, \Gamma', F_1 \lor F_2 \vdash \Delta, \Delta'}\ (\lor\text{L})$$

$$\frac{\Gamma, F_1 \vdash \Delta \quad \Gamma', F_2 \vdash \Delta'}{\Gamma, \Gamma', F_1 \vee F_2 \vdash \Delta, \Delta'} \ (\vee L)$$

$$\frac{}{F \vdash F} \ (\text{Axiom}) \qquad \frac{F \vdash F'}{F\theta \vdash F'\theta} \ (\text{Subst}) \qquad \frac{\vdash F'}{F \vdash F'} \ (\text{WL})$$

$$\frac{F_1 \vdash F}{F_1 \wedge F_2 \vdash F} \ (\wedge L_1) \qquad \frac{F \vdash F_1}{F \vdash F_1 \vee F_2} \ (\vee R_1) \qquad \frac{F_1 \vdash F \quad F_2 \vdash F}{F_1 \vee F_2 \vdash F} \ (\vee L)$$

$$\frac{F_2 \vdash F}{F_1 \wedge F_2 \vdash F} \ (\wedge L_2) \qquad \frac{F \vdash F_2}{F \vdash F_1 \vee F_2} \ (\vee R_2) \qquad \frac{F \vdash F_1 \quad F \vdash F_2}{F \vdash F_1 \wedge F_2} \ (\wedge R)$$

Fig. 1. Sequent-calculus rules considered in this paper.

Instead, we use the simplified version in Fig. 1, which is derived by ($\vee$L) above and (CR) ($\frac{\Gamma \vdash F, F, \Delta}{\Gamma \vdash F, \Delta}$).

The rule of applying a production in Φ is defined as follows:

$$\frac{}{F \vdash P(t_1, \ldots, t_n)\theta} \ (\text{App } P_i) \qquad \frac{F \vdash A\theta}{F \vdash P(u_1, \ldots, u_n)\theta} \ (\text{App } P_j)$$

where $\frac{}{P(t_1, \ldots, t_n)}, \frac{A}{P(u_1, \ldots, u_n)} \in \Phi$ are the i- and j-th rules of P, respectively.

The rule for case distinctions based on productions in Φ is defined as follows:

$$\frac{A_1 \vdash F\{y_j \mapsto t_{1,j} \mid 1 \le j \le n\} \quad \ldots \quad A_k \vdash F\{y_j \mapsto t_{k,j} \mid 1 \le j \le n\}}{P(y_1, \ldots, y_n) \vdash F} \ (\text{Case } P)$$

where $\Phi|_P = \{\frac{A_i}{P(t_{i,1}, \ldots, t_{i,n})} \mid 1 \le i \le k\}$ for some k, and $\frac{A_i}{P(t_{i,1}, \ldots, t_{i,n})}$ is renamed as $Var(t_{i,1}, \ldots, t_{i,n}, A_i) \cap Var(F) = \emptyset$.

Next, for cyclic proofs, we define some notions. Note that given a function f, we write $f : X \rightharpoonup Y$ and $f : X \rightarrow Y$ if f is partial and total, respectively.

Definition 2.5 (derivation tree and bud/companion nodes [6]). *Let $\mathcal{S}eqs$ be the set of well-formed sequents in some language, $\mathcal{R}ules$ some set of rules, and n the maximum number of premises of any rule in $\mathcal{R}ules$. A derivation tree is a rooted tree $\mathcal{T}$ represented by a quadruple (V, s, r, p) such that*

- *V is a set of nodes,*
- *$s : V \rightarrow \mathcal{S}eqs$ is a mapping that assigns a sequent to a node,*
- *$r : V \rightharpoonup \mathcal{R}ules$ is a mapping that assigns a rule to a node,*
- *$p : V \rightharpoonup V^n$ is a mapping that assigns premises nodes to a node, where $p_j(v)$ denotes the j-th component of $p(v)$, and*
- *for all nodes $v \in V$, $p_j(v)$ is defined just in case $r(v)$ is a rule with m premises $(1 \le j \le m)$, and $\frac{s(p_1(v)) \ \ldots \ s(p_m(v))}{s(v)}$ is an instance of rule $r(v)$.*

Note that the edges of the derivation tree is $\{(v, p_j(v)) \mid v \in V, \ p_j(v) \text{ is defined}\}$. A node $v \in V$ is called

$$\dfrac{\dfrac{}{\text{(1.1)} \ \vdash N(0)} \text{(App } N_1) \quad \dfrac{\dfrac{\dfrac{\text{(1.2.1.1)} \ O(x) \vdash N(x) \ \dagger}{\text{(1.2.1)} \ O(y) \vdash N(y)} \text{(Subst)}}{\text{(1.2)} \ O(y) \vdash N(s(y))} \text{(App } N_2)}{\text{(1)} \ E(x) \vdash N(x) \ \ddagger} \text{(Case E)} \quad \dfrac{\dfrac{\dfrac{\text{(2.1.1.1)} \ E(x) \vdash N(x) \ \ddagger}{\text{(2.1.1)} \ E(y) \vdash N(y)} \text{(Subst)}}{\dfrac{\text{(2.1)} \ E(y) \vdash N(s(y))}{\text{(2)} \ O(x) \vdash N(x) \ \dagger}} \text{(App } N_2)}{} \text{(Case O)}}{\text{(ε)} \ E(x) \vee O(x) \vdash N(x)} \text{($\vee$L)}$$

Fig. 2. A cyclic proof for $E(x) \vee O(x) \vdash N(x)$ [6].

- a bud node *(of $\mathcal{T}$) if $r(v)$ is undefined, i.e., v is not the conclusion of any proof-rule instance in $\mathcal{T}$, and*
- a companion *for a bud node v' if $r(v)$ is defined and $s(v) = s(v')$.*

Note that a companion does not have to be an ancestor of its bud nodes.

For readability, in illustrating a derivation tree, we attach to each node a label as well as RI proofs; such labels are sequences of positive integers indicating positions in the tree.

Definition 2.6 (cyclic proof [6]). *A cyclic proof of a sequent $F \vdash F'$ is a pair $(\mathcal{T}, \xi)$ of a finite derivation tree $\mathcal{T} = (V, s, r, p)$ (with v_0 the root node) and a mapping $\xi : V \rightharpoonup V$ such that*

- *the codomain of s is the set of well-formed sequents,*
- *$s(v_0) = (F \vdash F')$,*
- *the codomain of r comprises the sequent calculus rules in this section, and*
- *every bud node v of $\mathcal{T}$ is assigned by ξ a companion, i.e., $\xi(v)$ is a companion.*

Theorem 2.7 ([6]). *If a sequent $F \vdash F'$ has a cyclic proof, then $F \models_\Phi F'$.*

Example 2.8. Consider the IDS Φ_2 in Example 2.3 again. Figure 2 illustrates a cyclic proof for $E(x) \vee O(x) \vdash N(x)$ [6]. Therefore, $E(x) \vee O(x) \models_{\Phi_2} N(x)$ holds.

3 From IDSs and Sequent-Calculus Rules into TRSs

In this section, we transform an IDS and sequent calculus rules into a TRS.

3.1 Transformation of IDSs into TRSs

First, we briefly recall a transformation of a GSC-terminating orthogonal IDS Φ into a terminating confluent TRS $\mathcal{R}_\Phi$ in [26, 27]. Logical connectives $\wedge, \vee, \neg$ are represented by $\mathsf{and}, \mathsf{or} : bool \times bool \to bool$, $\mathsf{not} : bool \to bool$, respectively, and for a formula F, $\widetilde{F}$ is terms representing F: $\widetilde{b} = b$ for $b \in \{\mathsf{true}, \mathsf{false}\}$, $\widetilde{A} = A$ for an atomic formula A, $\widetilde{\neg F} = \mathsf{not}(\widetilde{F})$, $\widetilde{F_1 \wedge F_2} = \mathsf{and}(\widetilde{F_1}, \widetilde{F_2})$, and $\widetilde{F_1 \vee F_2} = \mathsf{or}(\widetilde{F_1}, \widetilde{F_2})$.

We transform an orthogonal IDS Φ into a TRS $\mathcal{R}_\Phi$ as follows [26,27]:

$$\mathcal{R}_\Phi = \{\, A \to A' \mid \tfrac{A'}{A} \in \Phi \,\} \cup \{\, t \to \mathsf{false} \mid t \in Cop \,\} \cup \mathcal{R}_{pl}$$

where Cop is a finite set of $co\text{-}patterns$ [12] of $\{\, A \to A' \mid \tfrac{A'}{A} \in \Phi \}$, and

$$\mathcal{R}_{pl} = \left\{ \begin{array}{lll} \mathsf{and}(\mathsf{false},\mathsf{false}) \to \mathsf{false}, & \mathsf{or}(\mathsf{false},\mathsf{false}) \to \mathsf{false}, & \mathsf{not}(\mathsf{false}) \to \mathsf{true}, \\ \mathsf{and}(\mathsf{false},\mathsf{true}) \to \mathsf{false}, & \mathsf{or}(\mathsf{false},\mathsf{true}) \to \mathsf{true}, & \mathsf{not}(\mathsf{true}) \to \mathsf{false}, \\ \mathsf{and}(\mathsf{true},\mathsf{false}) \to \mathsf{false}, & \mathsf{or}(\mathsf{true},\mathsf{false}) \to \mathsf{true}, & \\ \mathsf{and}(\mathsf{true},\mathsf{true}) \to \mathsf{true}, & \mathsf{or}(\mathsf{true},\mathsf{true}) \to \mathsf{true} & \end{array} \right\}$$

Theorem 3.1 ([27]). *Let Φ is a GSC-terminating orthogonal. $\mathcal{R}_\Phi$ is a GSC-terminating, confluent, and quasi-reductive constructor TRS such that for any ground formula F,*

(1) $\Phi \models F$ if and only if $\widetilde{F} \to^*_{\mathcal{R}_\Phi} \mathsf{true}$, and

(2) $\Phi \not\models F$ if and only if $\widetilde{F} \to^*_{\mathcal{R}_\Phi} \mathsf{false}$.

Example 3.2 ([26,27]). We transform Φ_2 in Example 2.3 into the following TRS:

$$\mathcal{R}_{\Phi_2} = \left\{ \begin{array}{lll} \mathsf{N}(0) \to \mathsf{true}, & \mathsf{E}(0) \to \mathsf{true}, & \mathsf{O}(0) \to \mathsf{false}, \\ \mathsf{N}(\mathsf{s}(x)) \to \mathsf{N}(x), & \mathsf{E}(\mathsf{s}(x)) \to \mathsf{O}(x), & \mathsf{O}(\mathsf{s}(x)) \to \mathsf{E}(x) \end{array} \right\} \cup \mathcal{R}_{pl}$$

3.2 Transformation of Sequent-Calculus Rules into Rewrite Rules

In this section, we show rewrite rules for sequents and inference rules of sequent calculus.

As explained in Sect. 1, we represent a sequent $F \vdash F'$ by a term $\mathsf{seq}(\widetilde{F}, \widetilde{F'})$. Unlike [26,27], we introduce a sort $prop$ for sequents, i.e., $\mathsf{seq} : bool \times bool \to prop$. Let us consider an inference rule in the following form:

$$\frac{F_1 \vdash F_1' \quad F_2 \vdash F_2'}{F \vdash F'}$$

To show validity of $F \vdash F'$, we consider validity of $F_1 \vdash F_1'$ and $F_2 \vdash F_2'$. We can use and to represent such a meta logical-connective "and", but we avoid nests of sequents in the term representation such as $\mathsf{seq}(\mathsf{seq}(\mathsf{E}(x), \mathsf{O}(x)), \mathsf{N}(x))$, which are not necessary in our setting. To avoid such nests, we distinguish meta-logical connectives from logical connectives in formulas by means of $prop$. For meta truth-values, we prepare $\top : prop$ and $\bot : prop$. For meta conjunction, we prepare $\& : prop \times prop \to prop$, and we use infix notation for $\&$ under left-associativity. We define rewrite rules for seq, which are almost the same as those in [26,27], as follows:

$$\mathcal{R}_{seq} = \left\{ \begin{array}{llll} \mathsf{seq}(\mathsf{false},\mathsf{false}) \to \top, & \mathsf{seq}(\mathsf{false},\mathsf{true}) \to \top, & \bot \,\&\, \bot \to \bot, & \bot \,\&\, \top \to \bot, \\ \mathsf{seq}(\mathsf{true},\mathsf{false}) \to \bot, & \mathsf{seq}(\mathsf{true},\mathsf{true}) \to \top, & \top \,\&\, \bot \to \bot, & \top \,\&\, \top \to \top \end{array} \right\}$$

Note that $\top, \bot$ mean validity and invalidity of sequents, respectively.

Theorem 3.3. *For a GSC-terminating orthogonal IDS Φ, $\mathcal{R}_\Phi \cup \mathcal{R}_{seq}$ is a GSC-terminating, confluent, and quasi-reductive constructor TRS such that a sequent $F \vdash F'$ is valid w.r.t. Φ if and only if $\mathsf{seq}(\widetilde{F}, \widetilde{F'}) \approx \top$ is an inductive theorem of $\mathcal{R}_\Phi \cup \mathcal{R}_{seq}$.*

Proof (Sketch). The difference of $\mathcal{R}_\Phi \cup \mathcal{R}_{seq}$ from [26,27] is the use of sort *prop*, constants $\top, \bot$, and binary symbol $\&$. This difference does not affect the proof of the same claim in [26,27]. Note that as in [26,27], the proof of this theorem relies on Theorem 3.1. □

As described in Sect. 1, we need rewrite rules to simulate the application of some sequent-calculus rules in Fig. 1, except for rule (Subst) which is simulated by rule GENERALIZE. We transform an inference rule of the form $\frac{F_1 \vdash F_1' \quad \cdots \quad F_n \vdash F_n'}{F \vdash F'}$ into the following rewrite rule:

$$\mathsf{seq}(\widetilde{F}, \widetilde{F'}) \rightarrow \mathsf{seq}(\widetilde{F_1}, \widetilde{F_1'}) \& \cdots \& \mathsf{seq}(\widetilde{F_n}, \widetilde{F_n'})$$

Note that if $n = 0$, then the rule is $\mathsf{seq}(\widetilde{F}, \widetilde{F'}) \rightarrow \top$, and if $n = 1$, then it is $\mathsf{seq}(\widetilde{F}, \widetilde{F'}) \rightarrow \mathsf{seq}(\widetilde{F_1}, \widetilde{F_1'})$. For example, we transform rule ($\vee$L) in Fig. 1 into $\mathsf{seq}(\mathsf{or}(x, y), z) \rightarrow \mathsf{seq}(x, z) \& \mathsf{seq}(y, z)$. This rule (i.e., $\mathsf{seq}(\mathsf{or}(x, y), z) \approx \mathsf{seq}(x, z) \& \mathsf{seq}(y, z)$) is an inductive theorem of $\mathcal{R}_{pl} \cup \mathcal{R}_{seq}$ ($\subseteq \mathcal{R}_\Phi \cup \mathcal{R}_{seq}$). This means that to prove an equation to be an inductive theorem of $\mathcal{R}_\Phi$, we can use the above rule in an RI proof for the equation.

Theorem 3.4. *Let $\mathcal{R}$ be a quasi-reductive and terminating TRS over a signature Σ, and $\mathcal{R}'$ a TRS over Σ such that for each rule $\ell' \rightarrow r' \in \mathcal{R}'$, $\ell' \approx r'$ is an inductive theorem of $\mathcal{R}$. An equation $s \approx t$ over Σ is an inductive theorem of $\mathcal{R}$ if and only if it is an inductive theorem of $\mathcal{R} \cup \mathcal{R}'$.*

Proof. Since rules in $\mathcal{R}'$ are inductive theorems of $\mathcal{R}$, we have that $\leftrightarrow_{\mathcal{R}'} \subseteq \leftrightarrow_{\mathcal{R}}^* \subseteq \leftrightarrow_{\mathcal{R} \cup \mathcal{R}'}^*$ on ground terms. Therefore, this claim holds. □

For rules (Axiom), ($\vee$L), and ($\wedge$R) in Fig. 1, we define the following TRS:

$$\mathcal{R}_{scr} = \left\{ \begin{array}{ll} \text{(Axiom)} & \mathsf{seq}(x, x) \rightarrow \mathsf{true}, \\ (\vee\text{L}) & \mathsf{seq}(\mathsf{or}(x, y), z) \rightarrow \mathsf{seq}(x, z) \& \mathsf{seq}(y, z), \\ (\wedge\text{R}) & \mathsf{seq}(x, \mathsf{and}(y, z)) \rightarrow \mathsf{seq}(x, y) \& \mathsf{seq}(x, z) \end{array} \right\}$$

None of the other rules in Fig. 1 is an inductive theorem of $\mathcal{R}_{pl} \cup \mathcal{R}_{seq}$: Let us represent ($\wedge$L$_1$) by $\mathsf{seq}(\mathsf{and}(x, y), z) \rightarrow \mathsf{seq}(x, z)$; then, $\mathsf{seq}(\mathsf{and}(x, y), z) \approx \mathsf{seq}(x, z)$ is not an inductive theorem of $\mathcal{R}_{pl} \cup \mathcal{R}_{seq}$ because e.g., $\mathsf{seq}(\mathsf{and}(\mathsf{true}, \mathsf{false}), \mathsf{false})$ $\rightarrow_{\mathcal{R}_{pl} \cup \mathcal{R}_{seq}}^* \top$ and $\mathsf{seq}(\mathsf{true}, \mathsf{false}) \rightarrow_{\mathcal{R}_{pl} \cup \mathcal{R}_{seq}}^* \bot$. The treatment of ($\wedge$L$_1$), ($\wedge$L$_2$), ($\vee$R$_1$), and ($\vee$R$_2$) will be discussed in the conclusion.

Theorem 3.5. *If an equation $\mathsf{seq}(s, t) \approx \top$ is an inductive theorem of $\mathcal{R}_\Phi \cup \mathcal{R}_{seq} \cup \mathcal{R}_{scr}$, then it is an inductive theorem of $\mathcal{R}_\Phi \cup \mathcal{R}_{seq}$.*

Proof. For each rule $\ell \rightarrow r$ in $\mathcal{R}_{scr}$, $\ell \approx r$ is an inductive theorem of $\mathcal{R}_\Phi \cup \mathcal{R}_{seq}$. Therefore, by Theorem 3.4, this claim holds. □

Thanks to Theorem 3.5, we can use $\mathcal{R}_\Phi \cup \mathcal{R}_{seq} \cup \mathcal{R}_{scr}$ for RI proofs of equations to be proved inductive theorems of $\mathcal{R}_\Phi \cup \mathcal{R}_{seq}$.

In transforming a cyclic proof into an RI proof in Sect. 4, we need to ensure termination of $\mathcal{R}_\Phi \cup \mathcal{R}_{seq} \cup \mathcal{R}_{scr}$ with rewrite rules of the form $\mathsf{seq}(\ldots) \to \top$. To prove the termination, we use the following termination criterion.

Theorem 3.6 ([27]). *Let $\mathcal{R}_1$ and $\mathcal{R}_2$ be TRSs such that*

$$Cycles(EDG(\mathcal{R}_1)) \cup Cycles(EDG(\mathcal{R}_2)) \supseteq Cycles(EDG(\mathcal{R}_1 \cup \mathcal{R}_2))$$

where $Cycles(EDG(\mathcal{R}'))$ denotes the set of cycles in $EDG(\mathcal{R}')$. Then, both $\mathcal{R}_1$ and $\mathcal{R}_2$ are GSC-terminating if and only if $\mathcal{R}_1 \cup \mathcal{R}_2$ is so.

Theorem 3.7. *Let Φ be a GSC-terminating orthogonal IDS, and $\mathcal{H}$ be a TRS such that every rule in $\mathcal{H}$ is of the form $\mathsf{seq}(F, F') \to \top$. Then, $\mathcal{R}_\Phi \cup \mathcal{R}_{seq} \cup \mathcal{R}_{scr} \cup \mathcal{H}$ is GSC-terminating.*

Proof. It follows from Theorem 3.3 that $\mathcal{R}_\Phi \cup \mathcal{R}_{seq}$ is GSC-terminating. By definition, $\mathcal{R}_{seq} \cup \mathcal{H}$ is GSC-terminating, $Cycles(EDG(\mathcal{R}_\Phi)) = Cycles(EDG(\mathcal{R}_\Phi \cup \mathcal{R}_{seq}))$, and $Cycles(EDG(\mathcal{R}_{scr})) = Cycles(EDG(\mathcal{R}_{scr} \cup \mathcal{H}))$. Because of $\mathsf{seq} : bool \times bool \to prop$, $\mathcal{R}_{scr} \cup \mathcal{H}$ and $\mathcal{R}_\Phi \cup \mathcal{R}_{seq}$ do not affect edges of $EDG(\mathcal{R}_\Phi \cup \mathcal{R}_{seq})$ and $EDG(\mathcal{R}_{scr} \cup \mathcal{H})$, respectively, and hence $Cycles(EDG(\mathcal{R}_\Phi \cup \mathcal{R}_{seq} \cup \mathcal{R}_{scr} \cup \mathcal{H})) = Cycles(EDG(\mathcal{R}_\Phi)) \cup Cycles(EDG(\mathcal{R}_{scr} \cup \mathcal{H}))$. Therefore, it follows from Theorem 3.7 that $\mathcal{R}_\Phi \cup \mathcal{R}_{seq} \cup \mathcal{R}_{scr} \cup \mathcal{H}$ is GSC-terminating. □

4 Transformation of Cyclic Proofs into RI Proofs

In this section, we show our main result by means of a transformation of cyclic proofs into RI proofs.

4.1 Overview of Our Transformation

Using the cyclic proof in Fig. 2, we show our idea of transforming a cyclic proof into an RI proof. As described in Sect. 1, the transformation starts with the root of the cyclic proof, and proceeds step-by-step. The resulting RI proof is illustrated in Fig. 3.

The initial equation of the resulting RI proof is $\mathsf{seq}(\widetilde{F}, \widetilde{F'}) \approx \top$, equations in the RI proof are of the form $\mathsf{seq}(\widetilde{F}, \widetilde{F'}) \approx \top$ and thus, oriented rules are of the form $\mathsf{seq}(\widetilde{F}, \widetilde{F'}) \to \top$.

The application of $(\vee L)$ to the root node is transformed into steps (1)–(4), (*Case* E) for node (1) into step (4)–(5), (*Case* O) for node (2) into steps (5)–(8); (App E_1) for node (1.1) into steps (8)–(11); (App E_2) for node (1.2) into step (11)–(12); (Subst) for node (1.2.1) into step (12)–(13); bud node (1.2.1.1) with † into steps (13)–(15); (App N_2) for node (2.1) into step (15)–(16); (Subst) for node (2.1.1) into step (16)–(17); bud node (2.1.1.1) with ‡ into steps (17)–(19). Companions ‡,† are oriented and included in the second elements of RI processes.

$$(\{ \ (\varepsilon) \ \ \mathsf{seq}(\mathsf{or}(\mathsf{E}(x),\mathsf{O}(x)),\mathsf{N}(x))) \approx \top \ \},\emptyset) \tag{1}$$

$$\Rightarrow_{\mathsf{sR}} (\{ \ (\varepsilon) \ \ \mathsf{seq}(\mathsf{E}(x),\mathsf{N}(x)) \ \& \ \mathsf{seq}(\mathsf{O}(x),\mathsf{N}(x)) \approx \top \ \},\emptyset) \tag{2}$$

$$\Rightarrow_{\mathsf{p}} (\{ \ (\varepsilon), \ \ (1) \ \ \mathsf{seq}(\mathsf{E}(x),\mathsf{N}(x)) \approx \top, \ \ (2) \ \ \mathsf{seq}(\mathsf{O}(x),\mathsf{N}(x)) \approx \top \ \},\emptyset) \tag{3}$$

$$\Rightarrow_{\mathsf{d}} (\{ \ (1), \ \ (2) \ \},\emptyset) \tag{4}$$

$$\Rightarrow_{\mathsf{e}} \left(\left\{ \begin{matrix} (1.1) & \mathsf{seq}(\mathsf{true},\mathsf{N}(0)) & \approx \top, (2), \\ (1.2) & \mathsf{seq}(\mathsf{O}(y),\mathsf{N}(\mathsf{s}(y))) & \approx \top \end{matrix} \right\},\{ (\ddagger) \ \ \mathsf{seq}(\mathsf{E}(x),\mathsf{N}(x)) \to \top \}\right) \tag{5}$$

$$\Rightarrow_{\mathsf{e}} \left(\left\{ \begin{matrix} (1.1), (2.1) \ \mathsf{seq}(\mathsf{E}(y),\mathsf{N}(\mathsf{s}(y))) \approx \top, \\ (1.2), (2.2) \ \ \mathsf{seq}(\mathsf{false},\mathsf{N}(0)) \ \ \approx \top \end{matrix} \right\},\left\{ \begin{matrix} (\ddagger), \\ (\dagger) \ \mathsf{seq}(\mathsf{O}(x),\mathsf{N}(x)) \to \top \end{matrix} \right\}\right) \tag{6}$$

$$\Rightarrow_{\mathsf{sR}} (\{ \ (1.1), \ (2.1), \ (1.2), \ (2.2) \ \top \approx \top \ \},\{ (\ddagger), \ (\dagger) \ \}) \tag{7}$$

$$\Rightarrow_{\mathsf{d}} (\{ \ (1.1), \ (1.2), \ (2.1) \ \},\{ (\ddagger), \ (\dagger) \ \}) \tag{8}$$

$$\Rightarrow_{\mathsf{sR}} (\{ \ (1.1.1) \ \mathsf{seq}(\mathsf{true},\mathsf{true}) \approx \top, \ (1.2), \ (2.1) \ \},\{ (\ddagger), \ (\dagger) \ \}) \tag{9}$$

$$\Rightarrow_{\mathsf{sR}} (\{ \ (1.1.1) \ \top \approx \top, \ (1.2), \ (2.1) \ \},\{ (\ddagger), \ (\dagger) \ \}) \tag{10}$$

$$\Rightarrow_{\mathsf{d}} (\{ \ (1.2), \ (2.1) \ \},\{ (\ddagger), \ (\dagger) \ \}) \tag{11}$$

$$\Rightarrow_{\mathsf{sR}} (\{ \ (1.2.1) \ \mathsf{seq}(\mathsf{O}(y),\mathsf{N}(y)) \approx \top, \ (2.1) \ \},\{ (\ddagger), \ (\dagger) \ \}) \tag{12}$$

$$\Rightarrow_{\mathsf{g}} (\{ \ (1.2.1.1) \ \mathsf{seq}(\mathsf{O}(x),\mathsf{N}(x)) \approx \top, \ (2.1) \ \},\{ (\ddagger), \ (\dagger) \ \}) \tag{13}$$

$$\Rightarrow_{\mathsf{sH}} (\{ \ (1.2.1.1) \ \top \approx \top, \ (2.1) \ \},\{ (\ddagger), \ (\dagger) \ \}) \tag{14}$$

$$\Rightarrow_{\mathsf{d}} (\{ \ (2.1) \ \},\{ (\ddagger), \ (\dagger) \ \}) \tag{15}$$

$$\Rightarrow_{\mathsf{sR}} (\{ \ (2.1.1) \ \mathsf{seq}(\mathsf{E}(y),\mathsf{N}(y)) \approx \top \ \},\{ (\ddagger), \ (\dagger) \ \}) \tag{16}$$

$$\Rightarrow_{\mathsf{g}} (\{ \ (2.1.1.1) \ \mathsf{seq}(\mathsf{E}(x),\mathsf{N}(x)) \approx \top \ \},\{ (\ddagger), \ (\dagger) \ \}) \tag{17}$$

$$\Rightarrow_{\mathsf{sH}} (\{ \ (2.1.1.1) \ \top \approx \top \ \},\{ (\ddagger), \ (\dagger) \ \}) \tag{18}$$

$$\Rightarrow_{\mathsf{d}} (\emptyset,\{ (\ddagger), \ (\dagger) \ \}) \tag{19}$$

Fig. 3. An RI proof obtained from the cyclic proof in Fig. 2.

Steps (6)–(8) in Fig. 3 show that equations generated by rules of the form $\ell \to$ false can be dropped by SIMPLIFY and DELETE. In our setting, such equations can always be dropped. EXPAND is applied to $(\mathcal{E} \uplus \{\mathsf{seq}(P(s_1,\ldots,s_n),t) \approx \top\}, \mathcal{H})$ making a case distinction for $P(s_1,\ldots,s_n)$. For this reason, s, t, and p in the definition of EXPAND are $\mathsf{seq}(P(s_1,\ldots,s_n),t)$, $\top$, and 1, respectively, and all of the following side conditions hold:

- $p \in \mathcal{B}(s)$ (by definition), and
- $\mathcal{R}_\Phi \cup \mathcal{R}_{seq} \cup \mathcal{R}_{scr} \cup \mathcal{H} \cup \{\mathsf{seq}(s,t) \to \top\}$ is terminating (by Theorem 3.7).

This implies that the above side conditions can be dropped from the definition. For this reason, we simplify EXPAND, replacing it by the following one which is specialized to $\mathsf{seq}(\ldots) \approx \top$:

EXPAND$^+$ $(\mathcal{E} \uplus \{(\rho) \ \mathsf{seq}(P(s_1,\ldots,s_n),t) \simeq \top\}, \mathcal{H})$
$$\Rightarrow_{\mathsf{e}} (\mathcal{E} \cup \mathcal{E}', \mathcal{H} \cup \{\mathsf{seq}(P(s_1,\ldots,s_n),t) \to \top\})$$
where $\mathcal{E}' = \{(\rho.i) \ \mathsf{seq}(r\sigma,t\sigma) \approx \top \mid \sigma = mgu(P(s_1,\ldots,s_n),\ell), \ \ell \to r \in \mathcal{R}$ is the i-th rule of P, $r \neq$ false$\}$.

Table 1. A transformation of the application of rules in cyclic proofs into RI steps.

Rules $r(v)$ in cyclic proofs	RI steps	
(Case P)	EXPAND$^+$	($\Rightarrow_e$)
(App P_i) for inner nodes	SIMPLIFY with $P(\ldots) \rightarrow P'(\ldots) \in \mathcal{R}_\Phi$	($\Rightarrow_{sR}$)
(App P_i) for leaves	SIMPLIFY with $P(\ldots) \rightarrow$ true $\in \mathcal{R}_\Phi$ & DELETE	($\Rightarrow_{sR} \cdot \Rightarrow_d$)
bud nodes	SIMPLIFY with $\mathcal{H}$ & DELETE	($\Rightarrow_{sH} \cdot \Rightarrow_d$)
(Axiom), ($\vee$L), ($\wedge$R)	SIMPLIFY with $\mathcal{R}_{scr}$ & DELETE	($\Rightarrow_{sR} \cdot \Rightarrow_d$)
(Subst)	GENERALIZE	($\Rightarrow_g$)

For rules of the form $\ell \rightarrow$ false with $root(\ell) = P$, the equations of the form seq(false, $t\sigma$) $\approx \top$ are generated, and such equations are dropped by DELETE. For this reason, EXPAND$^+$ is a derived rule of EXPAND and DELETE.

In summary, the application of rules in cyclic proofs are simulated by RI steps as shown in Table 1.

4.2 Formulation of Our Transformation

In this section, we formulate a transformation of cyclic proofs into RI proofs. Since we can transform cyclic proof choosing nodes non-deterministically, the proof can be transformed into several RI proofs, and thus, the transformation is non-deterministic.

Definition 4.1 (transformation $\mathfrak{T}_\Phi$ of cyclic proofs into RI proofs). *Let Φ be a GSC-terminating orthogonal IDS. We define a transformation $\mathfrak{T}_\Phi$ of a cyclic proof $\mathcal{P} = ((V, s, r, p), \xi)$ with v_0 the root node into an RI proof as*

$$\mathfrak{T}_\Phi(\mathcal{P}) = \mathscr{T}_\Phi(V, (\{\widetilde{s(v_0)} \approx \top\}, \emptyset))$$

where $\mathscr{T}_\Phi$ takes a set of nodes in V and an RI process $(\mathcal{E}, \mathcal{H})$ as input and returns a sequence of RI processes, and is inductively defined as follows:

– $\mathscr{T}_\Phi(\emptyset, (\mathcal{E}, \mathcal{H})) = (\mathcal{E}, \mathcal{H})$,
– $\mathscr{T}_\Phi(\{v\} \uplus V', (\mathcal{E} \uplus \{\widetilde{s(v)} \simeq \top\}, \mathcal{H})) =$
  - $(\mathcal{E} \cup \{\widetilde{s(v)} \approx \top\}, \mathcal{H}) \Rightarrow_e \mathscr{T}_\Phi(V', (\mathcal{E} \cup \{\widetilde{(v_i)\ s(v_i)} \approx \top \mid 1 \leq i \leq n\}, \mathcal{H} \cup \{\widetilde{s(v)} \rightarrow \top\}))$ *if* $r(v) = (Case\ P)$, *where* $p(v) = v_1 \ldots v_n$,
  - $(\mathcal{E} \cup \{\widetilde{s(v)} \approx \top\}, \mathcal{H}) \Rightarrow_{sR} \mathscr{T}_\Phi(V', (\mathcal{E} \cup \{\widetilde{(v_1)\ s(v_1)} \approx \top\}, \mathcal{H}))$ *if* $r(v) = (App\ P_i)$ *and* v *is not a leaf, where* $p(v) = v_1,$[6]
  - $(\mathcal{E} \cup \{\widetilde{s(v)} \approx \top\}, \mathcal{H}) \Rightarrow^+_{sR} (\mathcal{E} \cup \{\top \approx \top\}, \mathcal{H}) \Rightarrow_d \mathscr{T}_\Phi(V', (\mathcal{E}, \mathcal{H}))$ *if either* $r(v) = (App\ P_i)$ *and* v *is a leaf or* $r(v) = (Axiom)$,
  - $(\mathcal{E} \cup \{\widetilde{s(v)} \approx \top\}, \mathcal{H}) \Rightarrow_{sH} (\mathcal{E} \cup \{\top \approx \top\}, \mathcal{H}) \Rightarrow_d \mathscr{T}_\Phi(V', (\mathcal{E}, \mathcal{H}))$ *if* v *is a bud node and V has no companion of v, i.e., $\xi(v) \notin V'$,*

---

[6] In this case, by definition, v has an exactly one child.

- $(\mathcal{E} \cup \{\widetilde{s(v)} \approx \top\}, \mathcal{H}) \Rightarrow_{sR} (\mathcal{E} \cup \{\widetilde{s(v_1) \,\&\, s(v_2)} \approx \top\}, \mathcal{H})$
  $\Rightarrow_p (\mathcal{E} \cup \{\widetilde{s(v_1) \,\&\, s(v_2)} \approx \top\} \cup \{(v_1)\ \widetilde{s(v_1)} \approx \top,\ (v_2)\ \widetilde{s(v_2)} \approx \top\}, \mathcal{H})$
  $\Rightarrow_d \mathscr{T}_\Phi(V', (\mathcal{E} \cup \{(v_1)\ \widetilde{s(v_1)} \approx \top,\ (v_2)\ \widetilde{s(v_2)} \approx \top\}, \mathcal{H}))$ *if $r(v)$ is either*
  $(\vee L)$ *or* $(\vee R)$, *where $p(v) = v_1 v_2$,*
- $(\mathcal{E} \cup \{\widetilde{s(v)} \approx \top\}, \mathcal{H}) \Rightarrow_g \mathscr{T}_\Phi(V', (\mathcal{E} \cup \{(v_1)\ \widetilde{s(v_1)} \approx \top\}, \mathcal{H}))$ *if $r(v) =$*
  (Subst), where $p(v) = v_1$,

where V' has no ancestor of v.

In the definition of $\mathscr{T}_\Phi$, we required that V' has no ancestor of v. This is because a node in $\mathcal{P}$ cannot be transformed before its parent. To transform a bud node v, we need to transform its companion in advance because the rule in $\mathcal{H}$ obtained from the companion is applied to $\widetilde{s(v)} \approx \top$ to be reduced to $\top \approx \top$. It would be usual to use the breadth-first search to choose nodes in applying $\mathscr{T}_\Phi$.

Theorem 4.2 (correctness of $\mathfrak{T}_\Phi$). *Let Φ be a GSC-terminating orthogonal IDS, $\mathcal{P} = ((V, s, r, p), \xi)$ a cyclic proof with v_0 the root node. Then, $\mathfrak{T}_\Phi(\mathcal{P})$ is an RI proof for $\widetilde{s(v_0)} \approx \top$.*

Proof. For $V' \subseteq V$, we denote the set $\{v \in V' \mid \text{the parent of } v \text{ is not in } V'\}$ by $anc(V')$. By definition, $\mathfrak{T}_\Phi(\mathcal{P}) = \mathscr{T}_\Phi(V, (\{\widetilde{s(v_0)} \approx \top\}, \emptyset)) = \mathscr{T}_\Phi(V, (\{\widetilde{s(v)} \approx \top \mid v \in anc(V)\}, \emptyset))$. It suffices to show that for a descendant-closed[7] set $V' \subseteq V$, $\mathcal{E} = \{\widetilde{s(v)} \approx \top \mid v \in anc(V')\}$, and $\mathcal{H} \supseteq \{\widetilde{s(\xi(v'))} \rightarrow \top \mid v' \in V', \xi(v') \text{ is defined}\}$, $\mathscr{T}_\Phi(V', (\mathcal{E}, \mathcal{H}))$ is an RI proof such that

- the head of the resulting sequence of $\mathscr{T}_\Phi(V', (\mathcal{E}, \mathcal{H}))$ is $(\mathcal{E}, \mathcal{H})$, and
- for each call of $\mathscr{T}_\Phi$ with $\mathscr{T}_\Phi(V_1, (\mathcal{E}_1, \mathcal{H}_1))$ during the computation,
  - $\mathcal{E}_1 = \{\widetilde{s(v_1)} \simeq \top \mid v_1 \in anc(V_1)\}$, and
  - $\mathcal{H}_1 \supseteq \mathcal{H} \cup \{\widetilde{s(\xi(v_1))} \rightarrow \top \mid v_1 \in V_1, \xi(v_1) \text{ is defined}\}$.

We prove this claim by induction on $|V'|$. Since the case where $V' = \emptyset$ is trivial, we consider the remaining case where $V' \neq \emptyset$. Let $V' = \{v\} \uplus V''$ and $\mathcal{E} = \mathcal{E}' \uplus \{\widetilde{s(v)} \simeq \top\}$ such that V'' has no ancestor of v. By definition, suppose that

$$\mathscr{T}_\Phi(\{v\} \uplus V'', (\mathcal{E}' \uplus \{\widetilde{s(v)} \simeq \top\}, \mathcal{H})) =$$
$$(\mathcal{E}' \uplus \{\widetilde{s(v)} \simeq \top\}, \mathcal{H}) \Rightarrow^* (\mathcal{E}'', \mathcal{H}'') \Rightarrow \mathscr{T}_\Phi(V'', (\mathcal{E}''', \mathcal{H}'''))$$

It follows from the definition of $\mathscr{T}_\Phi$ that $(\mathcal{E}' \uplus \{\widetilde{s(v)} \simeq \top\}, \mathcal{H}) \Rightarrow^* (\mathcal{E}'', \mathcal{H}'') \Rightarrow (\mathcal{E}''', \mathcal{H}''')$ is an RI step, and $\mathcal{E}''' = \{\widetilde{s(v'')} \simeq \top \mid v'' \in anc(V'')\}$. By induction hypothesis, $\mathscr{T}_\Phi(V'', (\mathcal{E}''', \mathcal{H}'''))$ is an RI proof such that

- the head of the resulting sequence of $\mathscr{T}_\Phi(V'', (\mathcal{E}''', \mathcal{H}'''))$ is $(\mathcal{E}''', \mathcal{H}''')$, and
- for each call of $\mathscr{T}_\Phi$ with $\mathscr{T}_\Phi(V_2, (\mathcal{E}_2, \mathcal{H}_2))$ during the computation,
  - $\mathcal{E}_2 = \{\widetilde{s(v_2)} \simeq \top \mid v_2 \in anc(V_2)\}$, and

---

[7] V' is *descendant-closed* if for any $v' \in V'$, all descendants v'' of v' are in V'.

- $\mathcal{H}_2 \supseteq \mathcal{H}''' \cup \{s(\widetilde{\xi(v_2)}) \to \top \mid v_2 \in V_2, \ \xi(v_2) \text{ is defined}\}$.

Note that if $V_2 = \emptyset$, then $\mathcal{E}_2 = \emptyset$, and thus, the RI proof ends with $(\emptyset, \mathcal{H}_2)$. Therefore, $\mathscr{T}_\Phi(\{v\} \uplus V'', (\mathcal{E}' \uplus \{\widetilde{s(v)} \simeq \top\}, \mathcal{H}))$ is an RI proof such that

- the head of the resulting sequence of $\mathscr{T}_\Phi(V', (\mathcal{E}, \mathcal{H}))$ is $(\mathcal{E}, \mathcal{H})$, and
- for each call of $\mathscr{T}_\Phi$ with $\mathscr{T}_\Phi(V_1, (\mathcal{E}_1, \mathcal{H}_1))$ during the computation,
  - $\mathcal{E}_1 = \{\widetilde{s(v_1)} \simeq \top \mid v_1 \in anc(V_1)\}$, and
  - $\mathcal{H}_1 \supseteq \mathcal{H} \cup \{s(\widetilde{\xi(v_1)}) \to \top \mid v_1 \in V_1, \ \xi(v_1) \text{ is defined}\}$.   □

Finally, we show our main result.

Theorem 4.3 (main result). *Let Φ be a GSC-terminating orthogonal IDS. If a sequent $F \vdash F'$ has a cyclic proof w.r.t. Φ, then there exists an RI proof of $\{\operatorname{seq}(\widetilde{F}, \widetilde{F'}) \approx \top\}$, i.e., $(\{\operatorname{seq}(\widetilde{F}, \widetilde{F'}) \approx \top\}, \emptyset) \Rightarrow^* (\emptyset, \mathcal{H})$ for some TRS $\mathcal{H}$.*

Proof. Let $\mathcal{P}$ be a cyclic proof for $F \vdash F'$. Then, by Theorem 4.2, $\mathfrak{T}_\Phi(\mathcal{P})$ is an RI proof for $\operatorname{seq}(\widetilde{F}, \widetilde{F'}) \approx \top$.   □

5   Conclusion

In this paper, under the assumptions (A1)–(A10), we proved that if a sequent $F \vdash F'$ has a cyclic proof w.r.t. a GSC-terminating orthogonal IDS Φ, then there exists an RI proof $(\{\operatorname{seq}(\widetilde{F}, \widetilde{F'}) \approx \top\}, \emptyset) \Rightarrow^* (\emptyset, \mathcal{H})$ for some TRS $\mathcal{H}$. To this end, we showed a transformation of cyclic proofs into RI proofs. Due to our restrictive assumptions, we limit the scope of cyclic proofs and the result in this paper does not imply that RI is more powerful than cyclic proof systems. For example, termination of given systems ($\mathcal{R}_\Phi \cup \mathcal{R}_{seq} \cup \mathcal{R}_{scr}$ in this paper) is necessary for RI proofs and we assume GSC-termination of IDSs (Φ in this paper), which is not necessary for cyclic proofs.

As future work for the comparison of RI with cyclic proof systems, under the same assumptions, we will show that for a sequent $F \vdash F'$, if there exists an RI proof for $\operatorname{seq}(\widetilde{F}, \widetilde{F'}) \approx \top$, then there exists a cyclic proof for the sequent. Since (Case P) of cyclic proof systems is only applicable to $P(\boldsymbol{y})$ of $P(\boldsymbol{y}) \vdash F'$, but EXPAND of RI is applicable to $\operatorname{seq}(C[P(\ldots)], F') \approx \top$ and $\operatorname{seq}(F, C[P(\ldots)]) \approx \top$ w.r.t. $P(\boldsymbol{y})$ below logical connective (e.g., $\neg P(\boldsymbol{y})$) in the first and second argument of seq. In addition, EXPAND can make a case distinction on $P(\boldsymbol{y})$ below a logical connective, e.g., $\neg P(\boldsymbol{y})$. Such a difference makes the transformation of RI proofs into cyclic proofs more difficult. Due to the difference, we will show that for an IDS Φ and a sequent $F \vdash F'$, if there exists an RI proof for $\operatorname{seq}(\widetilde{F}, \widetilde{F'})$, then there exists a cyclic proof for $\Gamma, F \vdash F'$ w.r.t. Φ' ($\supseteq \Phi$) such that Γ is a multiset of valid instances $Q(\boldsymbol{t})$ of new predicates Q, i.e., $Q(\boldsymbol{t})$ is valid w.r.t. $\Phi' \setminus \Phi$. Such a cyclic proof implies that $F \vdash F'$ is valid w.r.t. Φ. After showing the conjecture above, from the comparison, we will have some insights into differences between RI and cyclic proof systems w.r.t. e.g., inference rules.

Finally, we briefly discuss the possibility of relaxing assumptions (A1)–(A10).

(A1) As mentioned above, termination of given systems is necessary for RI, and thus, we have this assumption, limiting the scope of IDSs. Given a terminating IDS Φ, to ensure the existence of RI proofs, we have to ensure termination of $\mathcal{R}_\Phi \cup \mathcal{R}_{seq} \cup \mathcal{R}_{seq} \cup \mathcal{H}$ such that $\mathcal{H} \subseteq \{\mathsf{seq}(F, F') \to \top \mid F \vdash F'$ appears in a given cyclic proof$\}$. In relaxing GSC-termination of Φ to termination of $\{A \to A_i \mid \frac{A_1 \ \cdots \ A_n}{A} \in \Phi,\ 1 \le i \le n\}$, we have not established a method to to ensure termination of $\mathcal{R}_\Phi$ because termination is not modular in general and we have to take rules for co-patterns into account. On the other hand, GSC-termination is modular under some property (Theorem 3.6), and termination is proved by referring to dependency pairs only.

On the other hand, we will try to drop this assumption because cyclic proof systems work for coinductively defined predicates which are useful in applying inductive theorem proving to verification (cf. [24]). Termination of $\mathcal{R}_\Phi$ is necessary for Theorem 3.1 (2). Though, the transformation of cyclic proofs into RI proofs may not rely on Theorem 3.1 (2). Since equations corresponding to sequents are of the form $\mathsf{seq}(F, F') \approx \top$, validity of sequents may be reduced to *one-pass reachability* [18], a proof system of which is based on coinduction and is similar to RI. One of possibilities for coinductively defined predicates is to consider e.g., a one-pass reachability proof system instead of RI.

(A2) Orthogonality of Φ is assumed to compute co-patterns and to ensure confluence of $\mathcal{R}_\Phi$, which is necessary for Theorem 3.1 (2), as well as termination. In dropping (A1), we may also drop this assumption.

(A3) As described in Sect. 1, RI has been extended to LCTRSs. An extension of the result in this paper to RI for LCTRSs which can naturally deal with ordinary predicates may allow us to use ordinary predicates.

(A4) RI has been extended to *conditional rewriting* [4,5]. An extension of the result in this paper to RI for conditional rewriting may enable us to drop this assumption. For such an extension, we will refer to a transformation of Horn clauses into TRSs (cf. [7]) because IDSs can be considered Horn clauses.

(A5) As described in Sect. 1, the usual setting of RI cannot deal with existential quantifiers in equations. To overcome such a downside, RI for LCTRSs has been extended to existentially quantified equations [14]. An extension of the result in this paper to such a setting may allow us to consider cyclic proofs with quantifiers.

(A6) It would be very challenging to drop this assumption. We must have two possibilities: One is to leave (A6), and apply *cut elimination*—a transformation of proofs into an equivalent cut-free one—to cyclic proofs as much as possible in advance; the other is to generate a conditional rewrite rule for the *cut* rule, extending our result to conditional rewriting. It is known that cut elimination is not successful for all cyclic proofs [9,10], and the cut rule plays an important role in e.g., verifying software as well as quantifiers [23]. For these reasons, we would like to take the second approach above to dropping this assumption.

(A7) As mentioned in Sect. 1, this assumption is automatically implied by (A8). This is not for any technical reason.

(A8) To partially relax this assumption, we have to consider multisets Γ, Δ of formulas for a sequent $\Gamma \vdash \Delta$, extend our result to the setting of e.g., AC-TRSs. For the extension, we will adapt Theorem 3.6 to AC-termination. Note that the generalized subterm criterion is defined for AC-termination.

(A9) We did not allow cyclic proofs to have the application of $(\wedge L_1)$, $(\wedge L_2)$, $(\vee R_1)$, $(\vee R_2)$, and (WL). To deal with them, we have to show a stronger property of our RI setting. For the page limitation, we leave the property as future work, while we have already proved it.

(A10) One of possibilities to drop this assumption is to show that a cyclic proof is transformed into another one which satisfies this assumption. Under (A8), such a transformation would be possible. The case without (A8) would be challenging as future work.

We leave the above relaxation for future work.

Acknowledgement. We gratefully acknowledge the anonymous reviewers for their useful comments and suggestions to improve the paper.

References

1. Aoto, T.: Rewriting induction using termination checkers. In: Proceedings of the JSSST 24th Annual Conference, pp. 1–4. No. 3C-C (2007). http://www.nue.ie. niigata-u.ac.jp/~aoto/research/papers/report/itp.pdf. (in Japanese)

2. Aoto, T., Toyama, Y.: Ground confluence prover based on rewriting induction. In: Kesner, D., Pientka, B. (eds.) Proceedings of the 1st International Conference on Formal Structures for Computation and Deduction. LIPIcs, vol. 52, pp. 33:1–33:12. Schloss Dagstuhl - Leibniz-Zentrum für Informatik (2016). https://doi.org/10.4230/LIPIcs.FSCD.2016.33

3. Baader, F., Nipkow, T.: Term Rewriting and All That. Cambridge University Press, Cambridge (1998). https://doi.org/10.1017/CBO9781139172752

4. Bouhoula, A.: Automated theorem proving by test set induction. J. Symb. Comput. **23**(1), 47–77 (1997). https://doi.org/10.1006/jsco.1996.0076

5. Bouhoula, A., Jacquemard, F.: Sufficient completeness verification for conditional and constrained TRS. J. Appl. Log. **10**(1), 127–143 (2012). https://doi.org/10.1016/j.jal.2011.09.001

6. Brotherston, J.: Cyclic proofs for first-order logic with inductive definitions. In: Beckert, B. (ed.) TABLEAUX 2005. LNCS (LNAI), vol. 3702, pp. 78–92. Springer, Heidelberg (2005). https://doi.org/10.1007/11554554_8

7. Fu, P., Komendantskaya, E.: Operational semantics of resolution and productivity in Horn clause logic. Formal Aspects Comput. **29**(3), 453–474 (2016). https://doi.org/10.1007/s00165-016-0403-1

8. Fuhs, C., Kop, C., Nishida, N.: Verifying procedural programs via constrained rewriting induction. ACM Trans. Comput. Logic **18**(2), 14:1–14:50 (2017). https://doi.org/10.1145/3060143

9. Kimura, D., Nakazawa, K., Terauchi, T., Unno, H.: Failure of cut-elimination in cyclic proofs of separation logic. Comput. Softw. **37**(1), 39–52 (2020). https://doi.org/10.11309/jssst.37.1_39

10. Komendantskaya, E., Rozplokhas, D., Basold, H.: The new normal: We cannot eliminate cuts in coinductive calculi, but we can explore them. Theory Pract. Logic Program. **20**(6), 990–1005 (2020). https://doi.org/10.1017/S1471068420000423

11. Kop, C., Nishida, N.: Term rewriting with logical constraints. In: Fontaine, P., Ringeissen, C., Schmidt, R.A. (eds.) FroCoS 2013. LNCS (LNAI), vol. 8152, pp. 343–358. Springer, Heidelberg (2013). https://doi.org/10.1007/978-3-642-40885-4_24

12. Lazrek, A., Lescanne, P., Thiel, J.: Tools for proving inductive equalities, relative completeness, and omega-completeness. Inf. Comput. **84**(1), 47–70 (1990). https://doi.org/10.1016/0890-5401(90)90033-E

13. Mizutani, S., Nishida, N.: Transforming proof tableaux of Hoare logic into inference sequences of rewriting induction. In: Cirstea, H., Sabel, D. (eds.) Proceedings of the 4th International Workshop on Rewriting Techniques for Program Transformations and Evaluation. Electronic Proceedings in Theoretical Computer Science, vol. 265, pp. 35–51. Open Publishing Association (2018). https://doi.org/10.4204/EPTCS.265.4

14. Nishie, K., Nishida, N., Sakai, M.: Extending rewriting induction to existentially quantified equations. IEICE Tech. Rep. SS2019-17 Inst. Electron. Inf. Commun. Eng. 119(246), 25–30 (2019). (in Japanese)

15. Ohlebusch, E.: Advanced Topics in Term Rewriting. Springer, New York (2002). https://doi.org/10.1007/978-1-4757-3661-8

16. Reddy, U.S.: Term rewriting induction. In: Stickel, M.E. (ed.) CADE 1990. LNCS, vol. 449, pp. 162–177. Springer, Heidelberg (1990). https://doi.org/10.1007/3-540-52885-7_86

17. Reynolds, J.C.: Separation logic: a logic for shared mutable data structures. In: Proceedings of the 17th IEEE Symposium on Logic in Computer Science, pp. 55–74. IEEE Computer Society (2002). https://doi.org/10.1109/LICS.2002.1029817

18. Rosu, G., Stefanescu, A., Ciobâcă, Ş., Moore, B.M.: One-path reachability logic. In: Proceedings of the 28th Annual ACM/IEEE Symposium on Logic in Computer Science, pp. 358–367. IEEE Computer Society (2013). https://doi.org/10.1109/LICS.2013.42

19. Sato, H., Kurihara, M.: Multi-context rewriting induction with termination checkers. IEICE Trans. Inf. Syst. **93-D**(5), 942–952 (2010). https://doi.org/10.1587/transinf.E93.D.942

20. Stratulat, S.: A unified view of induction reasoning for first-order logic. In: Turing-100. The Alan Turing Centenary. EPiC Series in Computing, vol. 10, pp. 326–352. EasyChair (2012)

21. Stratulat, S.: Structural vs. cyclic induction: a report on some experiments with Coq. In: Davenport, J.H., et al. (eds.) Proceedings of the 18th International Symposium on Symbolic and Numeric Algorithms for Scientific Computing, pp. 29–36. IEEE (2016). https://doi.org/10.1109/SYNASC.2016.018

22. Terese: Term Rewriting Systems. No. 55 in Cambridge Tracts in Theoretical Computer Science. Cambridge University Press, Cambridge (2003)

23. Tsukada, T., Unno, H.: Software model-checking as cyclic-proof search. Proc. ACM Program. Lang. **6**, 1–29 (2022). https://doi.org/10.1145/3498725

24. Unno, H., Torii, S., Sakamoto, H.: Automating induction for solving horn clauses. In: Majumdar, R., Kunčak, V. (eds.) CAV 2017. LNCS, vol. 10427, pp. 571–591. Springer, Cham (2017). https://doi.org/10.1007/978-3-319-63390-9_30
25. Yamada, A., Sternagel, C., Thiemann, R., Kusakari, K.: AC dependency pairs revisited. In: Talbot, J., Regnier, L. (eds.) Proceedings of the 25th EACSL Annual Conference on Computer Science Logic. LIPIcs, vol. 62, pp. 8:1–8:16. Schloss Dagstuhl - Leibniz-Zentrum für Informatik (2016). https://doi.org/10.4230/LIPIcs.CSL.2016.8
26. Zhang, S., Nishida, N.: On transforming inductive definition sets into term rewrite systems. In: Nakano, K., Riesco, A. (eds.) Informal Proceedings of the 8th International Workshop on Rewriting Techniques for Program Transformations and Evaluation, pp. 1–10 (2021). https://www.ipl.riec.tohoku.ac.jp/wpte2021/Zhang21wpte.pdf
27. Zhang, S., Nishida, N.: Transforming orthogonal inductive definition sets into confluent term rewrite systems, November 2021, https://www.trs.css.i.nagoya-u.ac.jp/~nishida/DB/pdf/ZhangNishida_21_wpte21-journal-submission.pdf. An extended version of [26] under submission to a journal

Author Index

Printed in the United States
by Baker & Taylor Publisher Services